An Apology for the Life of Mr. Colley Cibber Written by Himself. A new ed. With Notes and Supplement by Robert W. Lowe

AN APOLOGY FOR THE LIFE OF
MR. COLLEY CIBBER.

VOLUME THE SECOND.

NOTE

510 *copies printed on this fine deckle-edge demy 8vo paper for England and America, with the portraits as India proofs after letters*

Each copy is numbered, and the type distributed

No 368

COLLEY CIBBER AS LORD FOPPINGTON

AN APOLOGY FOR THE LIFE OF

MR. COLLEY CIBBER

WRITTEN BY HIMSELF

A NEW EDITION WITH NOTES AND SUPPLEMENT

BY

ROBERT W. LOWE

WITH TWENTY-SIX ORIGINAL MEZZOTINT PORTRAITS BY
R. B. PARKES, AND EIGHTEEN ETCHINGS
BY ADOLPHE LALAUZE

IN TWO VOLUMES
VOLUME THE SECOND

LONDON
JOHN C. NIMMO
14, KING WILLIAM STREET, STRAND
MDCCCLXXXIX

Chiswick Press
PRINTED BY CHARLES WHITTINGHAM AND CO.
TOOKS COURT, CHANCERY LANE, LONDON, E.C.

CONTENTS.

CHAPTER X.
                                                                PAGE
THE RECRUITED ACTORS IN THE HAY-MARKET ENCOURAG'D
BY A SUBSCRIPTION, ETC.   1

CHAPTER XI.
SOME CHIMÆRICAL THOUGHTS OF MAKING THE STAGE
USEFUL, ETC. 24

CHAPTER XII.
A SHORT VIEW OF THE OPERA WHEN FIRST DIVIDED FROM
THE COMEDY, ETC 50

CHAPTER XIII
THE PATENTEE, HAVING NOW NO ACTORS, REBUILDS THE
NEW THEATRE IN LINCOLNS-INN-FIELDS, ETC. . . 97

CHAPTER XIV.
THE STAGE IN ITS HIGHEST PROSPERITY, ETC. . . . 117

CHAPTER XV.
SIR RICHARD STEELE SUCCEEDS COLLIER IN THE THEATRE-
ROYAL, ETC. 161

CHAPTER XVI.

THE AUTHOR STEPS OUT OF HIS WAY. PLEADS HIS
  THEATRICAL CAUSE IN CHANCERY, ETC. 192

SUPPLEMENTARY CHAPTER 257
BIBLIOGRAPHY OF COLLEY CIBBER 289
A BRIEF SUPPLEMENT TO COLLEY CIBBER, ESQ; HIS LIVES
  OF THE LATE FAMOUS ACTORS AND ACTRESSES . . 299
MEMOIRS OF ACTORS AND ACTRESSES 319

LIST OF MEZZOTINT PORTRAITS.

NEWLY ENGRAVED BY R. B. PARKES.

VOLUME THE SECOND.

	PAGE
I. COLLEY CIBBER, in the character of "Sir Novelty Fashion, newley created Lord Foppington," in Vanbrugh's play of "The Relapse; or, Virtue in Danger." From the painting by J. Grisoni. The property of the Garrick Club	*Frontispiece*
II OWEN SWINEY. After the painting by John Baptist Vanloo	54
III. ANNE OLDFIELD. From the picture by Jonathan Richardson	70
IV. THEOPHILUS CIBBER, in the character of "Antient Pistol"	86
V. HESTER SANTLOW (Mrs. Barton Booth). After an original picture from the life	104
VI. ROBERT WILKS After the painting by John Ellys, 1732	122
VII. RICHARD STEELE. From the painting by Jonathan Richardson, 1712	172
VIII. BARTON BOOTH. From the picture by George White	206
IX. SUSANNA MARIA CIBBER. After a painting by Thomas Hudson	222
X. CHARLES FLEETWOOD. "Sir Fopling Flutter Arrested." "Drawn from a real Scene." John Dixon *ad vivum del et fect*	254
XI ALEXANDER POPE, at the age of 28. After the picture by Sir Godfrey Kneller, painted in 1716	272
XII SUSANNA MARIA CIBBER, in the character of Cordelia, "King Lear," act iii. After the picture by Peter Van Bleeck	288
XIII. CAVE UNDERHILL, in the character of Obadiah, "The Fanatic Elder." After the picture by Robert Bing, 1712	306

LIST OF CHAPTER HEADINGS.

NEWLY ETCHED FROM CONTEMPORARY DRAWINGS BY
ADOLPHE LALAUZE.

VOLUME THE SECOND.

X. SCENE ILLUSTRATING CIBBER'S "CARELESS HUSBAND." After the picture by Philip Mercier.

XI. COFFEE-HOUSE SCENE OF CIBBER'S DAY, "drawn from the life" by G. Vander Gucht

XII. SCENE ILLUSTRATING "THE ITALIAN OPERA," WITH SENESINO, CUZZONI, &c From a contemporary design.

XIII. SCENE ILLUSTRATING FARQUHAR'S "RECRUITING OFFICER" After the picture by Philip Mercier.

XIV. SCENE ILLUSTRATING ADDISON'S "CATO" After the contemporary design by Lud. du Guernier.

XV. SCENE ILLUSTRATING VANBRUGH AND CIBBER'S "PROVOKED HUSBAND." After the contemporary design by J. Vanderbank.

XVI. SCENE ILLUSTRATING VANBRUGH'S "PROVOKED WIFE." After the contemporary design by Arnold Vanhaecken.

XVII. "THE STAGE MUTINY," with portraits of Theophilus Cibber as "Antient Pistol," Mrs. Wilks, and others, in character; Colley Cibber as Poet Laureate, with his lap filled with bags of money. From a pictorial satire of the time.

XVIII. ANTHONY ASTON'S "THE FOOL'S OPERA."

AN APOLOGY FOR THE LIFE OF MR. COLLEY CIBBER, &c.

CHAPTER X.

The recruited Actors in the Hay-Market *encourag'd by a Subscription.* Drury-Lane *under a particular Menagement. The Power of a Lord-Chamberlain over the Theatres consider'd. How it had been formerly exercis'd. A Digression to Tragick Authors.*

HAVING shewn the particular Conduct of the Patentee in refusing so fair an Opportunity of securing to himself both Companies under his sole Power and Interest, I shall now lead the Reader, after a short View of what pass'd in this new Establishment of the *Hay-Market* Theatre, to the Accidents that the Year following compell'd the same Patentee to receive both Companies, united, into the *Drury-Lane* Theatre, notwithstanding his Disinclination to it.

It may now be imagin'd that such a Detachment of Actors from *Drury-Lane* could not but give a new Spirit to those in the *Hay-Market*; not only by enabling them to act each others Plays to better Advantage, but by an emulous Industry which had lain too long inactive among them, and without which they plainly saw they could not be sure of Subsistence. Plays by this means began to recover a good Share of their former Esteem and Favour; and the Profits of them in about a Month enabled our new Menager to discharge his Debt (of something more than Two hundred Pounds) to his old Friend the Patentee, who had now left him and his Troop in trust to fight their own Battles. The greatest Inconvenience they still laboured under was the immoderate Wideness of their House, in which, as I have observ'd, the Difficulty of Hearing may be said to have bury'd half the Auditors Entertainment. This Defect seem'd evident from the much better Reception several new Plays (first acted there) met with when they afterwards came to be play'd by the same Actors in *Drury-Lane:* Of this Number were the *Stratagem*[1] and the *Wife's Resent-*

---

[1] That is, "The Beaux' Stratagem," by Farquhar, produced 8th March, 1707. Cibber played the part of Gibbet.

ment;[1] to which I may add the *Double Gallant*.[2] This last was a Play made up of what little was tolerable in two or three others that had no Success, and were laid aside as so much Poetical Lumber; but by collecting and adapting the best Parts of them all into one Play, the *Double Gallant* has had a Place every Winter amongst the Publick Entertainments these Thirty Years. As I was only the Compiler of this Piece I

[1] "Lady's Last Stake; or, the Wife's Resentment," a comedy by Cibber, produced 13th December, 1707.

LORD WRONGLOVE	Mr. Wilks.
SIR GEORGE BRILLANT	Mr. Cibber.
SIR FRIENDLY MORAL	Mr. Keene.
LADY WRONGLOVE	Mrs. Barry.
LADY GENTLE	Mrs. Rogers.
MRS. CONQUEST	Mrs. Oldfield.
MISS NOTABLE	Mrs. Cross.

[2] "The Double Gallant; or, the Sick Lady's Cure," a comedy by Cibber, produced 1st November, 1707.

SIR SOLOMON SADLIFE	Mr. Johnson.
CLERIMONT	Mr. Booth.
CARELESS	Mr. Wilks.
ATALL	Mr. Cibber.
CAPTAIN STRUT	Mr. Bowen.
SIR SQUABBLE SPLITHAIR	Mr. Norris.
SAUNTER	Mr. Pack.
OLD MR. WILFUL	Mr. Bullock.
SIR HARRY ATALL	Mr. Cross.
SUPPLE	Mr. Fairbank.
LADY DAINTY	Mrs. Oldfield.
LADY SADLIFE	Mrs. Crosse.
CLARINDA	Mrs. Rogers.
SYLVIA	Mrs. Bradshaw.
WISHWELL	Mrs. Saunders.
SITUP	Mrs. Brown.

did not publish it in my own Name; but as my having but a Hand in it could not be long a Secret, I have been often treated as a Plagiary on that Account: Not that I think I have any right to complain of whatever would detract from the Merit of that sort of Labour, yet a Cobler may be allow'd to be useful though he is not famous:[1] And I hope a Man is not blameable for doing a little Good, tho' he cannot do as much as another? But so it is—Twopenny Criticks must live as well as Eighteenpenny Authors![2]

While the Stage was thus recovering its former Strength, a more honourable Mark of Favour was shewn to it than it was ever known before or since to have receiv'd. The then Lord *Hallifax* was not only the Patron of the Men of Genius of this Time, but had likewise a generous Concern for the Reputation and Prosperity of the Theatre, from whence the most elegant Dramatick Labours of the Learned, he knew, had often shone in their brightest Lustre. A Proposal therefore was drawn up and addressed to that Noble Lord for his Approbation and Assistance to raise a publick Subscription for Reviving Three Plays of the best Authors, with the full Strength of the Company; every Subscriber to have Three Tickets for the first Day of each Play for

---

[1] The plays from which Cibber compiled "The Double Gallant" are "Love at a Venture," "The Lady's Visiting Day," and "The Reformed Wife" (Genest, ii. 389).

[2] Eighteenpence was for many years the recognized price of plays when published.

his single Payment of Three Guineas. This Subscription his Lordship so zealously encouraged, that from his Recommendation chiefly, in a very little time it was compleated. The Plays were *Julius Cæsar* of *Shakespear*; the *King and no King* of *Fletcher*, and the Comic Scenes of *Dryden's Marriage à la mode* and of his *Maiden Queen* put together;[1] for it was judg'd that, as these comic Episodes were utterly independent of the serious Scenes they were originally written to, they might on this occasion be as well Episodes either to the other, and so make up five livelier Acts between them: At least the Project so well succeeded, that those comic Parts have never since been replaced, but were continued to be jointly acted as one Play several Years after.

By the Aid of this Subscription, which happen'd in 1707, and by the additional Strength and Industry of this Company, not only the Actors (several of which were handsomely advanc'd in their Sallaries) were duly paid, but the Menager himself, too, at the Foot of his Account, stood a considerable Gainer.

[1] These were played on 14th January, 21st January, and 4th February, 1707, in the order Cibber gives them. The alteration of Dryden's plays was done by Cibber, and was called "Marriage à la Mode; or, the Comical Lovers."

CELADON	Mr. Cibber.
PALAMEDE	Mr. Wilks.
RHODOPHIL	Mr. Booth.
MELANTHA	Mrs. Bracegirdle.
FLORIMEL	Mrs. Oldfield.
DORALICE	Mrs. Porter.

I have not seen a copy of this, so take the cast from Genest.

At the same time the Patentee of *Drury-Lane* went on in his usual Method of paying extraordinary Prices to Singers, Dancers, and other exotick Performers, which were as constantly deducted out of the sinking Sallaries of his Actors: 'Tis true his Actors perhaps might not deserve much more than he gave them; yet, by what I have related, it is plain he chose not to be troubled with such as visibly had deserv'd more: For it seems he had not purchas'd his Share of the Patent to mend the Stage, but to make Money of it: And to say Truth, his Sense of every thing to be shewn there was much upon a Level with the Taste of the Multitude, whose Opinion and whose Money weigh'd with him full as much as that of the best Judges. His Point was to please the Majority, who could more easily comprehend any thing they *saw* than the daintiest things that could be said to them. But in this Notion he kept no medium; for in my Memory he carry'd it so far that he was (some few Years before this time) actually dealing for an extraordinary large Elephant at a certain Sum for every Day he might think fit to shew the tractable Genius of that vast quiet Creature in any Play or Farce in the Theatre (then standing) in *Dorset-Garden*. But from the Jealousy which so formidable a Rival had rais'd in his Dancers, and by his Bricklayer's assuring him that if the Walls were to be open'd wide enough for its Entrance it might endanger the fall of the House, he gave up his Project, and with it so hopeful a Prospect of making the Receipts of the Stage run higher than all the Wit and Force of the best Writers had ever yet rais'd them to.[1]

About the same time of his being under this Disappointment he put in Practice another Project of as new, though not of so bold a Nature; which was his introducing a Set of Rope-dancers into the same Theatre; for the first Day of whose Performance he had given out some Play in which I had a material Part: But I was hardy enough to go into the Pit and acquaint the Spectators near me, that I hop'd they would not think it a Mark of my Disrespect to them, if I declin'd acting upon any Stage that was brought to so low a Disgrace as ours was like to be by that Day's Entertainment. My Excuse was so well taken that I never after found any ill Consequences, or heard of the least Disapprobation of it: And the whole Body of Actors, too, protesting against such an Abuse of their Profession, our cautious Master was too much alarm'd and intimidated to repeat it.

After what I have said, it will be no wonder that all due Regards to the original Use and Institution of the Stage should be utterly lost or neglected: Nor was the Conduct of this Menager easily to be alter'd while he had found the Secret of making Money out

---

[1] An elephant was introduced into the pantomime of "Harlequin and Padmanaba," at Covent Garden, 26th December, 1811. Genest points out that one had appeared at Smock Alley Theatre, Dublin, in 1771-2.

of Disorder and Confusion: For however strange it may seem, I have often observ'd him inclin'd to be cheerful in the Distresses of his Theatrical Affairs, and equally reserv'd and pensive when they went smoothly forward with a visible Profit. Upon a Run of good Audiences he was more frighted to be thought a Gainer, which might make him accountable to others, than he was dejected with bad Houses, which at worst he knew would make others accountable to him: And as, upon a moderate Computation, it cannot be supposed that the contested Accounts of a twenty Year's Wear and Tear in a Play-house could be fairly adjusted by a Master in Chancery under four-score Years more, it will be no Surprize that by the Neglect, or rather the Discretion, of other Proprietors in not throwing away good Money after bad, this Hero of a Menager, who alone supported the War, should in time so fortify himself by Delay, and so tire his Enemies, that he became sole Monarch of his Theatrical Empire, and left the quiet Possession of it to his Successors.

If these Facts seem too trivial for the Attention of a sensible Reader, let it be consider'd that they are not chosen Fictions to *entertain*, but Truths necessary to *inform* him under what low Shifts and Disgraces, what Disorders and Revolutions, the Stage labour'd before it could recover that Strength and Reputation wherewith it began to flourish towards the latter End of Queen *Anne*'s Reign; and which it continued to enjoy for a Course of twenty Years following. But let us resume our Account of the new Settlement in the *Hay-Market*.

It may be a natural Question why the Actors whom *Swiney* brought over to his Undertaking in the *Hay-Market* would tie themselves down to limited Sallaries? for though he as their Menager was obliged to make them certain Payments, it was not certain that the Receipts would enable him to do it; and since their own Industry was the only visible Fund they had to depend upon, why would they not for that Reason insist upon their being Sharers as well of possible Profits as Losses? How far in this Point they acted right or wrong will appear from the following State of their Case.

It must first be consider'd that this Scheme of their Desertion was all concerted and put in Execution in a Week's Time, which short Warning might make them overlook that Circumstance, and the sudden Prospect of being deliver'd from having seldom more than half their Pay was a Contentment that had bounded all their farther Views. Besides, as there could be no room to doubt of their receiving their full Pay previous to any Profits that might be reap'd by their Labour, and as they had no great Reason to apprehend those Profits could exceed their respective Sallaries so far as to make them repine at them, they might think it but reasonable to let the Chance of any extraordinary Gain be on the Side of their Leader and Director. But farther, as this Scheme had the Approbation of the Court, these Actors in reality had it not in their Power to alter any Part of it: And what induced the Court to encourage it was, that by having the Theatre and its Menager more immediately dependent on the Power of the Lord Chamberlain, it was not doubted but the Stage would be recover'd into such a Reputation as might now do Honour to that absolute Command which the Court or its Officers seem'd always fond of having over it.

Here, to set the Constitution of the Stage in a clearer Light, it may not be amiss to look back a little on the Power of a Lord Chamberlain, which, as may have been observ'd in all Changes of the Theatrical Government, has been the main Spring without which no Scheme of what kind soever could be set in Motion. My Intent is not to enquire how far by Law this Power has been limited or extended; but merely as an Historian to relate Facts to gratify the Curious, and then leave them to their own Reflections: This, too, I am the more inclin'd to, because there is no one Circumstance which has affected the Stage wherein so many Spectators, from those of the highest Rank to the Vulgar, have seem'd more positively knowing or less inform'd in.

Though in all the Letters Patent for acting Plays, *&c.* since King *Charles* the *First*'s Time there has been no mention of the Lord Chamberlain, or of any Subordination to his Command or Authority, yet it was still taken for granted that no Letters Patent, by the bare Omission of such a great Officer's Name, could have superseded or taken out of his Hands that Power which Time out of Mind he always had exercised over the Theatre.¹ The common Opinions then abroad were, that if the Profession of Actors was unlawful, it was not in the Power of the Crown to license it; and if it were not unlawful, it ought to be free and independent as other Professions; and that a Patent to exercise it was only an honorary Favour from the Crown to give it a better Grace of Recommendation to the Publick. But as the Truth of this Question seem'd to be wrapt in a great deal of Obscurity, in the old Laws made in former Reigns relating to Players, &c. it may be no Wonder that the best Companies of Actors should be desirous of taking Shelter under the visible Power of a Lord Chamberlain who they knew had at his Pleasure favoured and protected or born hard upon them: But be all this as it may, a Lord Chamberlain (from whencesoever his Power might be derived) had till of later Years had always an implicit Obedience paid to it: I shall now give some few Instances in what manner it was exercised.

What appear'd to be most reasonably under his Cognizance was the licensing or refusing new Plays,

[1] In Mr. Percy Fitzgerald's "New History of the English Stage" (ii. 436) he gives an interesting memorandum by the Hon Sir Spencer Ponsonby-Fane regarding this point. It begins: "That the Chamberlain's authority proceeded from the Sovereign alone is clear, from the fact that no Act of Parliament, previous to the 10 Geo. II., c. 28 (passed in 1737), alludes to his licensing powers, though he was constantly exercising them."

or striking out what might be thought offensive in them: Which Province had been for many Years assign'd to his inferior Officer, the Master of the Revels; yet was not this License irrevocable; for several Plays, though acted by that Permission, had been silenced afterwards. The first Instance of this kind that common Fame has deliver'd down to us, is that of the *Maid's Tragedy* of *Beaumont* and *Fletcher*, which was forbid in King *Charles* the *Second*'s time, by an Order from the Lord Chamberlain. For what Reason this Interdiction was laid upon it the Politicks of those Days have only left us to guess. Some said that the killing of the King in that Play, while the tragical Death of King *Charles* the *First* was then so fresh in People's Memory, was an Object too horribly impious for a publick Entertainment. What makes this Conjecture seem to have some Foundation, is that the celebrated *Waller*, in Compliment to that Court, alter'd the last Act of this Play (which is printed at the End of his Works) and gave it a new Catastrophe, wherein the Life of the King is loyally saved, and the Lady's Matter made up with a less terrible Reparation. Others have given out, that a repenting Mistress, in a romantick Revenge of her Dishonour, killing the King in the very Bed he expected her to come into, was shewing a too dangerous Example to other *Evadnes* then shining at Court in the same Rank of royal Distinction; who, if ever their Consciences should have run equally mad, might have had frequent Opportunities of putting the Expiation of their Frailty into the like Execution. But this I doubt is too deep a Speculation, or too ludicrous a Reason, to be relied on; it being well known that the Ladies then in favour were not so nice in their Notions as to think their Preferment their Dishonour, or their Lover a Tyrant: Besides, that easy Monarch loved his Roses without Thorns; nor do we hear that he much chose to be himself the first Gatherer of them.[1]

The *Lucius Junius Brutus* of *Nat. Lee*[2] was in the same Reign silenced after the third Day of Acting it; it being objected that the Plan and Sentiments of it had too boldly vindicated, and might enflame republican Principles.

A Prologue (by *Dryden*) to the *Prophetess* was forbid by the Lord *Dorset* after the first Day of its being spoken.[3] This happen'd when King *William* was prosecuting the War in *Ireland*. It must be

---

[1] Langbaine, in his "Account of the English Dramatick Poets," 1691, says (p. 212): "*Maids Tragedy*, a Play which has always been acted with great Applause at the King's Theatre; and which had still continu'd on the English Stage, had not King *Charles* the Second, for some particular Reasons forbid its further Appearance during his Reign. It has since been reviv'd by Mr. *Waller*, the last Act having been wholly alter'd to please the Court."

I think there can be little doubt that the last reason suggested by Cibber was the real cause of the prohibition.

[2] Produced at Dorset Garden, 1681.

[3] Produced at Dorset Garden, 1690. See *ante*, vol. i. p. 187. I presume that the lines alluded to by Cibber are.—

"Never content with what you had before,
But true to change, and Englishmen all o'er."

confess'd that this Prologue had some familiar, metaphorical Sneers at the Revolution itself; and as the Poetry of it was good, the Offence of it was less pardonable.

The Tragedy of *Mary* Queen of *Scotland*[1] had been offer'd to the Stage twenty Years before it was acted: But from the profound Penetration of the Master of the Revels, who saw political Spectres in it that never appear'd in the Presentation, it had lain so long upon the Hands of the Author; who had at last the good Fortune to prevail with a Nobleman to favour his Petition to Queen *Anne* for Permission to have it acted: The Queen had the Goodness to refer the Merit of his Play to the Opinion of that noble Person, although he was not her Majesty's Lord Chamberlain; upon whose Report of its being every way an innocent Piece, it was soon after acted with Success.

Reader, by your Leave——I will but just speak a Word or two to any Author that has not yet writ one Line of his next Play, and then I will come to my Point again——What I would say to him is this —Sir, before you set Pen to Paper, think well and principally of your Design or chief Action, towards

---

[1] In the "Biographia Dramatica" (iii. 24) the following note appears: "Mary Queen of Scotland. A play under this title was advertised, among others, as sold by Wellington, in St. Paul's Churchyard, in 1703." But the work Cibber refers to is "The Island Queens; or, the Death of Mary Queen of Scots," a tragedy by John Banks, printed in 1684, but not produced till 6th March, 1704, when it was played at Drury Lane as "The Albion Queens."

which every Line you write ought to be drawn, as to its Centre: If we can say of your finest Sentiments, This or That might be left out without maiming the Story, you would tell us, depend upon it, that fine thing is said in a wrong Place; and though you may urge that a bright Thought is not to be resisted, you will not be able to deny that those very fine Lines would be much finer if you could find a proper Occasion for them: Otherwise you will be thought to take less Advice from *Aristotle* or *Horace* than from Poet *Bays* in the *Rehearsal*, who very smartly says—*What the Devil is the Plot good for but to bring in fine things?* Compliment the Taste of your Hearers as much as you please with them, provided they belong to your Subject, but don't, like a dainty Preacher who has his Eye more upon this World than the next, leave your Text for them. When your Fable is good, every Part of it will cost you much less Labour to keep your Narration alive, than you will be forced to bestow upon those elegant Discourses that are not absolutely conducive to your Catastrophe or main Purpose: Scenes of that kind shew but at best the unprofitable or injudicious Spirit of a Genius. It is but a melancholy Commendation of a fine Thought to say, when we have heard it, *Well! but what's all this to the Purpose?* Take, therefore, in some part, Example by the Author last mention'd! There are three Plays of his, The *Earl* of *Essex*,[1] *Anna*

---

[1] "The Unhappy Favourite; or, the Earl of Essex," produced at the Theatre Royal, 1682.

Bullen,[1] and *Mary Queen of Scots*, which, tho' they are all written in the most barren, barbarous Stile that was ever able to keep Possession of the Stage, have all interested the Hearts of his Auditors. To what then could this Success be owing, but to the intrinsick and naked Value of the well-conducted Tales he has simply told us? There is something so happy in the Disposition of all his Fables; all his chief Characters are thrown into such natural Circumstances of Distress, that their Misery or Affliction wants very little Assistance from the Ornaments of Stile or Words to speak them. When a skilful Actor is so situated, his bare plaintive Tone of Voice, the Cast of Sorrow from his Eye, his slowly graceful Gesture, his humble Sighs of Resignation under his Calamities: All these, I say, are sometimes without a Tongue equal to the strongest Eloquence. At such a time the attentive Auditor supplies from his own Heart whatever the Poet's Language may fall short of in Expression, and melts himself into every Pang of Humanity which the like Misfortunes in real Life could have inspir'd.

After what I have observ'd, whenever I see a Tragedy defective in its Fable, let there be never so many fine Lines in it; I hope I shall be forgiven if I impute that Defect to the Idleness, the weak Judgment, or barren Invention of the Author.

If I should be ask'd why I have not always my self follow'd the Rules I would impose upon others;

---

[1] "Virtue Betrayed; or, Anna Bullen," first acted at Dorset Garden, 1682.

I can only answer, that whenever I have not, I lie equally open to the same critical Censure. But having often observ'd a better than ordinary Stile thrown away upon the loose and wandering Scenes of an ill-chosen Story, I imagin'd these Observations might convince some future Author of how great Advantage a Fable well plann'd must be to a Man of any tolerable Genius.

All this I own is leading my Reader out of the way; but if he has as much Time upon his Hands as I have, (provided we are neither of us tir'd) it may be equally to the Purpose what he reads or what I write of. But as I have no Objection to Method when it is not troublesome, I return to my Subject.

Hitherto we have seen no very unreasonable Instance of this absolute Power of a Lord Chamberlain, though we were to admit that no one knew of any real Law, or Construction of Law, by which this Power was given him. I shall now offer some Facts relating to it of a more extraordinary Nature, which I leave my Reader to give a Name to.

About the middle of King *William*'s Reign an Order of the Lord Chamberlain was then subsisting that no Actor of either Company should presume to go from one to the other without a Discharge from their respective Menagers[1] and the Permission of

[1] Bellchambers notes here that this order was superfluous, because the prohibition was inserted in the Patents given to Davenant and Killigrew. But, whether superfluous or not, I find from the

the Lord Chamberlain. Notwithstanding such Order, *Powel*, being uneasy at the Favour *Wilks* was then rising into, had without such Discharge left the *Drury-Lane* Theatre and engag'd himself to that of *Lincolns-Inn-Fields:* But by what follows it will appear that this Order was not so much intended to do both of them *good*, as to do that which the Court chiefly favour'd (*Lincolns-Inn-Fields*) no harm.¹ For when *Powel* grew dissatisfy'd at his Station there too, he return'd to *Drury-Lane* (as he had before gone from it) without a Discharge: But halt a little! here, on this Side of the Question, the Order was to stand in force, and the same Offence against it now was not to be equally pass'd over. He was the next Day taken up by a Messenger and confin'd to the Porter's-Lodge, where, to the best of my Remembrance, he remain'd about two Days; when the Menagers of *Lincolns-Inn-Fields*, not thinking an Actor of his

---

Records of the Lord Chamberlain's Office that this order was frequently made. On 16th April, 1695, an edict was issued forbidding actors to desert from Betterton's company; on 25th July, 1695, desertions from either company were forbidden; and this latter order was reiterated on 27th May, 1697.

¹ I do not know whether it is merely a coincidence, but it is curious that, after Betterton got his License (on 25th March, 1695), an edict was issued that no one was to desert from his company to that of the Theatre Royal; while a general order against any desertion from either company to the other was not issued for more than three months after the first edict. The dates, as given in the Records of the Lord Chamberlain's Office, are 16th April and 25th July respectively. If this were intentional, it would form a curious commentary on Cibber's statement.

loose Character worth their farther Trouble, gave him up; though perhaps he was releas'd for some better Reason.[1] Upon this occasion, the next Day, behind the Scenes at *Drury-Lane*, a Person of great Quality in my hearing enquiring of *Powel* into the Nature of his Offence, after he had heard it, told him, That if he had had Patience or Spirit enough to have staid in his Confinement till he had given him Notice of it, he would have found him a handsomer way of coming out of it.

Another time the same Actor, *Powel*, was provok'd

---

[1] Genest supposes that this incident occurred about June, 1704. But the Lord Chamberlain's Records of that time contain no note of it, and Cibber's language scarcely bears the interpretation that three years elapsed between Powell's leaving Drury Lane and returning to it, as was the case at that time; for he was at Lincoln's Inn Fields for three seasons, 1702 to 1704. I find, however, a warrant, dated 14th November, 1705, to apprehend Powell for refusing to act his part at the Haymarket, so that the audience had to be dismissed, and for trying to raise a mutiny in the company. He was ordered to be confined in the Porter's Lodge until further notice. On the 24th November Rich was informed that Powell had deserted the Haymarket, and was warned not to engage him. Now these desertions must have followed each other pretty closely, for he was at Drury Lane in the beginning of 1705; at the Haymarket in April of the same year; and about six months later had deserted the latter. The sequel to this difficulty seems to be the silencing of Rich for receiving Powell, on 5th March in the fifth year of Queen Anne's reign, that is, 1707. Unless the transcriber of the Records has made a mistake in the year, Powell was thus suspended for about eighteen months. It will be noticed that Cibber does not say that he was acting the night after his release, but merely that he was behind the scenes.

at *Will's* Coffee-house, in a Dispute about the Playhouse Affairs, to strike a Gentleman whose Family had been sometimes Masters of it; a Complaint of this Insolence was, in the Absence of the Lord-Chamberlain, immediately made to the Vice-Chamberlain, who so highly resented it that he thought himself bound in Honour to carry his Power of redressing it as far as it could possibly go: For *Powel* having a Part in the Play that was acted the Day after, the Vice-Chamberlain sent an Order to silence the whole Company for having suffer'd *Powel* to appear upon the Stage before he had made that Gentleman Satisfaction, although the Masters of the Theatre had had no Notice of *Powel's* Misbehaviour: However, this Order was obey'd, and remain'd in force for two or three Days, 'till the same Authority was pleas'd or advis'd to revoke it.[1] From the Measures this injur'd Gentleman took for his Redress, it may be judg'd how far it was taken for granted that a Lord-Chamberlain had an absolute Power over the Theatre.

I shall now give an Instance of an Actor who had the Resolution to stand upon the Defence of his

---

[1] Among the Lord Chamberlain's Records is a copy of a decree suspending all performances at Drury Lane because Powell had been allowed to play. This is dated 3rd May, 1698. His offence was that he had drawn his sword on Colonel Stanhope and young Davenant. The suspension was removed the following day; but on the 19th of the same month Powell was forbidden to be received at either Drury Lane or Dorset Garden.

Liberty against the same Authority, and was reliev'd by it.

In the same King's Reign, *Dogget*, who tho', from a severe Exactness in his Nature, he could be seldom long easy in any Theatre, where Irregularity, not to say Injustice, too often prevail'd, yet in the private Conduct of his Affairs he was a prudent, honest Man. He therefore took an unusual Care, when he return'd to act under the Patent in *Drury-Lane*, to have his Articles drawn firm and binding: But having some Reason to think the Patentee had not dealt fairly with him, he quitted the Stage and would act no more, rather chusing to lose his whatever unsatisfy'd Demands than go through the chargeable and tedious Course of the Law to recover it. But the Patentee, who (from other People's Judgment) knew the Value of him, and who wanted, too, to have him sooner back than the Law could possibly bring him, thought the surer way would be to desire a shorter Redress from the Authority of the Lord-Chamberlain.[1] Accordingly, upon his Complaint a Messenger was immediately dispatch'd to *Norwich*, where *Dogget* then was, to bring him up in Custody: But doughty *Dogget*, who had Money in his Pocket and the Cause of Liberty at his Heart, was not in the least intimidated

[1] A warrant was issued to apprehend Dogget and take him to the Knight Marshall's Prison, on 23rd November, 1697, his offence being desertion of the company of Drury Lane and Dorset Garden. The Records contain no note as to the termination of the matter; but this is, beyond doubt, the occasion referred to by Cibber.

by this formidable Summons. He was observ'd to obey it with a particular Chearfulness, entertaining his Fellow-traveller, the Messenger, all the way in the Coach (for he had protested against Riding) with as much Humour as a Man of his Business might be capable of tasting. And as he found his Charges were to be defray'd, he, at every Inn, call'd for the best Dainties the Country could afford or a pretended weak Appetite could digest. At this rate they jollily roll'd on, more with the Air of a Jaunt than a Journey, or a Party of Pleasure than of a poor Devil in Durance. Upon his Arrival in Town he immediately apply'd to the Lord Chief Justice *Holt* for his *Habeas Corpus*. As his Case was something particular, that eminent and learned Minister of the Law took a particular Notice of it: For *Dogget* was not only discharg'd, but the Process of his Confinement (according to common Fame) had a Censure pass'd upon it in Court, which I doubt I am not Lawyer enough to repeat! To conclude, the officious Agents in this Affair, finding that in *Dogget* they had mistaken their Man, were mollify'd into milder Proceedings, and (as he afterwards told me) whisper'd something in his Ear that took away *Dogget's* farther Uneasiness about it.

By these Instances we see how naturally Power only founded on Custom is apt, where the Law is silent, to run into Excesses, and while it laudably pretends to govern others, how hard it is to govern itself. But since the Law has lately open'd its

Mouth, and has said plainly that some Part of this Power to govern the Theatre shall be, and is plac'd in a proper Person; and as it is evident that the Power of that white Staff, ever since it has been in the noble Hand that now holds it, has been us'd with the utmost Lenity, I would beg leave of the murmuring Multitude who frequent the Theatre to offer them a simple Question or two, *viz.* Pray, Gentlemen, how came you, or rather your Fore-fathers, never to be mutinous upon any of the occasional Facts I have related? And why have you been so often tumultuous upon a Law's being made that only confirms a less Power than was formerly exercis'd without any Law to support it? You cannot, sure, say such Discontent is either just or natural, unless you allow it a Maxim in your Politicks that Power exercis'd *without* Law is a less Grievance than the same Power exercis'd *according* to Law!

Having thus given the clearest View I was able of the usual Regard paid to the Power of a Lord-Chamberlain, the Reader will more easily conceive what Influence and Operation that Power must naturally have in all Theatrical Revolutions, and particularly in the complete Re-union of both Companies, which happen'd in the Year following.

CHAPTER XI.

Some Chimærical Thoughts of making the Stage useful: Some, to its Reputation. The Patent unprofitable to all the Proprietors but one. A fourth Part of it given away to Colonel Brett. *A Digression to his Memory. The two Companies of Actors re-united by his Interest and Menagement. The first Direction of Operas only given to Mr.* Swiney.

FROM the Time that the Company of Actors in the *Hay-Market* was recruited with those from *Drury-Lane,* and came into the Hands of their new Director, *Swiney,* the Theatre for three or four Years following suffer'd so many Convulsions, and was thrown every other Winter under such different Interests and Menagement before it came to a firm and lasting Settlement, that I am doubtful if the most candid Reader will have Patience to go through a full and fair Account of it: And yet I would fain flatter my self that those who are not too wise to frequent the Theatre (or have Wit enough to distinguish what sort of Sights there either do Honour or Disgrace to it) may think their national Diversion no contemptible Subject for a more able Historian than I pretend to be: If I have any particular Qualification for the Task more than another it is that I have been an ocular Witness of the several Facts that are to fill up the rest of my Volume, and am perhaps the only Person living (however unworthy) from whom the same Materials can be collected; but let them come from whom they may, whether at best they will be worth reading, perhaps a Judgment may be better form'd after a patient Perusal of the following Digression.

In whatever cold Esteem the Stage may be among the Wise and Powerful, it is not so much a Reproach to those who contentedly enjoy it in its lowest Condition, as that Condition of it is to those who (though they cannot but know to how valuable a publick Use a Theatre, well establish'd, might be rais'd) yet in so many civiliz'd Nations have neglected it. This perhaps will be call'd thinking my own wiser than all the wise Heads in *Europe*. But I hope a more humble Sense will be given to it; at least I only mean, that if so many Governments have their Reasons for their Disregard of their Theatres, those

Reasons may be deeper than my Capacity has yet been able to dive into: If therefore my simple Opinion is a wrong one, let the Singularity of it expose me: And tho' I am only building a Theatre in the Air, it is there, however, at so little Expence and in so much better a Taste than any I have yet seen, that I cannot help saying of it, as a wiser Man did (it may be) upon a wiser Occasion:

— *Si quid novisti rectius istis,*
Candidus imperti ; si non —   Hor.[1]

Give me leave to play with my Project in Fancy.

I say, then, that as I allow nothing is more liable to debase and corrupt the Minds of a People than a licentious Theatre, so under a just and proper Establishment it were possible to make it as apparently the School of Manners and of Virtue. Were I to collect all the Arguments that might be given for my Opinion, or to inforce it by exemplary Proofs, it might swell this short Digression to a Volume; I shall therefore trust the Validity of what I have laid down to a single Fact that may be still fresh in the Memory of many living Spectators. When the Tragedy of *Cato* was first acted,[2] let us call to mind the noble Spirit of Patriotism which that Play then infus'd into the Breasts of a free People that crowded to it; with what affecting Force was that most elevated of Human Virtues recommended? Even the false Pretenders to it felt an unwilling Conviction,

---

[1] Horace, *Epis.*, i. 6, 68.   [2] At Drury Lane, 14th April, 1713.

and made it a Point of Honour to be foremost in their Approbation; and this, too, at a time when the fermented Nation had their different Views of Government. Yet the sublime Sentiments of Liberty in that venerable Character rais'd in every sensible Hearer such conscious Admiration, such compell'd Assent to the Conduct of a suffering Virtue, as even *demanded* two almost irreconcileable Parties to embrace and join in their equal Applauses of it.[1] Now, not to take from the Merit of the Writer, had that Play never come to the Stage, how much of this valuable Effect of it must have been lost? It then could have had no more immediate weight with the Publick than our poring upon the many ancient Authors thro' whose Works the same Sentiments have been perhaps less profitably dispers'd, tho' amongst Millions of Readers; but by bringing such Sentiments to the Theatre and into Action, what a superior Lustre did they shine with? There *Cato* breath'd again in Life; and though he perish'd in the Cause of Liberty, his Virtue was victorious, and left the Triumph of it in the Heart of every melting Spectator. If Effects like these are laudable, if the Representation of such Plays can carry Conviction with so much Pleasure to the Understanding, have

---

[1] This is a pretty way of putting what Johnson, in his Life of Addison, afterwards stated in the well-known words: "The Whigs applauded every line in which Liberty was mentioned, as a satire on the Tories; and the Tories echoed every clap to show that the satire was unfelt." In the next paragraph Johnson describes the play as "supported by the emulation of factious praise."

they not vastly the Advantage of any other Human Helps to Eloquence? What equal Method can be found to lead or stimulate the Mind to a quicker Sense of Truth and Virtue, or warm a People into the Love and Practice of such Principles as might be at once a Defence and Honour to their Country? In what Shape could we listen to Virtue with equal Delight or Appetite of Instruction? The Mind of Man is naturally free, and when he is compell'd or menac'd into any Opinion that he does not readily conceive, he is more apt to doubt the Truth of it than when his Capacity is led by Delight into Evidence and Reason. To preserve a Theatre in this Strength and Purity of Morals is, I grant, what the wisest Nations have not been able to perpetuate or to transmit long to their Posterity: But this Difficulty will rather heighten than take from the Honour of the Theatre: The greatest Empires have decay'd for want of proper Heads to guide them, and the Ruins of them sometimes have been the Subject of Theatres that could not be themselves exempt from as various Revolutions: Yet may not the most natural Inference from all this be, That the Talents requisite to form good Actors, great Writers, and true Judges were, like those of wise and memorable Ministers, as well the Gifts of Fortune as of Nature, and not always to be found in all Climes or Ages. Or can there be a stronger modern Evidence of the Value of Dramatick Performances than that in many Countries where the Papal Religion prevails the Holy Policy (though it allows not to an Actor Christian Burial) is so conscious of the Usefulness of his Art that it will frequently take in the Assistance of the Theatre to give even Sacred History, in a Tragedy, a Recommendation to the more pathetick Regard of their People. How can such Principles, in the Face of the World, refuse the Bones of a Wretch the lowest Benefit of Christian Charity after having admitted his Profession (for which they deprive him of that Charity) to serve the solemn Purposes of Religion? How far then is this Religious Inhumanity short of that famous Painter's, who, to make his *Crucifix* a Master-piece of Nature, stabb'd the Innocent Hireling from whose Body he drew it; and having heighten'd the holy Portrait with his last Agonies of Life, then sent it to be the consecrated Ornament of an Altar? Though we have only the Authority of common Fame for this Story, yet be it true or false the Comparison will still be just. Or let me ask another Question more humanly political.

How came the *Athenians* to lay out an Hundred Thousand Pounds upon the Decorations of one single Tragedy of *Sophocles?*[1] Not, sure, as it was merely a Spectacle for Idleness or Vacancy of Thought to gape at, but because it was the most rational, most instructive and delightful Composition that Human Wit had yet arrived at, and consequently the most worthy to be the Entertainment of a wise and warlike Nation: And it may be still a Question whether

[1] I confess I do not know Cibber's authority for this statement.

the *Sophocles* inspir'd this Publick Spirit, or this Publick Spirit inspir'd the *Sophocles*?[1]

But alas! as the Power of giving or receiving such Inspirations from either of these Causes seems pretty well at an End, now I have shot my Bolt I shall descend to talk more like a Man of the Age I live in: For, indeed, what is all this to a common *English* Reader? Why truly, as *Shakespear* terms it— *Caviare to the Multitude!*[2] Honest *John Trott* will tell you, that if he were to believe what I have said of the *Athenians*, he is at most but astonish'd at it; but that if the twentieth Part of the Sum I have mentioned were to be apply'd out of the Publick money to the Setting off the best Tragedy the nicest Noddle in the Nation could produce, it would probably raise the Passions higher in those that did Not like it than in those that did; it might as likely meet with an Insurrection as the Applause of the People, and so, mayhap, be fitter for the Subject of a Tragedy than for a publick Fund to support it. ———Truly, Mr. *Trott*, I cannot but own that I am very much of your Opinion: I am only concerned that the Theatre has not a better Pretence to the Care and further Consideration of those Governments where it is tolerated; but as what I have said

---

[1] "The Laureat" abuses Cibber for this sentence, declaring that he evidently considered "Sophocles" to be the name of a tragedy. But Cibber's method of expression, though curious, does not justify this attack.

[2] "Caviare to the general."—"Hamlet," act ii. sc. 2.

will not probably do it any great Harm, I hope I have not put you out of Patience by throwing a few good Wishes after an old Acquaintance.

To conclude this Digression. If for the Support of the Stage what is generally shewn there must be lower'd to the Taste of common Spectators; or if it is inconsistent with Liberty to mend that Vulgar Taste by making the Multitude less merry there; or by abolishing every low and senseless Jollity in which the Understanding can have no Share; whenever, I say, such is the State of the Stage, it will be as often liable to unanswerable Censure and manifest Disgraces. Yet there *was* a Time, not yet out of many People's Memory, when it subsisted upon its own rational Labours; when even Success attended an Attempt to reduce it to Decency; and when Actors themselves were hardy enough to hazard their Interest in pursuit of so dangerous a Reformation. And this Crisis I am my self as impatient as any tir'd Reader can be to arrive at. I shall therefore endeavour to lead him the shortest way to it. But as I am a little jealous of the badness of the Road, I must reserve to myself the Liberty of calling upon any Matter in my way, for a little Refreshment to whatever Company may have the Curiosity or Goodness to go along with me.

When the sole Menaging Patentee at *Drury-Lane* for several Years could never be persuaded or driven to any Account with the Adventurers, Sir *Thomas Skipwith* (who, if I am rightly inform'd, had an equal

Share with him[1]) grew so weary of the Affair that he actually made a Present of his entire Interest in it upon the following Occasion.

Sir *Thomas* happen'd in the Summer preceding the Re-union of the Companies to make a Visit to an intimate Friend of his, Colonel *Brett*, of *Sandywell*, in *Gloucestershire*; where the Pleasantness of the Place, and the agreeable manner of passing his Time there, had raised him to such a Gallantry of Heart, that in return to the Civilities of his Friend the Colonel he made him an Offer of his whole Right in the Patent; but not to overrate the Value of his Present, told him he himself had made nothing of it these ten Years: But the Colonel (he said) being a greater Favourite of the People in Power, and (as he believ'd) among the Actors too, than himself was, might think of some Scheme to turn it to Advantage, and in that Light, if he lik'd it, it was at

[1] Malone supposes that Skipwith acquired his shares from the Killigrew family, but in the indenture by which he transferred his interest to Brett, it seems as if he had acquired part of it from Alexander Davenant, and the remainder by buying up shares of the original Adventurers. The indenture will be found at length in Mr. Percy Fitzgerald's "New History of the English Stage," i. 252. Skipwith is described in the "Biog. Dram." (i. 487) as "a weak, vain, conceited coxcomb." The proportion in which the shares were divided among the various holders is shown by the "Opinion" of Northey and Raymond, in 1711, to have been this: Three-twentieths belonged to Charles Killigrew. The remainder was divided into tenths, of which two-tenths belonged to Rich; the other eight parts were owned by the Mortgagees or Adventurers If Cibber's supposition is correct, two of these parts belonged to Shipwith.

his Service. After a great deal of Raillery on both sides of what Sir *Thomas* had *not* made of it, and the particular Advantages the Colonel was likely to make of it, they came to a laughing Resolution That an Instrument should be drawn the next Morning of an Absolute Conveyance of the Premises. A Gentleman of the Law well known to them both happening to be a Guest there at the same time, the next Day produced the Deed according to his Instructions, in the Presence of whom and of others it was sign'd, seal'd, and deliver'd to the Purposes therein contain'd.[1]

This Transaction may be another Instance (as I have elsewhere observed) at how low a Value the Interests in a Theatrical License were then held, tho' it was visible from the Success of *Swiney* in that very Year that with tolerable Menagement they could at no time have fail'd of being a profitable Purchase.

The next Thing to be consider'd was what the Colonel should do with his new Theatrical Commission, which in another's Possession had been of so little Importance. Here it may be necessary to premise that this Gentleman was the first of any Consideration since my coming to the Stage with whom I had contracted a Personal Intimacy; which might be the Reason why in this Debate my Opinion had some Weight with him: Of this Intimacy, too, I am the more tempted to talk from the natural Pleasure

[1] It is dated 6th October, 1707.

of calling back in Age the Pursuits and happy Ardours of Youth long past, which, like the Ideas of a delightful Spring in a Winter's Rumination, are sometimes equal to the former Enjoyment of them. I shall, therefore, rather chuse in this Place to gratify my self than my Reader, by setting the fairest Side of this Gentleman in view, and by indulging a little conscious Vanity in shewing how early in Life I fell into the Possession of so agreeable a Companion: Whatever Failings he might have to others, he had none to me; nor was he, where he had them, without his valuable Qualities to balance or soften them. Let, then, what was not to be commended in him rest with his Ashes, never to be rak'd into: But the friendly Favours I received from him while living give me still a Pleasure in paying this only Mite of my Acknowledgment in my Power to his Memory. And if my taking this Liberty may find Pardon from several of his fair Relations still living, for whom I profess the utmost Respect, it will give me but little Concern tho' my critical Readers should think it all Impertinence.

This Gentleman, then, *Henry*, was the eldest Son of *Henry Brett*, Esq; of *Cowley*, in *Gloucestershire*, who coming early to his Estate of about Two Thousand a Year, by the usual Negligences of young Heirs had, before this his eldest Son came of age, sunk it to about half that Value, and that not wholly free from Incumbrances. Mr. *Brett*, whom I am speaking of, had his Education, and I might say, ended it, at the University of *Oxford*; for tho' he was settled some time after at the *Temple*, he so little followed the Law there that his Neglect of it made the Law (like some of his fair and frail Admirers) very often follow *him*. As he had an uncommon Share of Social Wit and a handsom Person, with a sanguine Bloom in his Complexion, no wonder they persuaded him that he might have a better Chance of Fortune by throwing such Accomplishments into the gayer World than by shutting them up in a Study. The first View that fires the Head of a young Gentleman of this modish Ambition just broke loose from Business, is to cut a Figure (as they call it) in a Side-box at the Play, from whence their next Step is to the *Green Room* behind the Scenes, sometimes their *Non ultra*. Hither at last, then, in this hopeful Quest of his Fortune, came this Gentleman-Errant, not doubting but the fickle Dame, while he was thus qualified to receive her, might be tempted to fall into his Lap. And though possibly the Charms of our Theatrical Nymphs might have their Share in drawing him thither, yet in my Observation the most visible Cause of his first coming was a more sincere Passion he had conceived for a fair fullbottom'd Perriwig which I then wore in my first Play of the *Fool in Fashion* in the Year 1695.[1] For it is to be noted that the *Beaux* of those Days were of a quite different Cast from the modern Stamp, and had

[1] As noted vol. i. p. 213, January, 1695, Old Style; that is, January, 1696.

more of the Stateliness of the Peacock in their Mien than (which now seems to be their highest Emulation) the pert Air of a Lapwing. Now, whatever Contempt Philosophers may have for a fine Perriwig, my Friend, who was not to despise the World, but to live in it, knew very well that so material an Article of Dress upon the Head of a Man of Sense, if it became him, could never fail of drawing to him a more partial Regard and Benevolence than could possibly be hoped for in an ill-made one.[1] This perhaps may soften the grave Censure which so youthful a Purchase might otherwise have laid upon him: In a Word, he made his Attack upon this Perriwig, as your young Fellows generally do upon a Lady of Pleasure, first by a few familiar Praises of her Person, and then a civil Enquiry into the Price of it. But upon his observing me a little surprized at the Levity of his Question about a Fop's Perriwig, he began to railly himself with so much Wit and Humour upon the Folly of his Fondness for it, that he struck me with an equal Desire of granting any thing in my

[1] Davies ("Dram. Misc.," iii. 84) says: "The heads of the English actors were, for a long time, covered with large full-bottomed perriwigs, a fashion introduced in the reign of Charles II., which was not entirely disused in public till about the year 1720. Addison, Congreve, and Steele, met at Button's coffee-house, in large, flowing, flaxen wigs, Booth, Wilks, and Cibber, when full-dressed, wore the same. Till within these twenty-five years, our Tamerlanes and Catos had as much hair on their heads as our judges on the bench . . . I have been told, that he [Booth] and Wilks bestowed forty guineas each on the exorbitant thatching of their heads."

Power to oblige so facetious a Customer. This singular Beginning of our Conversation, and the mutual Laughs that ensued upon it, ended in an Agreement to finish our Bargain that Night over a Bottle.

If it were possible the Relation of the happy Indiscretions which passed between us that Night could give the tenth Part of the Pleasure I then received from them, I could still repeat them with Delight: But as it may be doubtful whether the Patience of a Reader may be quite so strong as the Vanity of an Author, I shall cut it short by only saying that single Bottle was the Sire of many a jolly Dozen that for some Years following, like orderly Children, whenever they were call'd for, came into the same Company. Nor, indeed, did I think from that time, whenever he was to be had, any Evening could be agreeably enjoy'd without him.[1] But the long continuance of our Intimacy perhaps may be thus accounted for.

He who can taste Wit in another may in some sort be said to have it himself: Now, as I always

---

[1] "The Laureat," p. 66, relates with great acrimony an anecdote of Colonel Brett's reproving Cibber harshly for his treatment of an author who had submitted a play to him. Cibber is said to have opened the author's MS, and, having read two lines only, to have returned it to him saying, "Sir, it will not do." Going to Button's, he related his exploit with great glee, but was rebuked in the strongest terms by Colonel Brett, who is said to have put him to shame before the whole company. This is related as having occurred many years after the time Cibber now writes of, the suggestion being that Brett did not consider Cibber as a friend

had, and (I bless my self for the Folly) still have a quick Relish of whatever did or can give me Delight: This Gentleman could not but see the youthful Joy I was generally raised to whenever I had the Happiness of a *Tête à tête* with him; and it may be a moot Point whether Wit is not as often inspired by a proper Attention as by the brightest Reply to it. Therefore, as he had Wit enough for any two People, and I had Attention enough for any four, there could not well be wanting a sociable Delight on either side. And tho' it may be true that a Man of a handsome Person is apt to draw a partial Ear to every thing he says; yet this Gentleman seldom said any thing that might not have made a Man of the plainest Person agreeable. Such a continual Desire to please, it may be imagined, could not but sometimes lead him into a little venial Flattery rather than not succeed in it. And I, perhaps, might be one of those Flies that was caught in this Honey. As I was then a young successful Author and an Actor in some unexpected Favour, whether deservedly or not imports not; yet such Appearances at least were plausible Pretences enough for an amicable Adulation to enlarge upon, and the Sallies of it a less Vanity than mine might not have been able to resist. Whatever this Weakness on my side might be, I was not alone in it; for I have heard a Gentleman of Condition say, who knew the World as well as most Men that live in it, that let his Discretion be ever so much upon its Guard, he never fell into Mr. *Brett*'s

Company without being loth to leave it or carrying away a better Opinion of himself from it. If his Conversation had this Effect among the Men; what must we suppose to have been the Consequence when he gave it a yet softer turn among the Fair Sex? Here, now, a *French* Novellist would tell you fifty pretty Lies of him; but as I chuse to be tender of Secrets of that sort, I shall only borrow the good Breeding of that Language, and tell you in a Word, that I knew several Instances of his being *un Homme à bonne Fortune*. But though his frequent Successes might generally keep him from the usual Disquiets of a Lover, he knew this was a Life too liquorish to last; and therefore had Reflexion enough to be govern'd by the Advice of his Friends to turn these his Advantages of Nature to a better use.

Among the many Men of Condition with whom his Conversation had recommended him to an Intimacy, Sir *Thomas Skipwith* had taken a particular Inclination to him; and as he had the Advancement of his Fortune at Heart, introduced him where there was a Lady[1] who had enough in her Power to disencumber him of the World and make him every way easy for Life.

While he was in pursuit of this Affair, which no time was to be lost in (for the Lady was to be in

[1] This was the Countess of Macclesfield, the supposed mother of Richard Savage, who had a large fortune in her own right, of which she was not deprived on her divorce from the Earl of Macclesfield Shortly after her divorce, probably about 1698, she married Brett. She lived to be eighty, or over it, dying 11th October, 1753.

Town but for three Weeks) I one Day found him idling behind the Scenes before the Play was begun. Upon sight of him I took the usual Freedom he allow'd me, to rate him roundly for the Madness of not improving every Moment in his Power in what was of such consequence to him. Why are you not (said I) where you know you only should be? If your Design should once get Wind in the Town, the Ill-will of your Enemies or the Sincerity of the Lady's Friends may soon blow up your Hopes, which in your Circumstances of Life cannot be long supported by the bare Appearance of a Gentleman.
——But it is impossible to proceed without some Apology for the very familiar Circumstance that is to follow——Yet, as it might not be so trivial in its Effect as I fear it may be in the Narration, and is a Mark of that Intimacy which is necessary should be known had been between us, I will honestly make bold with my Scruples and let the plain Truth of my Story take its Chance for Contempt or Approbation.

After twenty Excuses to clear himself of the Neglect I had so warmly charged him with, he concluded them with telling me he had been out all the Morning upon Business, and that his Linnen was too much soil'd to be seen in Company. Oh, ho! said I, is that all? Come along with me, we will soon get over that dainty Difficulty: Upon which I haul'd him by the Sleeve into my Shifting-Room, he either staring, laughing, or hanging back all the way. There, when I had lock'd him in, I began to strip off my upper Cloaths, and bad him do the same; still he either did not, or would not seem to understand me, and continuing his Laugh, cry'd, What! is the Puppy mad? No, no, only positive, said I; for look you, in short, the Play is ready to begin, and the Parts that you and I are to act to Day are not of equal consequence; mine of young *Reveller* (in *Greenwich-Park*[1]) is but a Rake; but whatever you may be, you are not to appear so; therefore take my Shirt and give me yours; for depend upon't, stay here you shall not, and so go about your Business. To conclude, we fairly chang'd Linnen, nor could his Mother's have wrap'd him up more fortunately; for in about ten Days he marry'd the Lady.[2] In a Year or two after his Marriage he was chosen a Member of that Parliament which was sitting when

[1] A comedy by Mountfort the actor, originally played at the Theatre Royal, 1691. The part of Young Reveller was then taken by the author, and we have no record of Cibber's playing it before 1708; but from this anecdote he must have done so ten years earlier.

[2] In Boswell's Life of Johnson (i. 174) there is a note by Boswell himself:—

"Miss Mason, after having forfeited the title of Lady Macclesfield by divorce, was married to Colonel Brett, and, it is said, was well known in all the polite circles. Colley Cibber, I am informed, had so high an opinion of her taste and judgement as to genteel life, and manners, that he submitted every scene of his *Careless Husband* to Mrs. Brett's revisal and correction. Colonel Brett was reported to be too free in his gallantry with his Lady's maid. Mrs. Brett came into a room one day in her own house, and found the Colonel and her maid both fast asleep in two chairs. She tied a white handkerchief round her husband's neck,

King *William* dy'd. And, upon raising of some new Regiments, was made Lieutenant-Colonel to that of Sir *Charles Hotham*. But as his Ambition extended not beyond the Bounds of a Park Wall and a pleasant Retreat in the Corner of it, which with too much Expence he had just finish'd, he, within another Year, had leave to resign his Company to a younger Brother.

This was the Figure in Life he made when Sir *Thomas Skipwith* thought him the most proper Person to oblige (if it could be an Obligation) with the Present of his Interest in the Patent. And from these Anecdotes of my Intimacy with him, it may be less a Surprise, when he came to Town invested with this new Theatrical Power, that I should be the first Person to whom he took any Notice of it. And notwithstanding he knew I was then engag'd, in another Interest, at the *Hay-Market*, he desired we might consider together of the best Use he could make of it, assuring me at the same time he should think it of none to himself unless it could in some Shape be turn'd to my Advantage. This friendly Declaration, though it might be generous in him to make, was not needful to incline me in whatever might be honestly in my Power, whether by Interest or Negotiation, to serve him. My first Advice,

which was a sufficient proof that she had discovered his intrigue; but she never at any time took notice of it to him. This incident, as I am told, gave occasion to the well-wrought scene of Sir Charles and Lady Easy and Edging."

therefore, was, That he should produce his Deed to the other Menaging Patentee of *Drury-Lane*, and demand immediate Entrance to a joint Possession of all Effects and Powers to which that Deed had given him an equal Title. After which, if he met with no Opposition to this Demand (as upon sight of it he did not) that he should be watchful against any Contradiction from his Collegue in whatever he might propose in carrying on the Affair, but to let him see that he was determin'd in all his Measures. Yet to heighten that Resolution with an Ease and Temper in his manner, as if he took it for granted there could be no Opposition made to whatever he had a mind to. For that this Method, added to his natural Talent of Persuading, would imperceptibly lead his Collegue into a Reliance on his superior Understanding, That however little he car'd for Business he should give himself the Air at least of Enquiry into what *had* been done, that what he intended to do might be thought more considerable and be the readier comply'd with: For if he once suffer'd his Collegue to seem wiser than himself, there would be no end of his perplexing him with absurd and dilatory Measures; direct and plain Dealing being a Quality his natural Diffidence would never suffer him to be Master of; of which his not complying with his Verbal Agreement with *Swiney*, when the *Hay-Market* House was taken for both their Uses, was an Evidence. And though some People thought it Depth and Policy in him to keep things often in

Confusion, it was ever my Opinion they over-rated his Skill, and that, in reality, his Parts were too weak for his Post, in which he had always acted to the best of his Knowledge. That his late Collegue, Sir *Thomas Shipwith*, had trusted too much to his Capacity for this sort of Business, and was treated by him accordingly, without ever receiving any Profits from it for several Years: Insomuch that when he found his Interest in such desperate Hands he thought the best thing he could do with it was (as he saw) to give it away. Therefore if he (Mr. *Brett*) could once fix himself, as I had advis'd, upon a different Foot with this hitherto untractable Menager, the Business would soon run through whatever Channel he might have a mind to lead it. And though I allow'd the greatest Difficulty he would meet with would be in getting his Consent to a Union of the two Companies, which was the only Scheme that could raise the Patent to its former Value, and which I knew this close Menager would secretly lay all possible Rubs in the way to; yet it was visible there was a way of reducing him to Compliance: For though it was true his Caution would never part with a Straw by way of Concession, yet to a high Hand he would give up any thing, provided he were suffer'd to keep his Title to it: If his Hat were taken from his Head in the Street, he would make no farther Resistance than to say, *I am not willing to part with it.* Much less would he have the Resolution openly to oppose any just

Measures, when he should find one, who with an equal Right to his and with a known Interest to bring them about, was resolv'd to go thro' with them.

Now though I knew my Friend was as thoroughly acquainted with this Patentee's Temper as myself, yet I thought it not amiss to quicken and support his Resolution, by confirming to him the little Trouble he would meet with, in pursuit of the Union I had advis'd him to; for it must be known that on our side Trouble was a sort of Physick we did not much care to take: But as the Fatigue of this Affair was likely to be lower'd by a good deal of Entertainment and Humour, which would naturally engage him in his dealing with so exotick a Partner, I knew that this softening the Business into a Diversion would lessen every Difficulty that lay in our way to it.

However copiously I may have indulg'd my self in this Commemoration of a Gentleman with whom I had pass'd so many of my younger Days with Pleasure, yet the Reader may by this Insight into his Character, and by that of the other Patentee, be better able to judge of the secret Springs that gave Motion to or obstructed so considerable an Event as that of the Re-union of the two Companies of Actors in 1708.[1] In Histories of more weight, for want of such Particulars we are often deceiv'd in the true Causes of Facts that most concern us to be let into; which sometimes makes us ascribe to Policy, or false

[1] See note, vol. i. p. 301.

Appearances of Wisdom, what perhaps in reality was the mere Effect of Chance or Humour.

Immediately after Mr. *Brett* was admitted as a joint Patentee, he made use of the Intimacy he had with the Vice-Chamberlain to assist his Scheme of this intended Union, in which he so far prevail'd that it was soon after left to the particular Care of the same Vice-Chamberlain to give him all the Aid and Power necessary to the bringing what he desired to Perfection. The Scheme was, to have but one Theatre for Plays and another for Operas, under separate Interests. And this the generality of Spectators, as well as the most approv'd Actors, had been some time calling for as the only Expedient to recover the Credit of the Stage and the valuable Interests of its Menagers

As the Condition of the Comedians at this time is taken notice of in my *Dedication* of the *Wife's Resentment* to the Marquis (now Duke) of *Kent*, and then Lord-Chamberlain, which was publish'd above thirty Years ago,[1] when I had no thought of ever troubling the World with this Theatrical History, I see no Reason why it may not pass as a Voucher of the Facts I am now speaking of; I shall therefore give them in the very Light I then saw them. After some Acknowledgment for his Lordship's Protection of our (*Hay-Market*) Theatre, it is further said——

" The Stage has, for many Years, 'till of late,

---

[1] 1707. See note on page 3 of this vol.

" groan'd under the greatest Discouragements, which
" have been very much, if not wholly, owing to the
" Mismenagement of those that have aukwardly
" govern'd it. Great Sums have been ventur'd upon
" empty Projects and Hopes of immoderate Gains,
" and when those Hopes have fail'd, the Loss has
" been tyrannically deducted out of the Actors
" Sallary. And if your Lordship had not redeem'd
" them—*This is meant of our being suffer'd to come
" over to* Swiney——they were very near being
" wholly laid aside, or, at least, the Use of their
" Labour was to be swallow'd up in the pretended
" Merit of Singing and Dancing."

What follows relates to the Difficulties in dealing with the then impracticable Menager, *viz.*

" —And though your Lordship's Tenderness of
" oppressing is so very just that you have rather
" staid to convince a Man of your good Intentions
" to him than to do him even a Service against his
" Will; yet since your Lordship has so happily begun
" the Establishment of the separate Diversions, we
" live in hope that the same Justice and Resolution
" will still persuade you to go as successfully through
" with it. But while any Man is suffer'd to confound
" the Industry and Use of them by acting publickly
" in opposition to your Lordship's equal Intentions,
" under a false and intricate Pretence of not being
" able to comply with them, the Town is likely to
" be more entertain'd with the private Dissensions
" than the publick Performance of either, and the

"Actors in a perpetual Fear and Necessity of petitioning your Lordship every Season for new Relief."

Such was the State of the Stage immediately preceding the time of Mr. *Brett*'s being admitted a joint Patentee, who, as he saw with clearer Eyes what was its evident Interest, left no proper Measures unattempted to make this so long despair'd-of Union practicable. The most apparent Difficulty to be got over in this Affair was, what could be done for *Swiney* in consideration of his being oblig'd to give up those Actors whom the Power and Choice of the Lord-Chamberlain had the Year before set him at the Head of, and by whose Menagement those Actors had found themselves in a prosperous Condition. But an Accident at this time happily contributed to make that Matter easy The Inclination of our People of Quality for foreign Operas had now reach'd the Ears of *Italy*, and the Credit of their Taste had drawn over from thence, without any more particular Invitation, one of their capital Singers, the famous Signior *Cavaliero Nicolini:* From whose Arrival, and the Impatience of the Town to hear him, it was concluded that Operas being now so completely provided could not fail of Success, and that by making *Swiney* sole Director of them the Profits must be an ample Compensation for his Resignation of the Actors. This Matter being thus adjusted by *Swiney*'s Acceptance of the Opera only to be perform'd at the *Hay-Market* House, the

Actors were all order'd to return to *Drury-Lane*, there to remain (under the Patentees) her Majesty's only Company of Comedians.[1]

[1] The edict which ordered this division of plays and operas is dated 31st December, 1707. Each theatre is ordered to confine itself to its own sphere on pain of being silenced; and no other theatre is permitted to be built. A copy of the edict is given by Mr. Percy Fitzgerald ("New History," i. 258), but it is not a *verbatim* copy of the original in the Lord Chamberlain's Office, though it contains all that is of importance in it.

CHAPTER XII.

A short View of the Opera when first divided from the Comedy. Plays recover their Credit. The old Patentee uneasy at their Success. Why. The Occasion of Colonel Brett's *throwing up his Share in the Patent. The Consequences of it. Anecdotes of* Goodman *the Actor. The Rate of favourite Actors in his Time. The Patentees, by endeavouring to reduce their Price, lose them all a second time. The principal Comedians return to the* Hay-Market *in Shares with* Swiney. *They alter that Theatre. The original and present Form of the Theatre in* Drury-Lane *compar'd. Operas fall off. The Occasion of it. Farther Observations upon them. The Patentee dispossess'd of* Drury-Lane *Theatre. Mr.* Collier, *with a new License, heads the Remains of that Company.*

PLAYS and Operas being thus established upon separate Interests,[1] they were now left to make

[1] At the Union, 1707-8, the Lord Chamberlain took measures

the best of their way into Favour by their different Merit. Although the Opera is not a Plant of our Native Growth, nor what our plainer Appetites are fond of, and is of so delicate a Nature that without excessive Charge it cannot live long among us; especially while the nicest *Connoisseurs* in Musick fall into such various Heresies in Taste, every Sect pretending to be the true one: Yet, as it is call'd a Theatrical Entertainment, and by its Alliance or Neutrality has more or less affected our Domestick Theatre, a short View of its Progress may be allow'd a Place in our History.

After this new Regulation the first Opera that appear'd was *Pyrrhus*. Subscriptions at that time were not extended, as of late, to the whole Season, but were limited to the first Six Days only of a new Opera. The chief Performers in this were *Nicolini*, *Valentini*, and Mrs. *Tofts*;[1] and for the inferior Parts the best that were then to be found. Whatever Praises may have been given to the most famous Voices that have been heard since *Nicolini*, upon the whole I cannot but come into the Opinion that still prevails among several Persons of Condition who are able to give a Reason for their liking, that no Singer since his Time has so justly and grace-

to assert his supremacy. Under date 6th January, 1708, he orders that no actors are to be engaged at Drury-Lane who are not Her Majesty's servants, and he therefore directs the managers to send a list of all actors to be sworn in.

[1] Bellchambers notes that Mrs Tofts "sang in English, while her associates responded in Italian."

fully acquitted himself in whatever Character he appear'd as *Nicolini*. At most the Difference between him and the greatest Favourite of the Ladies, *Farinelli*, amounted but to this, that he might sometimes more exquisitely surprize us, but *Nicolini* (by pleasing the Eye as well as the Ear) fill'd us with a more various and *rational* Delight. Whether in this Excellence he has since had any Competitor, perhaps will be better judg'd by what the Critical Censor of *Great Britain* says of him in his 115th *Tatler, viz.*

" *Nicolini* sets off the Character he bears in an
" Opera by his Action, as much as he does the
" Words of it by his Voice; every Limb and Finger
" contributes to the Part he acts, insomuch that a
" deaf Man might go along with him in the Sense
" of it. There is scarce a beautiful Posture in an
" old Statue which he does not plant himself in, as
" the different Circumstances of the Story give occa-
" sion for it— He performs the most ordinary
" Action in a manner suitable to the Greatness of
" his Character, and shews the Prince even in the
" giving of a Letter or dispatching of a Message,
" *&c.*" [1]

[1] The whole passage regarding Nicolini is —

"I went on *Friday* last to the Opera, and was surprised to find a thin House at so noble an Entertainment, till I heard that the Tumbler was not to make his Appearance that Night. For my own Part, I was fully satisfied with the Sight of an Actor, who, by the Grace and Propriety of his Action and Gesture, does Honour to an human Figure, as much as the other vilifies and degrades

His Voice at this first time of being among us (for he made us a second Visit when it was impair'd) had all that strong, clear Sweetness of Tone so lately admir'd in *Senesino*. A blind Man could scarce have distinguish'd them; but in Volubility of Throat the former had much the Superiority. This so excellent Performer's Agreement was Eight Hundred Guineas for the Year, which is but an eighth Part more than half the Sum that has since been given to several that could never totally surpass him: The Consequence of which is, that the Losses by Operas, for several Seasons, to the End of the Year 1738, have been so great, that those Gentlemen of Quality who last undertook the Direction of them, found it ridiculous any longer to entertain the Publick at so extravagant

it. Every one will easily imagine I mean Signior *Nicolini*, who sets off the Character he bears in an Opera by his Action, as much as he does the Words of it by his Voice. Every Limb, and every Finger, contributes to the Part he acts, insomuch that a deaf Man might go along with him in the Sense of it. There is scarce a beautiful Posture in an old Statue which he does not plant himself in, as the different Circumstances of the Story give Occasion for it. He performs the most ordinary Action in a Manner suitable to the Greatness of his Character, and shows the Prince even in the giving of a Letter, or the dispatching of a Message. Our best Actors are somewhat at a Loss to support themselves with proper Gesture, as they move from any considerable Distance to the Front of the Stage, but I have seen the Person of whom I am now speaking, enter alone at the remotest Part of it, and advance from it with such Greatness of Air and Mien, as seemed to fill the Stage, and at the same Time commanded the Attention of the Audience with the Majesty of his Appearance."—"Tatler," No 115, January 3rd, 1710.

an Expence, while no one particular Person thought himself oblig'd by it.

Mrs. *Tofts*,[1] who took her first Grounds of Musick here in her own Country, before the *Italian* Taste had so highly prevail'd, was then not an Adept in it:[2] Yet whatever Defect the fashionably Skilful might find in her manner, she had, in the general Sense of her Spectators, Charms that few of the most learned Singers ever arrive at. The Beauty of her fine proportion'd Figure, and exquisitely sweet, silver Tone of her Voice, with that peculiar, rapid Swiftness of her Throat, were Perfections not

---

[1] An excellent account of Mrs. Tofts is given by Mr. Henry Morley in a note on page 38 of his valuable edition of the "Spectator." She was the daughter of one of Bishop Burnet's household, and had great natural gifts. In 1709 she was obliged to quit the stage, her mental faculties having failed; but she afterwards recovered, and married Mr. Joseph Smith, a noted art patron, who was appointed English Consul at Venice. Her intellect again became disordered, and she died about the year 1760

[2] Cibber's most notorious blunder in language was made in this sentence. In his first edition he wrote "was then *but* an Adept in it," completely reversing the meaning of the word "Adept." Fielding ("Champion," 22nd April, 1740) declares Cibber to be a most absolute Master of English, "for surely he must be absolute Master of that whose Laws he can trample under Feet, and which he can use as he pleases. This Power he hath exerted, of which I shall give a *barbarous* Instance in the Case of the poor Word *Adept*. . . . This Word our great *Master* hath tortured and wrested to signify a *Tyro* or *Novice*, being directly contrary to the Sense in which it hath been hitherto used" It is of course conceivable that the error was a printer's error not corrected in reading the proof.

OWEN SWINEY.

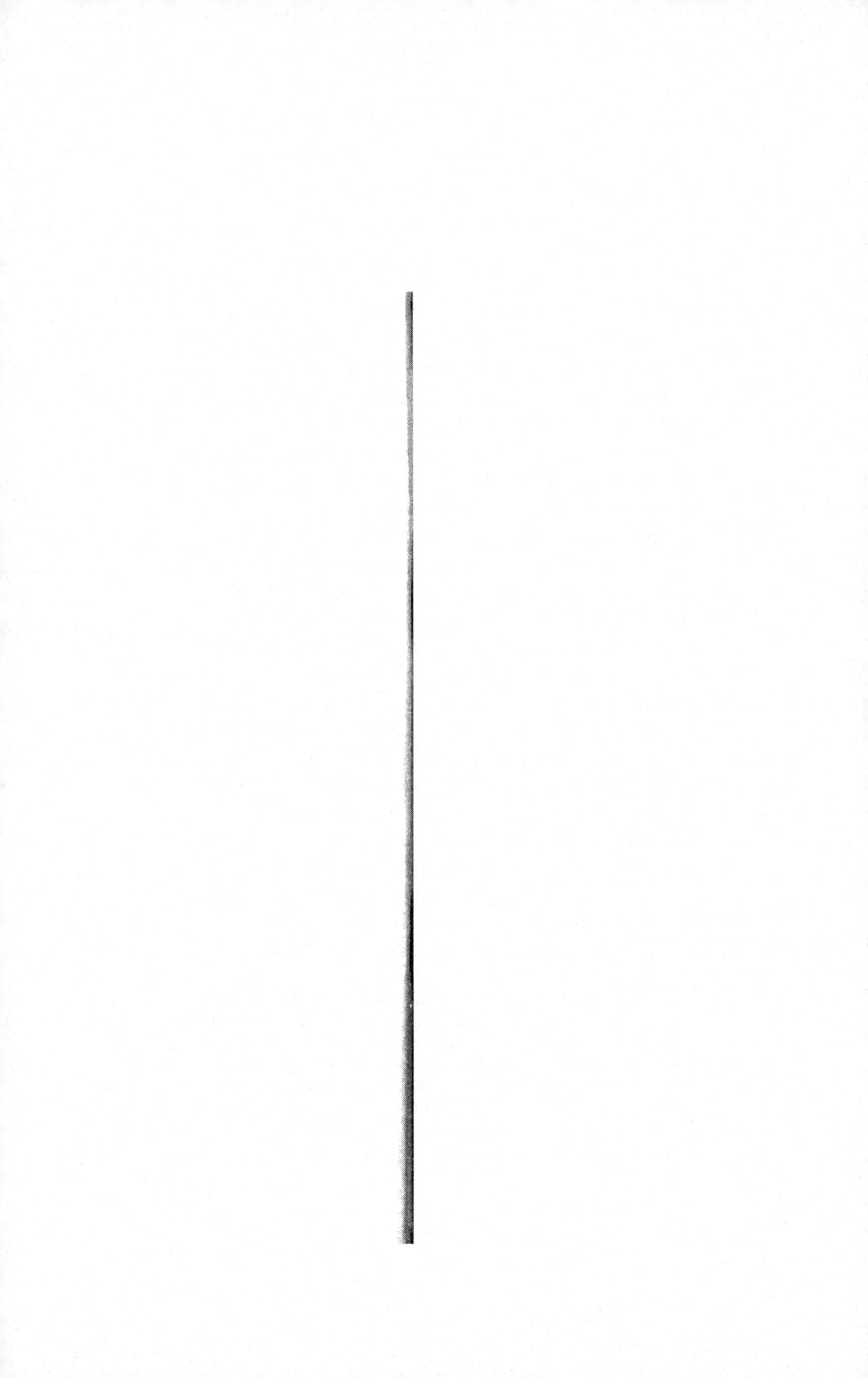

to be imitated by Art or Labour. *Valentini* I have already mention'd, therefore need only say farther of him, that though he was every way inferior to *Nicolini*,[1] yet, as he had the Advantage of giving us our first Impression of a good Opera Singer, he had still his Admirers, and was of great Service in being so skilful a Second to his Superior.

Three such excellent Performers in the same kind of Entertainment at once, *England* till this Time had never seen : Without any farther Comparison, then, with the much dearer bought who have succeeded them, their Novelty at least was a Charm that drew vast Audiences of the fine World after them. *Swiney*, their sole Director, was prosperous, and in one Winter a Gainer by them of a moderate younger Brother's Fortune. But as Musick, by so profuse a Dispensation of her Beauties, could not always supply our dainty Appetites with equal Variety, nor for ever please us with the same Objects, the Opera, after one luxurious Season, like the fine Wife of a roving Husband, began to loose its Charms, and every Day discover'd to our Satiety Imperfections which our former Fondness had been blind to . But of this I shall observe

---

[1] Nicolini was the stage name of the Cavalier Nicolo Grimaldi. Dr. Burney says: "This great singer, and still greater actor, was a Neapolitan; his voice was at first a *soprano*, but afterwards descended into a fine *contralto*" He first appeared, about 1694, in Rome, and paid his first visit to England in 1708. Valentini Urbani was a *castrato*, his voice was not so strong as Nicolini's, but his action was so excellent that his vocal defects were not noticed.—" General History of Music," 1789, iv. 207, 205.

more in its Place : in the mean time, let us enquire into the Productions of our native Theatre.

It may easily be conceiv'd, that by this entire Re-union of the two Companies Plays must generally have been perform'd to a more than usual Advantage and Exactness : For now every chief Actor, according to his particular Capacity, piqued himself upon rectifying those Errors which during their divided State were almost unavoidable. Such a Choice of Actors added a Richness to every good Play as it was then serv'd up to the publick Entertainment: The common People crowded to them with a more joyous Expectation, and those of the higher Taste return'd to them as to old Acquaintances, with new Desires after a long Absence. In a Word, all Parties seem'd better pleas'd but he who one might imagine had most Reason to be so, the (lately) sole menaging Patentee. He, indeed, saw his Power daily mould'ring from his own Hands into those of Mr. *Brett*,[1] whose

[1] Colonel Brett, by an indenture dated 31st March, 1708, made Wilks, Estcourt, and Cibber, his deputies in the management of the theatre. Genest (11. 405) says this was probably " 31st March, 1708, Old Style," by which I suppose he means March, 1709. But I cannot see why he should think this. Brett entered into management in January, 1708, and was probably out of it by March, 1709. It may be that Genest supposes that this indenture marks the end of Brett's connection with the theatre , whereas it was probably one of his first actions. It will be remembered that he stated his intention of benefitting Cibber by taking the Patent (see *ante*, p 42). A copy of the indenture is given by Mr. Percy Fitzgerald ("New History," 11. 443). It is dated 31st March in the seventh year of Queen Anne's reign, that is, 1708.

Gentlemanly manner of making every one's Business easy to him, threw their old Master under a Disregard which he had not been us'd to, nor could with all his happy Change of Affairs support. Although this grave Theatrical Minister of whom I have been oblig'd to make such frequent mention, had acquired the Reputation of a most profound Politician by being often incomprehensible, yet I am not sure that his Conduct at this Juncture gave us not an evident Proof that he was, like other frail Mortals, more a Slave to his Passions than his Interest; for no Creature ever seem'd more fond of Power that so little knew how to use it to his Profit and Reputation; otherwise he could not possibly have been so discontented, in his secure and prosperous State of the Theatre, as to resolve at all Hazards to destroy it. We shall now see what infallible Measures he took to bring this laudable Scheme to Perfection.

He plainly saw that, as this disagreeable Prosperity was chiefly owing to the Conduct of Mr. *Brett*, there could be no hope of recovering the Stage to its former Confusion but by finding some effectual Means to make Mr. *Brett* weary of his Charge: The most probable he could for the Present think of, in this Distress, was to call in the Adventurers (whom for many Years, by his Defence in Law, he had kept out) now to take care of their visibly improving Interests.[1] This fair Appearance of Equity being

[1] On p. 328 of vol. i, Cibber says that Rich (about 1705) had led the Adventurers "a Chace in Chancery several years." From

known to be his own Proposal, he rightly guess'd would incline these Adventurers to form a Majority of Votes on his Side in all Theatrical Questions, and consequently become a Check upon the Power of Mr. *Brett*, who had so visibly alienated the Hearts of his Theatrical Subjects, and now began to govern without him. When the Adventurers, therefore, were re-admitted to their old Government, after having recommended himself to them by proposing to make some small Dividend of the Profits (though he did not design that Jest should be repeated) he took care that the Creditors of the Patent, who were then no inconsiderable Body, should carry off the every Weeks clear Profits in proportion to their several Dues and Demands. This Conduct, so speciously just, he had Hopes would let Mr. *Brett* see that his Share in the Patent was not so valuable an Acquisition as perhaps he might think it; and probably make a Man of his Turn to Pleasure soon weary of the little Profit and great Plague it gave him. Now, though these might be all notable Expedients, yet I

the petition presented in 1709 against the order silencing Rich, we learn that the principal Adventurers were: Lord Guilford, Lord John Harvey, Dame Alice Brownlow, Mrs. Shadwell, Sir Edward Smith, Bart., Sir Thomas Skipwith, Bart., George Sayer, Charles Killegrew, Christopher Rich, Charles Davenant, John Metcalf, Thomas Goodall, Ashburnham Toll, Ashburnham Frowd, William East, Richard Middlemore, Robert Gower, and William Collier. It is curious that everyone who has reproduced this list has, as far as I know, mistaken the name "Frowd," calling it "Trowd." The earliest reproduction of the list of names which I know is in the "Dramatic Censor," 1811, col. 111.

cannot say they would have wholly contributed to Mr. *Brett*'s quitting his Post, had not a Matter of much stronger Moment, an unexpected Dispute between him and Sir *Thomas Skipwith*, prevailed with him to lay it down: For in the midst of this flourishing State of the Patent, Mr. *Brett* was surpriz'd with a Subpœna into Chancery from Sir *Thomas Skipwith*, who alledg'd in his Bill that the Conveyance he had made of his Interest in the Patent to Mr. *Brett* was only intended in Trust. (Whatever the Intent might be, the Deed it self, which I then read, made no mention of any Trust whatever.) But whether Mr. *Brett*, as Sir *Thomas* farther asserted, had previously, or after the Deed was sign'd, given his Word of Honour that if he should ever make the Stage turn to any Account or Profit, he would certainly restore it: That, indeed, I can say nothing to; but be the Deed valid or void, the Facts that apparently follow'd were, that tho' Mr. *Brett* in his Answer to this Bill absolutely deny'd his receiving this Assignment either in Trust or upon any limited Condition of what kind soever, yet he made no farther Defence in the Cause. But since he found Sir *Thomas* had thought fit on any Account to sue for the Restitution of it, and Mr. *Brett* being himself conscious that, as the World knew he had paid no Consideration for it, his keeping it might be misconstrued, or not favourably spoken of; or perhaps finding, tho' the Profits were great, they were constantly swallowed up (as has been observ'd) by the previous Satisfaction of old Debts, he grew so tir'd of the Plague and Trouble the whole Affair had given him, and was likely still to engage him in, that in a few Weeks after he withdrew himself from all Concern with the Theatre, and quietly left Sir *Thomas* to find his better Account in it. And thus stood this undecided Right till, upon the Demise of Sir *Thomas*, Mr. *Brett* being allow'd the Charges he had been at in this Attendance and Prosecution of the Union, reconvey'd this Share of the Patent to Sir *George Skipwith*, the Son and Heir of Sir *Thomas*.[1]

Our Politician, the old Patentee, having thus fortunately got rid of Mr. *Brett*, who had so rashly brought the Patent once more to be a profitable Tenure, was now again at Liberty to chuse rather to lose all than not to have it all to himself.

I have elsewhere observ'd that nothing can so effectually secure the Strength, or contribute to the Prosperity of a good Company, as the Directors of it having always, as near as possible, an amicable Understanding with three or four of their best Actors, whose good or ill-will must naturally make a wide Difference in their profitable or useless manner of serving them: While the Principal are kept reasonably easy the lower Class can never be troublesome without hurting themselves: But when a valuable Actor is hardly treated, the Master must be a very

---

[1] I do not know when Sir Thomas Skipwith died; but in 1709 the petition of the Adventurers, &c, is signed by, among others, Sir Thomas Skipwith.

cunning Man that finds his Account in it. We shall now see how far Experience will verify this Observation.

The Patentees thinking themselves secure in being restor'd to their former absolute Power over this now only Company, chose rather to govern it by the Reverse of the Method I have recommended: For tho' the daily Charge of their united Company amounted not, by a good deal, to what either of the two Companies now in *Drury-Lane* or *Covent-Garden* singly arises, they notwithstanding fell into their former Politicks of thinking every Shilling taken from a hired Actor so much clear Gain to the Proprietor: Many of their People, therefore, were actually, if not injudiciously, reduced in their Pay, and others given to understand the same Fate was design'd them; of which last Number I my self was one; which occurs to my Memory by the Answer I made to one of the Adventurers, who, in Justification of their intended Proceeding,[1] told me that my Sallary, tho' it should be less than it was by ten Shillings a Week, would still be more than ever *Goodman* had, who was a better Actor than I could pretend to be: To which I reply'd, This may be true, but then you know, Sir, it is as true that *Goodman* was forced to go upon the High-way for

---

[1] This anecdote shows that Rich had some sort of Committee of Shareholders to aid (or hinder) him. Subsequent experience has shown, as witness the Drury Lane Committee at the beginning of this century, how disastrous such form of management is.

a Livelihood. As this was a known Fact of *Goodman*, my mentioning it on that Occasion I believe was of Service to me; at least my Sallary was not reduced after it. To say a Word or two more of *Goodman*, so celebrated an Actor in his Time, perhaps may set the Conduct of the Patentees in a clearer Light. Tho' *Goodman* had left the Stage before I came to it, I had some slight Acquaintance with him. About the Time of his being expected to be an Evidence against Sir *John Fenwick* in the Assassination-Plot,[1] in 1696, I happen'd to meet him at Dinner at Sir *Thomas Skipwith*'s, who, as he was an agreeable Companion himself, liked *Goodman* for the same Quality. Here it was that *Goodman*, with-

[1] Dr Doran ("Their Majesties' Servants," 1888 edition, i. 103) gives the following account of Goodman's connection with this plot:—

"King James having saved Cardell's neck, Goodman, out of pure gratitude, perhaps, became a Tory, and something more, when William sat in the seat of his father-in-law. After Queen Mary's death, Scum was in the Fenwick and Charnock plot to kill the King. When the plot was discovered, Scum was ready to peach. As Fenwick's life was thought by his friends to be safe if Goodman could be bought off and got out of the way, the rogue was looked for, at the *Fleece*, in Covent Garden, famous for homicides, and at the robbers' and the revellers' den, the *Dog*, in Drury Lane. Fenwick's agent, O'Bryan, erst soldier and highwayman, now a Jacobite agent, found Scum at the *Dog*, and would then and there have cut his throat, had not Scum consented to the pleasant alternative of accepting £500 a year, and a residence abroad. . . . Scum suddenly disappeared, and Lord Manchester, our Ambassador in Paris, inquired after him in vain. It is impossible to say whether the rogue died by an avenging hand, or starvation."

out Disguise or sparing himself, fell into a laughing Account of several loose Passages of *his* younger Life; as his being expell'd the University of *Cambridge* for being one of the hot-headed Sparks who were concern'd in the cutting and defacing the Duke of *Monmouth's* Picture, then Chancellor of that Place. But this Disgrace, it seems, had not disqualified him for the Stage, which, like the Sea-Service, refuses no Man for his Morals that is ablebodied: There, as an Actor, he soon grew into a different Reputation; but whatever his Merit might be, the Pay of a hired Hero in those Days was so very low that he was forced, it seems, to take the Air (as he call'd it) and borrow what Money the first Man he met had about him. But this being his first Exploit of that kind which the Scantiness of his Theatrical Fortune had reduced him to, King *James* was prevail'd upon to pardon him: Which *Goodman* said was doing him so particular an Honour that no Man could wonder if his Acknowledgment had carried him a little farther than ordinary into the Interest of that Prince But as he had lately been out of Luck in backing his old Master, he had now no way to get home the Life he was out upon his Account but by being under the same Obligations to King *William*.

Another Anecdote of him, though not quite so dishonourably enterprizing, which I had from his own Mouth at a different Time, will equally shew to what low Shifts in Life the poor Provision for good

Actors, under the early Government of the Patent, reduced them. In the younger Days of their Heroism, Captain *Griffin* and *Goodman* were confined by their moderate Sallaries to the Oeconomy of lying together in the same Bed and having but one whole Shirt between them: One of them being under the Obligation of a Rendezvous with a fair Lady, insisted upon his wearing it out of his Turn, which occasion'd so high a Dispute that the Combat was immediately demanded, and accordingly their Pretensions to it were decided by a fair Tilt upon the Spot, in the Room where they lay: But whether *Clytus* or *Alexander* was obliged to see no Company till a worse could be wash'd for him, seems not to be a material Point in their History, or to my Purpose.[1]

By this Rate of *Goodman*, who, 'till the Time of his quitting the Stage never had more than what is call'd forty Shillings a Week, it may be judg'd how cheap the Labour of Actors had been formerly; and the Patentees thought it a Folly to continue the higher Price, (which their Divisions had since raised them to) now there was but one Market for them; but alas! they had forgot their former fatal Mistake of squabbling with their Actors in 1695;[2] nor did

---

[1] This anecdote is valuable as establishing the identity of *Captain* Griffin with the Griffin who retired (temporarily) from the stage about 1688. See note on page 83 of vol. 1.

[2] When Betterton and his associates left the Theatre Royal and opened Lincoln's Inn Fields Theatre. See Chapter VI.

they make any Allowance for the Changes and Operations of Time, or enough consider the Interest the Actors had in the Lord Chamberlain, on whose Protection they might always rely, and whose Decrees had been less restrain'd by Precedent than those of a Lord Chancellor.

In this mistaken View of their Interest, the Patentees, by treating their Actors as Enemies, really made them so: And when once the Masters of a hired Company think not their Actors Hearts as necessary as their Hands, they cannot be said to have agreed for above half the Work they are able to do in a Day: Or, if an unexpected Success should, notwithstanding, make the Profits in any gross Disproportion greater than the Wages, the Wages will always have something worse than a Murmur at the Head of them, that will not only measure the Merit of the Actor by the Gains of the Proprietor, but will never naturally be quiet till every Scheme of getting into Property has been tried to make the Servant his own Master: And this, as far as Experience can make me judge, will always be in either of these Cases the State of our *English* Theatre. What Truth there may be in this Observation we are now coming to a Proof of.

To enumerate all the particular Acts of Power in which the Patentees daily bore hard upon *this* now only Company of Actors, might be as tedious as unnecessary; I shall therefore come at once to their most material Grievance, upon which they grounded their Complaint to the Lord Chamberlain, who, in the Year following, 1709, took effectual Measures for their Relief.

The Patentees observing that the Benefit-Plays of the Actors towards the latter End of the Season brought the most crowded Audiences in the Year, began to think their own Interests too much neglected by these partial Favours of the Town to their Actors, and therefore judg'd it would not be impolitick in such wholesome annual Profits to have a Fellow-feeling with them. Accordingly an *Indulto*[1] was laid of one Third out of the Profits of every Benefit for the proper Use and Behoof of the Patent.[2] But that a clear Judgment may be form'd of the Equity or Hardship of this Imposition, it will be necessary to shew from whence and from what Causes the Actors Claim to Benefits originally proceeded.

[1] Indulto—In Spain, a duty, tax, or custom, paid to the King for all goods imported.

[2] In the "Answer to Steele's State of the Case," 1720 (Nichols's ed. p 527), it is said "After Mr Rich was again restored to the management of the Play-house, he made an order to stop a certain proportion of the clear profits of every Benefit-play without exception; which being done, and reaching the chief Players as well as the underlings, zealous application was made to the Lord Chamberlain, to oblige Mr. Rich to return the money stopped to each particular. The dispute lasted some time, and Mr. Rich, not giving full satisfaction upon that head, was silenced; during the time of which silence, the chief Players, either by a new License, or by some former (which I cannot absolutely determine, my Memoirs being not at this time by me) set up for themselves, and got into the possession of the Play-house in Drury-lane."

During the Reign of King *Charles* an Actor's Benefit had never been heard of. The first Indulgence of this kind was given to Mrs. *Barry* (as has been formerly observed[1]) in King *James*'s Time, in Consideration of the extraordinary Applause that had followed her Performance: But there this Favour rested to her alone, 'till after the Division of the only Company in 1695, at which time the Patentees were soon reduced to pay their Actors half in good Words and half in ready Money. In this precarious Condition some particular Actors (however binding their Agreements might be) were too poor or too wise to go to Law with a Lawyer, and therefore rather chose to compound their Arrears for their being admitted to the Chance of having them made up by the Profits of a Benefit-Play. This Expedient had this Consequence; that the Patentees, tho' their daily Audiences might, and did sometimes mend, still kept the short Subsistance of their Actors at a stand, and grew more steady in their Resolution so to keep them, as they found them less apt to mutiny while their Hopes of being clear'd off by a Benefit were depending. In a Year or two these Benefits grew so advantageous that they became at last the chief Article in every Actor's Agreement.

Now though the Agreements of these united Actors I am speaking of in 1708 were as yet only Verbal, yet that made no difference in the honest Obligation to keep them: But as Honour at that

[1] See *ante*, vol. 1., p. 161.

time happen'd to have but a loose hold of their Consciences, the Patentees rather chose to give it the slip, and went on with their Work without it. No Actor, therefore, could have his Benefit fix'd 'till he had first sign'd a Paper signifying his voluntary Acceptance of it upon the above Conditions, any Claims from Custom to the contrary notwithstanding. Several at first refus'd to sign this Paper; upon which the next in Rank were offer'd on the same Conditions to come before the Refusers; this smart Expedient got some few of the Fearful the Preference to their Seniors; who, at last, seeing the Time was too short for a present Remedy, and that they must either come into the Boat or lose their Tide, were forc'd to comply with what they as yet silently resented as the severest Injury. In this Situation, therefore, they chose to let the principal Benefits be over, that their Grievances might swell into some bulk before they made any Application for Redress to the Lord-Chamberlain; who, upon hearing their general Complaint, order'd the Patentees to shew cause why their Benefits had been diminish'd one Third, contrary to the common Usage? The Patentees pleaded the sign'd Agreement, and the Actors Receipts of the other two Thirds, in Full Satisfaction. But these were prov'd to have been exacted from them by the Methods already mentioned. They notwithstanding insist upon them as lawful. But as Law and Equity do not always agree, they were look'd upon as unjust and arbitrary. Whereupon the Patentees were warn'd at their Peril to refuse the Actors full Satisfaction.¹ But here it was thought necessary that Judgment should be for some time respited, 'till the Actors, who had leave so to do, could form a Body strong enough to make the Inclination of the Lord-Chamberlain to relieve them practicable.

Accordingly *Swiney* (who was then sole Director of the Opera only) had Permission to enter into a private Treaty with such of the united Actors in *Drury-Lane* as might be thought fit to head a Company under their own Menagement, and to be Sharers with him in the *Hay-Market*. The Actors chosen for this Charge were *Wilks, Dogget*, Mrs. *Oldfield*, and Myself. But before I proceed, lest it should seem surprizing that neither *Betterton*, Mrs. *Barry*, Mrs. *Bracegirdle*, or *Booth* were Parties in this Treaty, it must be observ'd that *Betterton* was now Seventy-three, and rather chose, with the Infirmities of Age upon him, to rely on such Sallary as might be appointed him, than to involve himself in the Cares and Hurry that must unavoidably attend the Regulation of a new Company. As to the two celebrated Actresses I have named, this has been my first proper Occasion of making it known that they had both quitted the Stage the Year before this

¹ This warning is dated 30th April, 1709, and is a very peremptory document Rich's treasurer is ordered to pay the actors the full receipts of their benefits, under deduction only of £40 for the charges of the house. See the Order for Silence quoted *post*, page 73.

Transaction was thought of.[1] And *Booth* as yet was scarce out of his Minority as an Actor, or only in the Promise of that Reputation which, in about four or five Years after, he happily arriv'd at. However, at this Juncture he was not so far overlook'd as not to be offer'd a valuable Addition to his Sallary: But this he declin'd, being, while the Patentees were under this Distress, as much, if not more, in favour with their chief Menager as a Schematist than as an Actor: And indeed he appear'd, to my Judgment, more inclin'd to risque his Fortune in *Drury-Lane*, where he should have no Rival in Parts or Power, than on any Terms to embark in the *Hay-Market*, where he was sure to meet with Opponents in both.[2] However, this his Separation from our Interest when our All was at stake, afterwards kept his Advancement to a Share with us in our more successful Days longer postpon'd than otherwise it probably might have been.

When Mrs. *Oldfield* was nominated as a joint Sharer in our new Agreement to be made with *Swiney*, *Dogget*, who had no Objection to her Merit, insisted that our Affairs could never be upon a secure Foundation if there was more than one Sex admitted to

[1] Mrs. Bracegirdle retired in February, 1707. Mrs. Barry played up to the end of the season, 1708, that is, up to June, 1708. She does not seem to have been engaged in 1708-9, but she was a member of the Haymarket Company in 1709-10.

[2] From Chapter XVI it will be seen that Wilks's unfair partiality for John Mills, whom he forced into prominence at Booth's expense, was the leading reason for Booth's remaining with Rich.

the Menagement of them. He therefore hop'd that if we offer'd Mrs. *Oldfield* a *Carte Blanche* instead of a Share, she would not think herself slighted. This was instantly agreed to, and Mrs. *Oldfield* receiv'd it rather as a Favour than a Disobligation: Her Demands therefore were Two Hundred Pounds a Year certain, and a Benefit clear of all Charges, which were readily sign'd to. Her Easiness on this Occasion, some Years after, when our Establishment was in Prosperity, made us with less Reluctancy advance her Two Hundred Pounds to Three Hundred Guineas *per Annum*, with her usual Benefit, which, upon an Average, for several Years at least doubled that Sum.

When a sufficient number of Actors were engag'd under our Confederacy with *Swiney*, it was then judg'd a proper time for the Lord-Chamberlain's Power to operate, which, by lying above a Month dormant, had so far recover'd the Patentees from any Apprehensions of what might fall upon them from their late Usurpations on the Benefits of the Actors, that they began to set their Marks upon those who had distinguish'd themselves in the Application for Redress. Several little Disgraces were put upon them, particularly in the Disposal of Parts in Plays to be reviv'd, and as visible a Partiality was shewn in the Promotion of those in their Interest, though their Endeavours to serve them could be of no extraordinary use. How often does History shew us, in the same State of Courts, the same Politicks have been practis'd? All this while the other Party were passively silent, 'till one Day the Actor who particularly solicited their Cause at the Lord-Chamberlain's Office, being shewn there the Order sign'd for absolutely silencing the Patentees, and ready to be serv'd, flew back with the News to his Companions, then at a Rehearsal in which he had been wanted; when being call'd to his Part, and something hastily question'd by the Patentee for his Neglect of Business: This Actor, I say, with an erected Look and a Theatrical Spirit, at once threw off the Mask and roundly told him——*Sir, I have now no more Business Here than you have; in half an Hour you will neither have Actors to command nor Authority to employ them.*——The Patentee, who though he could not readily comprehend his mysterious manner of Speaking, had just a Glimpse of Terror enough from the Words to soften his Reproof into a cold formal Declaration, That *if he would not do his Work he should not be paid.*—But now, to complete the Catastrophe of these Theatrical Commotions, enters the Messenger with the Order of Silence in his Hand, whom the same Actor officiously introduc'd, telling the Patentee that the Gentleman wanted to speak with him from the Lord-Chamberlain. When the Messenger had deliver'd the Order, the Actor, throwing his Head over his Shoulder towards the Patentee, in the manner of *Shakespear*'s *Harry the Eighth* to Cardinal *Wolsey*, cry'd—*Read o'er that! and now—to Breakfast, with what Appetite you may.* Tho' these Words might be spoken in too vindictive and insulting a manner to be commended, yet, from the Fulness of a Heart injuriously treated and now reliev'd by that instant Occasion, why might they not be pardon'd?[1]

The Authority of the Patent now no longer subsisting, all the confederated Actors immediately walk'd out of the House, to which they never return'd 'till they became themselves the Tenants and Masters of it.

[1] The Order for Silence has never, I believe, been quoted. I therefore give it in full. The theatre closed on the 4th of June, 1709, which was Saturday, and did not open again under Rich's management, the Order for Silence being issued on the next Monday

"*Play House in Covent Garden silenc'd* Whereas by an Order dated the 30th day of Apr^{ll} last upon the petičõn of sev^{ll} Players &c: I did then direct and require you to pay to the respective Comedians who had benfit plays last winter the full receip^{ts} of such plays deducting only from each the sume of 40l. for the Charges of the House pursuant to the Articles made wth y^{m} at ye theatre in the Haymarkett and wch were promis^{d} to be made good upon their removall to the Theatre in Covent Garden.

"And whereas I am inform^{d} y^{t} in Contempt of the said Ord^{r} y^{u} still refuse to pay and detain from the s^{d} Comedians ye profits of y^{r} s^{d} benefit plays I do therefore for the s^{d} Contempt hereby silence you from further acting & require you not to perform any Plays or other Theatricall entertainm^{ts} till further Ord^{r}, And all her Maj^{ts} Sworn Comedians are hereby forbid to act any Plays at ye Theatre in Covent Gard^{n} or else where wthout my leave as they shall answer the contrary at their perill And &c Given &c this 6th day of June 1709 in the Eighth Year of her Majesty's Reign

(Signed) KENT

"To the Manager or Manag^{rs}
 of her Maj^{ts} Company of Comedi^{ns}
 for their Patentees."

I have copied this from the Lord Chamberlain's Records.

Here agen we see an higher Instance of the Authority of a Lord-Chamberlain than any of those I have elsewhere mentioned. From whence that Power might be deriv'd, as I have already said, I am not Lawyer enough to know; however, it is evident that a Lawyer obey'd it, though to his Cost; which might incline one to think that the Law was not clearly against it: Be that as it may, since the Law has lately made it no longer a Question, let us drop the Enquiry and proceed to the Facts which follow'd this Order that silenc'd the Patent.

From this last injudicious Disagreement of the Patentees with their principal Actors, and from what they had suffered on the same Occasion in the Division of their only Company in 1695, might we not imagine there was something of Infatuation in their Menagement? For though I allow Actors in general, when they are too much indulg'd, or govern'd by an unsteady Head, to be as unruly a Multitude as Power can be plagued with; yet there is a Medium which, if cautiously observed by a candid use of Power, making them always know, without feeling, their Superior, neither suffering their Encroachments nor invading their Rights, with an immoveable Adherence to the accepted Laws they are to walk by; such a Regulation, I say, has never fail'd, in my Observation, to have made them a tractable and profitable Society. If the Government of a well-establish'd Theatre were to be compar'd to that of a Nation, there is no one Act of Policy or Misconduct in the one or the other in which the Menager might not, in some parallel Case, (laugh, if you please) be equally applauded or condemned with the Statesman. Perhaps this will not be found so wild a Conceit if you look into the 193d *Tatler*, Vol. 4. where the Affairs of the State and those of the very Stage which I am now treating of, are, in a Letter from *Downs* the Promptor,[1] compar'd, and with a great deal of Wit

[1] "*Honoured Sir*, *July* 1 1710
"Finding by divers of your late Papers, that you are a Friend to the Profession of which I was many Years an unworthy Member, I the rather make bold to crave your Advice, touching a Proposal that has been lately made me of coming into Business, and the Sub-Administration of Stage Affairs. I have, from my Youth, been bred up behind the Curtain, and been a Prompter from the Time of the Restoration. I have seen many Changes, as well of Scenes as of Actors, and have known Men within my Remembrance arrive to the highest Dignities of the Theatre, who made their Entrance in the Quality of Mutes, Joynt-stools, Flower-pots, and Tapestry Hangings. It cannot be unknown to the Nobility and Gentry, That a Gentleman of the Inns of Court, and a deep Intriguer, had some Time since worked himself into the sole Management and Direction of the Theatre. Nor is it less notorious, That his restless Ambition, and subtle Machinations, did manifestly tend to the Extirpation of the good old *British* Actors, and the Introduction of foreign Pretenders; such as Harlequins, *French* Dancers, and *Roman* Singers; which, tho' they impoverish'd the Proprietors, and imposed on the Audience, were for some Time tolerated, by Reason of his dextrous Insinuations, which prevailed upon a few deluded Women, especially the Vizard Masks, to believe, that the Stage was in Danger. But his Schemes were soon exposed, and the Great Ones that supported him withdrawing their Favour, he made his *Exit*, and remained for a Season in Obscurity. During this Retreat the Machiavilian was not idle, but secretly fomented Divisions, and wrought over to his Side

and Humour, set upon an equal Foot of Policy. The Letter is suppos'd to have been written in the last Change of the Ministry in Queen *Anne*'s Time. I will therefore venture, upon the Authority of that Author's Imagination, to carry the Comparison as high as it can possibly go, and say, That as I remember one of our Princes in the last Century to have lost his Crown by too arbitrary a Use of his Power, though he knew how fatal the same Measures had been to his unhappy Father before him, why should we wonder that the same Passions taking Possession of Men in lower Life, by an equally impolitick Usage of their Theatrical Subjects, should have involved the Patentees in proportionable Calamities.

some of the inferior Actors, reserving a Trap Door to himself, to which only he had a Key This Entrance secured, this cunning Person, to compleat his Company, bethought himself of calling in the most eminent of Strollers from all Parts of the Kingdom. I have seen them all ranged together behind the Scenes, but they are many of them Persons that never trod the Stage before, and so very aukward and ungainly, that it is impossible to believe the Audience will bear them. He was looking over his Catalogue of Plays, and indeed picked up a good tolerable Set of grave Faces for Counsellors, to appear in the famous Scene of *Venice Preserved*, when the Danger is over, but they being but meer Outsides, and the Actors having a great Mind to play the *Tempest*, there is not a Man of them when he is to perform any Thing above Dumb Show is capable of acting with a good Grace so much as the Part of *Trincalo*. However, the Master persists in his Design, and is fitting up the old Storm, but I am afraid he will not be able to procure able Sailors or experienced Officers for Love or Money.

During the Vacation, which immediately follow'd the Silence of the Patent, both Parties were at leisure to form their Schemes for the Winter: For the Patentee would still hold out, notwithstanding his being so miserably maim'd or over-match'd: He had no more Regard to Blows than a blind Cock of the Game; he might be beaten, but would never yield; the Patent was still in his Possession, and the Broad-Seal to it visibly as fresh as ever: Besides, he had yet some Actors in his Service,[1] at a much cheaper

---

"Besides all this, when he comes to cast the Parts there is so great a Confusion amongst them for Want of proper Actors, that for my Part I am wholly discouraged. The Play with which they design to open is, *The Duke and no Duke,* and they are so put to it, That the master himself is to act the Conjurer, and they have no one for the General but honest *George Powell.*

"Now, Sir, they being so much at a Loss for the *Dramatis Personæ, viz.* the Persons to enact, and the whole Frame of the House being designed to be altered, I desire your Opinion, whether you think it advisable for me to undertake to prompt 'em· For tho' I can clash Swords when they represent a Battel, and have yet Lungs enough to huzza their Victories, I question, if I should prompt 'em right, whether they would act accordingly.—I am
"*Your Honour's most humble Servant,*
"J. DOWNES.

P.S. Sir, Since I writ this, I am credibly informed, That they design a New House in *Lincoln's-Inn-fields,* near the Popish Chapel, to be ready by *Michaelmas* next; which indeed is but repairing an Old one that has already failed. You know the honest Man who kept the Office is gone already."

[1] The chief actor who remained with Rich was Booth. Among the others were Powell, Bickerstaffe, Pack, Keene, Francis Leigh, Norris, Mrs. Bignell, Mrs. Moor, Mrs. Bradshaw, and Mrs. Knight.

Rate than those who had left him, the Sallaries of which last, now they would not work for him, he was not oblig'd to pay.[1] In this way of thinking, he still kept together such as had not been invited over to the *Hay-Market*, or had been influenc'd by *Booth* to follow his Fortune in *Drury-Lane*.

By the Patentee's keeping these Remains of his broken Forces together, it is plain that he imagin'd this Order of Silence, like others of the same Kind, would be recall'd, of course, after a reasonable time of Obedience had been paid to it: But, it seems, he had rely'd too much upon former Precedents; nor had his Politicks yet div'd into the Secret that the Court Power, with which the Patent had been so long and often at variance, had now a mind to take the publick Diversions more absolutely into their own Hands: Not that I have any stronger Reasons for this Conjecture than that the Patent never after this Order of Silence got leave to play during the Queen's Reign. But upon the Accession of his late Majesty, Power having then a different Aspect, the Patent found no Difficulty in being permitted to exercise its

---

[1] An interesting advertisement was published on Rich's behalf in July, 1709, which gives curious particulars regarding the actors' salaries I quote it from "Edwin's Eccentricities," i. 219-224, without altering the figures, which, as regards the pence, are rather eccentric:—

"ADVERTISEMENT CONCERNING THE POOR ACTORS, WHO, UNDER PRETENCE OF HARD USAGE FROM THE PATENTEES, ARE ABOUT TO DESERT THEIR SERVICE.

"Some persons having industriously spread about amongst the Quality and others, what small allowances the chief Actors have

former Authority for acting Plays, &c. which, however, from this time of their lying still, in 1709, did not happen 'till 1714, which the old Patentee never liv'd to see: For he dy'd about six weeks before the new-built Theatre in *Lincoln's-Inn-Fields* was open'd,[1] where the first Play acted was the *Recruiting Officer*, under the Menagement of his Heirs and Successors. But of that Theatre it is not yet time to give any further Account.

The first Point resolv'd on by the Comedians now re-established in the *Hay-Market*,[2] was to alter the

had this last Winter from the Patentees of Drury Lane Play-house, as if they had received no more than so many poor palatines; it was thought necessary to print the following Account.

"The whole company began to act on the 12th of October, 1708, and left off on the 26th of the same month, by reason of Prince

---

[1] It was opened 18th December, 1714.

[2] The Lord Chamberlain's Records enable an exact account to be given of the transactions which led to the formation of this Haymarket Company. After Rich was silenced, his actors petitioned the Lord Chamberlain on three separate occasions, namely, 10th June, 20th June, and 5th July, 1709, and in answer to their petitions, the Haymarket, which was then devoted solely to Opera, was permitted to be used for Plays also. In an Answer to the actors' petitions, the Lord Chamberlain permits the manager of the Haymarket to engage such of them as he wished, and to act Plays four times a week, the other days being devoted to Operas. This License is dated 8th July, 1709. This is, of course, only a formal sanction of the private arrangement mentioned by Cibber *ante* p. 69; and was resented by Booth and others who were in Rich's favour. They therefore petitioned the Queen direct, in despite of the Lord Chamberlain (see "Dramatic Censor," 1811, col. 112; Genest, ii. 426, Mr. Fitzgerald's "New History," i. 273), but no result followed, until Collier's advent, as is related further on.

Auditory Part of their Theatre, the Inconveniencies of which have been fully enlarged upon in a former Chapter. What embarrass'd them most in this Design, was their want of Time to do it in a more complete manner than it now remains in, otherwise they had brought it to the original Model of that in

George's illness and death; and began again the 14th of December following, and left off upon the Lord Chamberlain's order, on the 4th of June last, 1709. So acted, during that time, in all 135 days, which is 22 weeks and three days, accounting six acting days to a week.

	£	s.	d.
In that time			
To Mr. Wilkes, by salary, for acting, and taking care of the rehearsals; paid	168	6	8
By his Benefit play,	90	14	9
Total	259	1	5
To Mr. Betterton by salary, for acting, 4*l.* a week for himself, and 1*l.* a week for his wife, although she does not act; paid	112	10	0
By a benefit play at common prices, besides what he got by high prices, and Guineas; paid	76	4	5
	188	14	5
To Mr. Eastcourt, at 5*l.* a week salary, paid	112	10	0
By a benefit play, paid	51	8	6
	163	18	6
To Mr Cibber, at 5*l.* a week salary; paid	111	10	0
By a benefit play; paid	51	0	10
	162	10	10

Drury-Lane, only in a larger Proportion, as the wider Walls of it would require; as there are not many Spectators who may remember what Form the *Drury-Lane* Theatre stood in about forty Years ago, before the old Patentee, to make it hold more Money, took it in his Head to alter it, it were but Justice to

	£	s.	d.
To Mr. Mills, at 4*l*. a week for himself, and 1*l*. a week for his wife, for little or nothing	112	10	0
By a benefit play paid to him (not including therein what she got by a benefit play)	58	1	4
	170	11	4
To Mrs Oldfield, at 4*l* a week salary, which for 14 weeks and one day; she leaving off acting presently after her benefit (viz) on the 17th of March last, 1708, though the benefit was intended for her whole nine months acting, and she refused to assist others in their benefits, her salary for these 14 weeks and one day came to, and she was paid,	56	13	4
In January she required, and was paid ten guineas, to wear on the stage in some plays, during the whole season, a mantua petticoat that was given her for the stage, and though she left off three months before she should, yet she hath not returned any part of the ten guineas	10	15	0
And she had for wearing in some plays a suit of boys cloaths on the stage; paid	2	10	9
By a benefit play; paid	62	7	8
	132	6	7
Certainties in all	1077	3	8

lay the original Figure which Sir *Christopher Wren* first gave it, and the Alterations of it now standing, in a fair Light; that equal Spectators may see, if they were at their choice, which of the Structures would incline them to a Preference. But in this

" Besides which certain sums abovementioned, the same actors got by their benefit plays, as follows ·

	£	s.	d.
Note, that Mr. Betterton having had 76*l*. 4*s*. 5*d* as above mentioned, for two-thirds of the profits by a benefit play, reckoning his tickets for the boxes at 5*s*. a piece, the pit at 3*s*. the first gallery at 2*s*. and the upper gallery at 1*s* ——But the boxes, pit, and stage, laid together on his day, and no person admitted but by his tickets, the lowest at half a guinea a ticket, nay he had much more, for one lady gave him ten guineas, some five guineas, some two guineas, and most one guinea, supposing that he designed not to act any more, and he delivered tickets out for more persons, than the boxes, pit, and stage could hold, it is thought he cleared at least 450*l* over and besides the 76*l*. 4*s*. 5*d*.	450	0	0
'Tis thought Mr. Estcourt cleared 200*l*. besides the said 51*l*. 8*s* 6*d*.	200	0	0
That Mr. Wilkes cleared by Guineas, as it is thought, about 40*l*. besides the said 90*l*. 14*s*. 9*d*.	40	0	0
That Mr Cibber got by Guineas, as it is thought, about 50*l* besides the said 51*l* 0*s* 10*d*.	50	0	0
That Mr. Mills got by guineas about 20*l*. as it is thought, besides the said 58*l*. 1*s* 4*d*.	20	0	0
That Mrs. Oldfield, it is thought, got 120*l*. by guineas over and above the said 62*l*. 7*s*. 8*d*.	120	0	0
In all	880	0	0

Appeal I only speak to such Spectators as allow a good Play well acted to be the most valuable Entertainment of the Stage. Whether such Plays (leaving

"So that these six comedians, who are the unsatisfied people, have between the 12th of October and the 4th of June last, cleared in all the following sums:

	£	s	d.
Acted 100 times, Mr Wilkes certain	259	1	5
and more by computation	40	0	0
Both	299	1	5
Acted 16 times, Mr. Betterton certain	188	14	5
and more by computation	450	0	0
	638	14	5
Acted 52 times, Mr. Estcourt certain	163	18	6
and more by computation	200	0	0
	363	18	6
Acted 71 times, Mr. Cibber certain	162	10	10
and more by computation	50	0	0
	212	10	10
Acted — times, Mr Mills certain	170	11	4
and more by computation	20	0	0
	190	11	4
Acted 39 times, Mrs Oldfield certain	132	6	7
and more by computation	120	0	3
	252	6	7
In all	1957	3	2

the Skill of the dead or living Actors equally out of the Question) have been more or less recommended in their Presentation by either of these different Forms of that Theatre, is our present Matter of Enquiry.

It must be observ'd, then,[1] that the Area or Plat-

"Had not acting been forbid seven weeks on the occasion of Prince George's death, and my Lord Chamberlain forbad acting about five weeks before the tenth of July instant; each of these actors would have had twelve weeks salary more than is abovementioned.

"As to the certainties expressed in this paper, to be paid to the six Actors, the same are positively true. and as to the sums they got over and above such certainties, I believe the same to be true, according to the best of my computation.

"Witness my hand, who am Receiver and Treasurer at the Theatre Royal, Drury Lane,

"July 8th, 1709.   "ZACHARY BAGGS."

---

[1] The description of the shape of the stage which follows is interesting and valuable In early times the stage was a platform surrounded by the audience, not, as now, a picture framed by the proscenium. This is evident, not only from descriptive allusions, but from the two drawings which have come down to us of the interior of pre-Restoration theatres—De Witt's drawing of the Swan Theatre in 1596, reproduced in Herr Gaedertz's "Zur Kenntniss der altenglischen Buhne" (Bremen, 1888), and the well-known print of the Red Bull Theatre during the Commonwealth, which forms the frontispiece to Kirkman's "The Wits, or Sport upon Sport" (1672) In both of them the pit entirely surrounds the stage on three sides, while the fourth side also contains spectators in boxes placed above the entrance-doors By gradual modifications the shape of the stage has changed, till now the audience is confined to one side The doors used for entrances and exits, to which Cibber alludes, have disappeared comparatively recently. They may be seen, for instance, in Cruikshank's plates to Dickens's "Grimaldi."

form of the old Stage projected about four Foot forwarder, in a Semi-oval Figure, parallel to the Benches of the Pit; and that the former lower Doors of Entrance for the Actors were brought down between the two foremost (and then only) Pilasters; in the Place of which Doors now the two Stage-Boxes are fixt. That where the Doors of Entrance now are, there formerly stood two additional Side-Wings, in front to a full Set of Scenes, which had then almost a double Effect in their Loftiness and Magnificence.

By this Original Form, the usual Station of the Actors, in almost every Scene, was advanc'd at least ten Foot nearer to the Audience than they now can be; because, not only from the Stage's being shorten'd in front, but likewise from the additional Interposition of those Stage-Boxes, the Actors (in respect to the Spectators that fill them) are kept so much more backward from the main Audience than they us'd to be: But when the Actors were in Possession of that forwarder Space to advance upon, the Voice was then more in the Centre of the House, so that the most distant Ear had scarce the least Doubt or Difficulty in hearing what fell from the weakest Utterance: All Objects were thus drawn nearer to the Sense; every painted Scene was stronger; every grand Scene and Dance more extended; every rich or fine-coloured Habit had a more lively Lustre: Nor was the minutest Motion of a Feature (properly changing with the Passion or Humour it suited) ever lost, as they frequently must be in the Obscurity of too great a Distance: And how valuable an Advantage the Facility of hearing distinctly is to every well-acted Scene, every common Spectator is a Judge. A Voice scarce raised above the Tone of a Whisper, either in Tenderness, Resignation, innocent Distress, or Jealousy suppress'd, often have as much concern with the Heart as the most clamorous Passions; and when on any of these Occasions such affecting Speeches are plainly heard, or lost, how wide is the Difference from the great or little Satisfaction received from them? To all this a Master of a Company may say, I now receive Ten Pounds more than could have been taken formerly in every full House! Not unlikely. But might not his House be oftener full if the Auditors were oftener pleas'd? Might not every bad House too, by a Possibility of being made every Day better, add as much to one Side of his Account as it could take from the other? If what I have said carries any Truth in it, why might not the original Form of this Theatre be restor'd? but let this Digression avail what it may, the Actors now return'd to the *Hay-Market*, as I have observ'd, wanting nothing but length of Time to have govern'd their Alteration of that Theatre by this original Model of *Drury-Lane* which I have recommended. As their time therefore was short, they made their best use of it, they did something to it: They contracted its Wideness by three Ranges of Boxes on each side, and brought down its enormous high Ceiling within so proportionable a

Compass that it effectually cur'd those hollow Undulations of the Voice formerly complain'd of. The Remedy had its Effect; their Audiences exceeded their Expectation. There was now no other Theatre open against them;[1] they had the Town to themselves; they were their own Masters, and the Profits of their Industry came into their own Pockets.

Yet with all this fair Weather, the Season of their uninterrupted Prosperity was not yet arriv'd; for the great Expence and thinner Audiences of the Opera (of which they then were equally Directors) was a constant Drawback upon their Gains, yet not so far but that their Income this Year was better than in their late Station at *Drury-Lane*. But by the short Experience we had then had of Operas; by the high Reputation they seem'd to have been arriv'd at the Year before; by their Power of drawing the whole Body of Nobility as by Enchantment to their Solemnities; by that Prodigality of Expence at which they were so willing to support them; and from the late extraordinary Profits *Swiney* had made of them, what Mountains did we not hope from this Molehill? But alas! the fairy Vision was vanish'd; this bridal Beauty was grown familiar to the general Taste, and Satiety began to make Excuses for its want of Appetite. Or, what is still stranger, its

---

[1] The Haymarket opened on 15th September, 1709, and there was no rival theatre till 23rd November, when Drury Lane opened; but from this latter date till the end of the season both theatres were open.

late Admirers now as much valued their Judgment in being able to find out the Faults of the Performers, as they had before in discovering their Excellencies. The Truth is, that this kind of Entertainment being so entirely sensual, it had no Possibility of getting the better of our Reason but by its Novelty; and that Novelty could never be supported but by an annual Change of the best Voices, which, like the finest Flowers, bloom but for a Season, and when that is over are only dead Nose-gays. From this Natural Cause we have seen within these two Years even *Farinelli* singing to an Audience of five and thirty Pounds, and yet, if common Fame may be credited, the same Voice, so neglected in one Country, has in another had Charms sufficient to make that Crown sit easy on the Head of a Monarch, which the Jealousy of Politicians (who had their Views in his keeping it) fear'd, without some such extraordinary Amusement, his Satiety of Empire might tempt him a second time to resign.[1]

There is, too, in the very Species of an *Italian* Singer such an innate, fantastical Pride and Caprice, that the Government of them (here at least) is almost im-

---

[1] Bellchambers has here the following note:—"The monarch alluded to, I suppose, was Victor Amadeus, King of Sardinia. Carlo Broschi, better known by the name of Farinelli, was born in the dukedom of Modena, in 1705, and suffered emasculation, from an accident, when young. The Spanish king Ferdinand created him a knight of Calatrava, honoured him with his friendship, and added to his fortune. He returned to Italy on his patron's death, and died in 1782"

practicable. This Distemper, as we were not sufficiently warn'd or apprized of, threw our musical Affairs into Perplexities we knew not easily how to get out of. There is scarce a sensible Auditor in the Kingdom that has not since that Time had Occasion to laugh at the several Instances of it: But what is still more ridiculous, these costly Canary-Birds have sometimes infested the whole Body of our dignified Lovers of Musick with the same childish Animosities: Ladies have been known to decline their Visits upon account of their being of a different musical Party. *Cæsar* and *Pompey* made not a warmer Division in the *Roman* Republick than those Heroines, their Country Women, the *Faustina* and *Cuzzoni*, blew up in our Common-wealth of Academical Musick by their implacable Pretensions to Superiority.[1] And while this Greatness of Soul is their unalterable Virtue, it will never be practicable to make two capital Singers of the same Sex do as they should do in one Opera at the same time! no, not tho' *England* were to double the Sums it has already thrown after them. For even in their own

---

[1] Francesca Cuzzoni and Faustina Bordoni Hasse, whose famous rivalry in 1726 and 1727 is here referred to, were singers of remarkable powers. Cuzzoni's voice was a *soprano*, her rival's a *mezzo-soprano*, and while the latter excelled in brilliant execution, the former was supreme in pathetic expression. Dr. Burney ("History of Music," iv. 319) quotes from M. Quantz the statement that so keen was their supporters' party spirit, that when one party began to applaud their favourite, the other party hissed!

Country, where an extraordinary Occasion has called a greater Number of their best to sing together, the Mischief they have made has been proportionable; an Instance of which, if I am rightly inform'd, happen'd at *Parma*, where, upon the Celebration of the Marriage of that Duke, a Collection was made of the most eminent Voices that Expence or Interest could purchase, to give as complete an Opera as the whole vocal Power of *Italy* could form. But when it came to the Proof of this musical Project, behold! what woful Work they made of it! every Performer would be a *Cæsar* or Nothing; their several Pretensions to Preference were not to be limited within the Laws of Harmony; they would all choose their own Songs, but not more to set off themselves than to oppose or deprive another of an Occasion to shine: Yet any one would sing a bad Song, provided no body else had a good one, till at last they were thrown together, like so many feather'd Warriors, for a Battle-royal in a Cock-pit, where every one was oblig'd to kill another to save himself! What Pity it was these froward Misses and Masters of Musick had not been engag'd to entertain the Court of some King of *Morocco*, that could have known a good Opera from a bad one! with how much Ease would such a Director have brought them to better Order? But alas! as it has been said of greater Things,

Suis et ipsa Roma viribus ruit. Hor.[1]

[1] Horace, *Epod.* xvi. 2

Imperial *Rome* fell by the too great Strength of its own Citizens! So fell this mighty Opera, ruin'd by the too great Excellency of its Singers! For, upon the whole, it proved to be as barbarously bad as if Malice it self had composed it.

Now though something of this kind, equally provoking, has generally embarrass'd the State of Operas these thirty Years, yet it was the Misfortune of the menaging Actors at the *Hay-Market* to have felt the first Effects of it: The Honour of the Singer and the Interest of the Undertaker were so often at Variance, that the latter began to have but a bad Bargain of it. But not to impute more to the Caprice of those Performers than was really true, there were two different Accidents that drew Numbers from our Audiences before the Season was ended; which were another Company permitted to act in *Drury-Lane*,[1] and the long Trial of Doctor *Sacheverel* in *Westminster-Hall* [2] By the way, it must be observed that this Company was not under the Direction of the Patent (which continued still silenced) but was set up by a third Interest, with a License from Court. The Person to whom this new License was granted was *William Collier*, Esq.,

---

[1] See note on page 87.

[2] The trial opened on 27th February, 1710, and lasted for more than three weeks. The political excitement it caused must have done great harm to theatricals. Shadwell, in the Preface to "The Fair Quaker of Deal," mentioned *post*, page 95, says it was a success, "Notwithstanding the trial in Westminster-Hall, and the rehearsal of the new opera."

a Lawyer of an enterprizing Head and a jovial Heart; what sort of Favour he was in with the People then in Power may be judg'd from his being often admitted to partake with them those detach'd Hours of Life when Business was to give way to Pleasure: But this was not all his Merit, he was at the same time a Member of Parliament for *Truro* in *Cornwall*, and we cannot suppose a Person so qualified could be refused such a Trifle as a License to head a broken Company of Actors. This sagacious Lawyer, then, who had a Lawyer to deal with, observing that his Antagonist kept Possession of a Theatre without making use of it, and for which he was not obliged to pay Rent unless he actually *did* use it, wisely conceived it might be the Interest of the joint Landlords, since their Tenement was in so precarious a Condition, to grant a Lease to one who had an undisputed Authority to be liable, by acting Plays in it, to pay the Rent of it; especially when he tempted them with an Offer of raising it from three to four Pounds *per Diem*. His Project succeeded, the Lease was sign'd; but the Means of getting into Possession were to be left to his own Cost and Discretion. This took him up but little Time; he immediately laid Siege to it with a sufficient Number of Forces, whether lawless or lawful I forget, but they were such as obliged the old Governor to give it up; who, notwithstanding, had got Intelligence of his Approaches and Design time enough to carry off every thing that was worth moving, except a great

Number of old Scenes and new Actors that could not easily follow him.[1]

A ludicrous Account of this Transaction, under fictitious Names, may be found in the 99th *Tatler*, Vol. 2. which this Explanation may now render more intelligible to the Readers of that agreeable Author.[2]

[1] In the British Museum will be found a copy of the report by the Attorney-General and Solicitor-General, who were ordered by Queen Anne to inquire into this business. Rich declared that Collier broke into the theatre with an armed mob of soldiers, &c., but Collier denied the soldiers, though he admitted the breaking in. He gave as his authority for taking possession a letter signed by Sir James Stanley, dated 19th November, 1709, by which the Queen gave him authority to act, and required him not to allow Rich to have any concern in the theatre. His authority was appointed to run from 23rd November, 1709

[2] "Tatler," No. 99, 26th November, 1709 : "*Divito* [Rich] was too modest to know when to resign it, till he had the Opinion and Sentence of the Law for his Removal. . . . . The lawful Ruler [of Drury Lane] sets up an Attorney to expel an Attorney, and chose a Name dreadful to the Stage [that is Collier], who only seemed able to beat *Divito* out of his Intrenchments.

"On the 22d Instant, a Night of public Rejoycing, the Enemies of *Divito* made a Largess to the People of Faggots, Tubs, and other combustible Matter, which was erected into a Bonfire before the Palace Plentiful Cans were at the same time distributed among the Dependencies of that Principality, and the artful Rival of *Divito* observing them prepared for Enterprize, presented the lawful Owner of the neighbouring Edifice, and showed his Deputation under him. War immediately ensued upon the peaceful Empire of Wit and the Muses; The *Goths* and *Vandals* sacking *Rome* did not threaten a more barbarous Devastation of Arts and Sciences. But when they had forced their Entrance, the experienced *Divito* had detached all his Subjects, and evacuated all his Stores. The neighbouring Inhabitants report, That the Refuse of *Divito*'s Followers marched off the Night before disguised in

This other new License being now in Possession of the *Drury-Lane* Theatre, those Actors whom the Patentee ever since the Order of Silence had retain'd in a State of Inaction, all to a Man came over to the Service of *Collier*. Of these *Booth* was then the chief.[1] The Merit of the rest had as yet made no considerable Appearance, and as the Patentee had not left a Rag of their Cloathing behind him, they were but poorly equip'd for a publick Review; consequently at their first Opening they were very little able to annoy us. But during the Trial of *Sacheverel* our Audiences were extremely weaken'd by the better Rank of People's daily attending it: While, at the same time, the lower Sort, who were

Magnificence; Door-Keepers came out clad like Cardinals, and Scene-Drawers like Heathen Gods. *Divito* himself was wrapped up in one of his black Clouds, and left to the Enemy nothing but an empty Stage, full of Trap-Doors, known only to himself and his Adherents."

[1] Barton Booth, Theophilus Keen, Norris, John Bickerstaffe, George Powell, Francis Leigh, George Pack, Mrs. Knight, Mrs. Bradshaw, and Mrs Moore were Collier's chief performers As most of them had signed the petition in Rich's favour which I mentioned in a note on page 79, it is not wonderful that disturbances soon arose. Collier appointed Aaron Hill to manage the company, and his post seems to have been a somewhat lively one. On 14th June, 1710, the Lord Chamberlain's Records contain an entry which proves how rebellious the company were. Powell, Booth, Bickerstaffe, Keen, and Leigh, are stated to have defied and beaten Aaron Hill, to have broken open the doors of the theatre, and made a riot generally. For this Powell is discharged, and the others suspended. Mr. Fitzgerald (" New History," i. 308 *et seq*) quotes a letter from Hill, in which some account of this matter is given.

not equally admitted to that grand Spectacle, as eagerly crowded into *Drury-Lane* to a new Comedy call'd *The fair Quaker of Deal*. This Play having some low Strokes of natural Humour in it, was rightly calculated for the Capacity of the Actors who play'd it, and to the Taste of the Multitude who were now more disposed and at leisure to see it:[1] But the most happy Incident in its Fortune was the Charm of the fair Quaker which was acted by Miss *Santlow*, (afterwards Mrs. *Booth*) whose Person was then in the full Bloom of what Beauty she might pretend to: Before this she had only been admired as the most excellent Dancer, which perhaps might not a little contribute to the favourable Reception she now met with as an Actress, in this Character which so happily suited her Figure and Capacity: The gentle Softness of her Voice, the composed Innocence of her Aspect, the Modesty of her Dress,

---

[1] Charles Shadwell's " Fair Quaker of Deal" was produced at Drury Lane on 25th February, 1710 In the Preface the author says, "This play was written about three years since, and put into the hands of a famous Comedian belonging to the Haymarket Playhouse, who took care to beat down the value of it so much, as to offer the author to alter it fit to appear on the stage, on condition he might have half the profits of the third day, and the dedication entire; that is as much as to say, that it may pass for one of his, according to custom. The author not agreeing to this reasonable proposal, it lay in his hands till the beginning of this winter, when Mr. Booth read it, and liked it, and persuaded the author, that, with a little alteration, it would please the town" (Bell's edition) If, as is likely, Cibber is the actor referred to, his abuse of the play and the actors is not unintelligible.

the reserv'd Decency of her Gesture, and the Simplicity of the Sentiments that naturally fell from her, made her seem the amiable Maid she represented: In a Word, not the enthusiastick Maid of *Orleans* was more serviceable of old to the *French* Army when the *English* had distressed them, than this fair Quaker was at the Head of that dramatick Attempt upon which the Support of their weak Society depended.[1]

But when the Trial I have mention'd and the Run of this Play was over, the Tide of the Town beginning to turn again in our Favour, *Collier* was reduced to give his Theatrical Affairs a different Scheme; which advanced the Stage another Step towards that Settlement which, in my Time, was of the longest Duration.

---

[1] Hester Santlow, the "Santlow, fam'd for dance" of Gay, married Barton Booth. She appears to have retired from the stage about 1733. Genest (iii. 375) says, "she seems to have been a pleasing actress with no great powers." Her reputation was none of the best before her marriage, for she was said to have been the mistress of the Duke of Marlborough and of Secretary Craggs. See memoir of Booth.

CHAPTER XIII.

The Patentee, having now no Actors, rebuilds the new Theatre in Lincolns-Inn-Fields. A Guess at his Reasons for it. More Changes in the State of the Stage. The Beginning of its better Days under the Triumvirate of Actors. A Sketch of their governing Characters.

AS coarse Mothers may have comely Children, so Anarchy has been the Parent of many a good Government; and by a Parity of possible Consequences, we shall find that from the frequent Convulsions of the Stage arose at last its longest Settlement and Prosperity; which many of my Readers (or if I should happen to have but few of them, many of my Spectators at least) who I hope have not yet liv'd half their Time, will be able to remember.

Though the Patent had been often under Distresses, it had never felt any Blow equal to this unrevoked Order of Silence; which it is not easy to conceive could have fallen upon any other Person's Conduct than that of the old Patentee: For if he was conscious of his being under the Subjection of that Power which had silenc'd him, why would he incur the Danger of a Suspension by his so obstinate and impolitick Treatment of his Actors? If he thought such Power over him illegal, how came he to obey it now more than before, when he slighted a former Order that injoin'd him to give his Actors their Benefits on their usual Conditions?[1] But to do him Justice, the same Obstinacy that involv'd him in these Difficulties, at last preserv'd to his Heirs the Property of the Patent in its full Force and Value,[2] yet to suppose that he foresaw a milder use of Power in some future Prince's Reign might be more favourable to him, is begging at best but a cold Question. But whether he knew that this broken

[1] Genest (ii. 430) has the following outspoken character of Rich: "He seems in his public capacity of Patentee and Manager to have been a despicable character—without spirit to bring the power of the Lord Chamberlain to a legal test—without honesty to account to the other proprietors for the receipts of the theatre—without any feeling for his actors—and without the least judgment as to players and plays."

[2] Rich's Patent was revived, as Cibber states (p. 78), in 1714, when it was the property of his son, John Rich.

Condition of the Patent would not make his troublesome Friends the Adventurers fly from it as from a falling House, seems not so difficult a Question. Howèver, let the Reader form his own Judgment of them from the Facts that follow'd : It must therefore be observ'd, that the Adventurers seldom came near the House but when there was some visible Appearance of a Dividend : But I could never hear that upon an ill Run of Audiences they had ever returned or brought in a single Shilling, to make good the Deficiencies of their daily Receipts. Therefore, as the Patentee in Possession had alone, for several Years, supported and stood against this Uncertainty of Fortune, it may be imagin'd that his Accounts were under so voluminous a Perplexity that few of those Adventurers would have Leisure or Capacity enough to unravel them : And as they had formerly thrown away their Time and Money at law in a fruitless Enquiry into them, they now seem'd to have intirely given up their Right and Interest : And, according to my best Information, notwithstanding the subsequent Gains of the Patent have been sometimes extraordinary, the farther Demands or Claims of Right of the Adventurers have lain dormant above these five and twenty Years.[1]

---

[1] There is no more curious transaction in theatrical history than the acquisition of the entire right in the Patent by Rich and his son. Christopher Rich's share (see note on p. 32) was seventeen one-hundredths, or about one-sixth ; yet, by obstinate dishonesty, he succeeded in annexing the remainder.

Having shewn by what means *Collier* had dispossess'd this Patentee, not only of the *Drury-Lane* House, but likewise of those few Actors which he had kept for some time unemploy'd in it, we are now led to consider another Project of the same Patentee, which, if we are to judge of it by the Event, has shewn him more a Wise than a Weak Man; which I confess at the time he put it in Execution seem'd not so clear a Point: For notwithstanding he now saw the Authority and Power of his Patent was superseded, or was at best but precarious, and that he had not one Actor left in his Service, yet, under all these Dilemma's and Distresses, he resolv'd upon rebuilding the New Theatre in *Lincolns-Inn-Fields*, of which he had taken a Lease, at a low Rent, ever since *Betterton's* Company had first left it.[1] This Conduct seem'd too deep for my Comprehension! What are we to think of his taking this Lease in the height of his Prosperity, when he could have no Occasion for it? Was he a Prophet? Could he then foresee he should, one time or other, be turn'd out of *Drury-Lane*? Or did his mere Appetite of Architecture urge him to build a House, while he could not be sure he should ever have leave to make use of it? But of all this we may think as we please; whatever was his Motive, he, at his own Expence, in this Interval of his having nothing else to do, rebuilt that Theatre from the Ground, as it is now

[1] In March, 1705.

standing.[1] As for the Order of Silence, he seem'd little concern'd at it while it gave him so much uninterrupted Leisure to supervise a Work which he naturally took Delight in.

After this Defeat of the Patentee, the Theatrical Forces of *Collier* in *Drury-Lane*, notwithstanding their having drawn the Multitude after them for about three Weeks during the Trial of *Sacheverel*, had made but an indifferent Campaign at the end of the Season. *Collier* at least found so little Account in it, that it obliged him to push his Court-Interest (which, wherever the Stage was concern'd, was not inconsiderable) to support him in another Scheme; which was, that in consideration of his giving up the *Drury-Lane*, Cloaths, Scenes, and Actors, to *Swiney*

---

[1] There has been some doubt as to the locality of the theatre in Little Lincoln's Inn Fields, in which Betterton acted, one authority at least holding that he played in Gibbons' Tennis Court in Vere Street, Clare Market. But Cibber distinctly states that Rich rented the building which Betterton left in 1705, and old maps of London show clearly that Rich's theatre was in Portugal Street, just opposite the end of the then unnamed street, now called Carey Street. In "A New and Exact Plan of the Cities of London and Westminster," published 30th August, 1738, by George Foster, "The New Play House" is given as the name of this building, and it is worthy of notice that Cibber, a few lines above, writes of "the New Theatre in Lincoln's Inn Fields." See also vol i. p. 192, note 1, where I quote Downes, who calls Betterton's theatre the New Theatre in Lincoln's Inn Fields. About 1756 this house was made a barrack, it was afterwards an auction room; then the China Repository of Messrs Spode and Copeland, and was ultimately pulled down about 1848 to make room for the extension of the Museum of the Royal College of Surgeons.

and his joint Sharers in the *Hay-Market*, he (*Collier*) might be put into an equal Possession of the *Hay-Market* Theatre, with all the Singers, *&c.* and be made sole Director of the Opera. Accordingly, by Permission of the Lord Chamberlain, a Treaty was enter'd into, and in a few Days ratified by all Parties, conformable to the said Preliminaries.[1] This was that happy Crisis of Theatrical Liberty which the labouring Comedians had long sigh'd for, and which, for above twenty Years following, was so memorably fortunate to them.

However, there were two hard Articles in this Treaty, which, though it might be Policy in the Actors to comply with, yet the Imposition of them seem'd little less despotick than a Tax upon the Poor when a Government did not want it.

The first of these Articles was, That whereas the sole License for acting Plays was presum'd to be a more profitable Authority than that for acting Operas only, that therefore Two Hundred Pounds a Year should be paid to *Collier*, while Master of the Opera, by the Comedians; to whom a verbal Assurance was given by the *Plenipo's* on the Court-side, that while such Payment subsisted no other Company should be permitted to act Plays against them within the Liberties, *&c.* The other Article was, That on every *Wednesday* whereon an Opera could be per-

[1] The Licence to Swiney, Wilks, Cibber, and Dogget, for Drury Lane, is dated 6th November, 1710. In it Swiney's name is spelled "Swyny," and Cibber's "Cybber."

form'd, the Plays should, *toties quoties*, be silent at *Drury-Lane*, to give the Opera a fairer Chance for a full House.

This last Article, however partial in the Intention, was in its Effect of great Advantage to the sharing Actors: For in all publick Entertainments a Day's Abstinence naturally increases the Appetite to them: Our every *Thursday*'s Audience, therefore, was visibly the better by thus making the Day before it a Fast. But as this was not a Favour design'd us, this Prohibition of a Day, methinks, deserves a little farther Notice, because it evidently took a sixth Part of their Income from all the hired Actors, who were only paid in proportion to the Number of acting Days. This extraordinary Regard to Operas was, in effect, making the Day-labouring Actors the principal Subscribers to them, and the shutting out People from the Play every *Wednesday* many murmur'd at as an Abridgment of their usual Liberty. And tho' I was one of those who profited by that Order, it ought not to bribe me into a Concealment of what was then said and thought of it. I remember a Nobleman of the first Rank, then in a high Post, and not out of Court-Favour, said openly behind the Scenes——*It was shameful to take part of the Actors Bread from them to support the silly Diversion of People of Quality.* But alas! what was all this Grievance when weighed against the Qualifications of so grave and stanch a Senator as *Collier?* Such visible Merit, it seems, was to be made easy, tho' at the Expence of the—I had almost said, *Honour* of the Court, whose gracious Intention for the Theatrical Common-wealth might have shone with thrice the Lustre if such a paltry Price had not been paid for it. But as the Government of the Stage is but that of the World in Miniature, we ought not to have wonder'd that *Collier* had Interest enough to quarter the Weakness of the Opera upon the Strength of the Comedy. General good Intentions are not always practicable to a Perfection. The most necessary Law can hardly pass, but a Tenderness to some private Interest shall often hang such Exceptions upon particular Clauses, 'till at last it comes out lame and lifeless, with the Loss of half its Force, Purpose, and Dignity. As, for Instance, how many fruitless Motions have been made in Parliaments to moderate the enormous Exactions in the Practice of the Law? And what sort of Justice must that be call'd, which, when a Man has not a mind to pay you a Debt of Ten Pounds, it shall cost you Fifty before you can get it? How long, too, has the Publick been labouring for a Bridge at *Westminster?* But the Wonder that it was not built a Hundred Years ago ceases when we are told, That the Fear of making one End of *London* as rich as the other has been so long an Obstruction to it.[1] And though it might seem a still

---

[1] Westminster Bridge was authorized to be built in the face of virulent opposition from the Corporation of London, who feared that its existence would damage the trade of the City. Dr. Potter, Archbishop of Canterbury, and others interested, applied for an

HESTER SANTLOW

greater Wonder, when a new Law for building one had at last got over that Apprehension, that it should meet with any farther Delay; yet Experience has shewn us that the Structure of this useful Ornament to our Metropolis has been so clogg'd by private Jobs that were to be pick'd out of the Undertaking, and the Progress of the Work so disconcerted by a tedious Contention of private Interests and Endeavours to impose upon the Publick abominable Bargains, that a whole Year was lost before a single Stone could be laid to its Foundation. But Posterity will owe its Praises to the Zeal and Resolution of a truly Noble Commissioner, whose distinguish'd Impatience has broke thro' those narrow Artifices, those false and frivolous Objections that delay'd it, and has already began to raise above the Tide that future Monument of his Publick Spirit.[1]

How far all this may be allow'd applicable to the State of the Stage is not of so great Importance, nor so much my Concern, as that what is observ'd upon it should always remain a memorable Truth, to the Honour of that Nobleman. But now I go on: *Collier* being thus possess'd of his Musical Government, thought his best way would be to farm it out

---

Act of Parliament in 1736; the bridge was begun in 1738, and not finished till 1750, the opening ceremony being held on 17th November of that year. Until this time the only bridge was London Bridge. See "Old and New London," iii. 297.

[1] I presume the Noble Commissioner is the Earl of Pembroke, who laid the first stone of the bridge on 29th January, 1739.

to a Gentleman, *Aaron Hill*, Esq.[1] (who he had reason to suppose knew something more of Theatrical Matters than himself) at a Rent, if I mistake not, of Six Hundred Pounds *per Annum:* But before the Season was ended (upon what occasion, if I could remember, it might not be material to say) took it into his Hands again: But all his Skill and Interest could not raise the Direction of the Opera to so good a Post as he thought due to a Person of his Consideration · He therefore, the Year following, enter'd upon another high-handed Scheme, which, 'till the Demise of the Queen, turn'd to his better Account.

After the Comedians were in Possession of *Drury-Lane*, from whence during my time upon the Stage they never departed, their Swarm of Audiences exceeded all that had been seen in thirty Years before; which, however, I do not impute so much to the Excellence of their Acting as to their indefatigable Industry and good Menagement; for, as I have often said, I never thought in the general that we stood in any Place of Comparison with the eminent Actors before us; perhaps, too, by there being now an End of the frequent Divisions and Disorders that had from time to time broke in upon and frustrated their Labours, not a little might be contributed to their Success.

---

[1] Collier seems to have relied on Aaron Hill in all his theatrical enterprises, for, as previously noted, Hill had been manager for him at Drury Lane

Collier, then, like a true liquorish Courtier, observing the Prosperity of a Theatre, which he the Year before had parted with for a worse, began to meditate an Exchange of Theatrical Posts with *Swiney*, who had visibly very fair Pretensions to that he was in, by his being first chosen by the Court to regulate and rescue the Stage from the Disorders it had suffer'd under its former Menagers:[1] Yet *Collier* knew that sort of Merit could stand in no Competition with his being a Member of Parliament: He therefore had recourse to his Court-Interest (where meer Will and Pleasure at that time was the only Law that dispos'd of all Theatrical Rights) to oblige *Swiney* to let him be off from his bad Bargain for a better. To this it may be imagin'd *Swiney* demurr'd, and as he had Reason, strongly remonstrated against it: But as *Collier* had listed his Conscience under the Command of Interest, he kept it to strict Duty, and was immoveable; insomuch that Sir *John Vanbrugh*, who was a Friend to *Swiney*, and who, by his Intimacy with the People in Power, better knew the Motive of their Actions, advis'd *Swiney* rather to accept of the Change, than by a Non-compliance to hazard his being excluded from any Post or Concern in either of the Theatres: To conclude, it was not long before *Collier* had procured a new License for acting Plays, *&c.* for himself, *Wilks*, *Dogget*, and *Cibber*, exclusive of *Swiney*, who by this new Regula-

---

[1] At the end of the season 1708-9. See *ante*, p. 69.

tion was reduc'd to his *Hobson*'s Choice of the Opera.¹

Swiney being thus transferr'd to the Opera² in the sinking Condition *Collier* had left it, found the Receipts of it in the Winter following, 1711, so far short of the Expences, that he was driven to attend his Fortune in some more favourable Climate, where he remain'd twenty Years an Exile from his Friends and Country, tho' there has been scarce an *English* Gentleman who in his *Tour* of *France* or *Italy* has not renew'd or created an Acquaintance with him As this is a Circumstance that many People may have forgot, I cannot remember it without that Regard and Concern it deserves from all that know him: Yet it is some Mitigation of his Misfortune that since his Return to *England*, his grey Hairs and cheerful Disposition have still found a general Welcome among his foreign and former domestick Acquaintance.

Collier being now first-commission'd Menager with the Comedians, drove them, too, to the last Inch of a hard Bargain (the natural Consequence of all Treaties between Power and Necessity.) He not only demanded six hundred a Year neat Money, the Price at which he had farm'd out his Opera, and to make the Business a *Sine-cure* to him, but likewise insisted

---

¹ Collier's treatment of Swiney was so discreditable, that when he in his turn was evicted from Drury Lane (1714) we cannot help feeling gratified at his downfall.

² Swiney's Licence for the Opera is dated 17th April, 1712

upon a Moiety of the Two hundred that had been levied upon us the Year before in Aid of the Operas; in all 700*l*. These large and ample Conditions, considering in what Hands we were, we resolv'd to swallow without wry Faces; rather chusing to run any Hazard than contend with a formidable Power against which we had no Remedy: But so it happen'd that Fortune took better care of our Interest than we ourselves had like to have done: For had *Collier* accepted of our first Offer, of an equal Share with us, he had got three hundred Pounds a Year more by complying with it than by the Sum he imposed upon us, our Shares being never less than a thousand annually to each of us, 'till the End of the Queen's Reign in 1714. After which *Collier*'s Commission was superseded, his Theatrical Post, upon the Accession of his late Majesty, being given to Sir *Richard Steele*.[1]

From these various Revolutions in the Government of the Theatre, all owing to the Patentees mistaken Principle of increasing their Profits by too far enslaving their People, and keeping down the Price of good Actors (and I could almost insist that giving large Sallaries to bad Ones could not have had a worse Consequence) I say, when it is consider'd that the Authority for acting Plays, *&c.* was thought of so little worth that (as has been observ'd) Sir *Thomas*

---

[1] For a further account of Steele's being given a share of the Patent, which he got through Marlborough's influence, see the beginning of Chapter XV.

Skipwith gave away his Share of it, and the Adventurers had fled from it; that Mr. *Congreve*, at another time, had voluntarily resign'd it; and Sir *John Vanbrugh* (meerly to get the Rent of his new House paid) had, by Leave of the Court, farm'd out his License to *Swiney*, who not without some Hesitation had ventur'd upon it; let me say again, out of this low Condition of the Theatre, was it not owing to the Industry of three or four Comedians that a new Place was now created for the Crown to give away, without any Expence attending it, well worth the Acceptance of any Gentleman whose Merit or Services had no higher Claim to Preferment, and which *Collier* and Sir *Richard Steele*, in the two last Reigns, successively enjoy'd? Tho' I believe I may have said something like this in a former Chapter,[1] I am not unwilling it should be twice taken notice of.

We are now come to that firm Establishment of the Theatre, which, except the Admittance of *Booth* into a Share and *Dogget's* retiring from it, met with no Change or Alteration for above twenty Years after.

Collier, as has been said, having accepted of a certain Appointment of seven hundred *per Annum*, *Wilks*, *Dogget*, and Myself were now the only acting Menagers under the Queen's License; which being a Grant but during Pleasure oblig'd us to a Conduct that might not undeserve that Favour. At this

[1] See vol. 1 284-5

Time we were All in the Vigour of our Capacities as Actors, and our Prosperity enabled us to pay at least double the Sallaries to what the same Actors had usually receiv'd, or could have hoped for under the Government of the Patentees. *Dogget*, who was naturally an Oeconomist, kept our Expences and Accounts to the best of his Power within regulated Bounds and Moderation. *Wilks*, who had a stronger Passion for Glory than Lucre, was a little apt to be lavish in what was not always as necessary for the Profit as the Honour of the Theatre: For example, at the Beginning of almost every Season, he would order two or three Suits to be made or refresh'd for Actors of moderate Consequence, that his having constantly a new one for himself might seem less particular, tho' he had as yet no new Part for it. This expeditious Care of doing us good without waiting for our Consent to it, *Dogget* always look'd upon with the Eye of a Man in Pain: But I, who hated Pain, (tho' I as little liked the Favour as *Dogget* himself) rather chose to laugh at the Circumstance, than complain of what I knew was not to be cured but by a Remedy worse than the Evil. Upon these Occasions, therefore, whenever I saw him and his Followers so prettily dress'd out for an old Play, I only commended his Fancy; or at most but whisper'd him not to give himself so much trouble about others, upon whose Performance it would but be thrown away· To which, with a smiling Air of Triumph over my want of Penetration, he has reply'd—Why, now, that was what I really did it for! to shew others that I love to take care of them as well as of myself. Thus, whenever he made himself easy, he had not the least Conception, let the Expence be what it would, that we could possibly dislike it. And from the same Principle, provided a thinner Audience were liberal of their Applause, he gave himself little Concern about the Receipt of it. As in these different Tempers of my Brother-Menagers there might be equally something right and wrong, it was equally my Business to keep well with them both: And tho' of the two I was rather inclin'd to *Dogget's* way of thinking, yet I was always under the disagreeable Restraint of not letting *Wilks* see it: Therefore, when in any material Point of Menagement they were ready to come to a Rupture, I found it adviseable to think neither of them absolutely in the wrong; but by giving to one as much of the Right in his Opinion this way as I took from the other in that, their Differences were sometimes soft'ned into Concessions, that I have reason to think prevented many ill Consequences in our Affairs that otherwise might have attended them. But this was always to be done with a very gentle Hand; for as *Wilks* was apt to be easily hurt by Opposition, so when he felt it he was as apt to be insupportable. However, there were some Points in which we were always unanimous. In the twenty Years while we were our own Directors, we never had a Creditor that had occasion to come twice for his Bill; every *Monday* Morning discharged us of all Demands before we took a Shilling for our own Use. And from this time we neither ask'd any Actor, nor were desired by them, to sign any written Agreement (to the best of my Memory) whatsoever: The Rate of their respective Sallaries were only enter'd in our daily Pay-Roll; which plain Record every one look'd upon as good as City-Security: For where an honest Meaning is mutual, the mutual Confidence will be Bond enough in Conscience on both sides: But that I may not ascribe more to our Conduct than was really its Due, I ought to give Fortune her Share of the Commendation; for had not our Success exceeded our Expectation, it might not have been in our Power so throughly to have observ'd those laudable Rules of Oeconomy, Justice, and Lenity, which so happily supported us: But the Severities and Oppression we had suffer'd under our former Masters made us incapable of imposing them on others; which gave our whole Society the cheerful Looks of a rescued People. But notwithstanding this general Cause of Content, it was not above a Year or two before the Imperfection of human Nature began to shew itself in contrary Symptoms. The Merit of the Hazards which the Menagers had run, and the Difficulties they had combated in bringing to Perfection that Revolution by which they had all so amply profited in the Amendment of their general Income, began now to be forgotten; their Acknowledgments and thankful Promises of Fidelity were no more repeated, or scarce thought obligatory: Ease and Plenty by an habitual Enjoyment had lost their Novelty, and the Largeness of their Sallaries seem'd rather lessen'd than advanc'd by the extraordinary Gains of the Undertakers; for that is the Scale in which the hired Actor will always weigh his Performance; but whatever Reason there may seem to be in his Case, yet, as he is frequently apt to throw a little Self-partiality into the Balance, that Consideration may a good deal alter the Justness of it. While the Actors, therefore, had this way of thinking, happy was it for the Menagers that their united Interest was so inseparably the same, and that their Skill and Power in Acting stood in a Rank so far above the rest, that if the whole Body of private Men had deserted them, it would yet have been an easier matter for the Menagers to have pick'd up Recruits, than for the Deserters to have found proper Officers to head them. Here, then, in this Distinction lay our Security: Our being Actors ourselves was an Advantage to our Government which all former Menagers, who were only idle Gentlemen, wanted: Nor was our Establishment easily to be broken, while our Health and Limbs enabled us to be Joint-labourers in the Work we were Masters of.

The only Actor who, in the Opinion of the Publick, seem'd to have had a Pretence of being advanc'd to a Share with us was certainly *Booth:* But when it is consider'd how strongly he had oppos'd the Measures that had made us Menagers, by setting himself (as has been observ'd) at the Head of an opposite Interest,[1] he could not as yet have much to complain of: Beside, if the Court had thought him, now, an equal Object of Favour, it could not have been in our Power to have oppos'd his Preferment: This I mention, not to take from his Merit, but to shew from what Cause it was not as yet better provided for. Therefore it may be no Vanity to say, our having at that time no visible Competitors on the Stage was the only Interest that rais'd us to be the Menagers of it.

But here let me rest a while, and since at my time of Day our best Possessions are but Ease and Quiet, I must be content, if I will have Sallies of Pleasure, to take up with those only that are to be found in Imagination. When I look back, therefore, on the Storms of the Stage we had been toss'd in; when I consider that various Vicissitude of Hopes and Fears we had for twenty Years struggled with, and found ourselves at last thus safely set on Shore to enjoy the Produce of our own Labours, and to have rais'd those Labours by our Skill and Industry to a much fairer Profit, than our Task-masters by all their severe and griping Government had ever reap'd from them, a good-natur'd Reader, that is not offended at the Comparison of great things with small, will allow was a Triumph in proportion equal to those that have attended the

---

[1] That is, he had been the chief of Collier's Company at Drury Lane at his opening in November, 1709. See *ante*, p. 94.

most heroick Enterprizes for Liberty! What Transport could the first *Brutus* feel upon his Expulsion of the *Tarquins* greater than that which now danc'd in the Heart of a poor Actor, who, from an injur'd Labourer, unpaid his Hire, had made himself, without Guilt, a legal Menager of his own Fortune? Let the Grave and Great contemn or yawn at these low Conceits, but let me be happy in the Enjoyment of them! To this Hour my Memory runs o'er that pleasing Prospect of Life past with little less Delight than when I was first in the real Possession of it. This is the natural Temper of my Mind, which my Acquaintance are frequently Witnesses of: And as this was all the Ambition Providence had made my obscure Condition capable of, I am thankful that Means were given me to enjoy the Fruits of it.

—— Hoc est
Vivere bis, vitâ posse priore frui.[1]

Something like the Meaning of this the less learned Reader may find in my Title Page.

[1] Martial, x. 23, 7

CHAPTER XIV.

The Stage in its highest Prosperity. The Menagers not without Errors. Of what Kind. Cato first acted. What brought it to the Stage. The Company go to Oxford. Their Success and different Auditors there. Booth made a Sharer. Dogget objects to him. Quits the Stage upon his Admittance. That not his true Reason. What was. Dogget's Theatrical Character.

NOTWITHSTANDING the Menaging Actors were now in a happier Situation than their utmost Pretensions could have expected, yet it is not to be suppos'd but wiser Men might have mended it. As we could not all govern our selves, there were Seasons when we were not all fit to govern others. Our Passions and our Interest drew not always the same way. *Self* had a great Sway in our Debates: We had our Partialities; our Prejudices; our Favourites of less Merit; and our Jealousies of those who came too near us; Frailties which Societies of higher Consideration, while they are compos'd of Men, will not always be free from. To have been constantly capable of Unanimity had been a Blessing too great for our Station: One Mind among three People were to have had three Masters to one Servant; but when that one Servant is called three different ways at the same time, whose Business is to be done first? For my own Part, I was forced almost all my Life to give up my Share of him. And if I could, by Art or Persuasion, hinder others from making what I thought a wrong use of their Power, it was the All and utmost I desired. Yet, whatever might be our Personal Errors, I shall think I have no Right to speak of them farther than where the Publick Entertainment was affected by them. If therefore, among so many, some particular Actors were remarkable in any part of their private Lives, that might sometimes make the World merry without Doors, I hope my laughing Friends will excuse me if I do not so far comply with their Desires or Curiosity as to give them a Place in my History. I can only recommend such Anecdotes to the Amusement of a Noble Person, who (in case I' conceal them) does me the flattering Honour to threaten my Work with a Supplement. 'Tis enough for me that such Actors had their Merits to the Publick: Let those recite their Imperfections who are themselves without them: It is my Misfortune not to have that Qualification. Let us see then (whatever was amiss in it) how our Administration went forward.

When we were first invested with this Power, the Joy of our so unexpectedly coming into it kept us for some time in Amity and Good-Humour with one another: And the Pleasure of reforming the many false Measures, Absurdities, and Abuses, that, like Weeds, had suck'd up the due Nourishment from the Fruits of the Theatre, gave us as yet no leisure for private Dissentions. Our daily Receipts exceeded our Imagination: And we seldom met as a Board to settle our weekly Accounts without the Satisfaction of Joint-Heirs just in Possession of an unexpected Estate that had been distantly intail'd upon them. Such a sudden Change of our Condition it may be imagin'd could not but throw out of us a new Spirit in almost every Play we appear'd in: Nor did we ever sink into that common Negligence which is apt to follow Good-fortune: Industry we knew was the Life of our Business; that it not only conceal'd Faults, but was of equal Value to greater Talents without it; which the Decadence once of *Betterton*'s Company in *Lincoln's-Inn-Fields* had lately shewn us a Proof of.

This then was that happy Period, when both Actors and Menagers were in their highest Enjoyment of general Content and Prosperity. Now it was that the politer World, too, by their decent

Attention, their sensible Taste, and their generous Encouragements to Authors and Actors, once more saw that the Stage, under a due Regulation, was capable of being what the wisest Ages thought it *might* be, The most rational Scheme that Human Wit could form to dissipate with Innocence the Cares of Life, to allure even the Turbulent or Ill-disposed from worse Meditations, and to give the leisure Hours of Business and Virtue an instructive Recreation.

If this grave Assertion is less recommended by falling from the Pen of a Comedian, I must appeal for the Truth of it to the Tragedy of *Cato*, which was first acted in 1712.[1] I submit to the Judgment of those who were then the sensible Spectators of it, if the Success and Merit of that Play was not an Evidence of every Article of that Value which I have given to a decent Theatre? But (as I was observing) it could not be expected the Summer

---

[1] This is a blunder, which, by the way, Bellchambers does not correct. "Cato" was produced at Drury Lane on 14th April, 1713. The cast was —

CATO	Mr Booth
LUCIUS	Mr. Keen.
SEMPRONIUS	Mr. Mills
JUBA	Mr. Wilks.
SYPHAX	Mr Cibber.
PORTIUS	Mr. Powell.
MARCUS	Mr. Ryan.
DECIUS	Mr Bowman.
MARCIA	Mrs. Oldfield
LUCIA	Mrs. Porter

Days I am speaking of could be the constant Weather of the Year; we had our clouded Hours as well as our sun-shine, and were not always in the same Good-Humour with one another: Fire, Air, and Water could not be more vexatiously opposite than the different Tempers of the Three Menagers, though they might equally have their useful as well as their destructive Qualities. How variously these Elements in our several Dispositions operated may be judged from the following single Instance, as well as a thousand others, which, if they were all to be told, might possibly make my Reader wish I had forgot them.

Much about this time, then, there came over from *Dublin* Theatre two uncelebrated Actors to pick up a few Pence among us in the Winter, as *Wilks* had a Year or two before done on their side the Water in the Summer.[1] But it was not so clear to *Dogget* and myself that it was in their Power to do us the same Service in *Drury-Lane* as *Wilks* might have done them in *Dublin*. However, *Wilks* was so much a Man of Honour that he scorned to be outdone in

[1] "The Laureat" says these Irish actors were Elrington and Griffith, but I venture to think that Evans's name should be substituted for that of Griffith. All three came from Ireland to Drury Lane in 1714; but, while Elrington and Evans played many important characters, Griffith did very little. Again, I can find no record of the latter's benefit, but the others had benefits in the best part of the season. The fact that they had *separate* benefits makes my theory contradict Cibber on this one point; but what he says may have occurred in connection with one of the two benefits. Cibber's memory is not infallible.

the least Point of it, let the Cost be what it would to his Fellow-Menagers, who had no particular Accounts of Honour open with them. To acquit himself therefore with a better Grace, *Wilks* so order'd it, that his *Hibernian* Friends were got upon our Stage before any other Menager had well heard of their Arrival. This so generous Dispatch of their Affair gave *Wilks* a very good Chance of convincing his Friends that Himself was sole Master of the Masters of the Company. Here, now, the different Elements in our Tempers began to work with us. While *Wilks* was only animated by a grateful Hospitality to his Friends, *Dogget* was ruffled into a Storm, and look'd upon this Generosity as so much Insult and Injustice upon himself and the Fraternity. During this Disorder I stood by, a seeming quiet Passenger, and, since talking to the Winds I knew could be to no great Purpose (whatever Weakness it might be call'd) could not help smiling to observe with what officious Ease and Delight *Wilks* was treating his Friends at our Expence, who were scarce acquainted with them. For it seems all this was to end in their having a Benefit-Play in the Height of the Season, for the unprofitable Service they had done us without our Consent or Desire to employ them. Upon this *Dogget* bounc'd and grew almost as untractable as *Wilks* himself. Here, again, I was forc'd to clap my Patience to the Helm to weather this difficult Point between them: Applying myself therefore to the Person I imagin'd was most

likely to hear me, I desired *Dogget* "to consider that
" I must naturally be as much hurt by this vain and
" over-bearing Behaviour in *Wilks* as he could be;
" and that tho' it was true these Actors had no Pre-
" tence to the Favour design'd them, yet we could
" not say they had done us any farther Harm, than
" letting the Town see the Parts they had been
" shewn in, had been better done by those to whom
" they properly belong'd: Yet as we had greatly
" profited by the extraordinary Labour of *Wilks*, who
" acted long Parts almost every Day, and at least
" twice to *Dogget*'s once;[1] and that I granted it
" might not be so much his Consideration of our
" common Interest, as his Fondness for Applause,
" that set him to Work, yet even that Vanity, if he
" supposed it such, had its Merit to us; and as we
" had found our Account in it, it would be Folly
" upon a Punctilio to tempt the Rashness of a Man,
" who was capable to undo all he had done, by any
" Act of Extravagance that might fly into his Head:
" That admitting this Benefit might be some little
" Loss to us, yet to break with him upon it could not
" but be ten times of worse Consequence, than our
" overlooking his disagreeable manner of making the
" Demand upon us."

Though I found this had made *Dogget* drop the
Severity of his Features, yet he endeavoured still to
seem uneasy, by his starting a new Objection, which

[1] Genest's record gives Wilks about one hundred and fifty different characters, Dogget only about sixty.

was, That we could not be sure even of the Charge they were to pay for it: For *Wilks*, said he, you know, will go any Lengths to make it a good Day to them, and may whisper the Door-keepers to give them the Ready-money taken, and return the Account in such Tickets only as these Actors have not themselves disposed of. To make this easy too, I gave him my Word to be answerable for the Charge my self. Upon this he acceded, and accordingly they had the Benefit-Play. But so it happen'd (whether as *Dogget* had suspected or not, I cannot say) the Ready-money receiv'd fell Ten Pounds short of the Sum they had agreed to pay for it. Upon the *Saturday* following, (the Day on which we constantly made up our Accounts) I went early to the Office, and inquired if the Ten Pounds had yet been paid in; but not hearing that one Shilling of it had found its way thither, I immediately supply'd the Sum out of my own Pocket, and directed the Treasurer to charge it received from me in the deficient Receipt of the Benefit-Day. Here, now, it might be imagined, all this silly Matter was accommodated, and that no one could so properly say he was aggrieved as myself: But let us observe what the Consequence says—why, the Effect of my insolent interposing honesty prov'd to be this: That the Party most oblig'd was the most offended; and the Offence was imputed to me who had been Ten Pounds out of Pocket to be able to commit it: For when *Wilks* found in the Account how spitefully the Ten Pounds had been paid in, he took me aside into the adjacent Stone-Passage, and with some Warmth ask'd me, What I meant by pretending to pay in this Ten Pounds? And that, for his part, he did not understand such Treatment. To which I reply'd, That tho' I was amaz'd at his thinking himself ill-treated, I would give him a plain, justifiable Answer.——That I had given my Word to *Dogget* the Charge of the Benefit should be fully paid, and since his Friends had neglected it, I found myself bound to make it good. Upon which he told me I was mistaken if I thought he did not see into the bottom of all this—That *Dogget* and I were always endeavouring to thwart and make him uneasy; but he was able to stand upon his own Legs, and we should find he would not be used so: That he took this Payment of the Ten Pounds as an Insult upon him and a Slight to his Friends; but rather than suffer it he would tear the whole Business to pieces: That I knew it was in his Power to do it; and if he could not do a civil thing to a Friend without all this senseless Rout about it, he could be received in *Ireland* upon his own Terms, and could as easily mend a Company there as he had done here: That if he were gone, *Dogget* and I would not be able to keep the Doors open a Week; and, by G—, he would not be a Drudge for nothing. As I knew all this was but the Foam of the high Value he had set upon himself, I thought it not amiss to seem a little silently concerned, for the helpless Condition to which his Resentment of the Injury I have related was going to reduce us: For I knew I had a Friend in his Heart that, if I gave him a little time to cool, would soon bring him to Reason: The sweet Morsel of a Thousand Pounds a Year was not to be met with at every Table, and might tempt a nicer Palate than his own to swallow it, when he was not out of Humour. This I knew would always be of weight with him, when the best Arguments I could use would be of none. I therefore gave him no farther Provocation than by gravely telling him, We all had it in our Power to do one another a Mischief; but I believed none of us much cared to hurt ourselves; that if he was not of my Opinion, it would not be in my Power to hinder whatever new Scheme he might resolve upon; that *London* would always have a Play-house, and I should have some Chance in it, tho' it might not be so good as it had been, that he might be sure, if I had thought my paying in the Ten Pounds could have been so ill received, I should have been glad to have saved it. Upon this he seem'd to mutter something to himself, and walk'd off as if he had a mind to be alone. I took the Occasion, and return'd to *Dogget* to finish our Accounts. In about six Minutes *Wilks* came in to us, not in the best Humour, it may be imagined; yet not in so ill a one but that he took his Share of the Ten Pounds without shewing the least Contempt of it; which, had he been proud enough to have refused, or to have paid in himself, I might have thought he intended to make good his Menaces, and that the

Injury I had done him would never have been forgiven; but it seems we had different ways of thinking.

Of this kind, more or less delightful, was the Life I led with this impatient Man for full twenty Years. *Dogget*, as we shall find, could not hold it so long; but as he had more Money than I, he had not Occasion for so much Philosophy. And thus were our Theatrical Affairs frequently disconcerted by this irascible Commander, this *Achilles* of our Confederacy, who, I may be bold to say, came very little short of the Spirit *Horace* gives to that Hero in his—

Impiger, iracundus, inexorabilis, acer.[1]

This, then, is one of those Personal Anecdotes of our Variances, which, as our publick Performances were affected by it, could not, with regard to Truth and Justice, be omitted.

From this time to the Year 1712 my Memory (from which Repository alone every Article of what I write is collected) has nothing worth mentioning, 'till the first acting of the Tragedy of *Cato*.[2] As to the Play itself, it might be enough to say, That the Author and the Actors had their different Hopes of Fame and Profit amply answer'd by the Performance; but as its Success was attended with remarkable Consequences, it may not be amiss to trace it from its several Years Concealment in the Closet, to the Stage.

---

[1] Horace, *Ars Poetica*, 121.
[2] See note on page 120.

In 1703, nine Years before it was acted, I had the Pleasure of reading the first four Acts (which was all of it then written) privately with Sir *Richard Steele*: It may be needless to say it was impossible to lay them out of my Hand 'till I had gone thro' them, or to dwell upon the Delight his Friendship to the Author receiv'd upon my being so warmly pleas'd with them: But my Satisfaction was as highly disappointed when he told me, Whatever Spirit Mr. *Addison* had shewn in his writing it, he doubted he would never have Courage enough to let his *Cato* stand the Censure of an *English* Audience; that it had only been the Amusement of his leisure Hours in *Italy*, and was never intended for the Stage. This Poetical Diffidence[1] Sir *Richard* himself spoke of with some Concern, and in the Transport of his Imagination could not help saying, *Good God! what a Part would* Betterton *make of* Cato! But this was seven Years before *Betterton* died, and when *Booth* (who afterwards made his Fortune by acting it) was in his Theatrical Minority. In the latter end of Queen *Anne*'s Reign, when our National Politicks had changed Hands, the Friends of Mr. *Addison* then thought it a proper time to animate the Publick with the Sentiments of *Cato*, in a word, their Importunities were too warm to be resisted; and it was no sooner finish'd than hurried to the Stage, in *April*,

---

[1] Johnson (Life of Addison) terms this "the despicable cant of literary modesty"

1712,[1] at a time when three Days a Week were usually appointed for the Benefit Plays of particular Actors: But a Work of that critical Importance was to make its way through all private Considerations; nor could it possibly give place to a Custom, which the Breach of could very little prejudice the Benefits, that on so unavoidable an Occasion were (in part, tho' not wholly) postpon'd; it was therefore (*Mondays* excepted) acted every Day for a Month to constantly crowded Houses.[2] As the Author had made us a Present of whatever Profits he might have claim'd from it, we thought our selves oblig'd to spare no Cost in the proper Decorations of it. Its coming so late in the Season to the Stage prov'd of particular Advantage to the sharing Actors, because the Harvest of our annual Gains was generally over before the middle of *March*, many select Audiences being then usually reserv'd in favour to the Benefits of private Actors; which fixt Engagements naturally abated the Receipts of the Days before and after them: But this unexpected Aftercrop of *Cato* largely

---

[1] 14th April, 1713 See note on page 120.
[2] Mrs. Oldfield, Powell, Mills, Booth, Pinkethman, and Mrs Porter, had their benefits before "Cato" was produced. "Cato" was then acted twenty times—April 14th to May 9th—that is, every evening except Monday in each week, as Cibber states. On Monday nights the benefits continued—being one night in the week instead of three. Johnson, Keen, and Mrs. Bicknell had their benefits during the run of "Cato," and on May 11th the regular benefit performances recommenced, Mrs. Rogers taking her benefit on that night.

supplied to us those Deficiencies, and was almost equal to two fruitful Seasons in the same Year; at the Close of which the three menaging Actors found themselves each a Gainer of thirteen hundred and fifty Pounds: But to return to the first Reception of this Play from the Publick.

Although *Cato* seems plainly written upon what are called *Whig* Principles, yet the *Torys* of that time had Sense enough not to take it as the least Reflection upon their Administration; but, on the contrary, they seem'd to brandish and vaunt their Approbation of every Sentiment in favour of Liberty, which, by a publick Act of their Generosity, was carried so high, that one Day, while the Play was acting, they collected fifty Guineas in the Boxes, and made a Present of them to *Booth*, with this Compliment——*For his honest Opposition to a perpetual Dictator, and his dying so bravely in the Cause of Liberty:* What was insinuated by any Part of these Words is not my Affair;[1] but so publick a Reward had the Appearance of a laudable Spirit, which only such a Play as *Cato* could have inspired; nor could *Booth* be blam'd if, upon so particular a Distinction of his Merit, he began himself to set more Value upon it: How far he might carry it, in making use of the Favour he stood in with a certain Nobleman[2] then in Power at Court, was not difficult

---

[1] The Duke of Marlborough is the person pointed at

[2] Theo. Cibber ("Life of Booth," p 6) says that Booth in his early days as an actor became intimate with Lord Bolingbroke,

to penetrate, and indeed ought always to have been expected by the menaging Actors: For which of them (making the Case every way his own) could with such Advantages have contented himself in the humble Station of an hired Actor? But let us see how the Menagers stood severally affected upon this Occasion.

Dogget, who expected, though he fear'd not, the Attempt of what after happen'd, imagin'd he had thought of an Expedient to prevent it: And to cover his Design with all the Art of a Statesman, he insinuated to us (for he was a staunch *Whig*) that this Present of fifty Guineas was a sort of a *Tory* Triumph which they had no Pretence to; and that for his Part he could not bear that so redoubted a Champion for Liberty as *Cato* should be bought off to the Cause of a Contrary Party: He therefore, in the seeming Zeal of his Heart, proposed that the Menagers themselves should make the same Present to *Booth* which had been made him from the Boxes the Day before. This, he said, would recommend the Equality and liberal Spirit of our Menagement to the Town, and might be a Means to secure *Booth* more firmly in our Interest, it never having been known that the Skill of the best Actor had receiv'd so round a Reward or Gratuity in one Day

and that this "was of eminent advantage to Mr. *Booth*,—when, on his great Success in the Part of CATO (of which he was the original Actor) my Lord's Interest (then Secretary of State) established him as a Manager of the Theatre."

before. *Wilks*, who wanted nothing but Abilities to be as cunning as *Dogget*, was so charm'd with the Proposal that he long'd that Moment to make *Booth* the Present with his own Hands; and though he knew he had no Right to do it without my Consent, had no Patience to ask it; upon which I turned to *Dogget* with a cold Smile, and told him, that if *Booth* could be purchas'd at so cheap a Rate, it would be one of the best Proofs of his Oeconomy we had ever been beholden to: I therefore desired we might have a little Patience; that our doing it too hastily might be only making sure of an Occasion to throw the fifty Guineas away; for if we should be obliged to do better for him, we could never expect that *Booth* would think himself bound in Honour to refund them. This seem'd so absurd an Argument to *Wilks* that he began, with his usual Freedom of Speech, to treat it as a pitiful Evasion of their intended Generosity· But *Dogget*, who was not so wide of my Meaning, clapping his Hand upon mine, said, with an Air of Security, O! don't trouble yourself! there must be two Words to that Bargain; let me alone to menage that Matter *Wilks*, upon this dark Discourse, grew uneasy, as if there were some Secret between us that he was to be left out of. Therefore, to avoid the Shock of his Intemperance, I was reduc'd to tell him that it was my Opinion, that *Booth* would never be made easy by any thing we could do for him, 'till he had a Share in the Profits and Menagement; and that, as he did not want Friends to assist him, whatever his Merit might be before, every one would think, since his acting of *Cato*, he had now enough to back his Pretensions to it. To which *Dogget* reply'd, that nobody could think his Merit was slighted by so handsome a Present as fifty Guineas; and that, for his farther Pretensions, whatever the License might avail, our Property of House, Scenes, and Cloaths were our own, and not in the Power of the Crown to dispose of. To conclude, my Objections that the Money would be only thrown away, *&c.* were over-rul'd, and the same Night *Booth* had the fifty Guineas, which he receiv'd with a Thankfulness that made *Wilks* and *Dogget* perfectly easy, insomuch that they seem'd for some time to triumph in their Conduct, and often endeavour'd to laugh my Jealousy out of Countenance: But in the following Winter the Game happen'd to take a different Turn; and then, if it had been a laughing Matter, I had as strong an Occasion to smile at their former Security. But before I make an End of this Matter, I cannot pass over the good Fortune of the Company that followed us to the Act at *Oxford*, which was held in the intervening Summer: Perhaps, too, a short View of the Stage in that different Situation may not be unacceptable to the Curious.

After the Restoration of King *Charles*, before the *Cavalier* and *Round-head* Parties, under their new Denomination of *Whig* and *Tory*, began again to be politically troublesome, publick Acts at *Oxford* (as I find by the Date of several Prologues written by *Dryden*[1] for *Hart* on those Occasions) had been more frequently held than in later Reigns. Whether the same Party-Dissentions may have occasion'd the Discontinuance of them, is a Speculation not necessary to be enter'd into. But these Academical Jubilees have usually been look'd upon as a kind of congratulatory Compliment to the Accession of every new Prince to the Throne, and generally, as such, have attended them. King *James*,[2] notwithstanding his Religion, had the Honour of it; at which the Players, as usual, assisted. This I have only mention'd to give the Reader a Theatrical Anecdote of a Liberty which *Tony Leigh* the Comedian took with the Character of the well known *Obadiah Walker*,[3] then Head of *University College*, who in that Prince's Reign had turn'd *Roman Catholick:* The Circumstance is this.

In the latter End of the Comedy call'd the *Committee*, *Leigh*, who acted the Part of *Teague*, hauling in *Obadiah* with an Halter about his Neck, whom, according to his written Part, he was to threaten to hang for no better Reason than his refusing to drink

---

[1] There are five Prologues by Dryden spoken at Oxford, one in 1674, and the others probably about 1681.

[2] James II.

[3] Obadiah Walker, born 1616, died 1699, is famous only for the change of religion to which Cibber's anecdote refers. Macaulay ("History," 1858, ii 85-86) relates the story of his perversion, and in the same volume, page 283, refers to the incident here told by Cibber.

the King's Health, (but here *Leigh*) to justify his Purpose with a stronger Provocation, put himself into a more than ordinary Heat with his Captive *Obadiah*, which having heightened his Master's Curiosity to know what *Obadiah* had done to deserve such Usage, *Leigh*, folding his Arms, with a ridiculous Stare of Astonishment, reply'd—*Upon my Shoule, he has shange his Religion.* As the Merit of this Jest lay chiefly in the Auditors' sudden Application of it to the *Obadiah* of *Oxford*, it was received with all the Triumph of Applause which the Zeal of a different Religion could inspire. But *Leigh* was given to understand that the King was highly displeased at it, inasmuch as it had shewn him that the University was in a Temper to make a Jest of his Proselyte. But to return to the Conduct of our own Affairs there in 1712.[1]

It had been a Custom for the Comedians while at *Oxford* to act twice a Day; the first Play ending every Morning before the College Hours of dining, and the other never to break into the time of shutting their Gates in the Evening. This extraordinary Labour gave all the hired Actors a Title to double Pay, which, at the Act in King *William*'s Time, I had myself accordingly received there. But the present Menagers considering that, by acting only once a Day, their Spirits might be fresher for every single

---

[1] 1713. The performance on 23rd June, 1713, was announced as the last that season, as the company were obliged to go immediately to Oxford.

Performance, and that by this Means they might be able to fill up the Term of their Residence, without the Repetition of their best and strongest Plays; and as their Theatre was contrived to hold a full third more than the usual Form of it had done, one House well fill'd might answer the Profits of two but moderately taken up: Being enabled, too, by their late Success at *London*, to make the Journey pleasant and profitable to the rest of their Society, they resolved to continue to them their double Pay, notwithstanding this new Abatement of half their Labour. This Conduct of the Menagers more than answer'd their Intention, which was rather to get nothing themselves than not let their Fraternity be the better for the Expedition. Thus they laid an Obligation upon their Company, and were themselves considerably, though unexpected, Gainers by it. But my chief Reason for bringing the Reader to *Oxford* was to shew the different Taste of Plays there from that which prevail'd at *London*. A great deal of that false, flashy Wit and forc'd Humour, which had been the Delight of our Metropolitan Multitude, was only rated there at its bare intrinsick Value;[1] Applause was not to be purchased there

[1] Dryden writes, in one of his Prologues (about 1681), to the University of Oxford:—

"When our fop gallants, or our city folly,
Clap over-loud, it makes us melancholy:
We doubt that scene which does their wonder raise,
And, for their ignorance, contemn their praise.
Judge, then, if we who act, and they who write,

but by the true Sterling, the *Sal Atticum* of a Genius, unless where the Skill of the Actor pass'd it upon them with some extraordinary Strokes of Nature. *Shakespear* and *Johnson* had there a sort of classical Authority; for whose masterly Scenes they seem'd to have as implicit a Reverence as formerly for the Ethicks of *Aristotle*; and were as incapable of allowing Moderns to be their Competitors, as of changing their Academical Habits for gaudy Colours or Embroidery. Whatever Merit, therefore, some few of our more politely-written Comedies might pretend to, they had not the same Effect upon the Imagination there, nor were received with that extraordinary Applause they had met with from the People of Mode and Pleasure in *London*, whose vain Accomplishments did not dislike themselves in the Glass that was held to them: The elegant Follies of higher Life were not at *Oxford* among their Acquaintance, and consequently might not be so good Company to a learned Audience as Nature, in her plain Dress and unornamented, in her Pursuits and Inclinations seem'd to be.

The only distinguish'd Merit allow'd to any modern Writer[1] was to the Author of *Cato*, which

> Should not be proud of giving you delight.
> London likes grossly; but this nicer pit
> Examines, fathoms, all the depths of wit;
> The ready finger lays on every blot;
> Knows what should justly please, and what should not."

[1] In a Prologue by Dryden, spoken by Hart in 1674, at Oxford, the poet says:—

Play being the Flower of a Plant raised in that learned Garden, (for there Mr. *Addison* had his Education) what favour may we not suppose was due to him from an Audience of Brethren, who from that local Relation to him might naturally have a warmer Pleasure in their Benevolence to his Fame? But not to give more Weight to this imaginary Circumstance than it may bear, the Fact was, that on our first Day of acting it our House was in a manner invested, and Entrance demanded by twelve a Clock at Noon, and before one it was not wide enough for many who came too late for Places. The same Crowds continued for three Days together, (an uncommon Curiosity in that Place) and the Death of *Cato* triumph'd over the Injuries of *Cæsar* every where. To conclude, our Reception at *Oxford*, whatever our Merit might be, exceeded our Expectation. At our taking Leave we had the Thanks of the Vice-Chancellor for the Decency and Order observ'd by our whole Society, an Honour which had not always been paid upon the same Occasions, for at

> "None of our living poets dare appear;
> For Muses so severe are worshipped here,
> That, conscious of their faults, they shun the eye,
> And, as profane, from sacred places fly,
> Rather than see the offended God, and die."

Malone (Dryden's Prose Works, vol. i., part ii., p. 13) gives a letter from Dryden to Lord Rochester, in which he says· "Your Lordship will judge [from the success of these Prologues, &c.] how easy 'tis to pass anything upon an University, and how gross flattery the learned will endure."

the Act in King *William*'s Time I remember some Pranks of a different Nature had been complain'd of. Our Receipts had not only enabled us (as I have observ'd) to double the Pay of every Actor, but to afford out of them towards the Repair of St. *Mary*'s Church the Contribution of fifty Pounds: Besides which, each of the three Menagers had to his respective Share, clear of all Charges, one hundred and fifty more for his one and twenty Day's Labour, which being added to his thirteen hundred and fifty shared in the Winter preceding, amounted in the whole to fifteen hundred, the greatest Sum ever known to have been shared in one Year to that Time· And to the Honour of our Auditors here and elsewhere be it spoken, all this was rais'd without the Aid of those barbarous Entertainments with which, some few Years after (upon the Re-establishment of two contending Companies) we were forc'd to disgrace the Stage to support it.

This, therefore, is that remarkable Period when the Stage, during my Time upon it, was the least reproachable: And it may be worth the publick Observation (if any thing I have said of it can be so) that *One* Stage may, as I have prov'd it has done, very laudably support it self by such Spectacles only as are fit to delight a sensible People; but the equal Prosperity of *Two* Stages has always been of a very short Duration. If therefore the Publick should ever recover into the true Taste of that Time, and stick to it, the Stage must come into it, or *starve*; as, whenever the general Taste is vulgar, the Stage must come down to it to *live*.——But I ask Pardon of the Multitude, who, in all Regulations of the Stage, may expect to be a little indulg'd in what they like: If therefore they *will* have a May-pole, why, the Players must *give* them a May-pole, but I only speak in case they should keep an old Custom of changing their Minds, and by their Privilege of being in the *wrong*, should take a Fancy, by way of Variety, of being in the *right*——Then, in such a Case, what I have said may appear to have been no intended Design against their Liberty of judging for themselves.

After our Return from *Oxford*, *Booth* was at full Leisure to solicit his Admission to a Share in the Menagement,[1] in which he succeeded about the Beginning of the following Winter: Accordingly a new License (recalling all former Licenses) was issued, wherein *Booth*'s Name was added to those of the other Menagers.[2] But still there was a Difficulty in his Qualification to be adjusted; what Considera-

---

[1] Theo Cibber ("Life of Booth," p. 7) says that Colley Cibber and Booth "used frequently to set out, after Play (in the Month of *May*) to *Windsor*, where the *Court* then was, to push their different Interests." Chetwood ("History," p. 93) states that the other Patentees "to prevent his solliciting his Patrons at Court, then at *Windsor*, gave out Plays every Night, where Mr *Booth* had a principal Part. Notwithstanding this Step, he had a Chariot and Six of a Nobleman's waiting for him at the End of every Play, that whipt him the twenty Miles in three Hours, and brought him back to the Business of the Theatre the next Night."

[2] The new Licence was dated 11th November, 1713. Dogget's name was of course included as well as Booth's.

tion he should allow for an equal Title to our Stock of Cloaths, Scenes, &c. without which the License was of no more use than the Stock was without the License; or, at least, if there were any Difference, the former Menagers seem'd to have the Advantage in it; the Stock being intirely theirs, and three Parts in four of the License; for *Collier*, though now but a fifth Menager, still insisted on his former Appointment of 700*l.* a Year, which in Equity ought certainly to have been proportionably abated: But Court-Favour was not always measur'd by *that* Yard; *Collier*'s Matter was soon out of the Question; his Pretensions were too visible to be contested; but the Affair of *Booth* was not so clear a Point: The Lord Chamberlain, therefore, only recommended it to be adjusted among our selves; which, to say the Truth, at that Time was a greater Indulgence than I expected. Let us see, then, how this critical Case was handled.

Wilks was of Opinion, that to set a good round Value upon our Stock, was the only way to come near an Equivalent for the Diminution of our Shares, which the Admission of *Booth* must occasion: But *Dogget* insisted that he had no mind to dispose of any Part of his Property, and therefore would set no Price upon it at all. Though I allow'd that Both these Opinions might be grounded on a good deal of Equity, yet I was not sure that either of them was practicable; and therefore told them, that when they could Both agree which of them could be made so, they might rely on my Consent in any Shape. In the mean time I desired they would consider, that as our License subsisted only during Pleasure, we could not pretend that the Queen might not recall or alter it: But that to speak out, without mincing the matter on either Side, the Truth was plainly this: That *Booth* had a manifest Merit as an Actor; and as he was not supposed to be a *Whig*, it was as evident that a good deal for that Reason a Secretary of State had taken him into his Protection, which I was afraid the weak Pretence of our invaded Property would not be able to contend with: That his having signaliz'd himself in the Character of *Cato* (whose Principles the *Tories* had affected to have taken into their own Possession) was a very popular Pretence of making him free of the Stage, by advancing him to the Profits of it. And, as we had seen that the Stage was frequently treated as if it was not suppos'd to have any Property at all, this Favour intended to *Booth* was thought a right Occasion to avow that Opinion by disposing of its Property at Pleasure: But be that as it might, I own'd it was not so much my Apprehensions of what the *Court* might do, that sway'd me into an Accommodation with *Booth*, as what the *Town*, (in whose Favour he now apparently stood) might think *ought* to be done: That there might be more danger in contesting their arbitrary Will and Pleasure than in disputing this less terrible Strain of the Prerogative. That if *Booth* were only impos'd upon us from his Merit to the Court, we were then in the Condition of other Subjects: Then, indeed, Law, Right, and Possession might have a tolerable Tug for our Property: But as the Town would always look upon his Merit to *them* in a stronger Light, and be Judges of it themselves, it would be a weak and idle Endeavour in us not to sail with the Stream, when we might possibly make a Merit of our cheerfully admitting him: That though his former Opposition to our Interest might, between Man and Man, a good deal justify our not making an earlier Friend of him; yet that was a Disobligation out of the Town's Regard, and consequently would be of no weight against so approv'd an Actor's being preferr'd. But all this notwithstanding, if they could both agree in a different Opinion, I would, at the Hazard of any Consequence, be guided by it.

Here, now, will be shewn another Instance of our different Tempers: *Dogget* (who, in all Matters that concern'd our common Weal and Interest, little regarded our Opinion, and even to an Obstinacy walk'd by his own) look'd only out of Humour at what I had said, and, without thinking himself oblig'd to give any Reason for it, declar'd he would maintain his Property. *Wilks* (who, upon the same Occasions, was as remarkably ductile, as when his Superiority on the Stage was in question he was assuming and intractable) said, for his Part, provided our Business of acting was not interrupted, he did not care what we did: But, in short, he was for playing on, come what would of it. This last Part of his Declaration

I did not dislike, and therefore I desir'd we might all enter into an immediate Treaty with *Booth*, upon the Terms of his Admission. *Dogget* still sullenly reply'd, that he had no Occasion to enter into any Treaty. *Wilks* then, to soften him, propos'd that, if I liked it, *Dogget* might undertake it himself. I agreed. No! he would not be concern'd in it. I then offer'd the same Trust to *Wilks*, if *Dogget* approv'd of it. *Wilks* said he was not good at making of Bargains, but if I was willing, he would rather leave it to me. *Dogget* at this rose up and said, we might both do as we pleas'd, but that nothing but the Law should make him part with his Property—and so went out of the Room. After which he never came among us more, either as an Actor or Menager.[1]

By his having in this abrupt manner abdicated his Post in our Government, what he left of it naturally devolv'd upon *Wilks* and myself. However, this did not so much distress our Affair as I have Reason to believe *Dogget* thought it would: For though by our Indentures tripartite we could not dispose of his Property without his Consent; Yet those Indentures could not oblige us to fast because he had no Appetite; and if the Mill did not grind, we could have no Bread: We therefore determin'd, at any Hazard, to keep our Business still going, and that our safest way would be to make the best Bargain we could with *Booth*; one Article of which was to be, That *Booth* should stand equally answerable with

---

[1] This must have been in November, 1713

us to *Dogget* for the Consequence: To which *Booth* made no Objection, and the rest of his Agreement was to allow us Six Hundred Pounds for his Share in our Property, which was to be paid by such Sums as should arise from half his Profits of Acting, 'till the whole was discharg'd: Yet so cautious were we in this Affair, that this Agreement was only Verbal on our Part, tho' written and sign'd by *Booth* as what intirely contented him: However, Bond and Judgment could not have made it more secure to him; for he had his Share, and was able to discharge the Incumbrance upon it by his Income of that Year only. Let us see what *Dogget* did in this Affair after he had left us.

Might it not be imagin'd that *Wilks* and Myself, by having made this Matter easy to *Booth*, should have deserv'd the Approbation at least, if not the Favour of the Court that had exerted so much Power to prefer him? But shall I be believed when I affirm that *Dogget*, who had so strongly oppos'd the Court in his Admission to a Share, was very near getting the better of us both upon that Account, and for some time appeared to have more Favour there than either of us? Let me tell out my Story, and then think what you please of it.

Dogget, who was equally oblig'd with us to act upon the Stage, as to assist in the Menagement of it, tho' he had refus'd to do either, still demanded of us his whole Share of the Profits, without considering what Part of them *Booth* might pretend to from our late Concessions. After many fruitless Endeavours to bring him back to us, *Booth* join'd with us in making him an Offer of half a Share if he had a mind totally to quit the Stage, and make it a *Sinecure*. No! he wanted the whole, and to sit still himself, while we (if we pleased) might work for him or let it alone, and none of us all, neither he nor we, be the better for it. What we imagin'd encourag'd him to hold us at this short Defiance was, that he had laid up enough to live upon without the Stage (for he was one of those close Oeconomists whom Prodigals call a Miser) and therefore, partly from an Inclination as an invincible *Whig* to signalize himself in defence of his Property, and as much presuming that our Necessities would oblige us to come to his own Terms, he was determin'd (even against the Opinion of his Friends) to make no other Peace with us But not being able by this inflexible Perseverance to have his wicked Will of us, he was resolv'd to go to the Fountain-head of his own Distress, and try if from thence he could turn the Current against us. He appeal'd to the Vice-Chamberlain,[1] to whose Direction the adjusting of all these Theatrical Difficulties was then committed: But there, I dare say, the Reader does not expect he should meet with much Favour: However, be that as it may; for whether any regard was had to his having some Thousands in his Pocket; or that he was consider'd as a Man who would or could make

[1] The Right Hon Thomas Coke.

more Noise in the Matter than Courtiers might care for: Or what Charms, Spells, or Conjurations he might make use of, is all Darkness to me; yet so it was, he one way or other play'd his part so well, that in a few Days after we received an Order from the Vice-Chamberlain, positively commanding us to pay *Dogget* his whole Share, notwithstanding we had complain'd before of his having withdrawn himself from acting on the Stage, and from the Menagement of it. This I thought was a dainty Distinction, indeed! that *Dogget*'s Defiance of the Commands in favour of *Booth* should be rewarded with so ample a *Sine-cure*, and that we for our Obedience should be condemn'd to dig in the Mine to pay it him! This bitter Pill, I confess, was more than I could down with, and therefore soon determin'd at all Events never to take it. But as I had a Man in Power to deal with, it was not my business to speak *out* to him, or to set forth our Treatment in its proper Colours. My only Doubt was, Whether I could bring *Wilks* into the same Sentiments (for he never car'd to litigate any thing that did not affect his Figure upon the Stage.) But I had the good Fortune to lay our Condition in so precarious and disagreeable a Light to him, if we submitted to this Order, that he fir'd before I could get thro' half the Consequences of it; and I began now to find it more difficult to keep him within Bounds than I had before to alarm him. I then propos'd to him this Expedient: That we should draw up a Remonstrance, neither seeming to refuse or comply with this Order; but to start such Objections and perplexing Difficulties that should make the whole impracticable: That under such Distractions as this would raise in our Affairs we could not be answerable to keep open our Doors, which consequently would destroy the Fruit of the Favour lately granted to *Booth*, as well as of This intended to *Dogget* himself. To this Remonstrance we received an Answer in Writing, which varied something in the Measures to accommodate Matters with *Dogget*. This was all I desir'd; when I found the Style of *Sic jubeo* was alter'd, when this formidable Power began to *parley* with us, we knew there could not be much to be fear'd from it: For I would have remonstrated 'till I had died, rather than have yielded to the roughest or smoothest Persuasion, that could intimidate or deceive us. By this Conduct we made the Affair at last too troublesome for the Ease of a Courtier to go thro' with. For when it was consider'd that the principal Point, the Admission of *Booth*, was got over, *Dogget* was fairly left to the Law for Relief.[1]

---

[1] The dates regarding this quarrel with Dogget are very difficult to fix satisfactorily In the collection of Mr. Francis Harvey of St. James's Street are some valuable letters by Dogget in connection with this matter. From these, and from Mr. Percy Fitzgerald's "New History" (i 352-358), I have made up a list of dates, which, however, I give with all reserve. We know from "The Laureat" that Dogget had some funds of the theatre in his hands when he ceased acting, and this fact makes a Petition by Cibber and Wilks, that he should account with them for money, intelligible. This is dated 16th January, 1714—it cannot be 1713,

Upon this Disappointment *Dogget* accordingly preferred a Bill in *Chancery* against us. *Wilks*, who hated all Business but that of entertaining the Publick, left the Conduct of our Cause to me; in which we had, at our first setting out, this Advantage of *Dogget*, that we had three Pockets to support our Expence, where he had but One. My first Direction to our Solicitor was, to use all possible Delay that the Law would admit of, a Direction that Lawyers seldom neglect; by this means we hung up our Plaintiff about two Years in *Chancery*, 'till we were at full Leisure to come to a Hearing before the Lord-Chancellor *Cooper*, which did not happen 'till after the Accession of his late Majesty. The Issue of it was this. *Dogget* had about fourteen Days allow'd him to make his Election whether he would

as Mr. Fitzgerald says, for Booth was not admitted then, and the quarrel had not arisen. Then follows a Petition from Cibber, Booth, and Wilks, dated 5th February, 1714, praying the Chamberlain to settle the dispute. Petitions by Dogget bear date 17th April, 1714, and, I think, 14th June, 1714. Mr Fitzgerald gives this latter date as 14th January, 1714, and certainly the date on the document itself is more like " Jan " than " June ; " but in the course of the Petition Dogget says that the season will end in a few days, which seems to fix June as the correct month The season 1713-14 ended 18th June, 1714. Next comes a Petition that Dogget should be compelled to act if he was to draw his share of the profits, which is dated 3rd November, 1714 In this case we are on sure ground, for the Petition is preserved among the Lord Chamberlain's Papers. Another Petition by Dogget, in which he talks of his being forced into Westminster Hall to obtain his rights, is dated " Jan. ye 6 1714," that is, 1715. After this, legal action was no doubt commenced, as related by Cibber.

return to act as usual: But he declaring, by his Counsel, That he rather chose to quit the Stage, he was decreed Six Hundred Pounds for his Share in our Property, with 15 *per Cent*. Interest from the Date of the last License: Upon the Receipt of which both Parties were to sign General-Releases, and severally to pay their own Costs. By this Decree, *Dogget*, when his Lawyer's Bill was paid, scarce got one Year's Purchase of what we had offer'd him without Law, which (as he surviv'd but seven Years after it) would have been an Annuity of Five Hundred Pounds and a *Sine Cure* for Life.[1]

Tho' there are many Persons living who know every Article of these Facts to be true: Yet it will be found that the strongest of them was not the strongest Occasion of *Dogget*'s quitting the Stage. If therefore the Reader should not have Curiosity enough to know how the Publick came to be depriv'd of so valuable an Actor, let him consider that he is not obliged to go through the rest of this Chapter, which I fairly tell him before-hand will only be fill'd up with a few idle Anecdotes leading to that Discovery.

After our Law-suit was ended, *Dogget* for some few Years could scarce bear the Sight of *Wilks* or myself; tho' (as shall be shewn) for different Reasons: Yet it was his Misfortune to meet with us almost every Day. *Button*'s Coffee-house, so celebrated in

---

[1] So full an account of Dogget is given by Cibber and by Aston, that I need only add, that he first appeared about 1691; and that he died in 1721.

the *Tatlers* for the Good-Company that came there, was at this time in its highest Request. *Addison, Steele, Pope*, and several other Gentlemen of different Merit, then made it their constant *Rendezvous*. Nor could *Dogget* decline the agreeable Conversation there, tho' he was daily sure to find *Wilks* or myself in the same Place to sour his Share of it: For as *Wilks* and He were differently Proud, the one rejoicing in a captious, over-bearing, valiant Pride, and the other in a stiff, sullen, Purse-Pride, it may be easily conceiv'd, when two such Tempers met, how agreeable the Sight of one was to the other. And as *Dogget* knew I had been the Conductor of our Defence against his Law-suit, which had hurt him more for the Loss he had sustain'd in his Reputation of understanding Business, which he valued himself upon, than his Disappointment had of getting so little by it; it was no wonder if I was intirely out of his good Graces, which I confess I was inclin'd upon any reasonable Terms to have recover'd; he being of all my Theatrical Brethren the Man I most delighted in: For when he was not in a Fit of Wisdom, or not over-concerned about his Interest, he had a great deal of entertaining Humour: I therefore, notwithstanding his Reserve, always left the Door open to our former Intimacy, if he were inclined to come into it. I never failed to give him my Hat and *Your Servant* wherever I met him; neither of which he would ever return for above a Year after; but I still persisted in my usual Salutation, without observing whether it was civilly received or not. This ridiculous Silence between two Comedians, that had so lately liv'd in a constant Course of Raillery with one another, was often smil'd at by our Acquaintance who frequented the same Coffee-house · And one of them carried his Jest upon it so far, that when I was at some Distance from Town he wrote me a formal Account that *Dogget* was actually dead. After the first Surprize his Letter gave me was over, I began to consider, that this coming from a droll Friend to both of us, might possibly be written to extract some Merriment out of my real belief of it: In this I was not unwilling to gratify him, and returned an Answer as if I had taken the Truth of his News for granted; and was not a little pleas'd that I had so fair an Opportunity of speaking my Mind freely of *Dogget*, which I did, in some Favour of his Character; I excused his Faults, and was just to his Merit. His Law-suit with us I only imputed to his having naturally deceived himself in the Justice of his Cause. What I most complain'd of was, his irreconcilable Disaffection to me upon it, whom he could not reasonably blame for standing in my own Defence; that not to endure me after it was a Reflection upon his Sense, when all our Acquaintance had been Witnesses of our former Intimacy, which my Behaviour in his Life-time had plainly shewn him I had a mind to renew. But since he was now gone (however great a Churl he was to me) I was sorry my Correspondent had lost him.

This Part of my Letter I was sure, if *Dogget's* Eyes were still open, would be shewn to him; if not, I had only writ it to no Purpose. But about a Month after, when I came to Town, I had some little Reason to imagine it had the Effect I wish'd from it: For one Day, sitting over-against him at the same Coffee-house where we often mixt at the same Table, tho' we never exchanged a single Syllable, he graciously extended his Hand for a Pinch of my Snuff: As this seem'd from him a sort of breaking the Ice of his Temper, I took Courage upon it to break Silence on my Side, and ask'd him how he lik'd it? To which, with a slow Hesitation naturally assisted by the Action of his taking the Snuff, he reply'd—*Umh! the best*—*Umh!*—*I have tasted a great while!*—If the Reader, who may possibly think all this extremely trifling, will consider that Trifles sometimes shew Characters in as strong a Light as Facts of more serious Importance, I am in hopes he may allow that my Matter less needs an Excuse than the Excuse itself does; if not, I must stand condemn'd at the end of my Story.——But let me go on.

After a few Days of these coy, Lady-like Compliances on his Side, we grew into a more conversable Temper: At last I took a proper Occasion, and desired he would be so frank with me as to let me know what was his real Dislike, or Motive, that made him throw up so good an Income as his Share with us annually brought him in? For though by our Admission of *Booth*, it might not probably amount to so much by a Hundred or two a Year as formerly, yet the Remainder was too considerable to be quarrel'd with, and was likely to continue more than the best Actors before us had ever got by the Stage. And farther, to encourage him to be open, I told him, If I had done any thing that had particularly disobliged him, I was ready, if he could put me in the way, to make him any Amends in my Power; if not, I desired he would be so just to himself as to let me know the real Truth without Reserve: But Reserve he could not, from his natural Temper, easily shake off. All he said came from him by half Sentences and *Inuendos*, as—No, he had not taken any thing particularly ill—for his Part, he was very easy as he was; but where others were to dispose of his Property as they pleas'd—if you had stood it out as I did, *Booth* might have paid a better Price for it. —You were too much afraid of the Court—but that's all over.—There were other things in the Playhouse. —No Man of Spirit.—In short, to be always pester'd and provok'd by a trifling Wasp—a—vain—shallow! —A Man would sooner beg his Bread than bear it. —(Here it was easy to understand him. I therefore ask'd him what he had to bear that I had not my Share of?) No! it was not the same thing, he said. —You can play with a Bear, or let him alone and do what he would, but I could not let him lay his Paws upon me without being hurt; you did not feel him as I did.—And for a Man to be cutting of Throats upon every Trifle at my time of Day!—If I had been as covetous as he thought me, may be I might have born it as well as you—but I would not be a Lord of the Treasury if such a Temper as *Wilks*'s were to be at the Head of it.—

Here, then, the whole Secret was out. The rest of our Conversation was but explaining upon it. In a Word, the painful Behaviour of *Wilks* had hurt him so sorely that the Affair of *Booth* was look'd upon as much a Relief as a Grievance, in giving him so plausible a Pretence to get rid of us all with a better Grace.

Booth too, in a little time, had his Share of the same Uneasiness, and often complain'd of it to me. Yet as we neither of us could then afford to pay *Dogget*'s Price for our Remedy, all we could do was to avoid every Occasion in our Power of inflaming the Distemper. So that we both agreed, tho' *Wilks*'s Nature was not to be changed, it was a less Evil to live with him than without him.

Tho' I had often suspected, from what I had felt myself, that the Temper of *Wilks* was *Dogget*'s real Quarrel to the Stage, yet I could never thoroughly believe it 'till I had it from his own Mouth. And I then thought the Concern he had shewn at it was a good deal inconsistent with that Understanding which was generally allow'd him. When I give my Reasons for it, perhaps the Reader will not have a better Opinion of my own: Be that as it may, I cannot help wondering that he who was so much more capable of Reflexion than *Wilks*, could sacrifice so valuable an Income to his Impatience of another's natural Frailty! And though my Stoical way of thinking may be no Rule for a wiser Man's Opinion, yet, if it should happen to be right, the Reader may make his Use of it. Why then should we not always consider that the Rashness of Abuse is but the false Reason of a weak Man? and that offensive Terms are only used to supply the want of Strength in Argument? Which, as to the common Practice of the sober World, we do not find every Man in Business is oblig'd to resent with a military Sense of Honour: Or if he should, would not the Conclusion amount to this? Because another wants Sense and Manners I am obliged to be a Madman: For such every Man is, more or less, while the Passion of Anger is in Possession of him. And what less can we call that proud Man who would put another out of the World only for putting him out of Humour? If Accounts of the Tongue were always to be made up with the Sword, all the Wisemen in the World might be brought in Debtors to Blockheads. And when Honour pretends to be Witness, Judge, and Executioner in its own Cause, if Honour were a Man, would it be an Untruth to say Honour is a very impudent Fellow? But in *Dogget*'s Case it may be ask'd, How was he to behave himself? Were passionate Insults to be born for Years together? To these Questions I can only answer with two or three more, Was he to punish himself because another was in the wrong? How many sensible Husbands endure the teizing Tongue of a froward Wife only because she is the weaker Vessel? And why should not a weak Man have the same Indulgence? Daily Experience will tell us that the fretful Temper of a Friend, like the Personal Beauty of a fine Lady, by Use and Cohabitation may be brought down to give us neither Pain nor Pleasure. Such, at least, and no more, was the Distress I found myself in upon the same Provocations, which I generally return'd with humming an Air to myself; or if the Storm grew very high, it might perhaps sometimes ruffle me enough to sing a little out of Tune. Thus too (if I had any ill Nature to gratify) I often saw the unruly Passion of the Aggressor's Mind punish itself by a restless Disorder of the Body.

What inclines me, therefore, to think the Conduct of *Dogget* was as rash as the Provocations he complain'd of, is that in some time after he had left us he plainly discover'd he had repented it. His Acquaintance observ'd to us, that he sent many a long Look after his Share in the still prosperous State of the Stage: But as his Heart was too high to declare (what we saw too) his shy Inclination to return, he made us no direct Overtures. Nor, indeed, did we care (though he was a golden Actor) to pay too dear for him: For as most of his Parts had been pretty well supply'd, he could not now be of his former Value to us. However, to shew the Town at least that he had not forsworn the Stage, he one Day con-

THE LIFE OF

descended to play for the Benefit of Mrs. *Porter*,[1] in the *Wanton Wife*, at which he knew his late Majesty was to be present.[2] Now (tho' I speak it not of my own Knowledge) yet it was not likely Mrs. *Porter* would have ask'd that Favour of him without some previous Hint that it would be granted. His coming among us for that Day only had a strong Appearance of his laying it in our way to make him Proposals, or that he hoped the Court or Town might intimate to us their Desire of seeing him oftener: But as he acted only to do a particular Favour, the Menagers ow'd him no Compliment for it beyond Common Civilities. And, as that might not be all he proposed by it, his farther Views (if he had any) came to nothing. For after this Attempt he never returned to the Stage.

To speak of him as an Actor · He was the most an Original, and the strictest Observer of Nature, of all his Contemporaries.[3] He borrow'd from none of them: His Manner was his own: He was a Pattern

---

[1] See memoir of Mrs. Porter at the end of this volume.

[2] On March 18th, 1717. Cibber is wrong in stating that this was Dogget's last appearance, for a week after he played Ben in "Love for Love" (March 25th, 1717), and made his last appearance, after the lapse of another week (April 1st, 1717), when he acted Hob in "The Country Wake."

[3] Downes ("Rosc Ang.," p 52) gives a quaint description of Dogget. "Mr. *Dogget*, On the Stage, he's very Aspectabund, wearing a Farce in his Face; his Thoughts deliberately framing his Utterance Congruous to his Looks: He is the only Comick Original now Extant Witness, *Ben. Solon, Nikin*, The *Jew* of *Venice*, &c."

to others, whose greatest Merit was that they had sometimes tolerably imitated him. In dressing a Character to the greatest Exactness he was remarkably skilful; the least Article of whatever Habit he wore seem'd in some degree to speak and mark the different Humour he presented; a necessary Care in a Comedian, in which many have been too remiss or ignorant. He could be extremely ridiculous without stepping into the least Impropriety to make him so. His greatest Success was in Characters of lower Life, which he improv'd from the Delight he took in his Observations of that Kind in the real World. In Songs, and particular Dances, too, of Humour, he had no Competitor. *Congreve* was a great Admirer of him, and found his Account in the Characters he expresly wrote for him. In those of *Fondlewife*, in his *Old Batchelor*, and *Ben*, in *Love for Love*, no Author and Actor could be more obliged to their mutual masterly Performances. He was very acceptable to several Persons of high Rank and Taste: Tho' he seldom car'd to be the Comedian but among his more intimate Acquaintance.

And now let me ask the World a Question. When Men have any valuable Qualities, why are the generality of our modern Wits so fond of exposing their Failings only, which the wisest of Mankind will never wholly be free from? Is it of more use to the Publick to know their Errors than their Perfections? Why is the Account of Life to be so unequally stated? Though a Man may be sometimes Debtor to Sense or Morality, is it not doing him Wrong not to let the World see, at the same time, how far he may be Creditor to both? Are Defects and Disproportions to be the only labour'd Features in a Portrait? But perhaps such Authors may know how to please the World better than I do, and may naturally suppose that what is delightful to themselves may not be disagreeable to others. For my own part, I confess myself a little touch'd in Conscience at what I have just now observ'd to the Disadvantage of my other Brother-Menager.

If, therefore, in discovering the true Cause of the Publick's losing so valuable an Actor as *Dogget*, I have been obliged to shew the Temper of *Wilks* in its natural Complexion, ought I not, in amends and Balance of his Imperfections, to say at the same time of him, That if he was not the most Correct or Judicious, yet (as *Hamlet* says of the King his Father) *Take him* for *All in All*, &c. he was certainly the most diligent, most laborious, and most useful Actor that I have seen upon the Stage in Fifty Years.[1]

---

[1] "The Laureat," p 83: "Thy Partiality is so notorious, with Relation to *Wilks*, that every one sees you never praise him, but to rail at him, and only oil your Hone, to whet your Razor."

CHAPTER XV.

Sir Richard Steele *succeeds* Collier *in the Theatre-Royal.* Lincoln's-Inn-Fields *House rebuilt. The Patent restored. Eight Actors at once desert from the King's Company. Why. A new Patent obtain'd by Sir* Richard Steele, *and assign'd in Shares to the menaging Actors of* Drury-Lane. *Of modern Pantomimes. The Rise of them. Vanity invincible and asham'd. The* Non-juror *acted. The Author not forgiven, and rewarded for it.*

UPON the Death of the Queen, Plays (as they always had been on the like Occasions) were silenc'd for six Weeks. But this happening on the first of *August*,[1] in the long Vacation of the Theatre, the Observance of that Ceremony, which at another

[1] 1714.

Juncture would have fallen like wet Weather upon their Harvest, did them now no particular Damage. Their License, however, being of course to be renewed, that Vacation gave the Menagers Time to cast about for the better Alteration of it: And since they knew the Pension of seven hundred a Year, which had been levied upon them for *Collier*, must still be paid to somebody, they imagined the Merit of a *Whig* might now have as good a Chance for getting into it, as that of a *Tory* had for being continued in it: Having no Obligations, therefore, to *Collier*, who had made the last Penny of them, they apply'd themselves to Sir *Richard Steele*, who had distinguished himself by his Zeal for the House of *Hanover*, and had been expell'd the House of Commons for carrying it (as was judg'd at a certain Crisis) into a Reproach of the Government. This we knew was his Pretension to that Favour in which he now stood at Court: We knew, too, the Obligations the Stage had to his Writings; there being scarce a Comedian of Merit in our whole Company whom his *Tatlers* had not made better by his publick Recommendation of them. And many Days had our House been particularly fill'd by the Influence and Credit of his Pen. Obligations of this kind from a Gentleman with whom they all had the Pleasure of a personal Intimacy, the Menagers thought could not be more justly return'd than by shewing him some warm Instance of their Desire to have him at the Head of them. We therefore beg'd him to use his Interest for the Renewal of our License, and that he would do us the Honour of getting our Names to stand with His in the same Commission. This, we told him, would put it still farther into his Power of supporting the Stage in that Reputation, to which his Lucubrations had already so much contributed; and that therefore we thought no Man had better Pretences to partake of its Success.[1]

[1] In the Dedication to Steele of "Ximena" (1719) Cibber warmly acknowledges the great service Steele had done to the theatre, not only in improving the tone of its performances, but also in the mere attracting of public attention to it. "How many a time," he says, "have we known the most elegant Audiences drawn together at a Day's Warning, by the Influence or Warrant of a single *Tatler*, when our best Endeavours without it, could not defray the Charge of the Performance." In the same Dedication Cibber's gratitude overstepped his judgment, in applying to Steele's generous acknowledgment of his indebtedness to Addison's help in his "Spectator," &c., Dryden's lines :—

"Fool that I was! upon my Eagle's Wings
I bore this Wren, 'till I was tir'd with soaring,
And now, he mounts above me——"

The following Epigram is quoted in "The Laureat," p. 76. It originally appeared in "Mist's Journal," 31st October, 1719 :—

"*Thus* Colley Cibber *to his Partner* Steele,
See here, Sir Knight, how I've outdone Corneille;
See here, how I, my Patron to inveigle,
Make Addison *a* Wren, *and you an* Eagle.
Safe to the silent Shades, we bid Defiance;
For living Dogs are better than dead Lions."

In one of his Odes, at which Johnson laughed (Boswell, i. 402 Cibber had the couplet :—

"Perch'd on the eagle's soaring wing,
The lowly linnet loves to sing."

Though it may be no Addition to the favourable Part of this Gentleman's Character to say with what Pleasure he receiv'd this Mark of our Inclination to him, yet my Vanity longs to tell you that it surpriz'd him into an Acknowledgment that People who are shy of Obligations are cautious of confessing. His Spirits took such a lively turn upon it, that had we been all his own Sons, no unexpected Act of filial Duty could have more endear'd us to him.

It must be observ'd, then, that as *Collier* had no Share in any Part of our Property, no Difficulties from that Quarter could obstruct this Proposal. And the usual Time of our beginning to act for the Winter-Season now drawing near, we press'd him not to lose any Time in his Solicitation of this new License. Accordingly Sir *Richard* apply'd himself to the Duke of *Marlborough*, the Hero of his Heart, who, upon the first mention of it, obtain'd it of his Majesty for Sir *Richard* and the former Mena-

---

"Ximena; or, the Heroic Daughter," produced on 28th November, 1712, was an adaptation of Corneille's "Cid." We do not know the cast of 1712, but that of 1718 (Drury Lane, 1st November) was the following —

DON FERDINAND	Mr. Mills.
DON ALVAREZ	Mr. Cibber.
DON GORMAZ	Mr. Booth.
DON CARLOS	Mr. Wilks.
DON SANCHEZ	Mr. Elrington.
DON ALONZO	Mr. Thurmond.
DON GARCIA	Mr. Boman.
XIMENA	Mrs. Oldfield.
BELZARA	Mrs. Porter.

gers who were Actors. *Collier* we heard no more of.[1]

The Court and Town being crowded very early in the Winter-Season, upon the critical Turn of Affairs so much expected from the *Hanover* Succession, the Theatre had its particular Share of that general Blessing by a more than ordinary Concourse of Spectators.

About this Time the Patentee, having very near finish'd his House in *Lincoln's-Inn Fields*, began to think of forming a new Company; and in the mean time found it necessary to apply for Leave to employ them. By the weak Defence he had always made against the several Attacks upon his Interest and former Government of the Theatre, it might be a Question, if his House had been ready in the Queen's Time, whether he would then have had the Spirit to ask, or Interest enough to obtain Leave to use it: But in the following Reign, as it did not appear he had done any thing to forfeit the Right of his Patent, he prevail'd with Mr. *Craggs* the Younger (afterwards Secretary of State) to lay his Case before the King, which he did in so effectual a manner that (as Mr. *Craggs* himself told me) his Majesty was pleas'd to say upon it, " That he remember'd when he had " been in *England* before, in King *Charles* his Time,

---

[1] A Royal Licence was granted on 18th October, 1714, to Steele, Wilks, Cibber, Dogget, and Booth. The theatre opened before the Licence was granted The first bill given by Genest is for 21st September, 1714.

" there had been two Theatres in *London*; and as
" the Patent seem'd to be a lawful Grant, he saw no
" Reason why Two Play-houses might not be con-
" tinued." [1]

The Suspension of the Patent being thus taken off, the younger Multitude seem'd to call aloud for two Play-houses! Many desired another, from the common Notion that *Two* would always create Emulation in the Actors (an Opinion which I have consider'd in a former Chapter). Others, too, were as eager for them, from the natural Ill-will that follows the Fortunate or Prosperous in any Undertaking. Of this low Malevolence we had, now and then, had remarkable Instances; we had been forced to dismiss an Audience of a hundred and fifty Pounds, from a Disturbance spirited up by obscure People, who never gave any better Reason for it, than that it was their Fancy to support the idle Complaint of one rival Actress against another, in their several Pretensions to the chief Part in a new Tragedy. But as this Tumult seem'd only to be the Wantonness of *English* Liberty, I shall not presume to lay any farther Censure upon it.[2]

Now, notwithstanding this publick Desire of re-

---

[1] Christopher Rich died before the theatre was opened, and it was under the management of John Rich, his son, that Lincoln's Inn Fields opened on 18th December, 1714, with "The Recruiting Officer." The company was announced as playing under Letters Patent granted by King Charles the Second.

[2] This refers to a riot raised by the supporters of Mrs Rogers, on Mrs. Oldfield's being cast for the character of Andromache in

establishing two Houses; and though I have allow'd the former Actors greatly our Superiors; and the Menagers I am speaking of not to have been without their private Errors: Yet under all these Disadvantages, it is certain the Stage, for twenty Years before this time, had never been in so flourishing a Condition: And it was as evident to all sensible Spectators that this Prosperity could be only owing to that better Order and closer Industry now daily observ'd, and which had formerly been neglected by our Predecessors. But that I may not impose upon the Reader a Merit which was not generally allow'd us, I ought honestly to let him know, that about this time the publick Papers, particularly *Mist*'s Journal, took upon them very often to censure our Menagement, with the same Freedom and Severity as if we had been so many Ministers of State: But so it happen'd, that these unfortunate Reformers of the World, these self-appointed *Censors*, hardly ever hit upon what was really wrong in us; but taking up Facts upon Trust, or Hear-say, piled up many a pompous Paragraph that they had ingeniously conceiv'd was sufficient to demolish our Administration, or at least to make us very uneasy in it; which, indeed, had so far its Effect, that my equally-injur'd Brethren, *Wilks* and *Booth*, often complain'd to me of these disagreeable Aspersions, and propos'd that some publick Answer might be made to them, which

Philips's tragedy of "The Distressed Mother," produced at Drury Lane on 17th March, 1712.

I always oppos'd by, perhaps, too secure a Contempt of what such Writers could do to hurt us; and my Reason for it was, that I knew but of one way to silence Authors of that Stamp; which was, to grow insignificant and good for nothing, and then we should hear no more of them: But while we continued in the Prosperity of pleasing others, and were not conscious of having deserv'd what they said of us, why should we gratify the little Spleen of our Enemies by wincing at it,[1] or give them fresh Opportunities to dine upon any Reply they might make to our publickly taking Notice of them? And though Silence might in some Cases be a sign of Guilt or Error confess'd, our Accusers were so low in their Credit and Sense, that the Content we gave the Publick almost every Day from the Stage ought to be our only Answer to them.

However (as I have observ'd) we made many Blots, which these unskilful Gamesters never hit: But the Fidelity of an Historian cannot be excus'd the Omission of any Truth which might make for the other Side of the Question. I shall therefore

---

[1] Cibber on one occasion manifested temper to a rather unexpected degree. In 1720, when Dennis published his attacks on Steele, in connection with his being deprived of the Patent, he accused Cibber of impiety and various other crimes and misdemeanours; and Cibber is said in the "Answer to the Character of Sir John Edgar" to have inserted the following advertisement in the "Daily Post": "Ten Pounds will be paid by Mr. CIBBER, of the Theatre Royal, to any person who shall (by a legal proof) discover the Author of a Pamphlet, intituled, 'The Characters and Conduct of Sir JOHN EDGAR, &c.'" (Nichols, p. 401.)

confess a Fact, which, if a happy Accident had not intervened, had brought our Affairs into a very tottering Condition. This, too, is that Fact which in a former Chapter I promis'd to set forth as a Sea-Mark of Danger to future Menagers in their Theatrical Course of Government.[1]

When the new-built Theatre in *Lincoln's-Inn Fields* was ready to be open'd, seven or eight Actors in one Day deserted from us to the Service of the Enemy,[2] which oblig'd us to postpone many of our best Plays for want of some inferior Part in them which these Deserters had been used to fill: But the Indulgence of the Royal Family, who then frequently honour'd us by their Presence, was pleas'd to accept of whatever could be hastily got ready for their Entertainment. And tho' this critical good Fortune prevented, in some measure, our Audiences falling so low as otherwise they might have done, yet it was not sufficient to keep us in our former Prosperity: For that Year our Profits amounted not to above a third Part of our usual Dividends; tho' in the following Year we intirely recover'd them. The Chief of these Deserters were *Keene, Bullock, Pack,*[3] *Leigh,* Son of the

---

[1] Cibber refers to his remarks (see vol. i. p. 191) on the conduct of the Patentees which caused Betterton's secession in 1694-5.

[2] In addition to Keen, Bullock (William), Pack, and Leigh, whom Cibber mentions a few lines after, Spiller and Christopher Bullock were among the deserters; and probably Cory and Knap. Mrs. Rogers, Mrs. Knight, and Mrs. Kent also deserted.

[3] George Pack is an actor of whom Chetwood ("History," p. 210) gives some account. He first came on the stage as a singer,

famous *Tony Leigh*,[1] and others of less note. 'Tis true, they none of them had more than a negative Merit, in being only able to do us more Harm by their leaving us without Notice, than they could do us Good by remaining with us: For though the best of them could not support a Play, the worst of them by their Absence could maim it; as the Loss of the least Pin in a Watch may obstruct its Motion. But to come to the true Cause of their Desertion: After my having discover'd the (long unknown) Occasion that drove *Dogget* from the Stage before his settled Inclination to leave it, it will be less incredible that these Actors, upon the first Opportunity to relieve themselves, should all in one Day have left us from the same Cause of Uneasiness. For, in a little time after, upon not finding their Expectations answer'd in *Lincoln's-Inn Fields*, some of them, who seem'd

---

performing the female parts in duets with Leveridge. His first appearance chronicled by Genest was at Lincoln's Inn Fields in 1700, as Westmoreland in the first part of "Henry IV." Chetwood says he was excellent as Marplot in "The Busy Body," Beau Maiden in "Tunbridge Walks," Beau Mizen in "The Fair Quaker of Deal," &c : "*indeed Nature seem'd to mean him for those Sort of Characters.*" On 10th March, 1722, he announced his last appearance on any stage; but he returned on 21st April and 7th May, 1724, on which latter date he had a benefit. Chetwood says that on his retirement he opened the Globe Tavern, near Charing-Cross, over against the Hay-market. When Chetwood wrote (1749) Pack was no longer alive.

[1] Francis Leigh There were several actors of the name of Leigh, and it is sometimes difficult to distinguish them This particular actor died about 1719

to answer for the rest, told me the greatest Grievance they had in our Company was the shocking Temper of *Wilks*, who, upon every, almost no Occasion, let loose the unlimited Language of Passion upon them in such a manner as their Patience was not longer able to support. This, indeed, was what we could not justify! This was a Secret that might have made a wholesome Paragraph in a critical News-Paper! But as it was our good Fortune that it came not to the Ears of our Enemies, the Town was not entertain'd with their publick Remarks upon it.[1]

After this new Theatre had enjoy'd that short Run of Favour which is apt to follow Novelty, their Audiences began to flag: But whatever good Opi-

---

[1] In the "Weekly Packet," 18th December, 1714, the following appears:—

"This Day the New Play-House in Lincolns-Inn Fields, is to be open'd and a Comedy acted there, call'd, The Recruiting Officer, by the Company that act under the Patent; tho' it is said, that some of the Gentlemen who have left the House in Drury-Lane for that Service, are order'd to return to their Colours, upon Pain of not exercising their Lungs elsewhere; which may in Time prove of ill Service to the Patentee, that has been at vast Expence to make his Theatre as convenient for the Reception of an Audience as any one can possibly be."

Genest remarks that this seems to show that the Lord Chamberlain threatened to interfere in the interests of Drury Lane. He adds: "Cibber's silence proves nothing to the contrary, as in more than one instance he does not tell the whole truth" (ii. 565). In defence of Cibber I may say that the Chamberlain's Records contain no hint that he threatened to interfere with the Lincoln's Inn Fields Theatre or its actors.

nion we had of our own Merit, we had not so good a one of the Multitude as to depend too much upon the Delicacy of their Taste: We knew, too, that this Company, being so much nearer to the City than we were, would intercept many an honest Customer that might not know a good Market from a bad one; and that the thinnest of their Audiences must be always taking something from the Measure of our Profits. All these Disadvantages, with many others, we were forced to lay before Sir *Richard Steele*, and farther to remonstrate to him, that as he now stood in *Collier*'s Place, his Pension of 700*l.* was liable to the same Conditions that *Collier* had receiv'd it upon; which were, that it should be only payable during our being the only Company permitted to act, but in case another should be set up against us, that then this Pension was to be liquidated into an equal Share with us; and which we now hoped he would be contented with. While we were offering to proceed, Sir *Richard* stopt us short by assuring us, that as he came among us by our own Invitation, he should always think himself oblig'd to come into any Measures for our Ease and Service: That to be a Burthen to our Industry would be more disagreeable to him than it could be to us; and as he had always taken a Delight in his Endeavours for our Prosperity, he should be still ready on our own Terms to continue them. Every one who knew Sir *Richard Steele* in his Prosperity (before the Effects of his Good-nature had brought him to Distresses) knew that this was

his manner of dealing with his Friends in Business: Another Instance of the same nature will immediately fall in my way.

When we proposed to put this Agreement into Writing, he desired us not to hurry ourselves; for that he was advised, upon the late Desertion of our Actors, to get our License (which only subsisted during Pleasure) enlarg'd into a more ample and durable Authority, and which he said he had Reason to think would be more easily obtain'd, if we were willing that a Patent for the same Purpose might be granted to him only, for his Life and three Years after, which he would then assign over to us. This was a Prospect beyond our Hopes; and what we had long wish'd for; for though I cannot say we had ever Reason to grieve at the Personal Severities or Behaviour of any one Lord-Chamberlain in my Time, yet the several Officers under them who had not the Hearts of Noblemen, often treated us (to use *Shakespear*'s Expression) with all the *Insolence* of *Office* that narrow Minds are apt to be elated with; but a Patent, we knew, would free us from so abject a State of Dependency. Accordingly, we desired Sir *Richard* to lose no time; he was immediately promised it: In the Interim, we sounded the Inclination of the Actors remaining with us; who had all Sense enough to know, that the Credit and Reputation we stood in with the Town, could not but be a better Security for their Sallaries, than the Promise of any other Stage put into Bonds could make good to them. In a few Days after, Sir *Richard* told us, that his Majesty being apprised that others had a joint Power with him in the License, it was expected we should, under our Hands, signify that his Petition for a Patent was preferr'd by the Consent of us all. Such an Acknowledgment was immediately sign'd, and the Patent thereupon pass'd the Great Seal; for which I remember the Lord Chancellor *Cooper*, in Compliment to Sir *Richard*, would receive no Fee.

We receiv'd the Patent *January* 19, 1715,[1] and (Sir *Richard* being obliged the next Morning to set out for *Burrowbridge* in *Yorkshire*, where he was soon after elected Member of Parliament) we were forced that very Night to draw up in a hurry ('till our Counsel might more adviseably perfect it) his Assignment to us of equal Shares in the Patent, with farther Conditions of Partnership:[2] But here I ought to take Shame to myself, and at the same time to give this second Instance of the Equity and Honour of Sir *Richard*: For this Assignment (which I had myself the hasty Penning of) was so worded, that it gave Sir *Richard* as equal a Title to our Property

---

[1] In both the first and second editions Cibber writes 1718, but this is so obviously a misprint that I correct the text. Steele was elected for Boroughbridge in the first Parliament of George I., which met 15th March, 1715.

[2] "The very night I received it, I participated the power and use of it, with relation to the profits that should arise from it, between the gentlemen who invited me into the Licence."—Steele, in "The Theatre," No. 8 [Nichols, p. 64].

as it had given us to his Authority in the Patent: But Sir *Richard*, notwithstanding, when he return'd to Town, took no Advantage of the Mistake, and consented in our second Agreement to pay us Twelve Hundred Pounds to be equally intitled to our Property, which at his Death we were obliged to repay (as we afterwards did) to his Executors; and which, in case any of us had died before him, the Survivors were equally obliged to have paid to the Executors of such deceased Person upon the same Account. But Sir *Richard's* Moderation with us was rewarded with the Reverse of *Collier's* Stiffness: *Collier*, by insisting on his Pension, lost Three Hundred Pounds a Year; and Sir *Richard*, by his accepting a Share in lieu of it, was, one Year with another, as much a Gainer.

The Grant of this Patent having assured us of a competent Term to be relied on, we were now emboldened to lay out larger Sums in the Decorations of our Plays.[1] Upon the Revival of *Dryden's All for Love*, the Habits of that Tragedy amounted to an Expence of near Six Hundred Pounds; a Sum unheard of, for many Years before, on the like Occa-

---

[1] The managers also expended money on the decoration of the theatre before the beginning of the next season after the Patent was granted. In the "Daily Courant," 6th October, 1715, they advertise: "His Majesty's Company of Comedians give Notice, That the Middle of next Week they will begin to act Plays, every day, as usual; they being oblig'd to lye still so long, to finish the New Decorations of the House"

sions.[1] But we thought such extraordinary Marks of our Acknowledgment were due to the Favours which the Publick were now again pouring in upon us. About this time we were so much in fashion, and follow'd, that our Enemies (who they were it would not be fair to guess, for we never knew them) made their Push of a good round Lye upon us, to terrify those Auditors from our Support whom they could not mislead by their private Arts or publick Invectives. A current Report that the Walls and Roof of our House were liable to fall, had got such Ground in the Town, that on a sudden we found our Audiences unusually decreased by it. *Wilks* was immediately for denouncing War and Vengeance on the Author of this Falshood, and for offering a Reward to whoever could discover him. But it was thought more necessary first to disprove the Falshood, and then to pay what Compliments might be thought

---

[1] This revival was on 2nd December, 1718. Dennis, whose "Invader of his Country" was, as he considered, unfairly postponed on account of this production, wrote to Steele —

"Well, Sir, when the winter came on, what was done by your Deputies? Why, instead of keeping their word with me, they spent above two months of the season in getting up "All for Love, or, the World well Lost," a Play which has indeed a noble first act, an act which ends with a scene becoming of the dignity of the Tragic Stage. But if HORACE had been now alive, and been either a reader or spectator of that entertainment, he would have passed his old sentence upon the Author.

'*Infelix operis summâ, quia ponere totum
Nesciet.*'" [*Ars Poetica*, 34]

Nichols' "Theatre," p 544

adviseable to the Author. Accordingly an Order from the King was obtained, to have our Tenement surveyed by Sir *Thomas Hewet*, then the proper Officer; whose Report of its being in a safe and sound Condition, and sign'd by him, was publish'd in every News-Paper.[1] This had so immediate an Effect, that our Spectators, whose Apprehensions had lately kept them absent, now made up our Losses by returning to us with a fresh Inclination and in greater Numbers.

When it was first publickly known that the New

---

[1] Cibber here skips a few years, for the report by Sir Thomas Hewitt is dated some years after the granting of the Patent. The text of it will be found in Nichols's "Theatre," p. 470:—

"My Lord, *Scotland-yard, Jan* 21, 1721.

"In obedience to his Majesty's commands signified to me by your Grace the 18th instant, I have surveyed the Play-house in Drury-lane, and took with me Mr. Ripley, Commissioner of his Majesty's Board of Works, the Master Bricklayer, and Carpenter: We examined all its parts with the greatest exactness we could; and found the Walls, Roofing, Stage, Pit, Boxes, Galleries, Machinery, Scenes, &c sound, and almost as good as when first built; neither decayed, nor in the least danger of falling; and when some small repairs are made, and an useless Stack of Chimnies (built by the late Mr Rich) taken down, the Building may continue for a long time, being firm, the Materials and Joints good, and no part giving way, and capable to bear much greater weight than is put on them.

"My Lord Duke,
"Your Grace's Most humble and obedient servant,
"Thomas Hewett.

"N B. The Stack of Chimnies mentioned in this Report (which were placed over the Stone Passage leading to the Boxes) are actually taken down."

Theatre would be open'd against us; I cannot help going a little back to remember the Concern that my Brother-Menagers express'd at what might be the Consequences of it. They imagined that now all those who wish'd Ill to us, and particularly a great Party who had been disobliged by our shutting them out from behind our Scenes, even to the Refusal of their Money,[1] would now exert themselves in any partial or extravagant Measures that might either hurt us or support our Competitors: These, too, were some of those farther Reasons which had discouraged them from running the hazard of continuing to Sir *Richard Steele* the same Pension which had been paid to *Collier*. Upon all which I observed to them, that, for my own Part, I had not the same Apprehensions; but that I foresaw as many good as bad Consequences from two Houses: That tho' the Novelty might possibly at first abate a little of our Profits; yet, if we slacken'd not our Industry, that Loss would be amply balanced by an equal Increase of our Ease and Quiet · That those turbulent Spirits which were always molesting us, would now have other Employment: That the question'd Merit of our Acting would now stand in a clearer Light when others were faintly compared to us: That though Faults might be found with the best Actors that ever were, yet the egregious Defects that would appear in others would now be the effectual means to make our Superiority shine, if we had any Pretence to it: And

[1] See *ante*, vol i p 234.

that what some People hoped might ruin us, would in the end reduce them to give up the Dispute, and reconcile them to those who could best entertain them.

In every Article of this Opinion they afterwards found I had not been deceived; and the Truth of it may be so well remember'd by many living Spectators, that it would be too frivolous and needless a Boast to give it any farther Observation.

But in what I have said I would not be understood to be an Advocate for two Play-houses: For we shall soon find that two Sets of Actors tolerated in the same Place have constantly ended in the Corruption of the Theatre; of which the auxiliary Entertainments that have so barbarously supply'd the Defects of weak Action have, for some Years past, been a flagrant Instance; it may not, therefore, be here improper to shew how our childish Pantomimes first came to take so gross a Possession of the Stage.

I have upon several occasions already observ'd, that when one Company is too hard for another, the lower in Reputation has always been forced to exhibit some new-fangled Foppery to draw the Multitude after them: Of these Expedients, Singing and Dancing had formerly been the most effectual;[1] but, at the Time I am speaking of, our *English* Musick had

---

[1] Cibber, vol. i p 94, relates how, when the King's Company proved too strong for their rivals, Davenant, "to make head against their Success, was forced to add Spectacle and Music to Action."

been so discountenanced since the Taste of *Italian* Operas prevail'd, that it was to no purpose to pretend to it.[1] Dancing therefore was now the only Weight in the opposite Scale, and as the New Theatre sometimes found their Account in it, it could not be safe for us wholly to neglect it. To give even Dancing therefore some Improvement, and to make it something more than Motion without Meaning, the Fable of *Mars* and *Venus*[2] was form'd into a connected Presentation of Dances in Character, wherein the Passions were so happily expressed, and the whole Story so intelligibly told by a mute Narration of Gesture only, that even thinking Spectators allow'd it both a pleasing and a rational Entertainment; though, at the same time, from our Distrust of its Reception, we durst not venture to decorate it with any extraordinary Expence of Scenes or Habits; but upon the Success of this Attempt it was rightly concluded, that if a visible Expence in both were added to something of the same Nature, it could not fail of drawing the Town proportionably after it. From this original Hint then (but every way unequal to it) sprung forth that Succession of monstrous Medlies that have so long infested the Stage, and which arose upon one another alternately, at both Houses

[1] In the season 1718-19, Rich at Lincoln's Inn Fields frequently produced French pieces and operas. He must have had a company of French players engaged.

[2] This is, no doubt, John Weaver's dramatic entertainment called "The Loves of Mars and Venus," which was published, as acted at Drury Lane, in 1717.

outvying in Expence, like contending Bribes on both sides at an Election, to secure a Majority of the Multitude. But so it is, Truth may complain and Merit murmur with what Justice it may, the Few will never be a Match for the Many, unless Authority should think fit to interpose and put down these Poetical Drams, these Gin-shops of the Stage, that intoxicate its Auditors and dishonour their Understanding with a Levity for which I want a Name.[1]

If I am ask'd (after my condemning these Fooleries myself) how I came to assent or continue my Share of Expence to them? I have no better Excuse for

[1] The following lines ("Dunciad," iii. verses 229-244) are descriptive of such pantomimes as Cibber refers to —

> "He look'd, and saw a sable Sorc'rer rise,
> Swift to whose hand a winged volume flies
> All sudden, Gorgons hiss, and dragons glare,
> And ten-horn'd fiends and giants rush to war.
> Hell rises, Heav'n descends, and dance on Earth,
> Gods, imps, and monsters, music, rage, and mirth,
> A fire, a jig, a battle, and a ball,
> Till one wide conflagration swallows all
> Thence a new world, to nature's laws unknown,
> Breaks out refulgent, with a heav'n its own
> Another Cynthia her new journey runs,
> And other planets circle other suns
> The forests dance, the rivers upward rise,
> Whales sport in woods, and dolphins in the skies,
> And last, to give the whole creation grace,
> Lo! one vast Egg produces human race."

The allusion in the last line is to "Harlequin Sorcerer," in which Harlequin is hatched from a large egg on the stage. See Jackson's "History of the Scottish Stage," pages 367-8, for description of John Rich's excellence in this scene.

my Error than confessing it. I did it against my Conscience! and had not Virtue enough to starve by opposing a Multitude that would have been too hard for me.¹ Now let me ask an odd Question: Had *Harry the Fourth* of *France* a better Excuse for changing his Religion?² I was still, in my Heart, as much as he could be, on the side of Truth and Sense, but with this difference, that I had their leave to quit them when they could not support me: For what Equivalent could I have found for my falling a Martyr to them? How far the Heroe or the Comedian was in the wrong, let the Clergy and the Criticks decide. Necessity will be as good a Plea for the one as the other. But let the Question go which way it will, *Harry* IV. has always been allow'd a great Man: And what I want of his Grandeur, you see by the Inference, Nature has amply supply'd to me in Vanity; a Pleasure which neither the Pertness of Wit or the Gravity of Wisdom will ever persuade me to part with. And why is there not as

---

[1] In the "Dunciad" (book iii verses 261-4) Pope writes:—
  "But lo! to dark encounter in mid air
  New wizards rise: here Booth, and Cibber there
  Booth in his cloudy tabernacle shrin'd,
  On grinning Dragons Cibber mounts the wind."

On these lines Cibber remarks, in his "Letter to Mr Pope," 1742 (page 37) "If you, figuratively, mean by this, that I was an Encourager of those Fooleries, you are mistaken; for it is not true: If you intend it literally, that I was Dunce enough to mount a Machine, there is as little Truth in that too."

[2] Henry of Navarre, of whom it has been said that he regarded religion mainly as a diplomatic instrument.

much Honesty in owning as in concealing it? For though to hide it may be Wisdom, to be without it is impossible; and where is the Merit of keeping a Secret which every Body is let into? To say we have no Vanity, then, is shewing a great deal of it; as to say we *have* a great deal cannot be shewing so much: And tho' there may be Art in a Man's accusing himself, even then it will be more pardonable than Self-commendation. Do not we find that even good Actions have their Share of it? that it is as inseparable from our Being as our Nakedness? And though it may be equally decent to cover it, yet the wisest Man can no more be without it, than the weakest can believe he was born in his Cloaths. If then what we say of ourselves be true, and not prejudicial to others, to be called vain upon it is no more a Reproach than to be called a brown or a fair Man. Vanity is of all Complexions; 'tis the growth of every Clime and Capacity; Authors of all Ages have had a Tincture of it; and yet you read *Horace, Montaign,* and Sir *William Temple,* with Pleasure. Nor am I sure, if it were curable by Precept, that Mankind would be mended by it! Could Vanity be eradicated from our Nature, I am afraid that the Reward of most human Virtues would not be found in this World! And happy is he who has no greater Sin to answer for in the next!

But what is all this to the Theatrical Follies I was talking of? Perhaps not a great deal; but it is to my Purpose; for though I am an Historian, I do not write to the Wise and Learned only; I hope to have Readers of no more Judgment than some of my *quondam* Auditors; and I am afraid they will be as hardly contented with dry Matters of Fact, as with a plain Play without Entertainments: This Rhapsody, therefore, has been thrown in as a Dance between the Acts, to make up for the Dullness of what would have been by itself only proper. But I now come to my Story again.

Notwithstanding, then, this our Compliance with the vulgar Taste, we generally made use of these Pantomimes but as Crutches to our weakest Plays: Nor were we so lost to all Sense of what was valuable as to dishonour our best Authors in such bad Company: We had still a due Respect to several select Plays that were able to be their own Support; and in which we found our constant Account, without painting and patching them out, like Prostitutes, with these Follies in fashion: If therefore we were not so strictly chaste in the other part of our Conduct, let the Error of it stand among the silly Consequences of Two Stages. Could the Interest of both Companies have been united in one only Theatre, I had been one of the Few that would have us'd my utmost Endeavour of never admitting to the Stage any Spectacle that ought not to have been seen there; the Errors of my own Plays, which I could not see, excepted. And though probably the Majority of Spectators would not have been so well pleas'd with a Theatre so regulated; yet Sense and Reason cannot lose their intrinsick Value because the Giddy and the Ignorant are blind and deaf, or numerous; and I cannot help saying, it is a Reproach to a sensible People to let Folly so publickly govern their Pleasures.

While I am making this grave Declaration of what I *would* have done had One only Stage been continued; to obtain an easier Belief of my Sincerity I ought to put my Reader in mind of what I *did* do, even after Two Companies were again establish'd.

About this Time *Jacobitism* had lately exerted itself by the most unprovoked Rebellion that our Histories have handed down to us since the *Norman* Conquest:[1] I therefore thought that to set the Authors and Principles of that desperate Folly in a fair Light, by allowing the mistaken Consciences of some their best Excuse, and by making the artful Pretenders to Conscience as ridiculous as they were ungratefully wicked, was a Subject fit for the honest Satire of Comedy, and what might, if it succeeded, do Honour to the Stage by shewing the valuable Use of it.[2] And considering what Numbers at that

[1] It is hardly necessary to note that this was the Scottish Rebellion of 1715; yet Bellchambers indicates the period as 1718.

[2] Cibber's most notorious play, "The Nonjuror," was produced at Drury Lane on 6th December, 1717. The cast was :—

SIR JOHN WOODVIL . .	Mr Mills.
COLONEL WOODVIL	. Mr. Booth
MR. HEARTLY .	. Mr. Wilks
DOCTOR WOLF . . .	. Mr. Cibber.
CHARLES	Mr Walker.
LADY WOODVIL . . .	. Mrs. Porter.
MARIA	Mrs. Oldfield.

time might come to it as prejudic'd Spectators, it may be allow'd that the Undertaking was not less hazardous than laudable.

To give Life, therefore, to this Design, I borrow'd the *Tartuffe* of *Moliere*, and turn'd him into a modern *Nonjuror*:[1] Upon the Hypocrisy of the *French* Character I ingrafted a stronger Wickedness, that of an *English* Popish Priest lurking under the Doctrine of our own Church to raise his Fortune upon the Ruin of a worthy Gentleman, whom his dissembled Sanctity had seduc'd into the treasonable Cause of a *Roman Catholick* Out-law. How this Design, in the Play, was executed, I refer to the Readers of it; it cannot be mended by any critical Remarks I can make in its favour: Let it speak for itself. All the Reason I had to think it no bad Performance was, that it was acted eighteen Days running,[2] and that the Party that were hurt by it (as I have been told) have not been the smallest Number of my back Friends ever since. But happy was it for this Play that the very Subject was its Protection; a few Smiles of silent Contempt were the utmost Disgrace that on the first Day of its Appearance it was thought safe to throw upon it; as the

---

[1] Genest (ii. 615) quotes the Epilogue to Sewell's "Sir Walter Raleigh," produced at Lincoln's Inn Fields 16th January, 1719 —

"Yet to write plays is easy, faith, enough,
As you have seen by—Cibber—in Tartuffe.
With how much wit he did your hearts engage!
He only stole the *play*,—he writ the *title-page*."

[2] Genest says it was acted twenty-three times

Satire was chiefly employ'd on the Enemies of the Government, they were not so hardy as to own themselves such by any higher Disapprobation or Resentment. But as it was then probable I might write again, they knew it would not be long before they might with more Security give a Loose to their Spleen, and make up Accounts with me. And to do them Justice, in every Play I afterwards produced they paid me the Balance to a Tittle.[1] But to none was I more beholden than that celebrated Author Mr. *Mist*, whose *Weekly Journal*,[2] for about fifteen Years following, scarce ever fail'd of passing some of his Party Compliments upon me: The State and the Stage were his frequent Parallels, and the Minister and *Minheer Keiber* the Menager were as constantly droll'd upon: Now, for my own Part, though I could never persuade my Wit to have an open Account with him (for as he had no Effects of his own, I did not think myself oblig'd to answer his Bills;) not-

[1] Genest remarks (ii. 616) that "Cibber deserved all the abuse and enmity that he met with—the Stage and the Pulpit ought NEVER to dabble in politics."

Theo. Cibber, in a Petition to the King, given in his "Dissertations" (Letter to Garrick, p. 29), says that his father's "Writings, and public Professions of Loyalty, created him many Enemies, among the Disaffected."

[2] "Mist's Weekly Journal" was an anti-Hanoverian sheet, which was prominent in opposition to the Protestant Succession. Nathaniel Mist, the proprietor, and, I suppose, editor, suffered sundry pains and penalties for his Jacobitism. In his Preface to the second volume of "Letters" selected from his paper, he relates how he had, among other things, suffered imprisonment and stood in the pillory.

withstanding, I will be so charitable to his real *Manes*, and to the Ashes of his Paper, as to mention one particular Civility he paid to my Memory, after he thought he had ingeniously kill'd me. Soon after the *Nonjuror* had receiv'd the Favour of the Town, I read in one of his Journals the following short Paragraph, *viz. Yesterday died Mr.* Colley Cibber, *late Comedian of the Theatre-Royal, notorious for writing the* Nonjuror. The Compliment in the latter part I confess I did not dislike, because it came from so impartial a Judge; and it really so happen'd that the former part of it was very near being true; for I had that very Day just crawled out, after having been some Weeks laid up by a Fever· However, I saw no use in being thought to be thoroughly dead before my Time, and therefore had a mind to see whether the Town cared to have me alive again: So the Play of the *Orphan* being to be acted that Day, I quietly stole myself into the Part of the *Chaplain*, which I had not been seen in for many Years before The Surprize of the Audience at my unexpected Appearance on the very Day I had been dead in the News, and the Paleness of my Looks, seem'd to make it a Doubt whether I was not the Ghost of my real Self departed · But when I spoke, their Wonder eas'd itself by an Applause; which convinc'd me they were then satisfied that my Friend *Mist* had told a *Fib* of me. Now, if simply to have shown myself in broad Life, and about my Business, after he had *notoriously* reported me dead, can be called a Reply, it was the only one which his Paper while alive ever drew from me. How far I may be vain, then, in supposing that this Play brought me into the Disfavour of so many Wits[1] and valiant Auditors as afterwards appear'd against me, let those who may think it worth their Notice judge. In the mean time, 'till I can find a better Excuse for their sometimes particular Treatment of me, I cannot easily give up my Suspicion: And if I add a more remarkable Fact, that afterwards confirm'd me in it, perhaps it may incline others to join in my Opinion.

On the first Day of the *Provok'd Husband*, ten Years after the *Nonjuror* had appear'd,[2] a powerful Party, not having the Fear of publick Offence or private Injury before their Eyes, appear'd most impetuously concern'd for the Demolition of it; in which they so far succeeded, that for some Time I gave it up for lost; and to follow their Blows, in the publick Papers of the next Day it was attack'd and triumph'd over as a dead and damn'd Piece; a swinging Criticism was made upon it in general invective Terms, for they disdain'd to trouble the

---

[1] There can be little doubt that the "Nonjuror" was one of the causes of Pope's enmity to Cibber. Pope's father was a Nonjuror. See "Epistle to Dr. Arbuthnot," where the poet says of his father:—

"No courts he saw, no suits would ever try,
Nor dar'd an oath, nor hazarded a lie."

[2] Produced 10th January, 1728. See vol I. p. 311, for list of characters, &c.

World with Particulars; their Sentence, it seems, was Proof enough of its deserving the Fate it had met with. But this damn'd Play was, notwithstanding, acted twenty-eight Nights together, and left off at a Receipt of upwards of a hundred and forty Pounds; which happen'd to be more than in fifty Years before could be then said of any one Play whatsoever.

Now, if such notable Behaviour could break out upon so successful a Play (which too, upon the Share Sir *John Vanbrugh* had in it, I will venture to call a good one) what shall we impute it to? Why may not I plainly say, it was not the Play, but Me, who had a Hand in it, they did not like? And for what Reason? if they were not asham'd of it, why did not they publish it? No! the Reason had publish'd itself, I was the Author of the *Nonjuror!* But, perhaps, of all Authors, I ought not to make this sort of Complaint, because I have Reason to think that that particular Offence has made me more honourable Friends than Enemies, the latter of which I am not unwilling should know (however unequal the Merit may be to the Reward) that Part of the Bread I now eat was given me for having writ the *Nonjuror*.[1]

And yet I cannot but lament, with many quiet Spectators, the helpless Misfortune that has so many Years attended the Stage! That no Law has had Force enough to give it absolute Protection! for

---

[1] Meaning, no doubt, that the post of Poet Laureate was given to him as a reward for his services to the Government.

'till we can civilize its Auditors, the Authors that write for it will seldom have a greater Call to it than Necessity; and how unlikely is the Imagination of the Needy to inform or delight the Many in Affluence? or how often does Necessity make many unhappy Gentlemen turn Authors in spite of Nature?

What a Blessing, therefore, is it! what an enjoy'd Deliverance! after a Wretch has been driven by Fortune to stand so many wanton Buffets of unmanly Fierceness, to find himself at last quietly lifted above the Reach of them!

But let not this Reflection fall upon my Auditors without Distinction; for though Candour and Benevolence are silent Virtues, they are as visible as the most vociferous Ill-nature; and I confess the Publick has given me more frequently Reason to be thankful than to complain.

CHAPTER XVI.

The Author steps out of his Way. Pleads his Theatrical Cause in Chancery. Carries it. Plays acted at Hampton-Court. Theatrical Anecdotes in former Reigns. Ministers and Menagers always censur'd. The Difficulty of supplying the Stage with good Actors consider'd. Courtiers and Comedians goverh'd by the same Passions. Examples of both. The Author quits the Stage. Why.

HAVING brought the Government of the Stage through such various Changes and Revolutions, to this settled State in which it continued to almost the Time of my leaving it;[1] it cannot be suppos'd that a Period of so much Quiet and so long a Train of Success (though happy for those who enjoy'd

[1] 1733.

it) can afford such Matter of Surprize or Amusement, as might arise from Times of more Distress and Disorder. A quiet Time in History, like a Calm in a Voyage, leaves us but in an indolent Station: To talk of our Affairs when they were no longer ruffled by Misfortunes, would be a Picture without Shade, a flat Performance at best. As I might, therefore, throw all that tedious Time of our Tranquillity into one Chasm in my History, and cut my Way short at once to my last Exit from the Stage, I shall at least fill it up with such Matter only as I have a mind should be known,[1] how few soever may have

---

[1] In leaping from 1717 to 1728, as Cibber does here, he omits to notice much that is of the greatest interest in stage history. Steele's connection with the theatre was of a chequered complexion, and it is curious as well as regrettable that an interested observer like Cibber should have simply ignored the great points which were at issue while Steele was a sharer in the Patent. In order to bridge over the chasm I give a bare record of Steele's transactions in connection with the Patent.

His first authority was a Licence granted to him and his partners, Wilks, Cibber, Dogget, and Booth, and dated October 18th, 1714. This was followed by a Patent, in Steele's name alone, for the term of his life, and three years after his death, which bore date January 19th, 1715. Cibber (p. 174) relates that Steele assigned to Wilks, Booth, and himself, equal shares in this Patent. All went smoothly for more than two years, until the appointment of the Duke of Newcastle (April 13th, 1717) as Lord Chamberlain. He seems soon to have begun to interfere in the affairs of the theatre. Steele, in the eighth number of "The Theatre," states that shortly after his appointment the Duke demanded that he should resign his Patent and accept a Licence in its place. This Steele naturally and rightly declined to do, and here the matter rested for many months. With reference to this

Patience to read it: Yet, as I despair not of some Readers who may be most awake when they think others have most occasion to sleep; who may be more pleas'd to find me languid than lively, or in the

it is interesting to note that among the Lord Chamberlain's Papers is the record of a consultation of the Attorney-General whether Steele's Patent made him independent of the Lord Chamberlain's authority. Unfortunately it is impossible to decide, from the terms of the queries put to the Attorney-General, whether these were caused by aggressive action on Steele's part, or merely by his defence of his rights

The next molestation was an order, dated December 19th, 1719, addressed to Steele, Wilks, and Booth, ordering them to dismiss Cibber, which they did His suspension, for it was nothing more, lasted till January 28th, 1720. Steele, in the seventh number of "The Theatre," January 23rd, 1720, alludes to his suspension as then existing, and in No. 12 talks of Cibber's being just restored to the "Begging Bridge," that is, the theatre. The allusion is to an Apologue by Steele ("Reader," No. II) which Cibber quotes, and applies to Steele, in his Dedication of "Ximena" to him. A peasant had succeeded in barricading, with his whole belongings, a bridge over which an enemy attempted to invade his native country. He kept them back till his countrymen were roused; but when the forces of his friends attacked the enemy, the peasant's property was destroyed in the fray and he was left destitute. He received no compensation, but it was enacted that he and his descendants were alone to have the privilege of *begging* on this bridge Cibber applies this fable to the treatment of Steele by the Lord Chamberlain, and there can be no doubt that this Dedication must have caused great offence to that official, and contributed materially to Cibber's suspension, though Steele declared that the attack upon his partner was merely intended as an oblique attack on himself. The author of the "Answer to the Case of Sir Richard Steele," 1720 (Nichols's ed , p. 532), says that Cibber had offended the Duke by an attack on the King and the Ministry in the Dedication of his "Ximena" to Steele He also says that when the Chamberlain wanted a certain actor to play a part which belonged to one of the managers, Cibber flatly refused to allow

wrong than in the right, why should I scruple (when it is so easy a Matter too) to gratify their particular Taste by venturing upon any Error that I like, or the Weakness of my Judgment misleads me to com-

him, and was thereupon silenced. (The actor is said to have been Elrington, and the part Torrismond, but I doubt if Elrington was at Drury Lane in 1719-20) A recent stage historian curiously says that the play which gave offence was "The Nonjuror," which is about as likely as that a man should be accused of high treason because he sang "God Save the Queen!"

Steele then, being made to understand that the attack on Cibber was the beginning of evil directed against himself, wrote to two great Ministers of State, and presented a Petition to the King on January 22nd, 1720, praying to be protected from molestation by the Lord Chamberlain. The result of this action was a revocation of Steele's Licence (*not* his Patent specially, which is curious) dated January 23rd, 1720; and on the next Monday, the 25th, an Order for Silence was sent to the managers and actors at Drury Lane. The theatre accordingly remained closed Monday, Tuesday, and Wednesday, January 25th to 27th, 1720, and on the 28th re-opened, Wilks, Cibber, and Booth having made their submission and received a Licence dated the previous day.

On the 4th of March following the actors of Drury Lane were sworn at the Lord Chamberlain's office, "pursuant to an Order occasioned by their acting in obedience to his Majesty's Licence, lately granted, exclusive of a Patent formerly obtained by Sir Richard Steele, Knight" The tenor of the Oath was, that as his Majesty's Servants they should act subservient to the Lord Chamberlain, Vice-Chamberlain, and Gentleman-Usher in Waiting. Whether Steele took any steps to test the legality of this treatment is doubtful; but, on the accession of his friend Walpole to office, he was restored to his position at the head of the theatre On May 2nd, 1721, Cibber and his partners were ordered to account with Steele for his past and present share of the profits of the theatre, as if all the regulations from which his name had been excluded had never been made. This edict is signed by the Duke of Newcastle, and must, I fancy, have been rather a bitter pill for that nobleman. How Steele subsequently conducted himself,

mit? I think, too, I have a very good Chance for my Success in this passive Ambition, by shewing myself in a Light I have not been seen in.

By your Leave then, Gentlemen! let the Scene open, and at once discover your Comedian at the Bar! There you will find him a Defendant, and pleading his own Theatrical Cause in a Court of *Chancery:* But, as I chuse to have a Chance of pleasing others as well as of indulging you, Gentlemen; I must first beg leave to open my Case to them; after which my whole Speech upon that Occasion shall be at your Mercy.

In all the Transactions of Life, there cannot be a more painful Circumstance, than a Dispute at Law with a Man with whom we have long liv'd in an agreeable Amity· But when Sir *Richard Steele,* to get himself out of Difficulties, was oblig'd to throw his Affairs into the Hands of Lawyers and Trustees, that Consideration, then, could be of no weight: The Friend, or the Gentleman, had no more to do in the Matter! Thus, while Sir *Richard* no longer acted from himself, it may be no Wonder if a Flaw was found in our Conduct for the Law to make Work

and how much interest he took in the theatre, Cibber very fully relates in the next few pages After Steele's death a new Patent was granted to Cibber, Wilks, and Booth, as will be related further on. It may be noted here, however, that the date of the new Patent proves conclusively that Steele's grant was never superseded. The new power was dated July 3rd, 1731, but it did not take effect till September 1st, 1732, exactly three years after Steele's death, according to the terms of his original Patent.

with. It must be observed, then, that about two or three Years before this Suit was commenc'd, upon Sir *Richard*'s totally absenting himself from all Care and Menagement of the Stage (which by our Articles of Partnership he was equally and jointly oblig'd with us to attend) we were reduc'd to let him know that we could not go on at that Rate; but that if he expected to make the Business a *sine-Cure*, we had as much Reason to expect a Consideration for our extraordinary Care of it; and that during his Absence we therefore intended to charge our selves at a Sallary of 1*l*. 13*s*. 4*d*. every acting Day (unless he could shew us Cause to the contrary) for our Menagement: To which, in his compos'd manner, he only answer'd; That to be sure we knew what was fitter to be done than he did; that he had always taken a Delight in making us easy, and had no Reason to doubt of our doing him Justice. Now whether, under this easy Stile of Approbation, he conceal'd any Dislike of our Resolution, I cannot say. But, if I may speak my private Opinion, I really believe, from his natural Negligence of his Affairs, he was glad, at any rate, to be excus'd an Attendance which he was now grown weary of. But, whether I am deceiv'd or right in my Opinion, the Fact was truly this, that he never once, directly nor indirectly, complain'd or objected to our being paid the above-mention'd daily Sum in near three Years together; and yet still continued to absent himself from us and our Affairs. But notwithstanding he had seen and done all this with his Eyes open ; his Lawyer thought here was still a fair Field for a Battle in Chancery, in which, though his Client might be beaten, he was sure his Bill must be paid for it: Accordingly, to work with us he went. But, not to be so long as the Lawyers were in bringing this Cause to an Issue, I shall at once let you know, that it came to a Hearing before the late Sir *Joseph Jekyll*, then Master of the Rolls, in the Year 1726.[1] Now, as the chief Point in dispute was, of what Kind or Importance the Business of a Menager was, or in what it principally consisted; it could not be suppos'd that the most learned Council could be so well appriz'd of the Nature of it, as one who had himself gone through the Care and Fatigue of it. I was therefore encourag'd by our Council to speak to that particular Head myself; which I confess I was glad he suffer'd me to undertake; but when I tell you that two of the learned Council against us came afterwards to be successively Lord-Chancellors,

---

[1] This is one of Cibber's bad blunders. The Case was heard in 1728. Genest (iii 208) refers to the *St. James's Evening Post's* mention of the hearing , and, in the Burney MSS in the British Museum, a copy of the paragraph is given. It is not, however, a cutting, but a manuscript copy. " Saty. Feb. 17. There was an hearing in the Rolls Chapel in a Cause between Sir Richard Steele, Mr Cibber, Mr. Wilks, and others belonging to Drury-Lane Theatre, which held five hours—one of which was taken up by a speech of Mr. Wilks, which had so good an effect, that the Cause went against Sir Richard Steele "—St. James's Evening Post, Feb. 17 to Feb 20, 1728 In its next issue, Feb 20 to Feb. 22, it corrects the blunder which it had made in attributing Cibber's speech to Wilks

it sets my Presumption in a Light that I still tremble to shew it in: But however, not to assume more Merit from its Success than was really its Due, I ought fairly to let you know, that I was not so hardy as to deliver my Pleading without Notes, in my Hand, of the Heads I intended to enlarge upon; for though I thought I could conquer my Fear, I could not be so sure of my Memory: But when it came to the critical Moment, the Dread and Apprehension of what I had undertaken so disconcerted my Courage, that though I had been us'd to talk to above Fifty Thousand different People every Winter, for upwards of Thirty Years together; an involuntary and unaffected Proof of my Confusion fell from my Eyes; and, as I found myself quite out of my Element, I seem'd rather gasping for Life than in a condition to cope with the eminent Orators against me. But, however, I soon found, from the favourable Attention of my Hearers, that my Diffidence had done me no Disservice: And as the Truth I was to speak to needed no Ornament of Words, I delivered it in the plain manner following, *viz.*

In this Cause, Sir, I humbly conceive there are but two Points that admit of any material Dispute. The first is, Whether Sir *Richard Steele* is as much obliged to do the Duty and Business of a Menager as either *Wilks*, *Booth*, or *Cibber*. And the second is, Whether by Sir *Richard*'s totally withdrawing himself from the Business of a Menager, the Defendants are justifiable in charging to each of themselves the 1*l.* 13*s.* 4*d. per Diem* for their particular Pains and Care in carrying on the whole Affairs of the Stage without any Assistance from Sir *Richard Steele.*

As to the First, if I don't mistake the Words of the Assignment, there is a Clause in it that says, All Matters relating to the Government or Menagement of the Theatre shall be concluded by a Majority of Voices. Now I presume, Sir, there is no room left to alledge that Sir *Richard* was ever refused his Voice, though in above three Years he never desir'd to give it · And I believe there will be as little room to say, that he could have a Voice if he were not a Menager. But, Sir, his being a Menager is so self-evident, that it is amazing how he could conceive that he was to take the Profits and Advantages of a Menager without doing the Duty of it. And I will be bold to say, Sir, that his Assignment of the Patent to *Wilks, Booth,* and *Cibber,* in no one Part of it, by the severest Construction in the World, can be wrested to throw the heavy Burthen of the Menagement only upon their Shoulders. Nor does it appear, Sir, that either in his Bill, or in his Answer to our Cross-Bill, he has offer'd any Hint, or Glimpse of a Reason, for his withdrawing from the Menagement at all; or so much as pretend, from the time complained of, that he ever took the least Part of his Share of it. Now, Sir, however unaccountable this Conduct of Sir *Richard* may seem, we will still allow that he had some Cause for it, but whether or no that Cause was a reasonable one your Honour will the better judge, if I may be indulged in the Liberty of explaining it.

Sir, the Case, in plain Truth and Reality, stands thus: Sir *Richard*, though no Man alive can write better of Oeconomy than himself, yet, perhaps, he is above the Drudgery of practising it: Sir *Richard*, then, was often in want of Money; and while we were in Friendship with him, we often assisted his Occasions: But those Compliances had so unfortunate an Effect, that they only heightened his Importunity to borrow more, and the more we lent, the less he minded us, or shew'd any Concern for our Welfare. Upon this, Sir, we stopt our Hands at once, and peremptorily refus'd to advance another Shilling 'till by the Balance of our Accounts it became due to him. And this Treatment (though, we hope, not in the least unjustifiable) we have Reason to believe so ruffled his Temper, that he at once was as short with us as we had been with him; for, from that Day, he never more came near us: Nay, Sir, he not only continued to neglect what he *should* have done, but actually did what he ought *not* to have done: He made an Assignment of his Share without our Consent, in a manifest Breach of our Agreement: For, Sir, we did not lay that Restriction upon ourselves for no Reason: We knew, before-hand, what Trouble and Inconvenience it would be to unravel and expose our Accounts to Strangers, who, if they were to do us no hurt by divulging our Secrets, we were sure could do us no good by keeping them. If Sir *Richard* had had our common Interest at heart, he would have been as warm in it as we were, and as tender of hurting it: But supposing his assigning his Share to others may have done us no great Injury, it is, at least, a shrewd Proof that he did not care whether it did us any or no. And if the Clause was not strong enough to restrain him from it in Law, there was enough in it to have restrain'd him in Honour from breaking it. But take it in its best Light, it shews him as remiss a Menager in our Affairs as he naturally was in his own. Suppose, Sir, we had all been as careless as himself, which I can't find he has any more Right to be than we have, must not our whole Affair have fallen to Ruin? And may we not, by a parity of Reason, suppose, that by his Neglect a fourth Part of it *does* fall to Ruin? But, Sir, there is a particular Reason to believe, that, from our want of Sir *Richard*, more than a fourth Part *does* suffer by it: His Rank and Figure in the World, while he gave us the Assistance of them, were of extraordinary Service to us: He had an easier Access, and a more regarded Audience at Court, than our low Station of Life could pretend to, when our Interest wanted (as it often did) a particular Solicitation there. But since we have been deprived of him, the very End, the very Consideration of his Share in our Profits is not perform'd on his Part. And will Sir *Richard*, then, make us no Compensation for so valuable a Loss in our Interests, and so palpable an Addition to our Labour? I am afraid, Sir, if we were all to be as indolent in the Menaging-Part as Sir *Richard* presumes he has a Right to be; our Patent would soon run us as many Hundreds in Debt, as he had (and still seems willing to have) his Share of, for doing of nothing.

Sir, our next Point in question is whether *Wilks*, *Booth*, and *Cibber* are justifiable in charging the 1*l.* 13*s.* 4*d. per diem* for their extraordinary Menagement in the Absence of Sir *Richard Steele.* I doubt, Sir, it will be hard to come to the Solution of this Point, unless we may be a little indulg'd in setting forth what is the daily and necessary Business and Duty of a Menager. But, Sir, we will endeavour to be as short as the Circumstances will admit of.

Sir, by our Books it is apparent that the Menagers have under their Care no less than One Hundred and Forty Persons in constant daily Pay: And among such Numbers, it will be no wonder if a great many of them are unskilful, idle, and sometimes untractable; all which Tempers are to be led, or driven, watch'd, and restrain'd by the continual Skill, Care, and Patience of the Menagers. Every Menager is oblig'd, in his turn, to attend two or three Hours every Morning at the Rehearsal of Plays and other Entertainments for the Stage, or else every Rehearsal would be but a rude Meeting of Mirth and Jollity. The same Attendance is as necessary at every Play during the time of its publick Action, in which one or more of us have constantly been punctual, whether we have had any part in the Play then acted or not. A Menager ought to be at the Reading of every new Play when it is first offer'd to the Stage, though there are seldom one of those Plays in twenty which, upon hearing, proves to be fit for it; and upon such Occasions the Attendance must be allow'd to be as painfully tedious as the getting rid of the Authors of such Plays must be disagreeable and difficult. Besides this, Sir, a Menager is to order all new Cloaths, to assist in the Fancy and Propriety of them, to limit the Expence, and to withstand the unreasonable Importunities of some that are apt to think themselves injur'd if they are not finer than their Fellows. A Menager is to direct and oversee the Painters, Machinists, Musicians, Singers, and Dancers; to have an Eye upon the Door-keepers, Under-Servants, and Officers that, without such Care, are too often apt to defraud us, or neglect their Duty.

And all this, Sir, and more, much more, which we hope will be needless to trouble you with, have we done every Day, without the least Assistance from Sir *Richard*, even at times when the Concern and Labour of our Parts upon the Stage have made it very difficult and irksome to go through with it.

In this Place, Sir, it may be worth observing that Sir *Richard*, in his Answer to our Cross-Bill, seems to value himself upon *Cibber*'s confessing, in the Dedication of a Play which he made to Sir *Richard*, that he (Sir *Richard*) had done the Stage very considerable Service by leading the Town to our Plays, and filling our Houses by the Force and Influence of his *Tatlers*.[1] But Sir *Richard* forgets that those *Tatlers* were written in the late Queen's Reign, long before he was admitted to a Share in the Play-house: And in truth, Sir, it was our real Sense of those Obligations, and Sir *Richard*'s assuring us they should be continued, that first and chiefly inclin'd us to invite him to share the Profits of our Labours, upon such farther Conditions as in his Assignment of the Patent to us are specified. And, Sir, as *Cibber*'s publick Acknowledgment of those Favours is at the same time an equal Proof of Sir *Richard*'s *Power* to continue them ; so, Sir, we hope it carries an equal Probability that, without his Promise to *use* that Power, he would never have been thought on, much less have been invited by us into a Joint-Menagement of the Stage, and into a Share of the Profits : And, indeed, what Pretence could he have form'd for asking a Patent from the Crown, had he been possess'd of no eminent Qualities but in common with other Men? But, Sir, all these Advantages, all these Hopes, nay, Certainties of greater Profits from those great Qualities, have we been utterly depriv'd of by the wilful and unexpected Neglect of Sir *Richard*. But we find, Sir, it is a common thing in the Practice of Mankind to justify one Error by committing another · For Sir *Richard* has not only refused us the extraordinary Assistance which he is able and

[1] This was in the Dedication to "Ximena." The passage will be found quoted by me in a note on page 163 of this volume.

bound to give us; but, on the contrary, to our great Expence and Loss of Time, now calls us to account, in this honourable Court, for the Wrong we have done him, in not doing his Business of a Menager for nothing. But, Sir, Sir *Richard* has not met with such Treatment from us: He has not writ Plays for us for *Nothing*, we paid him very well, and in an extraordinary manner, for his late Comedy of the *Conscious Lovers:* And though, in writing that Play, he had more Assistance from one of the Menagers [1] than becomes me to enlarge upon, of which Evidence has been given upon Oath by several of our Actors; yet, Sir, he was allow'd the full and particular Profits of that Play as an Author, which amounted to Three Hundred Pounds, besides about Three Hundred more which he received as a Joint-Sharer of the general Profits that arose from it. Now, Sir, though the Menagers are not all of them able to write Plays, yet they have all of them been able to do (I won't say as good, but at least) as profitable a thing. They have invented and adorn'd a Spectacle that for Forty Days together has brought more Money to the House than the best Play that ever was writ. The Spectacle I mean, Sir, is that of the Coronation-Ceremony of *Anna Bullen:* [2] And though we allow a

---

[1] Cibber himself, of course.

[2] This Coronation was tacked to the play of "Henry VIII.," which was revived at Drury Lane on 26th October, 1727 Special interest attached to it on account of the recent Coronation of George II

good Play to be the more laudable Performance, yet, Sir, in the profitable Part of it there is no Comparison. If, therefore, our Spectacle brought in as much, or more Money than Sir *Richard*'s Comedy, what is there on his Side but Usage that intitles him to be paid for one, more than we are for t'other? But then, Sir, if he is so profitably distinguish'd for his Play, if we yield him up the Preference, and pay him for his extraordinary Composition, and take nothing for our own, though it turn'd out more to our common Profit; sure, Sir, while we do such extraordinary Duty as Menagers, and while he neglects his Share of that Duty, he cannot grudge us the moderate Demand we make for our separate Labour?

To conclude, Sir, if by our constant Attendance, our Care, our Anxiety (not to mention the disagreeable Contests we sometimes meet with, both within and without Doors, in the Menagement of our Theatre) we have not only saved the whole from Ruin, which, if we had all follow'd Sir *Richard*'s Example, could not have been avoided; I say, Sir, if we have still made it so valuable an Income to him, without his giving us the least Assistance for several Years past; we hope, Sir, that the poor Labourers that have done all this for Sir *Richard* will not be thought unworthy of their Hire.

How far our Affairs, being set in this particular Light, might assist our Cause, may be of no great Importance to guess; but the Issue of it was this: That Sir *Richard* not having made any Objection to what we had charged for Menagement for three Years together; and as our Proceedings had been all transacted in open Day, without any clandestine Intention of Fraud; we were allow'd the Sums in dispute above-mention'd; and Sir *Richard* not being advised to appeal to the Lord-Chancellor, both Parties paid their own Costs, and thought it their mutual Interest to let this be the last of their Lawsuits.

And now, gentle Reader, I ask Pardon for so long an Imposition on your Patience: For tho' I may have no ill Opinion of this Matter myself; yet to you I can very easily conceive it may have been tedious. You are, therefore, at your own Liberty of charging the whole Impertinence of it, either to the Weakness of my Judgment, or the Strength of my Vanity; and I will so far join in your Censure, that I farther confess I have been so impatient to give it you, that you have had it out of its Turn : For, some Years before this Suit was commenced, there were other Facts that ought to have had a Precedence in my History: But that, I dare say, is an Oversight you will easily excuse, provided you afterwards find them worth reading. However, as to that Point I must take my Chance, and shall therefore proceed to speak of the Theatre which was order'd by his late Majesty to be erected in the Great old Hall at *Hampton-Court*; where Plays were intended to have been acted twice a Week during the Summer-Season. But before the Theatre could be finish'd, above half the Month of *September* being elapsed, there were but seven Plays acted before the Court returned to *London*.[1] This throwing open a Theatre in a Royal Palace seem'd to be reviving the Old *English* hospitable Grandeur, where the lowest Rank of neighbouring Subjects might make themselves merry at Court without being laugh'd at themselves. In former Reigns, Theatrical Entertainments at the Royal Palaces had been perform'd at vast Expence, as appears by the Description of the Decorations in several of *Ben. Johnson*'s Masques in King *James* and *Charles the First*'s Time;[2] many curious and original Draughts of which, by Sir *Inigo Jones*, I have seen in the *Musæum* of our greatest Master and Patron of Arts and Architecture, whom it would be a needless Liberty to name.[3] But when our Civil Wars ended in the Decadence of Monarchy, it was then an Honour to the Stage to have fallen with it: Yet, after the Restoration of *Charles* II. some faint Attempts were made to revive these Theatrical Spectacles at Court; but I have met with no Account of above one Masque acted there by the Nobility; which was that of *Calisto*, written by *Crown*, the Author of Sir *Courtly Nice*. For what Reason *Crown* was chosen to that Honour

---

[1] This was in 1718. On 24th September, 1718, the bills announce "the same Entertainments that were performed yesterday before his Majesty at Hampton Court."

[2] In Whitelocke's "Memorials" there is an account of a Masque played in 1633, before Charles I. and his Queen, by the gentlemen of the Temple, which cost £21,000.

[3] The Earl of Burlington.

rather than *Dryden*, who was then Poet-Laureat and out of all Comparison his Superior in Poetry, may seem surprizing: But if we consider the Offence which the then Duke of *Buckingham* took at the Character of *Zimri* in *Dryden*'s *Absalom*, &c. (which might probably be a Return to his Grace's *Drawcansir* in the *Rehearsal*) we may suppose the Prejudice and Recommendation of so illustrious a Pretender to Poetry might prevail at Court to give *Crown* this Preference.[1] In the same Reign the King had his Comedians at *Windsor*, but upon a particular Establishment; for tho' they acted in St. *George*'s Hall, within the Royal Palace, yet (as I have been inform'd by an Eye-witness) they were permitted to take Money at the Door of every Spectator; whether this was an Indulgence, in Conscience I cannot say; but it was a common Report among the principal Actors, when I first came into the *Theatre-Royal*, in 1690, that there was then due to the Company from that Court about One Thousand Five Hundred Pounds for Plays commanded, *&c.* and yet it was the general Complaint, in that Prince's Reign, that he paid too much Ready-money for his Pleasures:

[1] "Calisto" was published in 1675. Genest (i. 181) says: "Cibber, with his usual accuracy as to dates, supposes that Crowne was selected to write a mask for the Court in preference to Dryden, through the influence of the Duke of Buckingham, who was offended at what Dryden had said of him in Absalom and Achitophel—Dryden's poem was not written till 1681—Lord Rochester was the person who recommended Crowne." I may add that Dryden furnished an Epilogue to "Calisto," which was not spoken.

But these Assertions I only give as I received them, without being answerable for their Reality. This Theatrical Anecdote, however, puts me in mind of one of a more private nature, which I had from old solemn *Boman*, the late Actor of venerable Memory.[1] *Boman*, then a Youth, and fam'd for his Voice, was appointed to sing some Part in a Concert of Musick at the private Lodgings of Mrs. *Gwin*; at which were only present the King, the Duke of *York*, and one or two more who were usually admitted upon those detach'd Parties of Pleasure. When the Performance was ended, the King express'd himself highly pleased, and gave it extraordinary Commendations: Then, Sir, said the Lady, to shew you don't speak like a Courtier, I hope you will make the Performers a handsome Present. The King said he had no Money about him, and ask'd the Duke if he had any? To which the Duke reply'd, I believe, Sir, not above a Guinea or two. Upon which the laughing Lady, turning to the People about her, and making bold with the King's common Expression, cry'd, *Od's Fish! what Company am I got into!*

---

[1] Boman, or Bowman, was born about 1651, and lived till 23rd March, 1739. He made his first appearance about 1673, and acted to within a few months of his death, having thus been on the stage for the extraordinary period of sixty-five years He was very sensitive on the subject of his age, and, if asked how old he was, only replied, that he was very well. Davies speaks highly of Boman's acting in his extreme old age ("Dram. Misc.," i. 286 and ii. 100). Mrs. Boman was the adopted daughter of Betterton.

Whether the reverend Historian of his *Own Time*,[1] among the many other Reasons of the same Kind he might have for stiling this Fair One the *indiscreetest and wildest Creature that ever was in a Court*, might know this to be one of them, I can't say: But if we consider her in all the Disadvantages of her Rank and Education, she does not appear to have had any criminal Errors more remarkable than her Sex's Frailty to answer for. And if the same Author, in his latter End of that Prince's Life, seems to reproach his Memory with too kind a Concern for her Support, we may allow that it becomes a Bishop to have had no Eyes or Taste for the frivolous Charms or playful *Badinage* of a King's Mistress: Yet, if the common Fame of her may be believ'd, which in my Memory was not doubted, she had less to be laid to her Charge than any other of those Ladies who were in the same State of Preferment: She never meddled in Matters of serious Moment, or was the Tool of working Politicians: Never broke into those amorous Infidelities which others in that grave Author are accus'd of; but was as visibly distinguish'd by her particular Personal Inclination to the King, as her Rivals were by their Titles and Grandeur. Give me leave to carry (perhaps the Partiality of) my Observation a little farther. The same Author, in the same Page, 263,[2] tells us, That " Another of the King's Mistresses, the Daughter of " a Clergyman, Mrs. *Roberts*, in whom her first

[1] Bishop Burnet. [2] First edition, vol. 1.

"Education had so deep a Root, that though she fell
"into many scandalous Disorders, with very dismal
"Adventures in them all, yet a Principle of Reli-
"gion was so deep laid in her, that tho' it did not
"restrain her, yet it kept alive in her such a constant
"Horror of Sin, that she was never easy in an ill
"course, and died with a great Sense of her former
"ill Life."

To all this let us give an implicit Credit: Here is the Account of a frail Sinner made up with a Reverend Witness! Yet I cannot but lament that this Mitred Historian, who seems to know more Personal Secrets than any that ever writ before him, should not have been as inquisitive after the last Hours of our other Fair Offender, whose Repentance I have been unquestionably inform'd, appear'd in all the contrite Symptoms of a Christian Sincerity. If therefore you find I am so much concern'd to make this favourable mention of the one, because she was a Sister of the *Theatre*, why may not—But I dare not be so presumptuous, so uncharitably bold, as to suppose the other was spoken better of merely because she was the Daughter of a *Clergyman*. Well, and what then? What's all this idle Prate, you may say, to the matter in hand? Why, I say your Question is a little too critical; and if you won't give an Author leave, now and then, to embellish his Work by a natural Reflexion, you are an ungentle Reader. But I have done with my Digression, and return to our Theatre at *Hampton-Court*, where I am not sure the Reader, be he ever so wise, will meet with any thing more worth his notice: However, if he happens to read, as I write, for want of something better to do, he will go on; and perhaps wonder when I tell him that

A Play presented at Court, or acted on a publick Stage, seem to their different Auditors a different Entertainment. Now hear my Reason for it. In the common Theatre the Guests are at home, where the politer Forms of Good-breeding are not so nicely regarded: Every one there falls to, and likes or finds fault according to his natural Taste or Appetite. At Court, where the Prince gives the Treat, and honours the Table with his own Presence, the Audience is under the Restraint of a Circle, where Laughter or Applause rais'd higher than a Whisper would be star'd at. At a publick Play they are both let loose, even 'till the Actor is sometimes pleas'd with his not being able to be heard for the Clamour of them. But this Coldness or Decency of Attention at Court I observ'd had but a melancholy Effect upon the impatient Vanity of some of our Actors, who seem'd inconsolable when their flashy Endeavours to please had pass'd unheeded: Their not considering where they were quite disconcerted them; nor could they recover their Spirits 'till from the lowest Rank of the Audience some gaping *John* or *Joan*, in the fullness of their Hearts, roar'd out their Approbation: And, indeed, such a natural Instance of honest Simplicity a Prince himself, whose Indulgence knows where to make Allowances, might reasonably smile at, and perhaps not think it the worst part of his Entertainment. Yet it must be own'd, that an Audience may be as well too much reserv'd, as too profuse of their Applause: For though it is possible a *Betterton* would not have been discourag'd from throwing out an Excellence, or elated into an Error, by his Auditors being too little or too much pleas'd, yet, as Actors of his Judgment are Rarities, those of less Judgment may sink into a Flatness in their Performance for want of that Applause, which from the generality of Judges they might perhaps have some Pretence to: And the Auditor, when not seeming to feel what ought to affect him, may rob himself of something more that he might have had by giving the Actor his Due, who measures out his Power to please according to the Value he sets upon his Hearer's Taste or Capacity. But, however, as we were not here itinerant Adventurers, and had properly but one Royal Auditor to please; after that Honour was attain'd to, the rest of our Ambition had little to look after: And that the King was often pleas'd, we were not only assur'd by those who had the Honour to be near him; but could see it, from the frequent Satisfaction in his Looks at particular Scenes and Passages: One Instance of which I am tempted to relate, because it was at a Speech that might more naturally affect a Sovereign Prince than any private Spectator. In *Shakespear's Harry the Eighth,* that King commands the Cardinal to write circular Letters of Indemnity into every County where the Payment of certain heavy Taxes had been disputed: Upon which the Cardinal whispers the following Directions to his Secretary *Crom-well*:

> ——— *A Word with you:*
> *Let there be Letters writ to every Shire*
> *Of the King's Grace and Pardon: The griev'd*
>   *Commons*
> *Hardly conceive of me.   Let it be nois'd*
> *That through* our Intercession *this Revokement*
> *And Pardon comes.*—*I shall anon advise you*
> *Farther in the Proceeding* ———

The Solicitude of this Spiritual Minister, in filching from his Master the Grace and Merit of a good Action, and dressing up himself in it, while himself had been Author of the Evil complain'd of, was so easy a Stroke of his Temporal Conscience, that it seem'd to raise the King into something more than a Smile whenever that Play came before him: And I had a more distinct Occasion to observe this Effect; because my proper Stand on the Stage when I spoke the Lines required me to be near the Box where the King usually sate.[1] In a Word, this Play is so true

---

[1] Davies ("Dram. Misc.," i. 365) says: "Wolsey's filching from his royal master the honour of bestowing grace and pardon on the subject, appeared so gross and impudent a prevarication, that, when this play was acted before George I. at Hampton-Court, about the year 1717, the courtiers laughed so loudly at this ministerial craft, that his majesty, who was unacquainted with the

a Dramatick Chronicle of an old *English* Court, and where the Character of *Harry the Eighth* is so exactly drawn, even to a humourous Likeness, that it may be no wonder why his Majesty's particular Taste for it should have commanded it three several times in one Winter.

This, too, calls to my Memory an extravagant Pleasantry of Sir *Richard Steele,* who being ask'd by a grave Nobleman, after the same Play had been presented at *Hampton-Court,* how the King lik'd it, reply'd, *So terribly well, my Lord, that I was afraid I should have lost all my Actors! For I was not sure the King would not keep them to fill the Posts at Court that he saw them so fit for in the Play.*

It may be imagin'd that giving Plays to the People at such a distance from *London* could not but be attended with an extraordinary Expence; and it was some Difficulty, when they were first talk'd of, to bring them under a moderate Sum; I shall therefore, in as few Words as possible, give a Particular of what Establishment they were then brought to, that in case the same Entertainments should at any time hereafter be call'd to the same Place, future Courts may judge how far the Precedent may stand good, or need an Alteration.

English language, asked the lord-chamberlain the meaning of their mirth; upon being informed of it, the king joined in a laugh of approbation." Davies adds that this scene "was not unsuitably represented by Colley Cibber;" but, in scenes requiring dignity or passion, he expresses an unfavourable opinion of Cibber's playing.

Though the stated Fee for a Play acted at *Whitehall* had been formerly but Twenty Pounds;[1] yet, as that hinder'd not the Company's acting on the same Day at the Publick Theatre, that Sum was almost all clear Profits to them: But this Circumstance not being practicable when they were commanded to *Hampton-Court*, a new and extraordinary Charge was unavoidable: The Menagers, therefore, not to inflame it, desired no Consideration for their own Labour, farther than the Honour of being employ'd in his Majesty's Commands; and, if the other Actors might be allow'd each their Day's Pay and travelling Charges, they should hold themselves ready to act any Play there at a Day's Warning: And that the Trouble might be less by being divided, the Lord-Chamberlain was pleas'd to let us know that the Houshold-Musick, the Wax Lights, and a *Chaise-Marine* to carry our moving Wardrobe to every different Play, should be under the Charge of the proper Officers Notwithstanding these Assistances, the Expence of every Play amounted to Fifty Pounds: Which Account, when all was over, was not only allow'd us, but his Majesty was graciously pleas'd to give the Menagers Two Hundred Pounds more for their particular Performance and Trouble in only

[1] From the Lord Chamberlain's Records it is clear that £10 was the fee for a play at Whitehall during the time of Charles I. If the performance was at Hampton Court, or if it took place at such a time of day as to prevent the ordinary playing at the theatre, £20 was allowed.

seven times acting.[1] Which last Sum, though it might not be too much for a Sovereign Prince to give, it was certainly more than our utmost Merit ought to have hop'd for: And I confess, when I receiv'd the Order for the Money from his Grace the Duke of *Newcastle*, then Lord-Chamberlain, I was so surpris'd, that I imagin'd his Grace's Favour, or Recommendation of our Readiness or Diligence, must have contributed to so high a Consideration of it, and was offering my Acknowledgments as I thought them due; but was soon stopt short by his Grace's Declaration, That we had no Obligations for it but to the King himself, who had given it from no other Motive than his own Bounty. Now whether we may suppose that Cardinal *Wolsey* (as you see *Shakespear* has drawn him) would silently have taken such low Acknowledgments to himself, perhaps may be as little worth consideration as my mentioning this Circumstance has been necessary. But if it is due to the Honour and Integrity of the (then) Lord-Chamberlain, I cannot think it wholly impertinent.

Since that time there has been but one Play given at *Hampton-Court*, which was for the Entertainment of the Duke of *Lorrain*; and for which his present

---

[1] The warrant for the payment of these performances is dated 15th November, 1718. The expenses incurred by the actors amounted to £374 1s. 8d, and the present given by the King, as Cibber states, was £200, the total payment being thus £574 1s 8d.

Majesty was pleased to order us a Hundred Pounds.

The Reader may now plainly see that I am ransacking my Memory for such remaining Scraps of Theatrical History as may not perhaps be worth his Notice: But if they are such as tempt me to write them, why may I not hope that in this wide World there may be many an idle Soul, no wiser than my self, who may be equally tempted to read them?

I have so often had occasion to compare the State of the Stage to the State of a Nation, that I yet feel a Reluctancy to drop the Comparison, or speak of the one without some Application to the other. How many Reigns, then, do I remember, from that of *Charles* the Second, through all which there has been, from one half of the People or the other, a Succession of Clamour against every different Ministry for the time being? And yet, let the Cause of this Clamour have been never so well grounded, it is impossible but that some of those Ministers must have been wiser and honester Men than others. If this be true, as true I believe it is, why may I not then say, as some Fool in a *French* Play does upon a like Occasion—*Justement, comme chez nous!* 'Twas exactly the same with our Menagement! let us have done never so well, we could not please every body: All I can say in our Defence is, that though many good Judges might possibly conceive how the State of the Stage might have been mended, yet the best of them never pretended to remember the Time when it was better[1] or could shew us the way to make their imaginary Amendments practicable.

For though I have often allow'd that our best Merit as Actors was never equal to that of our Predecessors, yet I will venture to say, that in all its Branches the Stage had never been under so just, so prosperous, and so settled a Regulation, for forty Years before, as it was at the Time I am speaking of. The most plausible Objection to our Administration seemed to be, that we took no Care to breed up young Actors to succeed us;[1] and this was imputed as the greater Fault, because it was taken for granted that it was a Matter as easy as planting so many Cabbages: Now, might not a Court as well be reproached for not breeding up a Succession of complete Ministers? And yet it is evident, that if Providence or Nature don't supply us with both, the State and the Stage will be but poorly supported. If a Man of an ample Fortune should take it into his Head to give a younger Son an extraordinary Allowance in order to breed him a great Poet, what might we suppose would be the Odds that his Trouble and Money would be all thrown away? Not more than it would be against the Master of a Theatre who should say, this or that young Man I will take care shall be an excellent Actor! Let it be our

---

[1] M Perrin, the late manager of the Theatre Français, was virulently attacked for giving *la jeune troupe* no opportunities, and so doing nothing to provide successors to the great actors of his time.

Excuse, then, for that mistaken Charge against us; that since there was no Garden or Market where accomplished Actors grew or were to be sold, we could only pick them up, as we do Pebbles of Value, by Chance: We may polish a thousand before we can find one fit to make a Figure in the Lid of a Snuff-Box. And how few soever we were able to produce, it is no Proof that we were not always in search of them: Yet, at worst, it was allow'd that our Deficiency of Men Actors was not so visible as our Scarcity of tolerable Women: But when it is consider'd, that the Life of Youth and Beauty is too short for the bringing an Actress to her Perfection; were I to mention, too, the many frail fair Ones I remember who, before they could arrive to their Theatrical Maturity, were feloniously stolen from the Tree, it would rather be thought our Misfortune than our Fault that we were not better provided.[1]

Even the Laws of a Nunnery, we find, are thought no sufficient Security against Temptations without Iron Grates and high Walls to inforce them; which the Architecture of a Theatre will not so properly admit of: And yet, methinks, Beauty that has not those artificial Fortresses about it, that has no Defence but its natural Virtue (which upon the Stage

[1] After the death of Wilks and Booth, and the retirement of Cibber, the stage experienced a period of dulness, which was the natural result of the want of good young talent in the lifetime of the old actors. Such periods seem to recur at stated intervals in the history of the stage.

SUSANNA MARIA CIBBER

has more than once been met with) makes a much more meritorious Figure in Life than that immur'd Virtue which could never be try'd. But alas! as the poor Stage is but the Show-glass to a Toy-shop, we must not wonder if now and then some of the Bawbles should find a Purchaser.

However, as to say more or less than Truth are equally unfaithful in an Historian, I cannot but own that, in the Government of the Theatre, I have known many Instances where the Merit of promising Actors has not always been brought forward, with the Regard or Favour it had a Claim to: And if I put my Reader in mind, that in the early Part of this Work I have shewn thro' what continued Difficulties and Discouragements I myself made my way up the Hill of Preferment, he may justly call it too strong a Glare of my Vanity: I am afraid he is in the right; but I pretend not to be one of those chaste Authors that know how to write without it: When Truth is to be told, it may be as much Chance as Choice if it happens to turn out in my Favour: But to shew that this was true of others as well as myself, *Booth* shall be another Instance. In 1707, when *Swiney* was the only Master of the Company in the *Hay-Market*; *Wilks*, tho' he was then but an hired Actor himself, rather chose to govern and give Orders than to receive them; and was so jealous of *Booth*'s rising, that with a high Hand he gave the Part of *Pierre*, in *Venice Preserv'd*, to *Mills* the elder, who (not to undervalue him) was out of Sight in the Pretensions that *Booth*, then young as he was, had to the same Part:[1] and this very Discouragement so strongly affected him, that not long after, when several of us became Sharers with *Swiney*, *Booth* rather chose to risque his Fortune with the old Patentee in *Drury-Lane*, than come into our Interest, where he saw he was like to meet with more of those Partialities.[2] And yet, again, *Booth* himself, when he came to be a Menager, would sometimes suffer his Judgment to be blinded by his Inclination to Actors whom the Town seem'd to have but an indifferent Opinion of. This again inclines me to ask another of my odd Questions, *viz.* Have we never seen the same passions govern a Court! How many white Staffs and great Places do we find, in our Histories, have been laid at the Feet of a Monarch, because they chose not to give way to a Rival in Power, or hold a second Place in his Favour? How many *Whigs* and *Tories* have chang'd their Parties, when their good or bad Pretensions have met with a Check to their higher Preferment?

Thus we see, let the Degrees and Rank of Men be ever so unequal, Nature throws out their Passions from the same Motives; 'tis not the Eminence or Lowliness of either that makes the one, when provok'd, more or less a reasonable Creature than the

---

[1] "Venice Preserved" was acted at the Haymarket on 22nd February, 1707, but Dr. Burney's MSS. do not give the cast. On 15th November, 1707, Pierre was played by Mills.

[2] For an account of this matter, see *ante*, page 70.

other: The Courtier and the Comedian, when their Ambition is out of Humour, take just the same Measures to right themselves.

If this familiar Stile of talking should, in the Nostrils of Gravity and Wisdom, smell a little too much of the Presumptuous or the Pragmatical, I will at least descend lower in my Apology for it, by calling to my Assistance the old, humble Proverb, *viz*. *'Tis an ill Bird that, &c.* Why then should I debase my Profession by setting it in vulgar Lights, when I may shew it to more favourable Advantages? And when I speak of our Errors, why may I not extenuate them by illustrious Examples? or by not allowing them greater than the greatest Men have been subject to? Or why, indeed, may I not suppose that a sensible Reader will rather laugh than look grave at the Pomp of my Parallels?

Now, as I am tied down to the Veracity of an Historian whose Facts cannot be supposed, like those in a Romance, to be in the Choice of the Author to make them more marvellous by Invention; if I should happen to sink into a little farther Insignificancy, let the simple Truth of what I have farther to say, be my Excuse for it. I am obliged, therefore, to make the Experiment, by shewing you the Conduct of our Theatrical Ministry in such Lights as on various Occasions it appear'd in.

Though *Wilks* had more Industry and Application than any Actor I had ever known, yet we found it possible that those necessary Qualities might sometimes be so misconducted as not only to make them useless, but hurtful to our Common-wealth;[1] for while he was impatient to be foremost in every thing, he frequently shock'd the honest Ambition of others, whose Measures might have been more serviceable, could his Jealousy have given way to them. His own Regards for himself, therefore, were, to avoid a disagreeable Dispute with him, too often complied with: But this leaving his Diligence to his own Conduct, made us, in some Instances, pay dearly for it: For Example; he would take as much, or more Pains, in forwarding to the Stage the Water-gruel Work of some insipid Author that happen'd rightly to make his Court to him,[2] than he would for the

---

[1] Davies ("Dram Misc.," iii. 255) has the following interesting statement regarding Cibber and Wilks, which he gives on Victor's authority:—

"However Colley may complain, in his Apology, of Wilks's fire and impetuosity, he in general was Cibber's great admirer; he supported him on all occasions, where his own passion or interest did not interpose; nay, he deprived the inoffensive Harry Carey of the liberty of the scenes, because he had, in common with others, made merry with Cibber in a song, on his being appointed poet laureat, saying at the same time, he was surprised at his impertinence, in behaving so improperly *to a man of such great merit*"

[2] John Dennis, in an advertisement to the "Invader of his Country," remarks on this foible He says:—

"I am perfectly satisfied that any Author who brings a Play to *Drury-Lane*, must, if 'tis a good one, be sacrificed to the Jealousie of this fine Writer, unless he has either a powerful Cabal, or unless he will flatter Mr. *Robert Wilks*, and make him believe that he is an excellent Tragedian." The "fine Writer" is, of course, Cibber

best Play wherein it was not his Fortune to be chosen for the best Character. So great was his Impatience to be employ'd, that I scarce remember, in twenty Years, above one profitable Play we could get to be reviv'd, wherein he found he was to make no considerable Figure, independent of him: But the *Tempest* having done Wonders formerly, he could not form any Pretensions to let it lie longer dormant: However, his Coldness to it was so visible, that he took all Occasions to postpone and discourage its Progress, by frequently taking up the morning-Stage with something more to his Mind. Having been myself particularly solicitous for the reviving this Play, *Dogget* (for this was before *Booth* came into the Menagement) consented that the extraordinary Decorations and Habits should be left to my Care and Direction, as the fittest Person whose Temper could jossle through the petulant Opposition that he knew *Wilks* would be always offering to it, because he had but a middling Part in it, that of *Ferdinand*: Notwithstanding which, so it happen'd, that the Success of it shew'd (not to take from the Merit of *Wilks*) that it was possible to have good Audiences without his extraordinary Assistance. In the first six Days of acting it we paid all our constant and incidental Expence, and shar'd each of us a hundred Pounds: The greatest Profit that in so little a Time had yet been known within my Memory! But, alas! what was paltry Pelf to Glory? That was the darling Passion of *Wilks*'s Heart! and not to advance in it was, to so jealous an Ambition, a painful Retreat, a mere Shade to his Laurels! and the common Benefit was but a poor Equivalent to his want of particular Applause! To conclude, not Prince *Lewis* of *Baden*, though a Confederate General with the Duke of *Marlborough*, was more inconsolable upon the memorable Victory at *Blenheim*, at which he was not present, than our Theatrical Hero was to see any Action prosperous that he was not himself at the Head of. If this, then, was an Infirmity in *Wilks*, why may not my shewing the same Weakness in so great a Man mollify the Imputation, and keep his Memory in Countenance.

This laudable Appetite for Fame in *Wilks* was not, however, to be fed without that constant Labour which only himself was able to come up to: He therefore bethought him of the means to lessen the Fatigue, and at the same time to heighten his Reputation; which was, by giving up now and then a Part to some raw Actor who he was sure would disgrace it, and consequently put the Audience in mind of his superior Performance: Among this sort of Indulgences to young Actors he happen'd once to make a Mistake that set his Views in a clear Light. The best Criticks, I believe, will allow that in *Shakespear*'s *Macbeth* there are, in the Part of *Macduff*, two Scenes, the one of Terror, in the second Act, and the other of Compassion, in the fourth, equal to any that dramatick Poetry has produc'd: These Scenes *Wilks* had acted with Success, tho' far short of that happier

Skill and Grace which *Monfort* had formerly shewn in them.[1] Such a Part, however, one might imagine would be one of the last a good Actor would chuse to part with: But *Wilks* was of a different Opinion; for *Macbeth* was thrice as long, had more great Scenes of Action, and bore the Name of the Play: Now, to be a second in any Play was what he did not much care for, and had been seldom us'd to. This Part of *Macduff*, therefore, he had given to one *Williams*, as yet no extraordinary, though a promising Actor.[2] *Williams*, in the Simplicity of his Heart, immediately

[1] "In the trajedy of *Mackbeth*, where *Wilks* acts the Part of a Man whose Family has been murder'd in his Absence, the Wildness of his Passion, which is run over in a Torrent of calamitous Circumstances; does but raise my Spirits and give me the Alarm, but when he skilfully seems to be out of Breath, and is brought too low to say more, and upon a second Reflection, cry, only wiping his Eyes, What, both my Children! Both, both my Children gone—There is no resisting a Sorrow which seems to have cast about for all the Reasons possible for its Consolation, but has no Recource. There is not one left, but both, both are murdered! Such sudden Starts from the Thread of the Discourse, and a plain Sentiment express'd in an artless Way, are the irresistible Strokes of Eloquence and Poetry"—"Tatler," No. 68, September 15th, 1709.

The extraordinary language of Macduff is quoted from Davenant's mutilation of Shakespeare's play. Obviously it is not Shakespeare's language.

[2] Charles Williams was a young actor of great promise, who died in 1731. On the production of Thomson's "Sophonisba" at Drury Lane, on February 28th, 1730, Cibber played Scipio, but was so hissed by a public that would not suffer him in tragic parts, that he resigned the character to Williams (See Note [1], vol. 1. page 179) This would seem to indicate that Williams was an actor of some position, for Scipio is a good part.

told *Booth* what a Favour *Wilks* had done him. *Booth*, as he had Reason, thought *Wilks* had here carried his Indulgence and his Authority a little too far; for as *Booth* had no better a Part in the same Play than that of *Banquo*, he found himself too much disregarded in letting so young an Actor take Place of him: *Booth*, therefore, who knew the Value of *Macduff*, proposed to do it himself, and to give *Banquo* to *Williams*; and to make him farther amends, offer'd him any other of his Parts that he thought might be of Service to him. *Williams* was content with the Exchange, and thankful for the Promise. This Scheme, indeed, (had it taken Effect) might have been an Ease to *Wilks*, and possibly no Disadvantage to the Play; but softly——That was not quite what we had a Mind to! No sooner, then, came this Proposal to *Wilks*, but off went the Masque and out came the Secret! For though *Wilks* wanted to be eas'd of the Part, he did not desire to be *excell'd* in it; and as he was not sure but that might be the case if *Booth* were to act it,[1] he wisely retracted his

---

[1] "In the strong expression of horror on the murder of the King, and the loud exclamations of surprize and terror, Booth might have exceeded the utmost efforts of Wilks. But, in the touches of domestic woe, which require the feelings of the tender father and the affectionate husband, Wilks had no equal His skill, in exhibiting the emotions of the overflowing heart with corresponding look and action, was universally admired and felt. His rising, after the suppression of his anguish, into ardent and manly resentment, was highly expressive of noble and generous anger."—"Dram Misc.," ii. 183

own Project, took *Macduff* again to himself, and while he liv'd never had a Thought of running the same Hazard by any farther Offer to resign it.

Here I confess I am at a Loss for a Fact in History to which this can be a Parallel! To be weary of a Post, even to a real Desire of resigning it; and yet to chuse rather to drudge on in it than suffer it to be well supplied (though to share in that Advantage) is a Delicacy of Ambition that *Machiavil* himself has made no mention of: Or if in old *Rome*, the Jealousy of any pretended Patriot equally inclin'd to abdicate his Office may have come up to it, 'tis more than my reading remembers.

As nothing can be more impertinent than shewing too frequent a Fear to be thought so, I will, without farther Apology, rather risque that Imputation than not tell you another Story much to the same purpose, and of no more consequence than my last. To make you understand it, however, a little Preface will be necessary.

If the Merit of an Actor (as it certainly does) consists more in the Quality than the Quantity of his Labour; the other Menagers had no visible Reason to think this needless Ambition of *Wilks*, in being so often and sometimes so unnecessarily employ'd, gave him any Title to a Superiority; especially when our Articles of Agreement had allow'd us all to be equal. But what are narrow Contracts to great Souls with growing Desires? *Wilks*, therefore, who thought himself lessen'd in appealing to any Judgment but his own, plainly discovered by his restless Behaviour (though he did not care to speak out) that he thought he had a Right to some higher Consideration for his Performance: This was often *Booth*'s Opinion, as well as my own. It must be farther observ'd, that he actually had a separate Allowance of Fifty Pounds a Year for writing our daily Play-Bills for the Printer: Which Province, to say the Truth, was the only one we car'd to trust to his particular Intendance, or could find out for a Pretence to distinguish him. But, to speak a plainer Truth, this Pension, which was no part of our original Agreement, was merely paid to keep him quiet, and not that we thought it due to so insignificant a Charge as what a Prompter had formerly executed. This being really the Case, his frequent Complaints of being a Drudge to the Company grew something more than disagreeable to us: For we could not digest the Imposition of a Man's setting himself to work, and then bringing in his own Bill for it. *Booth*, therefore, who was less easy than I was to see him so often setting a Merit upon this Quantity of his Labour, which neither could be our Interest or his own to lay upon him, proposed to me that we might remove this pretended Grievance by reviving some Play that might be likely to live, and be easily acted, without *Wilks*'s having any Part in it. About this time an unexpected Occasion offer'd itself to put our Project in practice: What follow'd our Attempt will be all (if any thing be) worth Observation in my Story.

In 1725 we were call'd upon, in a manner that could not be resisted, to revive the *Provok'd Wife*,[1] a Comedy which, while we found our Account in keeping the Stage clear of those loose Liberties it had formerly too justly been charg'd with, we had laid aside for some Years.[2] The Author, Sir *John Vanbrugh*, who was conscious of what it had too much of, was prevail'd upon[3] to substitute a new-written Scene in the Place of one in the fourth Act, where the Wantonness of his Wit and Humour had (originally) made a Rake[4] talk like a Rake in the borrow'd Habit of a Clergyman: To avoid which Offence, he clapt the same Debauchee into the Undress of a Woman of Quality: Now the Character and Profession of a Fine Lady not being so indelibly sacred as that of a Churchman, whatever Follies he expos'd in the Petticoat kept him at least clear of his former Prophaneness,

---

[1] This revival took place 11th January, 1726. The play was acted eleven times.

[2] Jeremy Collier specially attacked Vanbrugh and his comedies for their immorality and profanity, and for their abuse of the clergy. Even less strict critics than Collier considered Vanbrugh's pieces as more indecent than the average play. Thus the author of "Faction Display'd," 1704, writes:—

"*Van's* Baudy, Plotless Plays were once our boast,
But now the Poet's in the Builder lost."

[3] Davies ("Dram. Misc.," iii. 455) says that he supposes Cibber prevailed upon Vanbrugh to alter the disguise which Sir John Brute assumes from a clergyman's habit to that of a woman of fashion.

[4] Sir John Brute.

and were now innocently ridiculous to the Spectator.

This Play being thus refitted for the Stage, was, as I have observ'd, call'd for from Court and by many of the Nobility.[1] Now, then, we thought, was a proper time to come to an Explanation with *Wilks:* Accordingly, when the Actors were summon'd to hear the Play read and receive their Parts, I address'd myself to *Wilks*, before them all, and told him, That as the Part of *Constant*, which he seem'd to chuse, was a Character of less Action than he generally appear'd in, we thought this might be a good Occasion to ease himself by giving it to another.—Here he look'd grave.—That the Love-Scenes of it were rather serious than gay or humourous, and therefore might sit very well upon *Booth*.——Down dropt his Brow, and furl'd were his Features.—That if we were never to revive a tolerable Play without him, what would become of us in case of his Indisposition?——Here he pretended to stir the Fire.—That as he could have no farther Advantage or Advancement in his Station to hope for, his acting in this Play was but giving himself an unprofitable Trouble, which neither *Booth* or I desired to impose upon him.—Softly.—Now the Pill began to

---

[1] Cibber's meaning is not very clear, but if he intends to convey the idea that it was for this revival that Vanbrugh made these alterations, he is probably wrong, for when the play was revived at the Haymarket, on 19th January, 1706, it was announced as "with alterations."

gripe him.——In a Word, this provoking Civility plung'd him into a Passion which he was no longer able to contain; out it came, with all the Equipage of unlimited Language that on such Occasions his Displeasure usually set out with; but when his Reply was stript of those Ornaments, it was plainly this: That he look'd upon all I had said as a concerted Design, not only to signalize our selves by laying him aside, but a Contrivance to draw him into the Disfavour of the Nobility, by making it suppos'd his own Choice that he did not act in a Play so particularly ask'd for; but we should find he could stand upon his own Bottom, and it was not all our little caballing should get our Ends of him: To which I answer'd with some Warmth, That he was mistaken in our Ends; for Those, Sir, said I, you have answer'd already by shewing the Company you cannot bear to be left out of any Play. Are not you every Day complaining of your being over-labour'd? And now, upon our first offering to ease you, you fly into a Passion, and pretend to make that a greater Grievance than t'other: But, Sir, if your being In or Out of the Play is a Hardship, you shall impose it upon yourself: The Part is in your Hand, and to us it is a Matter of Indifference now whether you take it or leave it. Upon this he threw down the Part upon the Table, cross'd his Arms, and sate knocking his Heel upon the Floor, as seeming to threaten most when he said least; but when no body persuaded him to take it up again, *Booth*, not chusing to push the matter too far, but rather to split the difference of our Dispute, said, That, for his Part, he saw no such great matter in acting every Day; for he believed it the wholsomest Exercise in the World; it kept the Spirits in motion, and always gave him a good Stomach. Though this was, in a manner, giving up the Part to *Wilks*, yet it did not allow he did us any Favour in receiving it. Here I observ'd Mrs. *Oldfield* began to titter behind her Fan: But *Wilks* being more intent upon what *Booth* had said, reply'd, Every one could best feel for himself, but he did not pretend to the Strength of a Pack-horse; therefore if Mrs. *Oldfield* would chuse any body else to play with her,[1] he should be very glad to be excus'd: This throwing the Negative upon Mrs. *Oldfield* was, indeed, a sure way to save himself; which I could not help taking notice of, by saying, It was making but an ill Compliment to the Company to suppose there was but one Man in it fit to play an ordinary Part with her. Here Mrs. *Oldfield* got up, and turning me half round to come forward, said with her usual Frankness, Pooh! you are all a Parcel of Fools, to make such a rout about nothing! Rightly judging that the Person most out of humour would not be more displeas'd at her calling us all by the same Name. As she knew, too, the best way of ending the Debate would be to help the Weak; she said, she hop'd Mr. *Wilks* would not so far mind what had past as to refuse his acting the Part with

---

[1] Mrs. Oldfield played Lady Brute, whose lover Constant is.

her; for tho' it might not be so good as he had been us'd to, yet she believed those who had bespoke the Play would expect to have it done to the best Advantage, and it would make but an odd Story abroad if it were known there had been any Difficulty in that point among ourselves. To conclude, *Wilks* had the Part, and we had all we wanted; which was an Occasion to let him see, that the Accident or Choice of one Menager's being more employ'd than another would never be allow'd a Pretence for altering our Indentures, or his having an extraordinary Consideration for it.[1]

However disagreeable it might be to have this unsociable Temper daily to deal with; yet I cannot but say, that from the same impatient Spirit that had so often hurt us, we still drew valuable Advantages: For as *Wilks* seem'd to have no Joy in Life beyond his being distinguish'd on the Stage, we were not only sure of his always doing his best there himself, but of making others more careful than without the Rod of so irascible a Temper over them they would have been. And I much question if a more temperate or better Usage of the hired Actors could have so effectually kept them to Order. Not even *Betterton* (as we have seen) with all his good Sense, his great Fame and Experience, could, by being only a quiet Example of Industry himself, save his Company from falling, while neither Gentleness could

---

[1] Wilks played Constant; Booth, Heartfree; and Cibber, Sir John Brute.

govern or the Consideration of their common Interest reform them.¹ Diligence, with much the inferior Skill or Capacity, will beat the best negligent Company that ever came upon a Stage. But when a certain dreaming Idleness or jolly Negligence of Rehearsals gets into a Body of the Ignorant and Incapable (which before *Wilks* came into *Drury-Lane*, when *Powel* was at the Head of them, was the Case of that Company) then, I say, a sensible Spectator might have look'd upon the fallen Stage as *Portius* in the Play of *Cato* does upon his ruin'd Country, and have lamented it in (something near) the same Exclamation, *viz.*

— O ye Immortal Bards !
What Havock do these Blockheads make among
    your Works !
How are the boasted Labours of an Age
*Defac'd and tortur'd by Ungracious Action?*²

Of this wicked Doings *Dryden*, too, complains in one of his Prologues at that time, where, speaking of such lewd Actors, he closes a Couplet with the following Line, *viz.*

*And murder Plays, which they miscall Reviving.*³

---

¹ Cibber begins the seventh chapter of this work with an account of Betterton's troubles as a manager. See vol. i p 227. See also vol. i. p 315.

² "Ye Gods, what Havock does Ambition make
Among your Works !"—"Cato," act I. sc. I.

³ "And, in despair their empty pit to fill,
Set up some Foreign monster in a bill.

The great Share, therefore, that *Wilks*, by his exemplary Diligence and Impatience of Neglect in others, had in the Reformation of this Evil, ought in Justice to be remember'd; and let my own Vanity here take Shame to itself when I confess, That had I had half his Application, I still think I might have shewn myself twice the Actor that in my highest State of Favour I appear'd to be. But if I have any Excuse for that Neglect (a Fault which, if I loved not Truth, I need not have mentioned) it is that so much of my Attention was taken up in an incessant Labour to guard against our private Animosities, and preserve a Harmony in our Menagement, that I hope and believe it made ample Amends for whatever Omission my Auditors might sometimes know it cost me some pains to conceal. But Nature takes care to bestow her Blessings with a more equal Hand than Fortune does, and is seldom known to heap too many upon one Man: One tolerable Talent in an Individual is enough to preserve him from being good for nothing; and, if that was not laid to my Charge as an Actor, I have in this Light too, less to complain of than to be thankful for.

Before I conclude my History, it may be expected I should give some further View of these my last Cotemporaries of the Theatre, *Wilks* and *Booth*, in their different acting Capacities. If I were to paint

> Thus they jog on, still tricking, never thriving,
> And murdering plays, which they miscall reviving."
> "Address to Granville, on his Tragedy, *Heroic Love.*"

them in the Colours they laid upon one another, their Talents would not be shewn with half the Commendation I am inclined to bestow upon them, when they are left to my own Opinion. But People of the same Profession are apt to see themselves in their own clear Glass of Partiality, and look upon their Equals through a Mist of Prejudice. It might be imagin'd, too, from the difference of their natural Tempers, that *Wilks* should have been more blind to the Excellencies of *Booth* than *Booth* was to those of *Wilks*; but it was not so : *Wilks* would sometimes commend *Booth* to me ; but when *Wilks* excell'd, the other was silent :[1] *Booth* seem'd to think nothing valuable that was not tragically Great or Marvellous : Let that be as true as it may; yet I have often thought that, from his having no Taste of Humour himself,[2] he might be too much inclin'd to depreciate the Acting of it in others. The very slight Opinion

---

[1] "During Booth's inability to act, ... Wilks was called upon to play two of his parts—Jaffier, and Lord Hastings in Jane Shore. Booth was, at times, in all other respects except his power to go on the stage, in good health, and went among the players for his amusement His curiosity drew him to the playhouse on the nights when Wilks acted these characters, in which himself had appeared with uncommon lustre. All the world admired Wilks, except his brother-manager : amidst the repeated bursts of applause which he extorted, Booth alone continued silent."—Davies ("Dram Misc.," iii. 256).

[2] Aaron Hill, quoted by Victor in his "Life of Barton Booth," page 32, says · "The Passions which he found in Comedy were not strong enough to excite his Fire ; and what seem'd Want of Qualification, was only Absence of Impression."

which in private Conversation with me he had of *Wilks*'s acting Sir *Harry Wildair*, was certainly more than could be justified; not only from the general Applause that was against that Opinion (tho' Applause is not always infallible) but from the visible Capacity which must be allow'd to an Actor, that could carry such slight Materials to such a height of Approbation: For, though the Character of *Wildair* scarce in any one Scene will stand against a just Criticism; yet in the Whole there are so many gay and false Colours of the fine Gentleman, that nothing but a Vivacity in the Performance proportionably extravagant could have made them so happily glare upon a common Audience.

Wilks, from his first setting out, certainly form'd his manner of Acting upon the Model of *Monfort*;[1] as *Booth* did his on that of *Betterton*. But——*Haud passibus æquis:* I cannot say either of them came up to their Original. *Wilks* had not that easy regulated Behaviour, or the harmonious Elocution of the One, nor *Booth* that Conscious Aspect of Intelligence nor requisite Variation of Voice that made every Line the Other spoke seem his own natural self-deliver'd Sentiment: Yet there is still room for great Commendation of Both the first mentioned; which will not be so much diminish'd in my having said they were only excell'd by such Predecessors, as it will be

[1] Wilks can have seen Mountfort only in his early career, for he did not leave Ireland till, at least, 1692, and in that year Mountfort was killed.

rais'd in venturing to affirm it will be a longer time before any Successors will come near them. Thus one of the greatest Praises given to *Virgil* is, that no Successor in Poetry came so near *Him* as *He* himself did to *Homer*.

Though the Majority of Publick Auditors are but bad judges of Theatrical Action, and are often deceiv'd into their Approbation of what has no solid Pretence to it; yet, as there are no other appointed Judges to appeal to, and as every single Spectator has a Right to be one of them, their Sentence will be definitive, and the Merit of an Actor must, in some degree, be weigh'd by it: By this Law, then, *Wilks* was pronounced an Excellent Actor; which, if the few true Judges did not allow him to be, they were at least too candid to slight or discourage him. *Booth* and he were Actors so directly opposite in their Manner, that if either of them could have borrowed a little of the other's Fault, they would Both have been improv'd by it · If *Wilks* had sometimes too violent a Vivacity; *Booth* as often contented himself with too grave a Dignity· The Latter seem'd too much to heave up his Words, as the other to dart them to the Ear with too quick and sharp a Vehemence: Thus *Wilks* would too frequently break into the Time and Measure of the Harmony by too many spirited Accents in one Line; and *Booth*, by too solemn a Regard to Harmony, would as often lose the necessary Spirit of it : So that (as I have observ'd) could we have sometimes rais'd the one and sunk the other, they had both been nearer to the mark. Yet this could not be always objected to them: They had their Intervals of unexceptionable Excellence, that more than balanc'd their Errors. The Master-piece of *Booth* was *Othello:* There he was most in Character, and seemed not more to animate or please himself in it than his Spectators. 'Tis true he owed his last and highest Advancement to his acting *Cato:* But it was the Novelty and critical Appearance of that Character that chiefly swell'd the Torrent of his Applause: For let the Sentiments of a declaiming Patriot have all the Sublimity that Poetry can raise them to; let them be deliver'd, too, with the utmost Grace and Dignity of Elocution that can recommend them to the Auditor: Yet this is but one Light wherein the Excellence of an Actor can shine: But in *Othello* we may see him in the Variety of Nature. There the Actor is carried through the different Accidents of domestick Happiness and Misery, occasionally torn and tortur'd by the most distracting Passion that can raise Terror or Compassion in the Spectator. Such are the Characters that a Master Actor would delight in; and therefore in *Othello* I may safely aver that *Booth* shew'd himself thrice the Actor that he could in *Cato*. And yet his Merit in acting *Cato* need not be diminish'd by this Comparison.

Wilks often regretted that in Tragedy he had not the full and strong Voice of *Booth* to command and grace his Periods with: But *Booth* us'd to say, That if his Ear had been equal to it, *Wilks* had Voice enough to have shewn himself a much better Tragedian. Now, though there might be some Truth in this; yet these two Actors were of so mixt a Merit, that even in Tragedy the Superiority was not always on the same side: In Sorrow, Tenderness, or Resignation, *Wilks* plainly had the Advantage, and seem'd more pathetically to feel, look, and express his Calamity: But in the more turbulent Transports of the Heart, *Booth* again bore the Palm, and left all Competitors behind him. A Fact perhaps will set this Difference in a clearer Light. I have formerly seen *Wilks* act *Othello*,[1] and *Booth* the *Earl of Essex*,[2] in which they both miscarried: Neither the exclamatory Rage or Jealousy of the one, or the plaintive Distresses of the other, were happily executed, or became either of them; though in the contrary Characters they were both excellent.

When an Actor becomes and naturally Looks the Character he stands in, I have often observ'd it to have had as fortunate an Effect, and as much re-

---

[1] Wilks first played Othello in this country on June 22nd, 1710, for Cibber's benefit. Steele draws attention to the event in "Tatler," No 187, and in No 188 states his intention of stealing out to see it, "out of Curiosity to observe how *Wilks* and *Cibber* touch those Places where *Betterton* and *Sandford* so very highly excelled." Cibber was the Iago on this occasion. Steele probably found little to praise in either.

[2] The Earl of Essex, in Banks's "Unhappy Favourite," was one of Wilks's good parts, in which Steele ("Tatler," No. 14) specially praises him. Booth acted the part at Drury Lane on November 25th, 1709.

commended him to the Approbation of the common Auditors, as the most correct or judicious Utterance of the Sentiments: This was strongly visible in the favourable Reception *Wilks* met with in *Hamlet*, where I own the Half of what he spoke was as painful to my Ear as every Line that came from *Betterton* was charming;[1] and yet it is not impossible, could they have come to a Poll, but *Wilks* might have had a Majority of Admirers: However, such a Division had been no Proof that the Præeminence had not still remain'd in *Betterton*; and if I should add that *Booth*, too, was behind *Betterton* in *Othello*, it would be saying no more than *Booth* himself had Judgment and Candour enough to know and confess. And if both he and *Wilks* are allow'd, in the two above-mention'd Characters, a second Place to so great a Master as *Betterton*, it will be a Rank of Praise that the best Actors since my Time might have been proud of.

I am now come towards the End of that Time through which our Affairs had long gone forward in a settled Course of Prosperity. From the Visible Errors of former Menagements we had at last found the necessary Means to bring our private Laws and Orders into the general Observance and Approbation of our Society: Diligence and Neglect were under an equal Eye; the one never fail'd of its Reward, and the other, by being very rarely excus'd,

---

[1] See Cibber on Betterton's Hamlet and on Wilks's mistakes in the part, vol 1. page 100.

was less frequently committed. You are now to consider us in our height of Favour, and so much in fashion with the politer Part of the Town, that our House every *Saturday* seem'd to be the appointed Assembly of the First Ladies of Quality: Of this, too, the common Spectators were so well appriz'd, that for twenty Years successively, on that Day, we scarce ever fail'd of a crowded Audience; for which Occasion we particularly reserv'd our best Plays, acted in the best Manner we could give them.[1]

Among our many necessary Reformations; what not a little preserv'd to us the Regard of our Auditors, was the Decency of our clear Stage;[2] from whence we had now, for many Years, shut out those idle Gentlemen, who seem'd more delighted to be pretty Objects themselves, than capable of any Pleasure from the Play: Who took their daily Stands where they might best elbow the Actor, and come in for their Share of the Auditor's Attention. In many a labour'd Scene of the warmest Humour and of the most affecting Passion have I seen the best Actors disconcerted, while these buzzing Muscatos have been fluttering round their Eyes and Ears. How was it possible an Actor, so embarrass'd, should keep his Impatience from entering into that different

---

[1] In the Theatre Français a similar arrangement holds to this day, Tuesday being now the fashionable night. M. Perrin, the late manager, was accused of a too great attention to his *Abonnés du Mardi*, to the detriment of the theatre and of the general public.

[2] See *ante*, vol. i. page 234.

Temper which his personated Character might require him to be Master of?

Future Actors may perhaps wish I would set this Grievance in a stronger Light; and, to say the Truth, where Auditors are ill-bred, it cannot well be expected that Actors should be polite. Let me therefore shew how far an Artist in any Science is apt to be hurt by any sort of Inattention to his Performance.

While the famous *Corelli*,[1] at *Rome*, was playing some Musical Composition of his own to a select Company in the private Apartment of his Patron-Cardinal, he observed, in the height of his Harmony, his Eminence was engaging in a detach'd Conversation; upon which he suddenly stopt short, and gently laid down his Instrument: The Cardinal, surpriz'd at the unexpected Cessation, ask'd him if a String was broke? To which *Corelli*, in an honest Conscience of what was due to his Musick, reply'd, No, Sir, I was only afraid I interrupted Business. His Eminence, who knew that a Genius could never shew itself to Advantage where it had not its proper Regards, took this Reproof in good Part, and broke off his Conversation to hear the whole *Concerto* play'd over again.

Another Story will let us see what Effect a mistaken Offence of this kind had upon the *French*

---

[1] Arcangelo Corelli, a famous Italian musician, born 1653, died 1713, who has been called the father of modern instrumental music.

Theatre; which was told me by a Gentleman of the long Robe, then at *Paris*, and who was himself the innocent Author of it. At the Tragedy of *Zaire*, while the celebrated Mademoiselle *Gossin*[1] was delivering a Soliloquy, this Gentleman was seiz'd with a sudden Fit of Coughing, which gave the Actress some Surprize and Interruption; and his Fit increasing, she was forced to stand silent so long, that it drew the Eyes of the uneasy Audience upon him; when a *French* Gentleman, leaning forward to him, ask'd him, If this Actress had given him any particular Offence, that he took so publick an Occasion to resent it? The *English* Gentleman, in the utmost Surprize, assured him, So far from it, that he was a particular Admirer of her Performance; that his Malady was his real Misfortune, and if he apprehended any Return of it, he would rather quit his Seat than disoblige either the Actress or the Audience.

This publick Decency in their Theatre I have myself seen carried so far, that a Gentleman in their *second Loge*, or Middle-Gallery, being observ'd to sit forward himself while a Lady sate behind him, a loud Number of Voices call'd out to him from the Pit, *Place à la Dame! Place à la Dame!* When the

---

[1] Jeanne Catherine Gaussin, a very celebrated actress of the Comédie Française, was the original representative of Zaire, in Voltaire's tragedy, to which Cibber refers. She made her first Parisian appearance in 1731, she retired in 1763, and died on 9th June, 1767. Voltaire's "Zaire" owed much of its success to her extraordinary ability.

Person so offending, either not apprehending the Meaning of the Clamour, or possibly being some *John Trott* who fear'd no Man alive; the Noise was continued for several Minutes; nor were the Actors, though ready on the Stage, suffer'd to begin the Play 'till this unbred Person was laugh'd out of his Seat, and had placed the Lady before him.

Whether this Politeness observ'd at Plays may be owing to their Clime, their Complexion, or their Government, is of no great Consequence; but if it is to be acquired, methinks it is pity our accomplish'd Countrymen, who every Year import so much of this Nation's gawdy Garniture, should not, in this long Course of our Commerce with them, have brought over a little of their Theatrical Good-breeding too.

I have been the more copious upon this Head, that it might be judg'd how much it stood us upon to have got rid of those improper Spectators I have been speaking of: For whatever Regard we might draw by keeping them at a Distance from our Stage, I had observed, while they were admitted behind our Scenes, we but too often shew'd them the wrong Side of our Tapestry; and that many a tolerable Actor was the less valued when it was known what ordinary Stuff he was made of.

Among the many more disagreeable Distresses that are almost unavoidable in the Government of a Theatre, those we so often met with from the Persecution of bad Authors were what we could never intirely get rid of. But let us state both our Cases, and then see where the Justice of the Complaint lies. 'Tis true, when an ingenious Indigent had taken perhaps a whole Summer's Pains, *invitâ Minervâ*, to heap up a Pile of Poetry into the Likeness of a Play, and found, at last, the gay Promise of his Winter's Support was rejected and abortive, a Man almost ought to be a Poet himself to be justly sensible of his Distress! Then, indeed, great Allowances ought to be made for the severe Reflections he might naturally throw upon those pragmatical Actors, who had no Sense or Taste of good Writing. And yet, if his Relief was only to be had by his imposing a bad Play upon a good Set of Actors, methinks the Charity that first looks at home has as good an Excuse for its Coldness as the unhappy Object of it had a Plea for his being reliev'd at their Expence. But immediate Want was not always confess'd their Motive for Writing; Fame, Honour, and *Parnassian* Glory had sometimes taken a romantick Turn in their Heads; and then they gave themselves the Air of talking to us in a higher Strain—Gentlemen were not to be so treated! the Stage was like to be finely govern'd when Actors pretended to be Judges of Authors, *&c.* But, dear Gentlemen! if they were good Actors, why not? How should they have been able to act, or rise to any Excellence, if you supposed them not to feel or understand what you offer'd them? Would you have reduc'd them to the meer Mimickry of Parrots and Monkies, that can only prate, and play a great many pretty Tricks, without Reflection? Or how are you sure your Friend, the infallible Judge to whom you read your fine Piece, might be sincere in the Praises he gave it? Or, indeed, might not you have thought the best Judge a bad one if he had disliked it? Consider, too, how possible it might be that a Man of Sense would not care to tell you a Truth he was sure you would not believe! And if neither *Dryden, Congreve, Steele, Addison,* nor *Farquhar,* (if you please) ever made any Complaint of their Incapacity to judge, why is the World to believe the Slights you have met with from them are either undeserved or particular? Indeed! indeed, I am not conscious that we ever did you or any of your Fraternity the least Injustice![1] Yet this was not all we had to struggle with; to

---

[1] Cibber has been strongly censured for his treatment of authors. "The Laureat" gives the following account of an author's experiences: "*The Court sitting, Chancellor Cibber* (for the other two, like M———rs in *Chancery,* sat only for Form sake, and did not presume to judge) nodded to the Author to open his Manuscript. The Author begins to read, in which if he failed to please the *Corrector,* he wou'd condescend sometimes to read it for him: When, if the play strook him very warmly, as it wou'd if he found any Thing new in it, in which he conceived he cou'd particularly shine as an Actor, he would lay down his Pipe, (for the *Chancellor* always smoaked when he made a Decree) and cry, *By G—d there is something in this: I do not know but it may do; but I will play such a Part.* Well, when the Reading was finished, he made his proper Corrections and sometimes without any Propriety; nay, frequently he very much and very hastily maimed what he pretended to mend" (p. 95). The author also accuses Cibber of delighting in repulsing dramatic writers, which he called

supersede our Right of rejecting, the Recommendation, or rather Imposition, of some great Persons (whom it was not Prudence to disoblige) sometimes came in with a high Hand to support their Pretensions; and then, *cout que cout*, acted it must be! So when the short Life of this wonderful Nothing was over, the Actors were perhaps abus'd in a Preface for obstructing the Success of it, and the Town publickly damn'd us for our private Civility.[1]

I cannot part with these fine Gentlemen Authors without mentioning a ridiculous *Disgraccia* that befel one of them many Years ago: This solemn Bard, who, like *Bays*, only writ for Fame and Reputation; on the second Day's publick Triumph of his Muse,

"Choaking of Singing birds." However, in Cibber's defence, Genest's opinion may be quoted (iii 346): "After all that has been said against Chancellor Cibber, it does not appear that he often made a wrong decree. most of the good plays came out at Drury Lane—nor am I aware that Cibber is much to be blamed for rejecting any play, except the Siege of Damascus in the first instance."

[1] In the preface to "The Lunatick" (1705) the actors are roundly abused, but the most amusing attack on actors is in the following title-page "The Sham Lawyer: or the Lucky Extravagant. As it was *Damnably* Acted at the Theatre-Royal in Drury Lane" This play, by Drake, was played in 1697, and among the cast were Cibber, Bullock, Johnson, Haines, and Pinkethman.

Bellchambers notes. "Such was the case in Dennis's 'Comic Gallant,' where one of the actors, whom I believe to be Bullock, is most severely handled" I think he is wrong in imagining Bullock to be the actor criticised. Dennis says that Falstaffe was the character that was badly sustained, and I cannot believe Bullock's position would entitle him to play that part in 1702. Genest (ii. 250) suggests Powell as the delinquent

marching in a stately full-bottom'd Perriwig into the
Lobby of the House, with a Lady of Condition in
his Hand, when raising his Voice to the Sir *Fopling*
Sound, that *became the Mouth of a Man of Quality*,
and calling out—Hey! Box-keeper, where is my
Lady such-a-one's Servant, was unfortunately answer'd by honest *John Trott*, (which then happen'd
to be the Box-keeper's real Name) Sir, we have dismiss'd, there was not Company enough to pay
Candles. In which mortal Astonishment it may be
sufficient to leave him. And yet had the Actors
refus'd this Play, what Resentment might have been
thought too severe for them?

Thus was our Administration often censured for
Accidents which were not in our Power to prevent:
A possible Case in the wisest Governments. If,
therefore, some Plays have been preferr'd to the
Stage that were never fit to have been seen there,
let this be our best Excuse for it. And yet, if the
Merit of our rejecting the many bad Plays that
press'd hard upon us were weigh'd against the
few that were thus imposed upon us, our Conduct in
general might have more Amendments of the Stage
to boast of than Errors to answer for. But it is now
Time to drop the Curtain.

During our four last Years there happen'd so very
little unlike what has been said before, that I shall
conclude with barely mentioning those unavoidable
Accidents that drew on our Dissolution. The first,
that for some Years had led the way to greater, was

the continued ill State of Health that render'd *Booth*[1] incapable of appearing on the Stage. The next was the Death of Mrs. *Oldfield*,[2] which happen'd on the 23d of *October*, 1730. About the same Time, too, Mrs. *Porter*, then in her highest Reputation for Tragedy, was lost to us by the Misfortune of a dislocated Limb from the overturning of a *Chaise*.[3] And our last Stroke was the Death of *Wilks*, in *September* the Year following, 1731.[4]

[1] Cibber's account of Booth is so complete that there is little to be added to it. Booth was born in 1681, and was of a good English family He first appeared in Dublin in 1698, under Ashbury, but returned to England in 1700, and joined the Lincoln's Inn Fields Company. He followed the fortunes of Betterton until, as related by Cibber in Chapter XII., the secession of 1709 occurred. From that point to his retirement the only event demanding special notice is his marriage with Hester Santlow (see p 96 of this volume). This took place in 1719, and was the cause of much criticism and slander, some of which Bellchambers reproduces with evident gusto. I do not repeat his statements, because I consider them wildly extravagant. They are fully refuted by Booth's will, from the terms of which it is clear that his marriage was a happy one, and that he esteemed his wife as well as loved her. Booth's illness, to which Cibber refers above, seized him early in the season of 1726-27, and though after it he was able to play occasionally, he was never restored to health. His last appearance was on 9th January, 1728, but he lived till 10th May, 1733.

[2] See memoir of Mrs. Oldfield at end of volume.

[3] Mrs. Porter met with the accident referred to in the summer of 1731. See Davies, "Dram Misc.," iii. 495. She returned to the stage in January, 1733

[4] Wilks died 27th September, 1732. He was of English parentage, and was born near Dublin, whither his father had removed, about 1665. He was in a Government office, but

Notwithstanding such irreparable Losses; whether, when these favourite Actors were no more to be had, their Successors might not be better born with than they could possibly have hop'd while the former were in being; or that the generality of Spectators, from their want of Taste, were easier to be pleas'd than the few that knew better: Or that, at worst, our Actors were still preferable to any other Company of the several then subsisting: Or to whatever Cause it might be imputed, our Audiences were far less abated than our Apprehensions had suggested. So that, though it began to grow late in Life with me; having still Health and Strength enough to have been as useful on the Stage as ever, I was under no visible Necessity of quitting it: But so it happen'd that our surviving Fraternity having got some chimærical, and, as I thought, unjust Notions into their Heads, which, though I knew they were without much Difficulty to be surmounted; I chose not, at my time of Day, to enter into new Contentions; and as I found an Inclination in some of them to purchase the whole Power of the Patent into their own Hands; I did my best while I staid

---

about 1691 he gave this up, and went on the stage. After a short probation in Dublin he came over to London, and was engaged by Rich, with whom he remained till about 1695. He returned to Dublin, and became so great a favourite there, that it is said that the Lord Lieutenant issued a warrant to prevent his leaving again for London. However, he came to Drury Lane about 1698, and from that time his fortunes are closely interwoven with Cibber's, and are fully related by him.

with them to make it worth their while to come up to my Price; and then patiently sold out my Share to the first Bidder, wishing the Crew I had left in the Vessel a good Voyage.[1]

What Commotions the Stage fell into the Year following, or from what Provocations the greatest Part of the Actors revolted, and set up for themselves in the little House in the *Hay-Market*, lies not within the Promise of my Title Page to relate: Or, as it might set some Persons living in a Light they possibly might not chuse to be seen in, I will rather be thankful for the involuntary Favour they have done me, than trouble the Publick with private Complaints of fancied or real Injuries.

FINIS

---

[1] "The Laureat," p 96. "As to the Occasion of your parting with your Share of the Patent, I cannot think you give us the true Reason, for I have been very well inform'd, it was the Intention, not only of you, but of your Brother Menagers, as soon as you could get the great Seal to your Patent, (which stuck for some Time, the then Lord *Chancellor* not being satisfied in the Legality of the Grant) to dispose it to the best Bidder. This was at first kept as a Secret among you, but as soon as the Grant was compleated, you sold to the first who wou'd come up to your Price."

SUPPLEMENTARY CHAPTER.

BY ROBERT W. LOWE.

THE transaction to which Cibber alludes in his last paragraph is one with regard to which he probably felt that his conduct required some explanation. After the death of Steele, a Patent was granted to Cibber, Wilks, and Booth, empowering them to give plays at Drury Lane, or elsewhere, for a period of twenty-one years from 1st September, 1732.[1]

---

[1] Among the Lord Chamberlain's Papers is a copy of a warrant to prepare this Patent. It is dated 15th May, 1731, and the Patent itself is dated 3rd July, 1731, though it did not take effect till 1st September, 1732. The reason for this is noted on page 196.

Just after it came into operation Wilks died, and his share in the Patent became the property of his wife. Booth, shortly before his death, which occurred in May, 1733, sold half of his share for £2,500, to John Highmore, a gentleman who seems to have been a typical amateur manager, being possessed of some money, no judgment, and unbounded vanity. In making this purchase Highmore stipulated that, with half of Booth's share, he should receive the whole of his authority; and he accordingly exercised the same power of control as had belonged to Booth. Mrs. Wilks deputed Mr. John Ellys, the painter, to be her representative, so that Cibber had to manage the affairs of the theatre in conjunction with a couple of amateurs, both ignorant, and one certainly presumptuous also. He delegated his authority for a time to his scapegrace son, Theophilus, who probably made himself so objectionable that Highmore was glad to buy the father's share in the Patent also.[1] He paid three thousand guineas for it, thus purchasing a whole share for a sum not much exceeding that which he had paid for one-half. Highmore's first purchase took place in the autumn of 1732, his second somewhere about May, 1733; so that, when Drury

---

[1] "The Grub-Street Journal," 7th June, 1733, says: "One little Creature, only the Deputy and Representative of his Father, was turbulent enough to balk their Measures, and counterbalance all the Civility and Decency in the other scale. . . . . To remedy this, the Gentleman who bought into the Patent first, purchased his Father's Share, and set him down in the same obscure Place from whence he rose"

Lane opened for the season 1733-34, he possessed one-half of the three shares into which the Patent was divided. Mrs. Wilks retained her share, but Mrs. Booth had sold her remaining half-share to Henry Giffard,[1] the manager of Goodman's Fields Theatre, at which, eight years later, Garrick made his first appearance. Highmore had scarcely entered upon his fuller authority when a revolt was spirited up among his actors, the chief of whom left him in a body to open the little theatre in the Haymarket. Shameful to relate, the ringleader in this mutiny was Theophilus Cibber; and, what is still more disgraceful, Colley Cibber lent them his active countenance. Benjamin Victor, though a devoted friend of Colley Cibber, characterizes the transaction as most dishonest,[2] and there is no reason to doubt the accuracy of his information or the soundness of his judgment. Davies ("Life of Garrick," i. 76) states that Colley

[1] In "The Case of John Mills, James Quin," &c, given in Theo. Cibber's "Dissertations" (Appendix, p. 48), it is stated that "such has been the Inveteracy of some of the late Patentees to the Actors, that when Mrs *Booth*, Executrix of her late Husband, *Barton Booth*, Esq; sold her sixth part of the Patent to Mr. *Giffard*, she made him covenant, not to sell or assign it to Actors"

[2] "I must own, I was heartily disgusted with the Conduct of the Family of the *Cibbers* on this Occasion, and had frequent and violent Disputes with Father and Son, whenever we met! It appeared to me something shocking that the Son should immediately render void, and worthless, what the Father had just received Thirty-one Hundred and Fifty Pounds for, as a valuable Consideration."—Victor's "History," 1. 14

Cibber applied to the Duke of Grafton, then Lord Chamberlain, for a new License or Patent in favour of his son; but the Duke, on inquiring into the matter, was so disgusted at Cibber's conduct that he refused the application with strong expressions of disapprobation. The seceders had of course no Patent or License under which to act; but, from the circumstance that they took the name of Comedians of His Majesty's Revels, it is probable that they received a License from the Master of the Revels, Charles Henry Lee. Highmore, deserted by every actor of any importance except Miss Raftor (Mrs. Clive), Mrs. Horton, and Bridgwater, was at his wits' end. He summoned the seceders for an infringement of his Patent, but his case, tried on 5th November, 1733, was dismissed, apparently on some technical plea. He could not prevail upon the Lord Chamberlain to exert his authority to close the Haymarket, so he determined to try the efficacy of the Vagrant Act (12 Queen Anne) against the irregular performers. John Harper accordingly was arrested on 12th November, 1733, and committed to Bridewell. On the 20th of the same month he was tried before the Court of King's Bench as a rogue and vagabond; but, whether from the circumstance that Harper was a householder, or from a decision that playing at the Haymarket was not an act of vagrancy,[1] he was discharged upon his own recogni-

[1] Cibber, in Chapter VIII. (vol 1 p 283), alludes to this trial, and gives the first of these two suppositions as the reason of

zance, and the manager's action failed. He had therefore to bring actors from the country to make up his company; but of these Macklin was the only one who proved of any assistance, and the unfortunate Highmore, after meeting deficiencies of fifty or sixty pounds each week for some months, was forced to give up the struggle.[1] Another amateur then stepped into the breach—Charles Fleetwood, who purchased the shares of Highmore and Mrs. Wilks for little more than the former had paid for his own portion. Giffard seems to have retained his sixth of the Patent. Fleetwood first set about regaining the services of the seceders, and, as the majority of them were probably ashamed of following the leadership of Theophilus Cibber, he succeeded at once. The last performance at the Haymarket took place on 9th March, 1734, and on the 12th the deserters reappeared on Drury Lane stage. This transaction ended Colley Cibber's direct interference in the affairs of the theatre, and his only subsequent connection with the stage was as an actor. His first appearance after his retirement was on 31st October, 1734, when he played his great character of Bayes. During the season he acted Lord Foppington, Sir

---

Harper's acquittal, but Victor ("History," i. 24) says that he has been informed that this is an error.

[1] "He was a Man of Humanity and strict Honour; many Instances fatally proved, that his Word, when solemnly given, (which was his Custom) was sufficient for the Performance, though ever so injurious to himself."—Victor's "History," i 25

John Brute, Sir Courtly Nice, and Sir Fopling Flutter; and on 26th February, 1735, he appeared as Fondlewife for the benefit of his old friend and partner, Owen Swiney.[1] At the end of the season 1734-5, an arrangement was under consideration by which a committee of actors, including Mills, Johnson, Miller, Theo. Cibber, Mrs. Heron, Mrs. Butler, and others, were to rent Drury Lane from Fleetwood, for fifteen years, at £920 per annum; but the arrangement does not appear to have been carried out, and Fleetwood continued Patentee of Drury Lane until 1744-5.

The rival company, under the control of John Rich, acted at Lincoln's Inn Fields from 18th December, 1714, to 5th December, 1732, then they removed to the new Covent Garden Theatre, which was opened on 7th December with "The Way of the World." For several seasons both companies dragged along very uneventfully, so far as the artistic advancement of the stage was concerned, although the passing of the Licensing Act of 1737, already fully commented on, was an event of great historical importance. Artistically the period was one of rest, if not of retrogression; the methods of the older time were losing their meaning and vitality, and were becoming mere dry bones of tradition. The high priest of the stage was James Quin, a great actor, though not of the first order; and among the younger players perhaps the most notable was Charles

[1] See *ante*, Chapter IX. (vol. 1 p. 330, note [1]).

Macklin, rough in manner as in person, but full of genius and a thorough reformer. Garrick was the direct means of revolutionizing the methods of the theatre, and it was his genius that swept away the formality and dulness of the old school; but it ought to be remembered that the way was prepared for him by Charles Macklin, whose rescue of Shylock from low comedy was an achievement scarcely inferior to Garrick's greatest. During this dull period Cibber's appearances must have had an importance and interest, which, after Garrick's advent, they lacked.

In the season 1735-6 he acted Sir Courtly Nice and Bayes, and in the next season his play of " Papal Tyranny in the Reign of King John," a miserable mutilation of Shakespeare's " King John," was put in rehearsal at Drury Lane. But such a storm of ridicule and abuse arose when this play was announced, that Cibber withdrew it,[1] and it was not seen till 1745, when, the nation being in fear of a Popish Pretender, it was produced at Covent Garden from patriotic motives.

Cibber's implacable foe, Fielding, was one of the ringleaders in the attack on him for mutilating Shakespeare; and in his " Historical Register for

[1] "The clamour against the author, whose presumption was highly censured for daring to alter Shakspeare, increased to such a height, that Colley, who had smarted more than once for dabbling in tragedy, went to the playhouse, and, without saying a word to any body, took the play from the prompter's desk, and marched off with it in his pocket."—" Dram. Misc ," 1. 5.

1736,"[1] in which Colley is introduced as "Ground-Ivy,"[2] gives him the following excellent rebuke.—

"*Medley.* As *Shakspear* is already good enough for People of Taste, he must be alter'd to the Palates of those who have none; and if you will grant that, who can be properer to alter him for the worse?"

In 1738, having, as Victor says ("History," ii. 48), "Health and Strength enough to be as useful as ever," he agreed with Fleetwood to perform a round of his favourite characters. He was successful in comedy, but in tragedy he felt that his strength was no longer sufficient; and Victor relates that, going behind the scenes while the third act of "Richard III." was on, he was told in a whisper by the old man, "That he would give fifty Guineas to be then sitting in his easy Chair by his own Fire-side." Probably

---

[1] Produced at the Haymarket, 1737.
[2]   "Enter Ground-Ivy.
Ground. What are you doing here?
Apollo. I am casting the Parts in the Tragedy of King *John*
Ground. Then you are casting the Parts in a Tragedy that won't do.
Apollo. How, Sir! Was it not written by *Shakespear*, and was not *Shakespear* one of the greatest Genius's that ever lived?
Ground No, Sir, *Shakespear* was a pretty Fellow, and said some things that only want a little of my licking to do well enough, King *John*, as now writ, will not do——But a Word in your Ear, I will make him do.
Apollo How?
Ground By Alteration, Sir, it was a Maxim of mine when I was at the Head of Theatrical Affairs, that no Play, tho' ever so good, would do without Alteration"—"Historical Register," act iii. sc 1.

he never played in tragedy again until the production of his own "Papal Tyranny"—at least I cannot discover that he did. In 1740-1 he acted Fondlewife for the benefit of Chetwood, late prompter at Drury Lane, who was then imprisoned in the King's Bench for debt; and his reception was so favourable that he repeated the character a second and third time for his own profit.[1] Upon these occasions he spoke an "Epilogue upon Himself," which is given in "The Egotist" (p. 57 *et seq.*), and forms so good an epitome of Cibber's philosophy, besides giving an excellent specimen of his style, that I quote it at length :—

> "Now worn with Years, and yet in Folly strong,
> Now to act Parts, your Grandsires saw when Young!
> What could provoke me!—I was always wrong
> To hope, with Age, I could advance in Merit!
> Even Age well acted, asks a youthful Spirit
> To feel my Wants, yet shew 'em thus detected,
> Is living to the Dotage, I have acted!
> T' have acted only Once excus'd might be,
> When I but play'd the Fool for Charity!
> But fondly to repeat it!—Senseless Ninny!
> —No—now—as Doctors do—I touch the Guinea!
> And while I find my Doses can affect you,
> 'Twere greater Folly still, should I neglect you.
> Though this Excuse, at *White's* they'll not allow me,
> The Ralliers There, in Diff'rent Lights will shew me.
> They'll tell you There : I only act—sly Rogue!
> To play with *Cocky*![2]—O! the doting Dog!
> And howsoe'er an Audience might regard me,

---

[1] These appearances took place on January 12th, 13th, and 14th, 1741.

[2] Fondlewife's pet name for his wife Lætitia.

> One—*tiss ye Nykin*,[1] amply might reward me!
> Let them enjoy the Jest, with Laugh incessant!
> For True, or False, or Right, or Wrong, 'tis pleasant!
> Mixt, in the wisest Heads, we find some Folly;
> Yet I find few such happy Fools—as *Colley!*
> So long t'have liv'd the daily Satire's Stroke, ⎫
> Unmov'd by Blows, that might have fell'd an Oak, ⎬
> And yet have laugh'd the labour'd Libel to a Joke. ⎭
> Suppose such want of Feeling prove me dull!
> What's my Aggressor then—a peevish Fool!
> The strongest Satire's on a Blockhead lost;
> For none but Fools or Madmen strike a Post.
> If for my Folly's larger List you call,
> My Life has lump'd 'em! There you'll read 'em all.
> There you'll find Vanity, wild Hopes pursuing,
> A wide Attempt: to save the Stage from Ruin!
> There I confess, I have *out-done* my *own out-doing!*[2]
> As for what's left of Life, if still 'twill do;
> 'Tis at your Service, pleas'd while pleasing you
> But then, mistake me not! when you've enough,
> One slender House declares both Parties off:
> Or Truth in homely Proverb to advance,
> I pipe no longer than you care to dance."

The representative of Lætitia (or *Cocky*) alluded to in this Epilogue was Mrs. Woffington, with whom stage-history has identified the "Susannah" of the following well-known anecdote, which I quote from an attack upon Cibber, published in 1742, entitled "A Blast upon *Bays*; or, A New Lick at the Laureat." The author writes: "No longer ago than when the *Bedford Coffee house* was in Vogue, and Mr. *Cibber* was writing *An Apology for his own Life*, there was

---

[1] Lætitia's pet name for Fondlewife. See vol. i page 206.
[2] An allusion to his own phrase in the Preface to "The Provoked Husband." See vol. i. page 51.

one Mr. *S——* (the Importer of an expensive *Haymarket* Comedy) an old Acquaintance of Mr. *Cibber*, who, as well as he, retain'd a Smack of his antient Taste. In those Days there was also a fair smirking Damsel, whose name was *Susannah-Maria* * * *, who happen'd to have Charms sufficient to revive the decay'd Vigour of these two Friends. They equally pursued her, even to the *Hazard of their Health*, and were frequently seen dangling after her, with tottering Knees, at one and the same Time. You have heard, Sir, what a witty Friend of your own said once on this Occasion: *Lo! yonder goes* Susannah *and the two Elders*." Even Genest has applied this anecdote to Mrs. Woffington, but the only circumstance that lends confirmation to this view is the fact that Swiney (who is Mr. S——) left her his estate. Against this must be set the important points that Susannah Maria was not Mrs. Woffington's name, and that the joke depended for its neatness and applicability on the name Susannah. The narrator of the story, also, gives no hint that the damsel was the famous actress, as he certainly would have done; and, most important of all, it must be pointed out that at the period mentioned, that is, while Cibber was writing his "Apology," Mrs. Woffington had not appeared in London. The "Apology" was published in April, 1740, and had probably been completed in the preceding November; while Mrs. Woffington made her London *début* on 6th November, 1740.[1]

[1] The name "Susannah Maria" naturally suggests Susanna Maria Arne, the wife of Theo. Cibber; but the anecdote cannot refer to

During the season 1741-2, "At the particular desire of several persons of Quality," Cibber made a few appearances at Covent Garden; the purpose being, in all probability, to oppose the extraordinary attraction of Garrick at Goodman's Fields. In 1743-4 he played at the same theatre as Garrick, being engaged at Drury Lane for a round of his famous characters; but there is no record that Garrick and he appeared in the same play. For the new actor Cibber had, naturally enough, no great admiration. He must have resented deeply the alteration in the method of acting tragedy which Garrick introduced, and is always reported as having lost no opportunity of expressing his low opinion of the new school.[1]

His last appearances on the stage were in direct rivalry with his young opponent. As has been related, Cibber's alteration of "King John," which had been "burked" in 1736-7, was produced, from patriotic motives, in 1745. As the principal purpose

her, because she was married in 1734, some years before Cibber began his "Apology"

[1] Davies ("Dram. Misc.," iii. 501) says . "Mr Garrick asked him [Cibber] if he had not in his possession, a comedy or two of his own writing.—'What then?' said Cibber —'I should be glad to have the honour of bringing it into the world '—'Who have you to act it?'—'Why, there are (said Garrick) Clive and Pritchard, myself, and some others,' whom he named.—'No! (said the old man, taking a pinch of snuff, with great nonchalance) it won't do '" Davies (iii. 502) relates how Garrick drew on himself a rebuke from Cibber. Discussing in company the old school, "Garrick observed that the old style of acting was banishing the stage, and would not go down   'How do you know? (said Cibber); you never tried it.'"

of the alteration was to make King John resent the insolence of the Pope's Nuncio in a much more emphatic manner than he does in Shakespeare, it may easily be imagined how wretched a production Cibber's play is. Genest's criticism is not too strong when he says (iv. 161): "In a word, Cibber has on this occasion shown himself utterly void of taste, judgment and modesty—well might Fielding call him Ground-Ivy, and say that no man was better calculated to alter Shakspeare for the worse . . . . in the Epilogue (which was spoken by Mrs. Clive) Cibber speaks of himself with modesty, but in the dedication, being emboldened by the favourable reception of his Tragedy, he has the insolence to say '*I have endeavoured to make it more like a play than I found it in Shakspeare.*'" "Papal Tyranny" was produced at Covent Garden on 15th February, 1745,[1]

---

[1] "Papal Tyranny in the Reign of King John"

KING JOHN	Mr Quin.
ARTHUR, his Nephew	Miss J Cibber.
SALISBURY	Mr. Ridout.
PEMBROKE	Mr. Rosco.
ARUNDEL	Mr. Anderson
FALCONBRIDGE.	Mr Ryan.
HUBERT	Mr Bridgewater.
KING PHILIP ⎫	⎧ Mr. Hale.
LEWIS the Dauphin ⎬ of France . . .	⎨ Mr Cibber, Jun.
MELUN, a Nobleman ⎭	⎩ Mr. Cashell
PANDULPH, Legate from Pope Innocent .	Mr. Cibber, Sen.
ABBOT ⎫ of Angiers	⎧ Mr. Gibson.
GOVERNOR ⎭	⎩ Mr Carr.
LADY CONSTANCE	Mrs. Pritchard.
BLANCH, Niece to King John . . .	Mrs. Bellamy

and, in opposition to it, Shakespeare's play was put up at Drury Lane, with Garrick as King John, Macklin as Pandulph, and Mrs. Cibber (the great Mrs. Cibber, wife of Theophilus) as Constance. Cibber's play was, nevertheless, successful; the profit resulting to the author being, according to Victor, four hundred pounds, which he wisely laid out in a profitable annuity with Lord Mountford. In this play Cibber made his last appearance on the stage, on 26th February, 1745, on which day "Papal Tyranny" was played for the tenth time. "After which," says Victor ("History," ii. 49) "he retired to his easy Chair and his Chariot, to waste the Remains of Life with a chearful, contented Mind, without the least bodily Complaint, but that of a slow, unavoidable Decay."

His state of mind was probably the more "chearful and contented" because of his unquestionable success in his tilt with the formidable author of "The Dunciad," a success none the less certain at the time, that the enduring fame of Pope has caused Cibber's triumph over him to be lost sight of now. The progress of the quarrel between these enemies has already been related up to the publication of Cibber's "Apology" (see vol 1 p. 36), and on pages 21, 35, and 36 of the first volume of this edition will be found Cibber's perfectly good-natured and proper remarks on Pope's attacks on him. Whether the very fact that Cibber did not show temper irritated his opponent, I do not know; but it probably did so, for in the fourth book of "The Dunciad," published in 1742, Pope had another fling at his opponent (line 17) :—

"She mounts the throne : her head a cloud conceal'd,
In broad effulgence all below reveal'd ;
('Tis thus aspiring Dulness ever shines ·)
Soft on her lap her laureate son reclines."

And in line 532 he talks of "Cibberian forehead" as typical of unblushing impudence.

It is not surprising that this last attack exhausted Cibber's patience. He had hitherto received his punishment with good temper and good humour; but his powerful enemy had not therefore held his hand. He now determined to retaliate. Conscious of the diseased susceptibility of Pope to ridicule, he felt himself quite capable of replying, not with equal literary power, but with much superior practical effect. Accordingly in 1742 there appeared a pamphlet entitled "A Letter from Mr. Cibber, to Mr. Pope, inquiring into the motives that might induce him in his Satyrical Works, to be so frequently fond of Mr. Cibber's name." To it was prefixed the motto. "*Out of thy own Mouth will I judge thee.* Pref. to the *Dunciad*."

Cibber commences by stating that he had been persuaded to reply to Pope by his friends; who insisted that for him to treat his attacker any longer with silent disdain might be thought a confession of Dulness indeed. This is a highly probable statement; for an encounter between the vivacious Cibber and the thin-skinned Pope promised a wealth of amusement for those who looked on—a promise which was amply fulfilled. Cibber proceeds to assure Pope that, having entered the lists, he will not in future avoid the fray, but reply to every attack made on him.[1] He confesses his vast inferiority to Pope, but adds: " I own myself so contented a Dunce, that I would not have even your merited Fame in Poetry, if it were to be attended with half the fretful Solicitude you seem to have lain under to maintain it; of which the laborious Rout you make about it, in those Loads of Prose Rubbish, wherewith you have almost smother'd your *Dunciad*, is so sore a Proof." On page 17 of his " Letter" Cibber gives an interesting account of a quarrel between Pope and himself, to which he, with sufficient probability, attributes much of Pope's enmity. The passage is curious and important, so I quote it in full.—

" The Play of the *Rehearsal*, which had lain some few Years dormant, being by his present Majesty (then Prince of *Wales*) commanded to be revived, the Part of *Bays* fell to my share. To this Character there had always been allow'd such ludicrous Liberties of Observation, upon any thing new, or

---

[1] " *On* CIBBER'S *Declaration that he will have the last Word with Mr* POPE.

QUOTH *Cibber* to *Pope*, tho' in Verse you foreclose,
I'll have the last Word, for by G—d I'll write Prose.
Poor *Colley*, thy reas'ning is none of the strongest,
For know, the last Word is the Word that lasts longest."
"The Summer Miscellany," 1742

ALEXANDER POPE

remarkable, in the state of the Stage, as Mr. *Bays* might think proper to take. Much about this time, then, *The Three Hours after Marriage* had been acted without Success;[1] when Mr. *Bays*, as usual, had a fling at it, which, in itself, was no Jest, unless the Audience would please to make it one: But however, flat as it was, Mr. *Pope* was mortally sore upon it. This was the Offence. In this Play, two Coxcombs, being in love with a learned Virtuoso's Wife, to get unsuspected Access to her, ingeniously send themselves, as two presented Rarities, to the Husband, the one curiously swath'd up like an *Egyptian* Mummy, and the other slily cover'd in the Pasteboard Skin of a Crocodile: upon which poetical Expedient, I, Mr. *Bays*, when the two Kings of *Brentford* came from the Clouds into the Throne again, instead of what my Part directed me to say, made use of these Words, viz. 'Now, Sir, this Revolution, I had some Thoughts of introducing, by a quite different Contrivance; but my Design taking air, some of your sharp Wits, I found, had made use of it before me; otherwise I intended to have stolen one of them in, in the Shape of a *Mummy*, and t'other, in that of a *Crocodile.*' Upon which, I doubt, the Audience by the Roar of their Applause shew'd their proportionable Contempt of the Play they belong'd to. But why am I answerable for that? I did not lead them,

---

[1] This play was produced at Drury Lane, 16th January, 1717; and the performance of "The Rehearsal" referred to took place on the 7th February.

by any Reflection of my own, into that Contempt: Surely to have used the bare Word *Mummy*, and *Crocodile*, was neither unjust, or unmannerly; Where then was the Crime of simply saying there had been two such things in a former Play? But this, it seems, was so heinously taken by Mr. *Pope*, that, in the swelling of his Heart, after the Play was over, he came behind the Scenes, with his Lips pale and his Voice trembling, to call me to account for the Insult: And accordingly fell upon me with all the foul Language, that a Wit out of his Senses could be capable of——How durst I have the Impudence to treat any Gentleman in that manner? *&c. &c. &c.* Now let the Reader judge by this Concern, who was the true Mother of the Child! When he was almost choked with the foam of his Passion, I was enough recover'd from my Amazement to make him (as near as I can remember) this Reply, *viz.* ' Mr. *Pope*——You are so particular a Man, that I must be asham'd to return your Language as I ought to do · but since you have attacked me in so monstrous a Manner; This you may depend upon, that so long as the Play continues to be acted, I will never fail to repeat the same Words over and over again' Now, as he accordingly found I kept my Word, for several Days following, I am afraid he has since thought, that his Pen was a sharper Weapon than his Tongue to trust his Revenge with. And however just Cause this may be for his so doing, it is, at least, the only Cause my Conscience can charge me with. Now, as I might have concealed this Fact if my Conscience would have suffered me, may we not suppose, Mr. *Pope* would certainly have mention'd it in his *Dunciad*, had he thought it could have been of service to him?"

Cibber afterwards proceeds to criticise and reply to allusions to himself in Pope's works, some of which are in conspicuously bad taste. Cibber, of course, does not miss the obvious point that to attack his successful plays was a foolish proceeding on Pope's part, whose own endeavours as a dramatist had been completely unsuccessful, and who thus laid himself open to the charge of envy. Nor is this accusation so ridiculous as it may seem to readers of to-day, for a successful playwright was a notable public figure, and the delicious applause of the crowded theatre was eagerly sought by even the most eminent men. And again, it must be remembered that Pope's fame was not then the perfectly assured matter that it is now.

But Cibber's great point, which made his opponent writhe with fury, was a little anecdote—Dr. Johnson terms it "an idle story of Pope's behaviour at a tavern"—which raised a universal shout of merriment at Pope's expense. The excuse for its introduction was found in these lines from the "Epistle to Dr. Arbuthnot":—

>"Whom have I hurt? has poet yet or peer
>Lost the arch'd eyebrow or Parnassian sneer?
>And has not Colley still his lord and whore?
>His butchers Henley? his freemasons Moore?"

Cibber's anecdote cannot be defended on the ground of decency, but it is extremely ludicrous, and in the state of society then existing it must have been a knock-down blow to the unhappy subject of it. There can be little doubt that it was this pamphlet which Pope received on the occasion when the Richardsons visited him, as related by Johnson in his Life of the poet : " I have heard Mr. Richardson relate that he attended his father the painter on a visit, when one of Cibber's pamphlets came into the hands of Pope, who said, ' These things are my diversion.' They sat by him while he perused it, and saw his features writhing with anguish : and young Richardson said to his father, when they returned, that he hoped to be preserved from such diversion as had been that day the lot of Pope." How deeply Pope was galled by Cibber's ludicrous picture of him is manifested by the extraordinary revenge he took. And even now we can realize the bitterness of the provocation when we read the maliciously comic story of the vivacious Colley :—

"As to the first Part of the Charge, the *Lord*; Why—we have both had him, and sometimes the *same* Lord ; but as there is neither Vice nor Folly in keeping our Betters Company; the Wit or Satyr of the Verse! can only point at my Lord for keeping such *ordinary* Company. Well, but if so! then *why* so, good Mr. *Pope?* If either of us could be *good* Company, our being professed Poets, I hope would be no Objection to my Lord's sometimes making one with us? and though I don't pretend to write like you, yet all the Requisites to make a good Companion are not confined to Poetry! No, Sir, even a Man's inoffensive Follies and Blunders may sometimes have their Merits at the best Table; and in those, I am sure, you won't pretend to vie with me: Why then may not my Lord be as much in the Right, in his sometimes choosing *Colley* to laugh at, as at other times in his picking up *Sawney*, whom he can only admire?

"Thus far, then, I hope we are upon a par; for the Lord, you see, will fit either of us.

"As to the latter Charge, the *Whore*, there indeed, I doubt you will have the better of me; for I must own, that I believe I know more of *your* whoring than you do of *mine*; because I don't recollect that ever I made you the least Confidence of *my* Amours, though I have been very near an Eye-Witness of *Yours*—— By the way, gentle Reader, don't you think, to say only, *a Man has his Whore*, without some particular Circumstances to aggravate the Vice, is the flattest Piece of Satyr that ever fell from the formidable Pen of Mr. *Pope*? because (*defendit numerus*) take the first ten thousand Men you meet, and I believe, you would be no Loser, if you betted ten to one that every single Sinner of them, one with another, had been guilty of the same Frailty. But as Mr. *Pope* has so particularly picked me out of the Number to make an Example of: Why may I not take the same Liberty, and even single him out for another to keep me in Countenance? He must excuse me, then, if in what I am going to relate, I am reduced to make bold with a little private Conversation: But as he has shewn no Mercy to *Colley*, why should so unprovok'd an Aggressor expect any for himself? And if Truth hurts him, I can't help it. He may remember, then (or if he won't I will) when *Button's* Coffee-house was in vogue, and so long ago, as when he had not translated above two or three Books of *Homer*; there was a late young Nobleman (as much his *Lord* as mine) who had a good deal of wicked Humour, and who, though he was fond of having Wits in his Company, was not so restrained by his Conscience, but that he lov'd to laugh at any merry Mischief he could do them. This noble Wag, I say, in his usual *Gayetè de Cœur*, with another Gentleman still in Being,[1] one Evening shly seduced the celebrated Mr. *Pope* as a Wit, and myself as a Laugher, to a certain House of Carnal Recreation, near the *Hay-Market*; where his Lordship's Frolick propos'd was to slip his little *Homer*, as he call'd him, at a Girl of the Game, that he might see what sort of Figure a Man of his Size, Sobriety, and Vigour (in Verse) would make, when the frail Fit of Love had got into him; in which he so far succeeded, that the smirking Damsel, who serv'd us with Tea, happen'd to have Charms sufficient to tempt the

---

[1] The Earl of Warwick was the young nobleman, and it is said in Dillworth's "Life of Pope" that "the late Commissioner Vaughan" was the other gentleman

little-tiny Manhood of Mr. *Pope* into the next Room with her: at which you may imagine, his Lordship was in as much Joy, at what might happen within, as our small Friend could probably be in Possession of it: But I (forgive me all ye mortified Mortals whom his fell Satyr has since fallen upon) observing he had staid as long as without hazard of his Health he might, I,

Prick'd to it by foolish Honesty and Love,

As *Shakespear* says, without Ceremony, threw open the Door upon him, where I found this little hasty Hero, like a terrible *Tom Tit*, pertly perching upon the Mount of Love! But such was my Surprize, that I fairly laid hold of his Heels, and actually drew him down safe and sound from his Danger. My Lord, who staid tittering without, in hopes the sweet Mischief he came for would have been compleated, upon my giving an Account of the Action within, began to curse, and call me an hundred silly Puppies, for my impertinently spoiling the Sport, to which with great Gravity I reply'd; pray, my Lord, consider what I have done was, in regard to the Honour of our Nation! For would you have had so glorious a Work as that of making *Homer* speak elegant *English*, cut short by laying up our little Gentleman of a Malady, which his thin Body might never have been cured of? No, my Lord! *Homer* would have been too serious a Sacrifice to our Evening Merriment. Now as his *Homer* has since been so happily compleated, who can say, that the World may not have been obliged to the kindly Care of *Colley* that so great a Work ever came to Perfection?

" And now again, gentle Reader, let it be judged, whether the *Lord* and the *Whore* above-mentioned might not, with equal Justice, have been apply'd to sober *Sawney* the Satyrist, as to *Colley* the Criminal?

" Though I confess Recrimination to be but a poor Defence for one's own Faults; yet when the Guilty are Accusers, it seems but just, to make use of any Truth, that may invalidate their Evidence: I therefore hope, whatever the serious Reader may think amiss in this Story, will be excused, by my being so hardly driven to tell it."

In the remainder of Cibber's pamphlet there is not much that is of any importance, though an allusion to one of Pope's victims having hung up a birch in Button's Coffee House, wherewith to chastise his satirist, was skilfully calculated to rouse Pope's temper. Cibber thoroughly succeeded in this object,[1] perhaps to a degree that he rather regretted. Pope made no direct reply to his banter, but in the following year (1743) a new edition of "The Dunciad" appeared, in which Theobald was deposed from the throne of Dulness, and Cibber elevated in his place.

[1] "But Pope's irascibility prevailed, and he resolved to tell the whole English world that he was at war with Cibber; and, to show that he thought him no common adversary, he prepared no common vengeance, he published a new edition of the 'Dunciad,' in which he degraded Theobald from his painful pre-eminence, and enthroned Cibber in his stead."—Johnson's "Life of Pope."

By doing this Pope gratified his vengeance, but injured his poem, for the carefully painted peculiarities of Theobald, a slow and pedantic scholar, sat ill on the pert and vivacious Colley.[1] To this retaliation Cibber, as he had promised,[2] replied with another pamphlet, entitled "Another Occasional Letter from Mr. Cibber to Mr. Pope. Wherein the New Hero's Preferment to his Throne, in the *Dunciad*, seems not to be Accepted. And the Author of that Poem His more rightful Claim to it, is Asserted. With An Expostulatory Address to the Reverend Mr. W. W——n, Author of the new Preface, and Adviser in the curious Improvements of that Satire." The motto on the title-page was :—

"—— *Remember* Sauney's *Fate !*
Bang'd by the Blockhead, whom he strove to beat.
　　　　　　　　Parodie on Lord *Roscommon.*"

There is little that is of any note in this production, which is characterized by the same real or affected good-nature as marked the former pamphlet. The most interesting passages to us are those alluding to the effect of Cibber's previous attack, and exulting over Pope's distress at it. For instance (on page 7) :—

"And now, Sir, give me leave to be a little sur-

---

[1] "Unhappily the two heroes were of opposite characters, and Pope was unwilling to lose what he had already written; he has therefore depraved his poem by giving to Cibber the old books, the old pedantry, and the sluggish pertinacity of Theobald."—Johnson's "Life of Pope."

[2] See *ante*, p. 272.

priz'd at the impenetrable Skull of your Courage, that (after I had in my first Letter) so heartily teiz'd, and toss'd, and tumbled you through all the Mire, and Dirt, the madness of your Muse had been throwing at other People, it could still, so Vixen like, sprawl out the same feeble Paw of its Satyr, to have t'other Scratch at my Nose: But as I know the Vulgar (with whose Applause I humbly content my self) are apt to laugh when they see a curst Cat in a Kennel; so whenever I observe your *Grimalkin* Spirit shew but the least grinning Gasp of Life, I shall take the honest liberty of old *Towser* the House-dog, and merrily lift up my Leg to have a little more Game with you.

"Well Sir, in plainer Terms, I am now, you see, once more willing to bring Matters to an Issue, or (as the Boxers say) to answer your Challenge, and come to a Trial of Manhood with you; though by our slow Proceedings, we seem rather to be at *Law*, than at *Loggerheads* with one another; and if you had not been a blinder Booby, than my self, you would have sate down quietly, with the last black Eye I gave you: For so loath was I to squabble with you, that though you had been snapping, and snarling at me for twenty Years together, you saw, I never so much as gave you a single Growl, or took any notice of you. At last, 'tis true, in meer Sport for others, rather than from the least Tincture of Concern for my self, I was inticed to be a little wanton, not to say waggish, with your Character; by which having (you know) got the strong Laugh on my Side, I doubt I have so offended the Gravity, and Greatness of your Soul, that to secure your more ample Revenge, you have prudently taken the full Term of thirteen Months Consideration, before you would pour it, upon me! But at last, it seems, we have it, and now Souse! out comes your old *Dunciad*, in a new Dress, like fresh Gold, upon stale Gingerbread, sold out in Penny-worth's of shining King *Colley*, crown'd the Hero of Immortal Stupidity!"

And again (on page 15): "At your Peril be it, little Gentleman, for I shall have t'other Frisk with you, and don't despair that the very Notice I am now taking of you, will once more make your Fame fly, like a yelping Cur with a Bottle at his Tail, the Jest and Joy of every Bookseller's Prentice between *Wapping* and *Westminster!*"

To this pamphlet Pope, whose infirmities were very great, made no reply, and Cibber had, as he had vowed, the last word. Round the central articles of this quarrel a crowd of supplementary productions had gathered, a list of which will be found in the Bibliography of Cibber a few pages on.

Cibber's position of Poet Laureate furnished him with a steady income during his declining years, and his Odes were turned out as required, with mechanical precision and most unpoetic spirit. They were the standing joke of the pamphleteers and news-sheet writers, and were always accompanied with a running fire of banter and parody. Those curious in the matter will find excellent specimens, both of the Odes and the burlesques, in the early volumes of the "Gentleman's Magazine."

After the termination of his quarrel with Pope, Cibber's life was very uneventful; and, although it extended far beyond the allotted span, he continued to enjoy it to the very end. Horace Walpole greeted him one day, saying, "I am glad, Sir, to see you looking so well." "Egad, Sir," replied the old man, "at eighty-four it is well for a man that he can look at all." On 11th December, 1757, he died, having attained the great age of eighty-six.[1] Dr. Doran ("Their Majesties' Servants," 1888 edition, ii. 235) says: "I read in contemporary publications that there 'died at his house in Berkeley Square, Colley Cibber, Esq., Poet Laureate;'" and although it has been stated that he died at Islington, I see no reason to doubt Dr. Doran's explicit statement. Cibber was buried in the Danish Church, Wellclose Square.[2]

---

[1] It has been generally stated that Cibber died on 12th December, 1757, but "The Public Advertiser" of Monday, 12th December, announces his death as having occurred "Yesterday morning." The "Gentleman's Magazine" and the "London Magazine," in their issues for December, 1757, give the 11th as the date.

[2] Mr. Laurence Hutton, in his "Literary Landmarks of London" (p. 54), gives the following interesting particulars regarding Cibber's last resting-place: "Cibber was buried by the side of his father and mother, in a vault under the Danish Church, situated in Wellclose Square, Ratcliff Highway (since named St. George Street) This church, according to an inscription

So far as we know, only two of Cibber's children survived him, his ne'er-do-well son Theophilus, and his equally scapegrace daughter Charlotte, who married Charke the musician. The former was born in 1703, and was drowned in the winter of 1758, while crossing to Ireland to fulfil an engagement in Dublin. As an actor he was chiefly famous for playing Ancient Pistol, but he was also excellent in some of his father's characters, such as Lord Foppington, Bayes, and Sir Francis Wronghead. His private life was in the last degree disreputable, and especially so in his relations with his second wife, Susanna Maria Arne—the great Mrs. Cibber. The literature regarding Theophilus Cibber is considerable in quantity and curious in quality. Some account of it will be found in my "Bibliographical Account of English Theatrical Literature," pp. 52-55.

placed over the doorway, was built in 1696 by Caius Gabriel Cibber himself, by order of the King of Denmark, for the use of such of his Majesty's subjects as might visit the port of London. The church was taken down some years ago (1868-70), and St. Paul's Schools were erected on its foundation, which was left intact. Rev. Dan. Greatorex, Vicar of the Parish of St Paul, Dock Street, in a private note written in the summer of 1883, says :—

"'Colley Cibber and his father and mother were buried in the vault of the old Danish Church. When the church was removed, the coffins were all removed carefully into the crypt under the apse, and then bricked up. So the bodies are still there. The Danish Consul was with me when I moved the bodies. The coffins had perished except the bottoms. I carefully removed them myself personally, and laid them side by side at the back of the crypt, and covered them with earth.'"

Charlotte Charke, who was born about 1710, and died in April, 1760, was of no note as an actress. Her private life, however, was madly eccentric, and her autobiography, published in 1755, is a curious and scarce work.

Cibber's principal plays have been noted in the course of his "Apology;" but, for the sake of convenience, I give here a complete list of his regular dramatic productions :—

Love's Last Shift—Comedy—Produced at Drury Lane, 1696.

Woman's Wit—Comedy—Drury Lane, 1697.

Xerxes—Tragedy—Lincoln's Inn Fields, 1699.

Richard III.—Tragedy (alteration of Shakespeare's play)—Drury Lane, 1700.

Love Makes a Man—Comedy—Drury Lane, 1701.

The School Boy—Comedy—Drury Lane, 26th October, 1702.

She Would and She Would Not—Comedy—Drury Lane, 26th November, 1702.

The Careless Husband—Comedy—Drury Lane, 7th December, 1704.

Perolla and Izadora — Tragedy — Drury Lane, 3rd December, 1705.

The Comical Lovers — Comedy — Haymarket, 4th February, 1707.

The Double Gallant—Comedy—Haymarket, 1st November, 1707.

The Lady's Last Stake—Comedy—Haymarket, 13th December, 1707.

The Rival Fools—Comedy—Drury Lane, 11th January, 1709.

The Rival Queans — Comical-Tragedy — Haymarket, 29th June, 1710.

Ximena—Tragedy—Drury Lane, 28th November, 1712.

Venus and Adonis—Masque—Drury Lane, 1715.

Bulls and Bears—Farce—Drury Lane, 1st December, 1715.

Myrtillo—Pastoral Interlude—Drury Lane, 1716.

The Nonjuror—Comedy—Drury Lane, 6th December, 1717.

The Refusal—Comedy—Drury Lane, 14th February, 1721.

Cæsar in Egypt—Tragedy—Drury Lane, 9th December, 1724.

The Provoked Husband—Comedy (in conjunction with Vanbrugh)—Drury Lane, 10th January, 1728.

Love in a Riddle—Pastoral—Drury Lane, 7th January, 1729.

Damon and Phillida — Pastoral Farce — Haymarket, 1729.

Papal Tyranny in the Reign of King John—Tragedy (alteration of Shakespeare's "King John")—Covent Garden, 15th February, 1745.

Of these, his alteration of "Richard III." had practically undisputed possession of the stage, until the taste and judgment of Mr. Henry Irving gave us back the original play.[1] But in the provinces, when

---

[1] Shakespeare's "Richard III." was produced at the Lyceum

stars of the old school play a round of legitimate parts, the adulterated version still reigns triumphant, and the great effect of the night is got in Cibber's famous line :—

"Off with his head! So much for Buckingham!"

In "The Hypocrite," a comedy still played at intervals, Cibber's "Nonjuror" survives. Bickerstaffe, who was the author of the alteration, retained a very large portion of the original play, his chief change being the addition of the inimitable Mawworm.

That another of Cibber's plays survives is owing to the taste of an American manager and to the Theatre on 29th January, 1877. It was announced as "strictly the original text, without interpolations, but simply with such omissions and transpositions as have been found essential for dramatic representation." In Richard Mr Irving's great powers are seen to special advantage

The cast of Cibber's play in 1700 was—

KING HENRY VI., *designed for* . . .	Mr. Wilks.
EDWARD, PRINCE OF WALES . . .	Mrs. Allison.
RICHARD, DUKE OF YORK	Miss Chock.
RICHARD, DUKE OF GLOUCESTER . .	Mr. Cibber.
DUKE OF BUCKINGHAM	Mr Powel.
LORD STANLEY	Mr. Mills.
DUKE OF NORFOLK	Mr Simpson.
RATCLIFF	Mr. Kent.
CATESBY	Mr. Thomas.
HENRY, EARL OF RICHMOND . . .	Mr. Evans.
OXFORD	Mr. Fairbank.
QUEEN ELIZABETH	Mrs. Knight.
LADY ANN	Mrs. Rogers
CICELY	Mrs. Powel.

SUSANNA MARIA CIBBER AS CORDELIA.

genius of an American company of comedians. Mr. Augustin Daly's company includes among its repertory Cibber's comedy of "She Would and She Would Not," and has shown in London as well as in New York how admirable a comedy it is. It goes without saying to those who have seen this company, that much of the success was due to Miss Ada Rehan, who showed in Hypolita, as she has done in Katharine ("Taming of the Shrew"), that she is mistress of classical comedy as of modern touch-and-go farce.[1]

Cibber was the cause of quite a considerable literature, mostly abusive. The following list, taken from my "Bibliographical Account of English Theatrical Literature" (1888), is, I believe, a complete catalogue of all separate publications by, or relating to, Colley Cibber:—

A clue to the comedy of the Non-Juror. With some hints of consequence relating to that play. In a letter to N. Rowe, Esq; Poet Laureat to His Majesty. London (Curll): 1718. 8vo. 6d.

Cibber's "Non-Juror," produced at Drury-Lane, December 6, 1717, was written in favour of the Hanoverian succession. Rowe wrote the prologue, which was very abusive of Nonjurors. This tract is not an attack on the play, but a satire on, it is said, Bishop Hoadly.

A lash for the Laureat: or an address by way of Satyr; most humbly inscrib'd to the unparallel'd

---

[1] A beautiful Portfolio of Sketches of Mr. Daly's Company has been published, in which is a portrait of Miss Rehan as Hypolita, with a critical note by Mr Brander Matthews.

Mr. Rowe, on occasion of a late insolent Prologue to the Non-Juror. London (J. Morphew): 1718. folio. Title, 1 leaf. Pref. 1 leaf. pp. 8. 6d.

<small>A furious attack on Rowe on account of his Prologue. A tract of extreme rarity.</small>

A compleat key to the Non-Juror. Explaining the characters in that play, with observations thereon. By Mr. Joseph Gay. The second edioion (*sic*). London (Curll): 1718. 8vo. pp. 24 including title and half-title.

<small>3rd edition: 1718. Joseph Gay is a pseudonym Pope is said to be the author of the pamphlet, which is very unfriendly to Cibber.</small>

The Theatre-Royal turn'd into a mountebank's stage. In some remarks upon Mr. Cibber's quack-dramatical performance, called the Non-Juror. By a Non-Juror. London (Morphew): 1718. 8vo. Title 1 leaf. pp. 38. 6d.

The Comedy call'd the Non-Juror. Shewing the particular scenes wherein that hypocrite is concern'd. With remarks, and a key, explaining the characters of that excellent play. London (printed for J. L.): 1718 8vo. pp. 24, including title. 2d.

Some cursory remarks on the play call'd the Non-Juror, written by Mr. Cibber. In a letter to a friend. London (Chetwood) 1718. 8vo.

<small>Dated from Button's Coffee-House and signed "H. S." Very laudatory.</small>

A journey to London. Being part of a comedy written by the late Sir John Vanbrugh, Knt. and printed after his own copy : which (since his decease) has been made an intire play, by Mr. Cibber, and call'd The provok'd husband, &c. London (Watts) : 1728. 8vo. pp. 51, including title.

"The Provok'd Husband," by Vanbrugh and Cibber, was produced at Drury Lane, January 10, 1728; and though Cibber's Nonjuror enemies tried to condemn it, was very successful. This tract shows how much of the play was written by Vanbrugh.

Reflections on the principal characters in the Provoked Husband. London : 1728. 8vo.

An apology for the life of Mr. Colley Cibber, comedian, and late patentee of the Theatre-Royal. With an historical view of the stage during his own time. Written by himself. London (Printed by John Watts for the author) : 1740. 4to. Port.

Second edition, London, 1740, 8vo., no portrait; third edition, London, 1750, 8vo., portrait; fourth edition, 1756, 2 vols 12mo, portrait. A good edition was published, London, 1822, 8vo., with notes by E. Bellchambers and a portrait. The "Apology" forms one of Hunt's series of autobiographies, London, 1826. One of the most famous and valuable of theatrical books.

An apology for the life of Mr. T ...... C ......, comedian. Being a proper sequel to the Apology for the life of Mr. Colley Cibber, comedian. With an historical view of the stage to the present year. Supposed to be written by himself. In the stile and manner of the Poet Laureat. London (Mechell) : 1740. 8vo. 2s.

The object of this pamphlet, ascribed to Fielding, is chiefly to ridicule Colley Cibber's "Apology." Herman, 22s.

A brief supplement to Colley·Cibber, Esq; his lives of the late famous Actors and Actresses. *Si tu scis, melior ego.* By Anthony, Vulgò Tony Aston. Printed for the Author, N.P. (London) : N.D. (1747-8). 8vo. pp. 24 including title.

<small>A pamphlet of extreme rarity. Isaac Reed purchased a copy in 1769, and in 1795 he notes on it that, though he has had it twenty-six years, he has never seen another copy. Reed's copy was bought by Field for 65s, at whose sale, in 1827, Genest bought it for 36s.</small>

The tryal of Colley Cibber, comedian, &c. for writing a book intitled An apology for his life, &c. Being a thorough examination thereof; wherein he is proved guilty of High Crimes and Misdemeanors against the English language, and in characterising many persons of distinction. . . . Together with an indictment exhibited against Alexander Pope of Twickenham, Esq; for not exerting his talents at this juncture : and the arraignment of George Cheyne, Physician at Bath, for the Philosophical, Physical, and Theological heresies, uttered in his last book on Regimen. London (for the author). 1740. 8vo. pp. vii. 40. 1s.

<small>With motto—"Lo ! He hath written a Book !" The Dedication is signed "T. Johnson"</small>

The Laureat : or, the right side of Colley Cibber, Esq; containing explanations, amendments, and observations, on a book intituled, An apology for the life, and writings of Mr. Colley Cibber. Not written by himself. With some anecdotes of the Laureat, which he (thro' an excess of modesty) omitted. To which is added, The history of the life, manners and writings of Æsopus the tragedian, from a fragment of a Greek manuscript found in the Library of the Vatican ; interspers'd with observations of the translator. London (Roberts) : 1740. 8vo. 1s. 6d.

<small>A furious attack on Cibber. The Life of Æsopus is a burlesque Life of Cibber. Daniel. 7s. 6d.</small>

The history of the stage. In which is included, the theatrical characters of the most celebrated actors who have adorn'd the theatre. Among many others are the following, *viz.* Mr. Betterton, Mr. Montfort, Mr. Dogget, Mr. Booth, Mr. Wilks, Mr. Nokes. Mrs. Barry, Mrs. Montfort, Mrs. Gwin, Mrs. Bracegirdle, Mrs. Porter, Mrs. Oldfield. Together with, the theatrical life of Mr. Colly Cibber. London (Miller) : 1742. 8vo.

<small>A "boil-down" of Cibber's Apology.</small>

A letter from Mr. Cibber, to Mr. Pope, inquiring into the motives that might induce him in his satyrical works, to be so frequently fond of Mr. Cibber's name   London (Lewis) : 1742. 8vo. 1s.

<small>Second edition, London, 1744, 8vo.; reprinted, London, 1777, 8vo. The sting of this pamphlet lies in an anecdote told of Pope at a house of ill-fame, in retaliation for his line ·
"And has not Colley still his lord and whore?"</small>

A letter to Mr. C—b—r, on his letter to Mr. P....... London (Roberts) : 1742. 8vo. 26 pp. 6d.
<small>Very scarce. Abusive of Pope—laudatory towards Cibber.</small>

Difference between verbal and practical virtue. With a prefatory epistle from Mr. C...b...r to Mr. P. London (Roberts): 1742. Folio. Title 1 leaf: Epistle 1 leaf: pp. 7.

<small>Very rare. A rhymed attack on Pope.</small>

A blast upon Bays; or, a new lick at the Laureat. Containing, remarks upon a late tatling performance, entitled, A letter from Mr. Cibber to Mr. Pope, &c. *And lo there appeared an old woman!* Vide the Letter throughout. London (Robbins). 1742. 8vo. pp. 26. 6d.

<small>A bitter attack on Cibber.</small>

Sawney and Colley, a poetical dialogue: occasioned by a late letter from the Laureat of St. James's, to the Homer of Twickenham. Something in the manner of Dr. Swift. London (for J. H.): n.d. (1742). Folio. Title 1 leaf: pp. 21. 1s.

<small>Very scarce. A coarse and ferocious attack on Pope in rhyme.</small>

The egotist: or, Colley upon Cibber. Being his own picture retouch'd, to so *plain* a likeness, that no one, *now*, would have the face to own it, but himself. London (Lewis): 1743. 8vo. pp. 78 including title. 1s.

<small>Anonymous, but undoubtedly by Cibber himself.</small>

Another occasional letter from Mr. Cibber to Mr. Pope Wherein the new hero's preferment to his throne, in the Dunciad, seems not to be accepted. And the author of that poem his more rightful claim to it, is asserted. With an expostulatory address to the Reverend Mr. W. W———n, author of the new preface, and adviser in the curious improvements of that satire. By Mr. Colley Cibber. London (Lewis): 1744. 8vo. 1s.

<small>The Rev. W. W———n is Warburton. This tract was reprinted, Glasgow, n. d., 8vo. The two "Letters" were reprinted, London, 1777, with, I believe, a curious frontispiece representing the adventure related by Cibber at Pope's expense in the first "Letter." I am not certain whether the frontispiece was issued with the London or Glasgow reprint, having seen it in copies of both. In Bohn's "Lowndes" (1865) is mentioned a parody on this first "Letter," with the same title, except that "Mrs. Cibber's name" is substituted for "Mr. Cibber's name." Lowndes says: "A copy is described in Mr Thorpe's catalogue, p. iv, 1832, 'with the frontispiece of Pope surprized with Mrs. Cibber.'" I gravely doubt the existence of any such work, and fancy that this frontispiece is the one just mentioned, but wrongly described. Herman (two Letters, with scarce front), 40s.</small>

A letter to Colley Cibber, Esq; on his transformation of King John. London. 1745. 8vo.

<small>Cibber's mangling of "King John," entitled "Papal Tyranny in the Reign of King John," was produced at Covent Garden, February 15, 1745.</small>

A new book of the Dunciad: occasion'd by Mr. Warburton's new edition of the Dunciad complete. By a gentleman of one of the Inns of Court. With several of Mr. Warburton's own notes, and likewise Notes *Variorum*. London (J. Payne & J. Bouquet): 1750. 4to. 1s.

<small>Cibber dethroned and Warburton elevated to the throne of Dulness.</small>

Shakspere's tragedy of Richard III., considered dramatically and historically; and in comparison with Cibber's alteration as at present in use on the stage, in a lecture delivered to the members of the Liverpool Literary, Scientific and Commercial Institution, by Thos. Stuart, of the Theatre Royal. (Liverpool): n. d. (about 1850). 12mo.

Cibber published in 1747 a work entitled "The Character and Conduct of Cicero, considered from the history of his life by Dr. Middleton;" but it is of little value or interest.

A BRIEF SUPPLEMENT

TO

Colley Cibber, Esq;

HIS

LIVES

Of the late FAMOUS

ACTORS and ACTRESSES.

Si tu scis, melior ego.

By *ANTHONY,* } *ASTON.*
Vulgò *TONY*

Printed for the AUTHOR.

✻ ✻ ✻ ✻ ✻ ✻ ✻

M R. CIBBER *is guilty of Omission, that he hath not given us any Description of the several Personages'* Beauties, or Faults——Faults (*I say*) *of the several* ACTORS, &c. *for*
    Nemo sine crimine vivit.
Or, as the late Duke of Buckingham *says of* Characters, *that, to shew a Man not defective,*
———————————— were to draw
A faultless Monster, that the World ne'er saw.

✻ ✻ ✻ ✻ ✻ ✻ ✻

A BRIEF SUPPLEMENT

To COLLEY CIBBER, Esq; his

LIVES

OF THE LATE FAMOUS

ACTORS AND ACTRESSES.

MR. *BETTERTON* (although a superlative good Actor) labour'd under ill Figure, being clumsily made, having a great Head, a short thick Neck, stoop'd in the Shoulders, and had fat short Arms, which he rarely lifted higher than his Stomach. —His Left Hand frequently lodg'd in his Breast, between his Coat and Waist-coat, while, with his Right, he prepar'd his Speech.—His Actions were few, but just.—He had little Eyes, and a broad Face, a little Pock-fretten, a corpulent Body, and thick Legs, with large Feet.—He was better to meet, than to follow; for his Aspect was serious, venerable, and majestic; in his latter Time a little paralytic.—His Voice was low and grumbling; yet he could Tune it by an artful *Climax*, which enforc'd universal Attention, even from the *Fops* and *Orange-Girls*.—He was incapable of dancing, even in a Country-Dance; as was Mrs. *BARRY*: But their good Qualities were more than equal to their Deficiencies.—While Mrs. *BRACEGIRDLE* sung very agreeably in the LOVES of *Mars* and *Venus*, and danced in a Country-Dance, as well as Mr. *WILKS*, though not with so much Art and Foppery, but like a well-bred Gentlewoman.—Mr. *Betterton* was the most extensive Actor, from *Alexander* to Sir *John Falstaff*; but, in that last Character, he wanted the Waggery of *ESTCOURT*, the Drollery of *HARPER*, the Sallaciousness of *JACK EVANS*.—But, then, *Estcourt* was too trifling; *Harper* had too much of the *Bartholomew-Fair*; and *Evans* misplac'd his Humour.—Thus, you see what *Flaws* are in *bright Diamonds*:—And I have often wish'd that Mr. *Betterton* would have resign'd the Part of HAMLET to some young Actor, (who might have Personated, though not have Acted, it better) for, when he threw himself at *Ophelia's* Feet, he appear'd a little too grave for a young Student, lately come from the University of *Wirtemberg*; and his *Repartees* seem'd rather as *Apopthegms* from a *sage Philosopher*, than the *sporting Flashes* of a Young HAMLET; and no one else could have pleas'd the Town, he was so rooted in their Opinion.—His younger Cotemporary, (*Betterton* 63, *Powel* 40, Years old) *POWEL*, attempted several of *Betterton's* Parts, as *Alexander*, *Jaffier*, &c. but lost his Credit; as, in *Alexander*, he maintain'd not the Dignity of a King, but *Out-Heroded* HEROD; and in his poison'd, mad Scene, *out-rav'd all Probability*; while *Betterton* kept his Passion under, and shew'd it most (as Fume smoaks most, when stifled) *Betterton*, from the Time he was dress'd, to the End of the Play, kept his Mind in the same Temperament and Adaptness, as the present Character required.—If I was to write of him all Day, I should still remember fresh Matter in his Behalf; and, before I part with him, suffer this facetious Story of him, and a Country Tenant of his.

Mr. *Betterton* had a small Farm near *Reading*, in the County of *Berks*; and the Countryman came, in the Time of *Bartholomew-Fair*, to pay his Rent.— Mr. *Betterton* took him to the Fair, and going to one *Crawley's* Puppet-Shew, offer'd *Two Shillings* for himself and *Roger*, his Tenant.—*No, no, Sir,* said *Crawley*; *we never take Money of one another.* This affronted Mr. *Betterton* who threw down the Money, and they enter'd.—*Roger* was hugeously diverted with *Punch*, and bred a great Noise, saying, that he would drink with him, for he was a merry Fellow.—Mr. *Betterton* told him, he was only a Puppet, made up of *Sticks and Rags*: However, *Roger* still cried out, that he would go and drink with *Punch*.—When Master took him behind, where the Puppets hung up, he swore, he thought *Punch* had been alive.—*However*, said he, *though he be but* Sticks and Rags, *I'll give him Six-pence to drink my Health.*—At Night, Mr. *Betterton* went to the *Theatre*, when was play'd the ORPHAN; Mr. *Betterton* acting *Castalio*; Mrs. *Barry*, *Monimia*.——*Well* (said Master) *how dost like this Play*, Roger? *Why, I don't knows*, (says *Roger*) *its well enought for* Sticks and Rags.

To end with this *Phœnix* of the Stage, I must say of him, as *Hamlet* does of his Father: "He was a Man (take him for all in all) I cannot look upon his Like again."

His Favourite, Mrs. *BARRY*, claims the next in Æstimation. They were both never better pleas'd, than in Playing together.—Mrs. *Barry* outshin'd Mrs. *Bracegirdle* in the Character of ZARA in the *Mourning Bride*, altho' Mr. *Congreve* design'd Almeria for that Favour.—And yet, this fine Creature was not handsome, her Mouth op'ning most on the Right Side, which she strove to draw t'other Way, and, at Times, composing her Face, as if sitting to have her Picture drawn.—Mrs *Barry* was middle-siz'd, and had darkish Hair, light Eyes, dark Eye-brows, and was indifferently plump:—Her Face somewhat preceded her Action, as the latter did her Words, her Face ever expressing the Passions; not like the Actresses of late Times, who are afraid of putting their Faces out of the Form of Non-meaning, lest they should crack the Cerum, White-Wash, or other Cosmetic, trowel'd on. Mrs. *Barry* had a Manner of drawing out her Words, which became her, but not Mrs. *Braidshaw*, and Mrs. *Porter*, (Successors.)—— To hear her speak the following Speech in the ORPHAN, was a Charm:

I'm ne'er so well pleas'd, as when I hear thee speak,
And listen to the Music of thy Voice.

And again:

Who's he that speaks with a Voice so sweet,
As the Shepherd pipes upon the Mountain,
When all his little Flock are gath'ring round him?

Neither she, nor any of the Actors of those Times, had any Tone in their speaking, (too much, lately, in Use.)—In *Tragedy* she was solemn and august—in *Free Comedy* alert, easy, and genteel—pleasant in her Face and Action; filling the Stage with Variety of Gesture.—She was Woman to Lady *Shelton*, of *Norfolk*, (my Godmother)—when Lord *Rochester* took her on the Stage; where for some Time, they could make nothing of her.—She could neither sing, nor dance, no, not in a Country-Dance.

Mrs. *BRACEGIRDLE*, that *Diana* of the Stage, hath many Places contending for her Birth—The most received Opinion is, that she was the Daughter of a Coachman, Coachmaker, or Letter-out of Coaches, in the Town of *Northampton*.—But I am inclinable to my Father's Opinion, (who had a great Value for her reported Virtue) that she was a distant Relation, and came out of *Staffordshire*, from about *Walsal* or *Wolverhampton*.—She had many Assailants on her Virtue, as Lord *Lovelace*, Mr. *Congreve*, the last of which had her Company most; but she ever resisted his vicious Attacks, and, yet, was always uneasy at his leaving her; on which Observation he made the following Song:

> PIOUS Celinda *goes to Pray'rs*,
>   *Whene'er I ask the Favour;*
> *Yet, the tender Fool's in Tears,*
>   *When she believes I'll leave her.*
> *Wou'd I were free from this Restraint,*
>   *Or else had Power to win her!*
> *Wou'd she cou'd make of me a Saint,*
>   *Or I of her a Sinner!*

And, as Mr. *Durfey* alludes to it in his Puppet Song—in *Don Quixot*,

> *Since that our Fate intends*
>   *Our Amity shall be no dearer,*
> *Still let us kiss and be Friends,*
>   *And sigh we shall never come nearer.*

She was very shy of Lord *Lovelace's* Company, as being an engaging Man, who drest well: And as, every Day, his Servant came to her, to ask her how she did, she always return'd her Answer in the most obeisant Words and Behaviour, *That she was indifferent well, she humbly thank'd his Lordship.*—She was of a lovely Height, with dark-brown Hair and Eye-brows, black sparkling Eyes, and a fresh blushy Complexion; and, whenever she exerted herself, had an involuntary Flushing in her Breast, Neck and Face, having continually a chearful Aspect, and a fine Set of even white Teeth; never making an *Exit*, but that she left the Audience in an Imitation of her pleasant Countenance. Genteel Comedy was her chief Essay, and that too when in Men's Cloaths, in which she far surmounted all the Actresses of that and this Age.—Yet she had a Defect scarce perceptible, *viz.* her Right Shoulder a little protended, which, when in Men's Cloaths, was cover'd by a long or Campaign Peruke.—She was finely shap'd, and had very handsome Legs and Feet; and her Gait, or Walk, was free, manlike, and modest, when in Breeches.— Her Virtue had its Reward, both in Applause and *Specie*; for it happen'd, that as the Dukes of *Dorset* and *Devonshire*, Lord *Hallifax*, and other Nobles, over a Bottle, were all extolling Mrs. *Bracegirdle's* virtuous Behaviour, *Come*, says Lord *Hallifax—You all commend her Virtue, &c. but why do we not present this incomparable Woman with something worthy her Acceptance?* His Lordship deposited 200 Guineas, which the rest made up 800, and sent to her, with Encomiums on her Virtue.—She was, when on the *Stage*, diurnally Charitable, going often into *Clare-Market*, and giving Money to the poor unemploy'd Basket-women, insomuch that she could not pass that Neighbourhood without the thankful Acclamations of People of all Degrees; so that, if any Person had affronted her, they would have been in Danger of being kill'd directly; and yet this good Woman was an Actress.—She has been off the Stage these 26 Years or more, but was alive *July* 20. 1747; for I saw her in the *Strand, London*, then—with the Remains of charming *Bracegirdle*.

Mr. *SANDFORD*, although not usually deem'd an Actor of the first Rank, yet the Characters allotted him were such, that none besides, then, or since, ever topp'd; for his Figure, which was diminutive and mean, (being Round-shoulder'd, Meagre-fac'd, Spindle-shank'd, Splay-footed, with a sour Countenance, and long lean Arms) render'd him a proper Person to discharge *Jago, Foresight*, and *Ma'lignij*, in the VILLAIN. But he fail'd in succeeding in a fine Description of a triumphant Cavalcade, in *Alonzo*, in the MOURNING BRIDE, because his Figure was despicable, (although his Energy was, by his Voice and Action, enforc'd with great Soundness of Art, and Justice.)—This Person acted strongly with his Face,—and (as King *Charles* said) was the best Villain in the World.—He proceeded from the *Sandfords* of *Sandford*, that lies between *Whitchurch* and *Newport*, in Shropshire.—He would not be concern'd with Mr. *Betterton*, Mrs. *Barry, &c.* as a Sharer in the Revolt from *Drury-Lane* to *Lincoln's-*

CAVE UNDERHILL

Inn-Fields; but said, *This is my Agreement.*—To Samuel Sandford, *Gentleman*, Threescore Shillings a Week.——Pho! pho! *said Mr.* Betterton, *Three Pounds a Week.*——*No, no, said* Sandford;—*To* Samuel Sandford, *Gentleman*, Threescore Shillings a Week. For which *Cave Underhill*, who was a ¾ Sharer, would often jeer *Sandford*; saying, *Samuel Sandford, Gent. my Man.*——Go, you Sot, said *Sandford.*—To which t'other ever replied, *Samuel Sandford, my Man* Samuel.

CAVE UNDERHILL, and Mr. DOGGET, will be the next treated of.

CAVE UNDERHILL, though not the best Actor in the Course of Precedency, was more admired by the Actors than the Audience—there being then no Rivals in his dry, heavy, downright Way in Low Comedy.—His few Parts were, The first Grave-digger in HAMLET,—*Sancho Pancha*, in the first Part of DON QUIXOT,—*Ned Blunt*, in the ROVER,—*Jacomo*, in the LIBERTINE, and the *Host*, in the VILLAIN:—All which were dry, heavy Characters, except in *Jacomo*; in which, when he aim'd at any Archness, he fell into downright Insignificance.—He was about 50 Years of Age the latter End of King *William's* Reign, about six Foot high, long and broad-fac'd, and something more corpulent than this Author; his Face very like the *Homo Sylvestris*, or *Champanza*; for his Nose was flattish and short, and his Upper Lip very long and thick, with a wide

Mouth and short Chin, a churlish Voice, and awkward Action, (leaping often up with both Legs at a Time, when he conceived any Thing waggish, and afterwards hugging himself at the Thought.)——He could not enter into any serious Character, much more Tragedy; and was the most confin'd Actor I ever saw And could scarce be brought to speak a short *Latin* Speech in Don Quixot, when *Sancho* is made to say, *Sit bonus Populus, bonus ero Gubernator*; which he pronounced thus:

Shit bones and bobble arse,
Bones, and ears Goble Nature.

He was obliged to Mr. *Betterton* for thrusting him into the Character of *Merryman* in his *Wanton Wife*, or *Amorous Widow*; but *Westheart Cave* was too much of a Dullman.—His chief Atchievement was in *Lolpoop*, in the *'Squire of Alsatia*; where it was almost impossible for him to deviate from himself But he did great Injustice to Sir *Sampson Legend* in *Love for Love*, unless it had been true, that the Knight had been bred a Hog-driver.—In short, *Underhill* was far from being a good Actor—as appear'd by the late *Ben. Johnson's* assuming his Parts of *Jacomo*—the Grave-digger in *Hamlet*—and Judge *Grypus* in *Amphytrion*.—I know, Mr. *Underhill* was much cry'd up in his Time; but I am so stupid as not to know why.

Mr. *DOGGET*, indeed, cannot reasonably be so

censur'd; for whoever decry'd him, must inevitably have laugh'd much, whenever he saw him act.

Mr. *Dogget* was but little regarded, 'till he chopp'd on the Character of *Solon* in the *Marriage-Hater Match'd*; and from that he vegetated fast in the Parts of *Fondle-wife* in the *Old Batchelor—Colignii*, in the *Villain—Hob*, in the *Country Wake—*and *Ben* the Sailor, in *Love for Love.*—But, on a Time, he suffer'd himself to be expos'd, by attempting the serious Character of *Phorbas* in *Oedipus*, than which nothing cou'd be more ridiculous—for when he came to these Words—(*But, oh! I wish* Phorbas *had perish'd in that very Moment*)—the Audience conceived that it was spoke like *Hob* in his Dying-Speech.—They burst out into a loud Laughter; which sunk *Tom Dogget's* Progress in Tragedy from that Time.

Fœlix quem faciunt aliena pericula cautum.

But our present LAUREAT had a better Opinion of himself;—for, in a few Nights afterwards, *COLLEY*, at the old Theatre, attempted the same Character; but was hiss'd,—his Voice sounding like Lord *Foppington's—Ne Sutor ultra Crepidam.*

Mr. *Dogget* was a little, lively, spract Man, about the Stature of Mr. L———, Sen. Bookseller in B—h, but better built.—His Behaviour modest, chearful, and complaisant.—He sung in Company very agreeably, and in Public very comically.—He danc'd the *Cheshire Round* full as well as the fam'd Capt. *George*, but with much more Nature and Nimbleness.—I have had the Pleasure of his Conversation for one Year, when I travell'd with him in his strolling Company, and found him a Man of very good Sense, but illiterate, for he wrote me Word thus—*Sir, I will give you a* hole instead of (*whole*) *Share.*—He dress'd neat, and something fine—in a plain Cloth Coat, and a brocaded Waistcoat.—But he is so recent, having been so often at *Bath,*—*satis est.*—He gave his Yearly Water-Badge, out of a warm Principle, (being a *staunch Revolution-Whig.*)———I cannot part with this *Nonpareil,* without saying, that he was the most faithful, pleasant Actor that ever was—for he never deceiv'd his Audience—because, while they gaz'd at him, he was working up the Joke, which broke out suddenly in involuntary Acclamations and Laughter.—Whereas our modern Actors are fumbling the dull Minutes, keeping the gaping Pit in Suspence of something delightful a coming,—*Et parturiunt Montes, nascitur ridiculus Mus.*

He was the best Face-player and Gesticulator, and a thorough Master of the several Dialects, except the *Scots,* (for he never was in *Scotland*) but was, for all that, a most excellent *Sawney.* Whoever would see him pictur'd, may view his Picture, in the Character of *Sawney,* at the *Duke's Head* in *Lynn-Regis,* in *Norfolk.*——While I travell'd with him, each Sharer kept his Horse, and was every where respected as a Gentleman.

Jack Verbruggen, in Point of Merit, will salute you next.

JACK VERBRUGGEN, that rough Diamond, shone more bright than all the artful, polish'd Brillants that ever sparkled on our Stage.—(*JACK bore the BELL* away.)—He had the Words perfect at one View, and Nature directed 'em into Voice and Action, in which last he was always pleasing—his Person being tall, well-built and clean ; only he was a little In-kneed, which gave him a shambling Gate, which was a Carelessness, and became him.—His chief Parts were *Bajazet, Oroonoko, Edgar* in King *Lear, Wilmore* in the *Rover*, and *Cassius*, when Mr. *Betterton* play'd *Brutus* with him.—Then you might behold the grand Contest, *viz.* whether Nature or Art excell'd—*Verbruggen* wild and untaught, or *Betterton* in the Trammels of Instruction.—In *Edgar*, in King *Lear*, *Jack* shew'd his Judgment most, for his Madness was unlimited : Whereas he sensibly felt a Tenderness for *Cordelia*, in these Words, (speaking to her)—*As you did once know* Edgar !—And you may best conceive his manly, wild Starts, by these Words in *Oroonoko*,—*Ha! thou hast rous'd the Lyon [in] his Den; he stalks abroad, and the wild Forest trembles at his Roar* :—Which was spoke, like a Lyon, by *Oroonoko*, and *Jack Verbruggen*; for Nature was so predominant, that his second Thoughts never alter'd his prime Performance.—The late Marquess of *Hallifax* order'd *Oroonoko* to be taken from *George Powel*, saying to Mr. *Southern*, the Author,—That *Jack* was the unpolish'd Hero, and wou'd do it best.—In the *Rover*

(*Wilmore*) never were more beautiful Scenes than between him, and Mrs. *Bracegirdle*, in the Character of *Helena*; for, what with *Verbruggen's* untaught Airs, and her smiling Repartees, the Audience were afraid they were going off the Stage every Moment. —*Verbruggen* was Nature, without Extravagance—Freedom, without Licentiousness—and vociferous, without bellowing.——He was most indulgently soft, when he says to *Imoinda*,—*I cannot, as I wou'd, bestow thee*; *and, as I ought, I dare not*.—Yet, with all these Perfections, *Jack* did, and said, more silly Things than all the Actors besides; for he was drawn in at the common Cheat of Pricking at the Girdle, Cups and Balls, *&c.* and told his Wife one Day that he had found out a Way to raise a great Benefit.—*I hope*, said she, *you'll have your* Bills *printed in* Gold Letters.—*No, no, better than that*, said he ; *for I'll have the King's-Arms all in Gold Letters.*—As Mr. *Verbruggen* had Nature for his Directress in Acting, so had a known Singer, *Jemmy Bowen*, the same in Music :—He, when practising a Song set by Mr. PURCELL, some of the Music told him to grace and run a Division in such a Place. *O let him alone*, said Mr. *Purcell* ; *he will grace it more naturally than you, or I, can teach him*.—In short, an Actor, like a Poet,

Nascitur, non fit.

And this Author prizes himself on that Attempt, as he hath had the Judgment of all the best Critics

in the Character of *Fondlewife* in the *Old Batchelor*.
—*If you wou'd see Nature,* say they, *see* Tony
Aston—*if Art,* Colley Cibber;—and, indeed, I have
shed mock Tears in that Part often involuntarily.

Mrs. *VERBRUGGEN* claims a Place next. She
was all Art, and her Acting all acquir'd, but dress'd
so nice, it look'd like Nature. There was not a
Look, a Motion, but what were all design'd; and
these at the same Word, Period, Occasion, Incident,
were every Night, in the same Character, alike; and
yet all sat charmingly easy on her.—Her Face,
Motion, *&c.* chang'd at once . But the greatest, and
usual, Position was Laughing, Flirting her Fan, and
je ne scay quois,—with a Kind of affected Twitter.—
She was very loath to accept of the Part of *Weldon*
in *Oroonoko,* and that with just Reason, as being
obliged to put on Men's Cloaths—having thick Legs
and Thighs, corpulent and large Posteriours;—but
yet the Town (that respected her) compounded, and
receiv'd her with Applause; for she was the most
pleasant Creature that ever appear'd: Adding to
these, that she was a fine, fair Woman, plump, full-
featur'd; her Face of a fine, smooth Oval, full of
beautiful, well-dispos'd Moles on it, and on her Neck
and Breast.—Whatever she did was not to be call'd
Acting; no, no, it was what she represented . She
was neither more nor less, and was the most easy
Actress in the World. The late Mrs. OLDFIELD
borrow'd something of her Manner in free Comedy;

—as for Tragedy, Mrs. *Verbruggen* never attempted it. *Melanthe* was her Master-piece; and the Part of *Hillaria* in *Tunbridge-Walks* cou'd not be said to be Acted by any one but her.—Her Maiden-Name was *Percival*; and she was the Widow of Mr. *Mountford*, (who was kill'd by Lord *Mohun*) when Mr. *Verbruggen* married her.—She was the best Conversation possible; never captious, or displeas'd at any Thing but what was gross or indecent; for she was cautious, lest fiery *Jack* shou'd so resent it as to breed a Quarrel;—for he wou'd often say,—*Dammee! tho' I don't much value my Wife, yet no Body shall affront her, by G—d*; and his Sword was drawn on the least Occasion, which was much in Fashion at the latter End of King *William's* Reign;—at which Time I came on the Stage, when Mr. *Dogget* left it; and then the facetious *Joe Haines* was declining in Years and Reputation, tho' a good Actor and Poet, his Prologues exceeding all ever wrote.—[*Vide* Love and a Bottle]

JOE HAINES is more remarkable for the witty, tho' wicked, Pranks he play'd, and for his Prologues and Epilogues, than for Acting.—He was, at first, a Dancer.—After he had made his Tour of *France*, he narrowly escaped being seiz'd, and sent to the *Bastile*, for personating an *English* Peer, and running 3000 Livres in Debt in *Paris*; but, happily landing at *Dover*, he went to *London*, where in *Bartholomew-Fair*, he set up a Droll-Booth, and acted a new Droll, call'd, *The Whore of Babylon, the Devil, and the Pope.* This was in the first Year of King *James* II. when *Joe* was sent for, and roundly admonish'd, by Judge *Pollixfen* for it. *Joe* reply'd, *That he did it in Respect to his* Holiness; *for, whereas many ignorant People believed the* Pope *to be a* Beast, *he shew'd him to be a fine, comely old Gentleman, as he was*; *not with Seven Heads, and Ten Horns, as the* Scotch *Parsons describe him.* However, this Affair spoil'd *Joe's* expiring Credit; for next Morning, a Couple of Bailiffs seiz'd him in an Action of 20*l.* as the Bishop of *Ely* was passing by in his Coach.—Quoth *Joe* to the Bailiffs,—*Gentlemen, here's my Cousin, the Bishop of* Ely, *going into his House*; *let me but speak to him, and he'll pay the Debt and Charges.* The Bailiffs thought they might venture that, as they were within three or four Yards of him. So, up goes *Joe* to the Coach, pulling off his Hat, and got close to it. The Bishop order'd the Coach to stop, whilst *Joe* (close to his Ear) said softly, *My Lord, here are two poor Men, who have such great Scruples of Conscience, that, I fear, they'll hang themselves.*—Very well, *said the Bishop.* So, calling to the Bailiffs, he said, *You two Men, come to me To-morrow Morning, and I'll satisfy you.* The Men bow'd, and went away *Joe* (hugging himself with his fallacious Device) went also his Way. In the Morning, the Bailiffs (expecting the Debt and Charges) repair'd to the Bishop's; where being introduced,—*Well,* said the Bishop, *what are your*

Scruples of Conscience?—Scruples! (said the Bailiffs) *we have no Scruples: We are Bailiffs, my Lord, who, Yesterday, arrested your Cousin,* Joe Haines, *for* 20*l. Your Lordship promised to satisfy us To-day, and we hope your Lordship will be as good as your Word.*—The Bishop, reflecting that his Honour and Name would be expos'd, (if he complied not) paid the Debt and Charges.—There were two Parts of Plays (*Nol Bluff* in the *Old Batchelor*, and *Roger* in *Æsop*) which none ever touch'd but *Joe Haines*—I own, I have copied him in *Roger*, as I did Mr. *Dogget* in *Fondlewife*.—But, now, for another Story of him.

In the long Vacation, when Harlots, Poets, and Players, are all poor,—*Joe* walking in *Cross-Street*, by *Hatton-Garden*, sees a fine Venison-Pasty come out of *Glassop's*, a Pastry-Cook's Shop, which a Boy carried to a Gentleman's House thereby.—*Joe* watch'd it; and seeing a Gentleman knock at the Door, he goes to the Door, and ask'd him if he had knock'd at it. *Yes*, said the Gentleman; *the Door is open'd.* —In goes the Gentleman, and *Joe* after him, to the Dining-Room.—Chairs were set, and all ready for the Pasty. The Master of the House took *Joe* for the Gentleman's Friend, whom he had invited to Dinner; which being over, the Gentleman departed. *Joe* sat still.—Says the Master of the House to *Joe, Sir, I thought you would have gone with your Friend!* —*My Friend*, said *Joe*; *alas! I never saw him before in my Life.*—*No, Sir,* replied the other:

Pray, Sir, then how came you to Dinner here?—Sir, said *Joe, I saw a Venison-Pasty carried in here; and, by this Means, have din'd very heartily of it. My Name is* Joe Haines, (said he) *I belong to the* Theatre. —*Oh, Mr.* Haines, (continued the Gentleman) *you are very welcome; you are a Man of Wit*: *Come, bring t'other bottle*; which being finish'd, *Joe*, with good Manners, departed, and purposely left his Cane behind him, which he design'd to be an Introduction to another Dinner there: For, next Day, when they were gone to Dinner, *Joe* knock'd briskly at the Door, to call for his Cane, when the Gentleman of the House was telling a Friend of his the Trick he play'd the Day before —*Pray call Mr.* Haines *in*.— *So, Mr.* Haines, said he; *sit down, and partake of another Dinner.*—*To tell you the Truth*, said *Joe, I left my Cane Yesterday on purpose*: At which they all laugh'd.—Now *Joe* (altho' while greedily eating) was very attentive to a Discourse on Humanity begun, and continued, by the Stranger Gentleman; wherein he advanced, that every Man's Duty was to assist another, whether with Advice, Money, Cloaths, Food, or whatever else. This Sort of Principle suited *Joe's* End, as by the Sequel will appear. The Company broke up, and *Joe*, and the Gentleman, walk'd away, (*Joe* sighing as he went along.) The Gentleman said to him, *What do you sigh for?*—*Dear Sir*, (quoth *Joe*) *I fear my Landlord will, this Day, seize my Goods for only a Quarter's Rent, due last Week*.— *How much is the Money?* said the Gentleman.—

Fifty Shillings, said *Joe, and the Patentees owe me Ten Pounds, which will be paid next Week.*—*Come,* said the Gentleman, *I'll lend thee Fifty Shillings on your Note, to pay me faithfully in three Weeks.* Which *Joe,* with many Promises and Imprecations, sign'd.— But *Joe,* thereafter, had his Eyes looking out before him; and, whenever he saw the Gentleman, would carefully avoid him; which the Gentleman one Day perceiv'd, and going a-cross *Smithfield,* met *Joe* full in the Face, and, in the Middle of the *Rounds,* stopp'd him. Taking him by the Collar, *Sirrah,* said he, *pray pay me now, you impudent, cheating Dog, or I'll beat you into a Jelly.*—*Joe* fell down on his Knees, making a dismal Outcry, which drew a Mob about them, who enquir'd into the Occasion, which was told them; and they, upon hearing it, said to the Gentleman, *That the poor Man could not pay it, if he had it not.*—*Well,* said he, *let him kneel down, and eat up that thin Sirreverence, and I'll forgive him, and give up his Note.*—*Joe* promis'd he would, and presently eat it all up, smearing his Lips and Nose with the human Conserve. The Gentleman gave him his Note; when *Joe* ran and embrac'd him, kissing him, and bedaubing his Face, and setting the Mob a hollowing.

The SECOND PART *of their* LIVES, *with the Continuation of* JOE HAINES's *Pranks, the Author hopes a fresh Advance for.*——*In the* Interim, *he thanks his Friends.*

FINIS.

MEMOIRS OF THE ACTORS AND ACTRESSES MENTIONED BY CIBBER,

TAKEN FROM EDMUND BELLCHAMBERS'S EDITION OF THE "APOLOGY," 1822.

WILLIAM SMITH.

THIS judicious actor, who is said to have been originally a barrister, came into the Duke's Company, when acting under Sir William D'Avenant, in Lincoln's Inn Fields, about the year 1663. He rose soon after to the duties of *Buckingham*, in "King Henry the Eighth," and subsequently filled a range of characters distinguished by their variety and importance. *Sir William Stanley*, in Caryl's wretched play of the "English Princess," procured him additional estimation and applause, which were still farther enlarged by his performance of *Stanford* in Shadwell's "Sullen Lovers." Mr. Smith was the original *Chamont* in Otway's "Orphan," and played many parts of as much local consequence in pieces that are now forgotten.

Chetwood informs us that Mr. Smith was zealously attached to the interests of King James the Second, in whose army, attended by two servants, he entered as a volunteer. Upon the abdication of that monarch, he returned to the stage, by the persuasions of many friends, who admired his performances, and resumed his original part of *Wilmore* in the "Rover;" but having been received with considerable disapprobation, on account of his party

NOTE.—All passages enclosed in square brackets are by the present editor, who is also responsible for the notes marked (L.).

principles, the audience was dismissed, and he departed from public life in the manner already mentioned. It is difficult to reconcile these discrepancies Chetwood's minuteness looks like credibility, and Cibber has committed a mistake in stating that Mr. Smith "entirely quitted" the stage at this secession, he having returned in 1695, when at the earnest solicitations of his sincere friends Mr. Betterton and Mrs. Barry, strengthened by the influence of Congreve over many of his connections in high life, he consented to sustain the part of *Scandal* in that author's comedy of "Love for Love," upon its production at the new theatre in Little Lincoln's Inn Fields, when his inimitable performance imparted an extra charm to that admirable play Continued peals of applause attested the satisfaction which his auditors felt at the return of their old favourite, and it seems singular that Congreve should have wholly overlooked this memorable event, in the "prologue" at least, where the defection of Williams and Mrs. Mountfort is thus obscurely stated:

> Forbear your wonder, and the fault forgive
> If in our larger family we grieve
> One falling Adam, and one tempted Eve.

Mr. Smith continued on the stage till about twelve months after this period, when, according to Downes, having a long part in Banks's tragedy of "Cyrus," 1696, he fell sick on the fourth day of performance, and died from a cold, as Chetwood relates, occasioned by cramp, which having seized him while in bed, he rose to get rid of it, and remained so long in his naked condition, that a fever ensued from disordered lungs, and, in three days, put an end to his existence.

We have but a slender clue to the stage-management of Mr. Smith, which was exercised over the Duke's Company in Dorset-garden, conjointly with Betterton and Dr. D'Avenant, when the famous agreement which bears their signatures was concluded with Hart and Kynaston, for an union of the theatres. It has been said that Booth [who wrote an epitaph on Smith] applied to him for an engagement, which was refused from a fear of offending his relatives, but with that kindness of expression and deportment so warmly distinguished in his epitaph. This assertion, however, is unfounded, for when Mr. Smith died, Barton Booth was a Westminster scholar, and in the fourteenth year of his age; the character of this eminent comedian must, accordingly, have been drawn up from such intelligence as the writer acquired at a subsequent period.

It only remains to be remarked, that Chetwood has placed Mr. Smith's original return to the stage in the year 1692; but, not to insist upon the known looseness of this writer's information, let us ask if a political offence would be so vehemently remembered, after the lapse of four years, as to drive an estimable actor from the harmless pursuance of his ordinary duties? Cibber is doubtless correct in the floating date of this fact, which must have happened *previous* to the revolution. Mr. Smith was a principal actor in Lee's later tragedies, but in the "Princess of Cleve," 4to, 1689, we find the part he would naturally have played to Betterton's *Nemours*, supported by Mr. Williams.

Smith's value as an actor, may be immediately felt by a reference to the parts he enjoyed under Betterton, with whom he lived till death in the most cordial manner, enhancing his fame by honourable emulation, and promoting his interests by unbroken amity. No instance has been recorded of their dissention or dispute, and from the notice which Betterton extended to Booth, he very possibly communicated that high account of his departed friend, which the latter has recorded with such spirit and fidelity.

From Cibber's admission, it appears, that Smith's moral qualities and professional excellence, procured him an extensive reception among people of rank, a patronage which his polished manners continued to exact, till society, by his death, sustained one of its deepest deprivations. (B.) Chetwood's story is now incapable either of proof or disproof. The known facts about Smith's retirement are, that his name appears to Constantine the Great, to Courtine in Otway's "Atheist," and to Lorenzo in Southerne's "Disappointment," in 1684; that it then disappears, and does not again occur till 1695. It is probable that he retired in 1684, as it is unlikely that his name should not appear in one or other of the 1685 bills. (L.)

CHARLES HART.

Charles Hart was the great nephew of Shakspeare, his father, William, being the eldest son of our poet's sister Joan. Brought up as an apprentice under Robinson, a celebrated actor, he commenced his career, conformably to the practice of that time, by playing female parts, among which the *Duchess*, in Shirley's tragedy of the "Cardinal," was the first that exhibited his talents, or enhanced his reputation.

Puritanism having gathered great strength, opposed theatrical amusements as vicious and profane institutions, which it was at length enabled to abolish and suppress. On the 11th day of February, 1647,[1] and the subsequent 22d of October, two ordinances were issued by the Long Parliament, whereby all stage-players were made liable to punishment for following their usual occupation Before the appearance of this severe edict, most of the actors had gone into the army, and fought with distinguished spirit for their unfortunate master , when, however, his fate was determined, the surviving dependants on the drama were compelled to renew their former efforts, in pursuance of which they returned, just before the death of Charles, to act a few plays at the "Cockpit" theatre, where, while per-

[1] This is a specimen of that commonest of blunders, the confusing of the dates of the first month or two of the year. The edict was issued February, 1647-8, that is, 1648. What Bellchambers calls the "subsequent" October was therefore the preceding October. (L.)

forming the tragedy of "Rollo," they were taken into custody by soldiers, and committed to prison.¹ Upon this occasion, Hart, who had been a lieutenant of horse, under Sir Thomas Dallison, in Prince Rupert's own regiment, sustained the character of *Otto*, a part which he afterwards relinquished to Kynaston, in exchange for the fierce energies of his ambitious brother.

At the Restoration, Hart was enrolled among the company constituting his Majesty's Servants, by whom the new Theatre Royal, Drury-lane, was opened on the 8th of April, 1663, with Beaumont and Fletcher's play of the "Humourous Lieutenant," in which he sustained a principal character for twelve days of successive representation.

About the year 1667,² Hart introduced Mrs. Gwyn upon the dramatic boards, and has acquired the distinction of being ranked among that lady's first felicitous lovers, by having succeeded to Lacy, in the possession of her charms. Nell had been tutored for the stage by these admirers in conjunction, and after testifying her gratitude to both, passed into the hands of Lord Buckhurst, by whom she was transferred to the custody of King Charles the Second.

The principal parts, according to Downes, sustained by Mr. Hart, were *Arbaces*, in "King and No King;" *Amintor*, in the "Maid's Tragedy;" *Othello, Rolla, Brutus*, and *Alexander the Great*. Such was his attraction in all these characters, that, to use the language of that honest prompter, "if he acted in any one of these but once in a fortnight, the house was filled as at a new play; especially *Alexander*, he acting that with such grandeur and agreeable majesty, that one of the court was pleased to honour him with this commendation—'that Hart might teach any king on earth how to comport himself.'" His merit has also been specified as *Mosca*, in the "Fox," *Don John*, in the "Chances," and

---

[1] See "Historia Histrionica."

[2] Nell Gwyn made her first appearance not later than 1665. Pepys, on the 3rd of April, 1665, mentions "Pretty, witty Nell, at the King's House." (L.)

Wildblood, in an "Evening's Love;" which, however, according to the same authority, merely harmonised with his general efforts, in commanding a vast superiority over the best of his successors.

Rymer has said that Hart's action could throw a lustre round the meanest characters, and, by dazzling the eyes of the spectator, protect the poet's deformities from discernment. He was taller, and more genteelly shaped than Mohun, on which account he probably claimed the choice of parts, and was prescriptively invested with the attributes of youth and agility. He possessed a considerable share in the profits and direction of the theatre, which were divided among the principal performers; and besides his salary of £3 a week, and an allowance as a proprietor, amounting to six shillings and three-pence a day, is supposed to have occasionally cleared about £1000 per annum.

[On the 14th of October, 1681, a memorandum was signed between Dr. Charles Davenant, Betterton, and Smith, of the one part, and Hart and Kynaston, of the other, by which the two last mentioned, in consideration of five shillings each for every day on which there shall be a play at the Duke's Theatre, undertake to do all they can to break up the King's Company. The result of this agreement was the Union of 1682. This agreement is given in Gildon's "Life of Betterton" (p. 8), and in Genest (i. 369). I suppose it is a genuine document, but I confess to some doubts, based chiefly on my belief that Betterton was too honest to enter into so shabby an intrigue.]

Declining age had rendered Hart less fit for exertion than in the vigour of life, and certain of the young actors, such as Goodman and Clark, became impatient to get possession of his and Mohun's characters. A violent affliction, however, of the stone and gravel, compelled him to relinquish his professional efforts, and having stipulated for the payment of five shillings-a day, during the season,[1] he retired from the stage, and died a short time after.

---

[1] Should be for the remainder of his life. (L.)

Hart was always esteemed a constant observer of decency in manners, and the following anecdote will evince his respect for the clergy. That witty, but abandoned fellow, Jo Haynes, had persuaded a silly divine, into whose company he had unaccountably fallen, that the players were a set of people, who wished to be reformed, and wanted a Chaplain to the Theatre, an appointment for which, with a handsome yearly income, he could undertake to recommend him. He then directed the clergyman to summon his hearers, by tolling a bell to prayers every morning, a scheme, in pursuance of which Haynes introduced his companion, with a bell in his hand, behind the scenes, which he frequently rang, and cried out, audibly, "Players! players! come to prayers!" While Jo and some others were enjoying this happy contrivance, Hart came into the theatre, and, on discovering the imposition, was extremely angry with Haynes, whom he smartly reprehended, and having invited the clergyman to dinner, convinced him that this buffoon was an improper associate for a man of his function.[1]

[1] Vide Davies's "Dramatic Miscellanies," vol. iii p. 264.

Another anecdote of the same kind is found in a "Life of the late famous comedian, J. Haynes," 8vo. 1701, which, as it preserves a characteristic trait of this valuable actor, is worth repeating

"About this time [1673] there happened a small pick between Mr. Hart and Jo, upon the account of his late negotiation in France,* and there spending so much money to so little purpose, or, as I may more properly say, to no purpose at all.

"There happened to be one night a play acted, called 'Cataline's Conspiracy,' wherein there was wanting a great number of senators Now Mr. Hart being chief of the house, would oblige Jo to dress for one of these senators, although his salary, being 50s. per week, freed him from any such obligation. But Mr Hart, as I said before, being sole governor of the playhouse, and at a small variance with Jo, commands it, and the other must obey.

"Jo being vexed at the slight Mr. Hart had put upon him, found out this method of being revenged on him. He gets a Scaramouch dress,

* Soon after the theatre in Drury-lane was burnt down, Jan 1671-2, Haynes had been sent to Paris by Mr Hart and Mr Killegrew, to examine the machinery employed in the French Operas —*Malone*

MICHAEL MOHUN.

The life of Michael Mohun, though passed in its early stages beneath a different teacher, was chequered by the very shades which distinguished that of Hart, with whom he acquired his military distinctions, and reverted to a theatrical life. He was brought up with Shatterel, under Beeston, at the "Cock-pit," in Drury-lane, where, in Shirley's play of "Love's Cruelty," he sustained the part of *Bellamente*, among other female characters,[1] and held it even after the Restoration.

Having attained the rank of captain in the royal forces, Mohun went to Flanders upon the termination of the civil war, where he received pay as a major, and acquitted himself with distinguished credit. At the Restoration, he resumed his pristine duties, and became an able second to Hart, with whom he was equally admired for superlative knowledge of his arduous profession.

a large full ruff, makes himself whiskers from ear to ear, puts on his head a long Merry-Andrew's cap, a short pipe in his mouth, a little three-legged stool in his hand; and in this manner follows Mr Hart on the stage, sets himself down behind him, and begins to smoke his pipe, laugh, and point at him, which comical figure put all the house in an uproar, some laughing, some clapping, and some hollaing. Now Mr Hart, as those who knew him can aver, was a man of that exactness and grandeur on the stage, that let what would happen, he'd never discompose himself, or mind any thing but what he then represented, and had a scene fallen behind him, he would not at that time look back, to have seen what was the matter, which Jo knowing, remained still smoking. The audience continued laughing, Mr. Hart acting, and wondering at this unusual occasion of their mirth, sometimes thinking it some disturbance in the house, again that it might be something amiss in his dress at last turning himself toward the scenes, he discovered Jo in the aforesaid posture, whereupon he immediately goes off the stage, swearing he would never set foot on it again, unless Jo was immediately turned out of doors, which was no sooner spoke, but put in practice."

[1] Bellamente is not a female, but a male character. By referring to the mention of this matter in the "Historia Histrionica," it will at once be seen how Bellchambers's blunder was caused. (L.)

He is celebrated by Lord Rochester, as the great Æsopus of the stage; praise, which, though coming from one of so capricious a temper, may be relied on, since it is confirmed by more respectable testimony. He was particularly remarkable for the dignity of his deportment, and the elegance of his step, which mimics, said his lordship, attempted to imitate, though they could not reach the sublimity of his elocution. The Duke's comedians, it would seem, endeavoured to emulate his manner, when reduced by age and infirmity, a baseness which the same noble observer has thus warmly reprehended:—

> Yet these are they, who durst expose the Age
> Of the great Wonder of the English Stage.
> Whom Nature seem'd to form for your delight,
> And bid him speak, as she bid Shakespeare write.
> These Blades indeed are Cripples in their Art,
> Mimick his Foot, but not his speaking part.
> Let them the *Traytor* or *Volpone* try,
> Could they
> Rage like *Cethegus*, or like *Cassius* die?
> (Epilogue to Fane's "Love in the Dark.")

Mohun, from his inferior height and muscular form, generally acted grave, solemn, austere parts, though upon more than one occasion, as in *Valentine*, in "Wit without Money," and *Face*, in the "Alchemist,"—one of his most capital characters,—he was frequently seen in gay and buoyant assumptions to great advantage. He was singularly eminent as *Melantius*, in the "Maid's Tragedy;" *Mardonius*, in "King and No King;" *Clytus*, *Mithridates*, and the parts alluded to by Lord Rochester. No man had more skill in putting spirit and passion into the dullest poetry than Mohun, an excellence with which Lee was so delighted, that on seeing him act his own King of Pontus, he suddenly exclaimed, "O, Mohun, Mohun, thou little man of mettle, if I should write a hundred plays, I'd write a part for thy mouth!" And yet Lee himself was so exquisite a reader, that Mohun once threw down a part in despair of approaching the force of the author's expression. The "Tatler" has adverted to his singular science,[1] "in all his parts, too," says Downes," he was most accurate and correct;" and perhaps no encomium can transcend the honours of unbroken propriety.

About the year 1681, there are some reasons to suspect that the king's company was divided by feuds and animosities, which their adversaries in Dorset-garden so well improved, as to produce an union of the separate patents Hart and Kynaston were dexterously detached from their old associates, by the management of Betterton, whose conduct, though grounded upon maxims of policy, can derive no advantage from so unfair an expedient. Upon the completion of this nefarious treaty, Mohun, who found means to retain the services of Kynaston, with the remnant of the royal company, continued to act in defiance of the junction just concluded, as an independent body. Downes, in his "Roscius Anglicanus," so far as the imperfect structure of its sentences can be relied on, expressly asserts this; and yet if "the patentees of each company united patents, and, by so incorporating, the duke's company were made the king's, and immediately removed to the Theatre Royal in Drury-lane," what field did Mohun and his followers select for their operations, to pitch their tents, and hoist their standard? Till some period, at least, of the year 1682, this party were in possession of their antient domicile, as Mohun at that time, acted *Burleigh*, in Banks's "Unhappy Favourite," and sustained a principal character in Southern's "Loyal Brother," with, for his heroine, in both pieces, the famous Nell Gwyn[2]

---

[1] " My old friends Hart and Mohun, the one by his natural and proper force, the other *by his great skill and art*, never failed to send me home full of such ideas as affected my behaviour, and made me insensibly more courteous and human to my friends and acquaintance."— 'Tatler," No 99

[2] The following extract from a pamphlet, called "A Comparison

[Bellchambers is here very inaccurate. The union of 1682 was, no doubt, opposed by some of the King's Company, from November, 1681, when the memorandum between Davenant, Betterton, Hart, and others, was executed, and the date of the actual conclusion of the union. This is clearly indicated in Dryden's Prologue on the opening of Drury Lane by the united company on 16th November, 1682. But, whatever the opposition had been, it had ceased then, because in the cast of the "Duke of Guise," produced less than three weeks later, appear the names of Kynaston and Wiltshire, whom Bellchambers represents as supporting Mohun in his supposed opposition theatre. (L.)]

CARDELL GOODMAN.

Cardell Goodman, according to his own admissions, as detailed by Cibber elsewhere, was expelled the university of Cambridge, for certain political reasons, a disgrace, however, which did not disqualify him for the stage. He came

between the Two Stages," will amply evince the popular estimation in which Hart and Mohun were held:—

"The late Duke of Monmouth was a good judge of dancing, and a good dancer himself; when he returned from France, he brought with him St. André, then the best master in France. The duke presented him to the stage, the stage to gratify the duke admitted him, and the duke himself thought he would prove a mighty advantage to them, though he had nobody else of his opinion A day was published in the bills for him to dance, but not one more, besides the duke and his friends came to see him; the reason was, the plays were then so good, and Hart and Mohun acted them so well, that the audience would not be interrupted, for so short a time, though 'twas to see the best master in Europe"

I suspect that Mohun was born about the year 1625, from the circumstance of his acting *Bellamente*, the heroine of Shirley's "Love's Cruelty," in 1640, when he had probably reached, and could hardly have exceeded, the age of fifteen years (B.) As has been before pointed out, Bellamente is not a female character. He is the husband of Clariana, and could scarcely be played by a boy If Mohun represented the character in 1640, he must have been considerably older than Bellchambers imagines. (L.)

upon it, accordingly, by repairing to Drury-lane theatre, where Downes has recorded [what was probably] his first appearance, as *Polyperchon*, in the "Rival Queens," 4to. 1677. Here, although we cannot trace his success in any character of importance, Mr. Cibber has adverted to his rapid advances in reputation. He followed the fortunes of Mohun in opposing the united actors, but, about three years afterwards, resorted to them, (in 1685,) and sustained the hero of Lord Rochester's "Valentinian." It is about this period that his excellence must have blazed out as *Alexander the Great*, since Cibber, who went upon the stage in 1690, says Goodman had retired before the time of his appearance.

The highest salary enjoyed at that period we are now treating of, was six shillings and three pence per diem, a stipend that was by no means equal to the strong passions and large appetites of a gay, handsome, inconsiderate young fellow. He was consequently induced to commit a robbery on the highway, and sentenced upon detection, to make a summary atonement for his fatal error; but this being the first exploit of that kind to which the scantiness of his income had urged him, King James was persuaded to pardon him, a favour for which Goodman was so grateful, that, in the year 1696, he shared with Sir John Fenwick in a design to assassinate King William, who spared his life in consideration of the testimony he was to render against his accomplice. This condition, however, Goodman did not fulfil, as he withdrew clandestinely to the continent, to avoid giving evidence, and died in exile.

Having been selected as a fit instrument for her abandoned pleasures by the Duchess of Cleveland, Goodman, long before his death, became so happy in his circumstances, that he acted only at intervals, when his titled mistress most probably desired to see him; for he used to say, he would not even act *Alexander*, unless his Duchess were in front to witness the performance.

RICHARD ESTCOURT.

Richard Estcourt, according to the biographical notice of Chetwood, was born at Tewksbury, in Glostershire, in the year 1668, and received a competent education at the Latin grammar-school of his native town. Influenced by an early attachment to the stage, he left his father's house, in the fifteenth year of his age, with an itinerant company, and on reaching Worcester, to elude the possibility of detection, made his first appearance as *Roxana*, in the "Rival Queens." Having received a correct intimation of this theatrical purpose, his father sent to secure the fugitive, who slipped away in a suit of woman's clothes, borrowed from one of his kind-hearted companions, and travelled to Chipping-Norton, a distance of five-and-twenty miles, in the course of the day

To prevent such excursions for the future, he was quickly carried up to London, and apprenticed to an apothecary in Hatton-garden, with whom, according to some authorities, he continued till the expiration of his indentures, and duly entered into business; which, either from want of liking or success he soon afterwards renounced, and returned to his favourite avocation.[1] Chetwood, on the contrary, asserts that he broke away from his master's authority, and after strolling about England for two years, went over to Dublin, where his performances were sanctioned by ardent and universal applause

About the opening of the eighteenth century [that is, 18th October, 1704], Mr. Estcourt was engaged at Drury-lane Theatre, where he made his début as *Dominic*, in the "Spanish Friar," and established his efforts, it is said, by a close imitation of Leigh, the original possessor of that part. In the year 1705 [should be 1706], such was his merit or

---

[1] This account, though generally rejected, appears to me more deserving of credit than Chetwood's notoriously neglectful habits, in gleaning intelligence, or making assertion

reputation, that Farquhar selected him for *Sergeant Kite*, in the "Recruiting Officer," a character to which Downes has alluded in terms of unqualified praise. It is asserted in the "Biographia Dramatica," that Mr. Estcourt was "mostly indebted for his applause to his powers of mimicry, in which he was inimitable; and which not only at times afforded him opportunities of appearing a much better actor than he really was,—by enabling him to copy very exactly several performers of capital merit, whose manner he remembered and assumed,—but also, by recommending him to a very numerous acquaintance in private life, secured him an indulgence for faults in his public profession, that he might otherwise, perhaps, never have been pardoned." As if an actor, in defiance of peculiar incapacity, associated emulation, and public disgust, could maintain, for twelve successive years, the very highest station in the Drury-lane company, attainable by talents, such as he was only flattered with possessing!

That Estcourt was happy in a "very numerous acquaintance," there is no reason to conceal or deny. He was remarkable for the promptitude of his wit, and the permanence of his pleasantry, qualifications that recommended him to the most cordial intercourse with Addison, Steele, Parnell, who has honoured him in a Bacchanalian poem, by the name of Jocus, and other choice spirits of the age, who enjoyed the variety of his talents, and acknowledged the goodness of his heart. He was highly in favour with the great Duke of Marlborough, but those who know his grace's character, will hardly be surprised to learn that he did not improve his fortune by that dazzling distinction. Estcourt's honours, indeed, were strictly nominal, for though constituted providore of the Beef-steak Club,—an assemblage comprising the chief wits and greatest men of the nation,—he gained nothing by the office but their badge of employment,—a small golden gridiron, suspended from his neck by a bit of green riband.

If the foregoing remarks should be held sufficient to redeem his dramatic character from the obloquy with which it has so long been attended, the following anecdote will perhaps be accepted as ample evidence of his great talent for private mimicry.

Secretary Craggs, when very young, in company with some of his friends, went, with Estcourt, to Sir Godfrey Kneller's, and whispered to him that a gentleman present was able to give such a representation of many among his most powerful patrons, as would occasion the greatest surprise. Estcourt accordingly, at the artist's earnest desire, mimicked Lords Somers, Halifax, Godolphin, and others, so exactly, that Kneller was delighted, and laughed heartily at the imitations. Craggs gave a signal, as concerted, and Estcourt immediately mimicked Sir Godfrey himself, who cried out in a transport of ungovernable conviction, "Nay, there you are out, man! By G—, that's not me!"

About a twelvemonth before his death, having retired from the stage, Estcourt opened the Bumper tavern, in Covent-garden, and by enlarging his acquaintance, most probably shortened his days. He died in the year 1713 [should be 1712], and was buried near his brother comedian, Jo Haynes, in the church-yard of St. Paul's, Covent-garden.

Thomas Betterton.

Thomas Betterton was born in Tothill-street, Westminster, in the year 1635 [baptized 11th August, 1635], his father at that time being under-cook to King Charles the First. He received the rudiments of a genteel education, and testified such a propensity to literature, that it was the steadfast intention of his family to have had him qualified for some congenial employment This design, the confusion and violence of the times most probably prevented, though a fondness for reading induced them to consult his inclinations, and he was accordingly apprenticed to Mr. Rhodes, a respectable bookseller, residing at the Bible, in Charing-cross.

This person, who had been wardrobe-keeper to the theatre in Blackfriars, before the suppression of dramatic amusements, on General Monk's approach to London, in the year 1659, obtained a license from the [governing powers] to collect a company of actors, and employ them at the "Cockpit," in Drury-lane. Here, while Kynaston, his fellow-apprentice, sustained the principal female parts, Betterton was distinguished by the vigour and elegance of his manly personations. The fame of Beaumont and Fletcher was then at its zenith, and in their plays of the "Loyal Subject," and the "Mad Lover," added to "Pericles," the "Bondman," and the "Changeling," Mr. Betterton established the groundwork of his great reputation.

Sir William D'Avenant having been favoured with a patent before the civil wars broke out, obtained a renewal of that royal grant upon the Restoration, and in the spring of 1662 [should be June, 1661], after rehearsing various plays at Apothecaries'-hall, he opened a new theatre in Lincoln's-inn-fields, where Rhodes's comedians, with the addition of Harris, and three others, were sworn before the Lord Chamberlain, as servants of the crown, and honoured by the sanction of the Duke of York.

Here Sir William D'Avenant produced his "Siege of Rhodes," a play in two parts, embellished with such scenery and decorations as had never been before exhibited on the boards of a British theatre. The parts were strongly cast, and this drama, assisted by its splendid appendages, was represented for twelve days, successively, with unbounded approbation.

At this period Mr. Betterton first assumed the part of *Hamlet*, deriving considerable advantage from the hints of Sir William D'Avenant, to whom the acting of Taylor [who had been instructed by Shakespeare] had been formerly familiar. Downes expressly declares that this character enhanced Mr. Betterton's reputation to the utmost, and there is much collateral evidence to substantiate its brilliant superiority.[1]

Mr. Betterton was so favourably considered by Charles the Second, that, upon his performance of *Alvaro*, in "Love and Honour," he received that monarch's coronation-suit for the character, as a token of esteem. Public opinion kept pace with his efforts to secure it, and by evincing unparalleled talent in such diversified parts as *Mercutio, Sir Toby Belch*, and *Henry the Eighth*, (the last of which was adopted from his manager's remembrance of Lowin) he speedily attained to that eminence in his art, above which no human exertion can probably ascend.

At the king's especial command, it has been asserted by some of his biographers that Mr. Betterton went over to Paris to take a view of the French stage, and suggest such means as might ensure a corresponding improvement upon our own. They even go so far as to term him the first who publicly introduced our moving scenes, though Sir William D'Avenant, to whom that honour decidedly belongs, had attached them, less perfectly, perhaps, in 1658, to his "Cruelty of the Spaniards in Peru."

[1] "I have lately been told by a Gentleman who has frequently seen Mr. *Betterton* perform this Part of *Hamlet*, that he has observ'd his Countenance (which was naturally ruddy and sanguin) in this Scene of the fourth Act where his Father's Ghost appears, thro' the violent and sudden Emotions of Amazement and Horror, turn instantly on the Sight of his Father's Spirit, as pale as his Neckcloath, when every Article of his Body seem'd to be affected with a Tremor inexpressible; so that, had his Father's Ghost actually risen before him; he could not have been seized with more real Agonies; and this was felt so strongly by the Audience, that the Blood seemed to shudder in their Veins likewise, and they in some Measure partook of the Astonishment and Horror, with which they saw this excellent Actor affected."—"Laureat," 1740, p 31

—— "I have seen a pamphlet, written above forty years ago, by an intelligent man, who greatly extols the performance of Betterton in this last scene, commonly called the closet scene"—Davies's "Dramatic Miscellanies," vol. iii. p. 112, ed. 1784.

By or before 1663, Mr. Betterton had married Mrs. Saunderson, a performer in the same company, of matchless merit and unsullied virtue, though that event, by the "Biographia Dramatica," and other incautious compilations, is referred to the year 1670. This lady, it may be remarked, was single, while denominated mistress; the appellation of miss not being made familiar to the middle classes, till after the commencement of the ensuing century.

The duke's company, notwithstanding the favour and excellence to which Betterton, Harris, Smith, and other members were admitted, began to feel its want of attraction so forcibly, that Sir William D'Avenant was induced to try the effects of a new theatre, which was accordingly opened, with unparalleled magnificence, in Dorset-garden, Salisbury-court, notwithstanding an earnest opposition by the city of London, in November, 1671. Opinion, however, still inclining to their antagonists, dramatic operas were invented, and soon enabled the players at this place to achieve a triumph over merit unassisted by such expensive frivolity.

At the death of D'Avenant, on the 17th of April, 1668, Mr. Betterton succeeded to a portion of the management, and so great was the estimation in which both he and his lady were held, that in the year 1675, when a pastoral, called "Calisto; or, the Chaste Nymph," written by Mr. Crown, at the request of King Charles's consort, was to be performed at court by persons of the greatest distinction, they were appointed to instruct them in their respective parts. In 1682, an union was effected with the rival company, which Mr. Betterton continued to direct, till Rich, in 1690, obtained possession of the patent, and dispossessed him of importance and authority.

Exasperated by ill treatment, Mr. Betterton confederated with the principal performers to procure an independent license, which being granted by King William, they built a new theatre in Lincoln's-inn-fields, by subscription, and opened it on the 30th of April, 1695, with Congreve's comedy of "Love for Love."

In 1705, enfeebled by age and infirmity, this distinguished veteran transferred his license to Sir John Vanbrugh, who erected a handsome theatre in the Haymarket, at which, divested of influence or control, he accepted an engagement as an actor.

Mr. Betterton's salary never exceeded eighty shillings a-week, and having sustained the loss of more than £2,000, by a commercial venture to the East Indies, in 1692, necessity compelled him to pursue his professional avocations. On Thursday, April the 13th, 1709,[1] the play of "Love for Love" was performed for his benefit, an occasion which summoned Mrs. Barry and Mrs. Bracegirdle from their retirement, to aid this antient coadjutor by the resumption of those parts they had originally sustained. Congreve is said to have furnished a prologue, though withdrawn and never submitted to print, which was delivered by the latter lady, the former reciting an epilogue from the pen of Rowe, which remains in lasting testimony of his affectionate regard. From this address the following lines are worthy of transcription:

> But since, like friends to wit, thus throng'd you meet,
> Go on, and make the generous work complete;
> Be true to merit, and still own his cause,
> Find something for him more than bare applause.
> In just remembrance of your pleasures past,
> Be kind and give him a discharge at last,
> In peace and ease life's remnant let him wear,
> And hang his consecrated buskin here

This hint, however, proved unavailing, and "Old Thomas"

---

[1] In Gildon's "Life," &c., 1710, there is a copy of Rowe's "Epilogue," stated to have been spoken by Mrs. Barry "at the Theatre Royal, in Drury-lane, April the 7th," and this mistaken date has been perpetuated by the "Biographia Dramatica." [In spite of this contradiction of Gildon and the "Biographia Dramatica," they are right, and Bell-chambers is wrong. The date was 7th April, 1709.]

still continued to labour, when permitted by intermissions of disease, for that subsistence his age and his services should long before have secured.

Mr. Betterton accordingly performed at intervals in the course of the ensuing winter, and on the 25th of April, 1710 [should be 13th April], was admitted to another benefit, which, with the patronage bestowed upon its predecessor, is supposed to have netted nearly £1000. Upon this occasion, he was announced for his celebrated part of *Melantius*, in the "Maid's Tragedy," from the performance of which he ought, however, upon strict consideration, to have been deterred; for having been suddenly seized with the gout, a determination not to disappoint the expectancy of his friends, induced him to employ a repellatory medicine, which lessened the swelling of his feet, and permitted him to walk in slippers. He acted, accordingly, with peculiar spirit, and was received with universal applause; but such were the fatal effects of his laudable anxiety, that the distemper returned with unusual violence, ascended to his head, and terminated his existence, in three days from the date of this fatal assumption. On the 2nd of May his remains were deposited with much form in the cloisters of Westminster-abbey.

Mr. Betterton was celebrated for polite behaviour to the dramatic writers of his time, and distinguished by singular modesty, in not presuming to understand the chief points of any character they offered him, till their ideas had been asked, and, if possible, adopted. He is also praised in some verses published with the "State Poems," for extending pecuniary assistance to embarrassed writers, till the success of a doubtful production might enable them to remunerate their generous creditor. Indeed, Mr Betterton's benevolence was coupled with such magnanimity, that upon the death of that unhappy friend to whose counsels his little fortune had been sacrificed, he took charge of a surviving daughter, educated her at considerable expense, and not only made her an accomplished actress, but a valuable woman.[1]

Among many testimonies of deference to his judgment, and regard for his zeal, the tributes of Dryden and Rowe have been brilliantly recorded. He was naturally of a cheerful temper, with a pious reliance upon the dispensations of providence, and nothing can yield a higher idea of his great affability, than the effect his behaviour produced upon Pope, who must have been a mere boy, when first admitted to his society. He sat to the poet for his picture, which Pope painted in oil,[2] and so eager was the bard to perpetuate his memory, that he published a modernization of Chaucer's "Prologues," in this venerable favourite's name, though palpably the produce of his own elegant pen.[3] As an author, Mr. Betterton's labours were confined to the drama, and if his original pieces are not entitled to much praise, his alterations exhibit some judicious amendments

Edward Kynaston

Edward Kynaston made his first appearance in 1659, at the "Cockpit" in Drury-lane, under the management of Rhodes, to whom, in his trade of bookselling, he had previously been apprenticed. Here he took the lead in personating female parts, among which he sustained *Calis*, in the "Mad Lover;" *Ismenia*, in the "Maid in the Mill," the

---

[1] This lady, who was remarkably handsome, married Boman, the actor.

[2] This curiosity, I believe, is still preserved in the Earl of Mansfield's mansion, at Caen-wood.

[3] Pope, in the postscript of a letter to Cromwell, writes thus —

"—— This letter of death puts me in mind of poor Betterton's, over whom I would have this sentence of Tully for an epitaph, which will serve for his moral as well as his theatrical capacity :

'*Vitæ bene actæ jucundissima est recordatio.*'"

In another part of his correspondence, he intimates that Betterton's "remains" had been taken care of, alluding, I suppose, to this posthumous forgery.

heroine of Sir John Suckling's "Aglaura;" *Arthiope*, in the "Unfortunate Lovers;" and *Evadne*, in the "Maid's Tragedy." The three last of these parts have been distinguished by Downes and our author as the best of his efforts, and being then but a "mannish youth," he made a suitable representative of feminine beauty. Kynaston's *forte*, at this period, appears to have consisted in moving compassion and pity, " in which," says old Downes, "it has since been disputable among the judicious, whether any woman that succeeded him so sensibly touched the audience as he."

At the Restoration, when his majesty's servants re-opened the "Red Bull" playhouse, in St. John-street, next shifted to Gibbons's tennis-court, in Clare-market, and finally settled, in 1663, at their new theatre in Drury-lane, Kynaston was admitted to their ranks, and played *Peregrine*, in Jonson's comedy of the "Fox." He also held *Sir Dauphine*, a minor personage, in the same author's "Silent Woman," and soon after succeeded to *Otto*, in the "Duke of Normandy," a part which was followed by others of variety and importance

In derogation of Cibber's panegyric, we are assured by Davies, upon the authority of some old comedians, that, from his juvenile familiarity with female characters, Kynaston contracted some disagreeable tones in speaking, which resembled the whine or cant that genuine taste has at all times been impelled to explode. When George Powel was once discharging the intemperance of a recent debauch from his stomach, Kynaston asked him if he still felt sick. "How is it possible to be otherwise," said Powel, "when I hear you speak?" Much as Kynaston, however, might have been affected by the peculiarities of early practice, we cannot consent, upon evidence such as this, to rob him of the laurels that have sprung from respectable testimony.

In 1695 he followed the fortunes of Betterton to Lincoln's-inn-fields, and supported a considerable character in John Banks's "Cyrus the Great," produced the year after this removal The time of his retirement is not known, but it appears from our author that he continued upon the stage till his memory and spirit both began to fail him He had left it, however, before 1706, when Betterton and Underhill have been specified by Downes, as "being the only remains of the Duke of York's servants," at that time before the public. Kynaston died wealthy, and was buried in the church-yard of St Paul's, Covent-garden.

Kynaston bore a great resemblance to the noted Sir Charles Sidley, a similitude of which he was so proud, that he endeavoured to display it by the most particular expedients. On one occasion, he got a suit of laced clothes made in imitation of the baronet's, and appearing publicly in it, Sir Charles, whose wit very seldom atoned for his ill-nature, punished this vain propensity in his usual mischievous manner. He hired a bravo to accost Kynaston in the Park, one day when he wore his finery, pick a quarrel with him on account of a pretended affront from his prototype, and beat him unmercifully. This scheme was duly put in practice, and though Kynaston protested that he was not the person his antagonist took him for, the ruffian redoubled his blows, on account of what he affected to consider his scandalous falsehood. When Sir Charles Sidley was remonstrated with upon the cruelty of this transaction, he told the actor's friends that their pity was misplaced, for that Kynaston had not suffered so much in his bones as *he* had in his character, the whole town believing that it was he who had undergone the disgrace of this chastisement.

WILLIAM MOUNTFORT.

William Mountfort, according to Cibber's estimate, was born in 1660, and having, I suppose, joined the king's company at a very early age, about the year 1682, "grew," in the words of old Downes, "to the maturity of a good actor." At Drury-lane theatre, he sustained *Alfonso Corso*, in the "Duke of Guise," in 1682. His rise was so rapid, that in 1685 we find him selected for the hero of Crowne's "Sir Courtly Nice," "which," says Downes, "was so *nicely* performed," that none of his successors, but Colley Cibber, could equal him. Perhaps the last new character assumed by Mountfort was *Cleanthes*, in Dryden's "Cleomenes," a play to which he spoke the prologue

I here present the reader with a narrative of those circumstances attending the death of Mountfort, which have so long been misunderstood and misrepresented.

A Captain Richard Hill had made proposals of marriage to Mrs. Bracegirdle, which were declined from what Hill appeared to consider an injurious preference for Mountfort, between whom, though a married man, and the lady, at least a platonic attachment was often thought to subsist. Enraged at Mountfort's superior success, and affecting to treat him as the only obstacle to his wishes, Hill expressed a determination at various times, and before several persons, to be revenged upon him, and as it was proved upon the trial, coupled this threat with some of the bitterest invectives that could spring from brutal animosity. Among Hill's associates was Lord Mohun, a peer of very dissolute manners, whose extreme youth afforded but a faint palliative for his participation in the act of violence and debauchery to which Hill resorted. This nobleman, however, who seems to have felt a chivalric devotion to the interests of his friend, engaged with Hill in a cruel and perfidious scheme for the abduction of Mrs. Bracegirdle, whom Hill proposed to carry off, violate, and afterwards marry. They arranged with one Dixon, an owner of hackney carriages, to provide a coach and six horses to take them to Totteridge, and appointed him to wait with this conveyance over against the Horse-shoe tavern in Drury-lane. A small party of soldiers was also hired to assist in this notable exploit, and as Mrs. Bracegirdle, who had been supping at a Mr. Page's in Prince's-street, was going down Drury-lane towards her lodgings in Howard-street,

Strand, about ten o'clock at night, on Friday the 9th of December, 1692, two of these soldiers pulled her away from Mr Page, who was attending her home, nearly knocked her mother down, and tried to lift her into the vehicle. Her mother, upon whom the blow given by these ruffians had providentially made but a short impression, hung very obstinately about her neck, and prevented the success of their endeavours. While Mr. Page was calling loudly for assistance, Hill ran at him with his sword drawn, and again endeavoured to get Mrs. Bracegirdle into the coach, a task he was hindered from accomplishing, by the alarm that Page had successfully given. Company came up, on which Hill insisted on seeing Mrs. Bracegirdle home, and actually led her by the hand to the house in which she resided. Lord Mohun, who during this scuffle was seated quietly in the coach, joined Hill in Howard-street, the soldiers having been previously dismissed, and there they paraded, with their swords drawn, for about an hour and a half, before Mrs. Bracegirdle's door. Hill's scabbard, it ought to be remarked, was clearly proved to have been lost during the scuffle in Drury-lane, and Lord Mohun, when challenged by the watch, not only sheathed his weapon, but offered to surrender it. These were strong points at least in his lordship's favour, and deserve to be noted, because the prescriptive assertion that Mountfort was treacherously killed, is weakened by the establishment of those facts. Mrs. Brown, the mistress of the house where Mrs. Bracegirdle lodged, went out on her arrival, to expostulate with Lord Mohun and his confederate, and after exchanging a few words of no particular importance, dispatched her maid servant to Mountfort's house,[1] hard by in Norfolk-street, to apprise Mrs. Mountfort of the danger to which, in case of coming home, he would be subjected. Mrs. Mountfort sent in search of her husband, but without

---

[1] Mrs Brown swore she went herself, but appears to have been mistaken

success, and the watch on going their round, between eleven and twelve o'clock, found Lord Mohun and Hill drinking wine in the street, a drawer having brought it from an adjacent tavern. At this juncture Mrs. Brown, the landlady, hearing the voices of the watch, went to the door with a design of directing them to secure both Lord Mohun and Hill, and some conversation passed upon that subject, although her directions were not obeyed. Seeing Mountfort, just as he had turned the corner into Howard-street, and was apparently coming towards her house, Mrs Brown hurried out to meet him, and mention his danger, but he would not stop, so as to allow her time for the slightest communication. On gaining the spot where Lord Mohun stood, Hill being a little farther off, he saluted his lordship with great respect, and was received by him with unequivocal kindness Lord Mohun hinted to Mountfort that he had been sent for by Mrs. Bracegirdle, in consequence of her projected seizure, a charge which Mountfort immediately denied Lord Mohun then touched upon the affair, and Mountfort expressed a hope, with some warmth, that he would not vindicate Hill's share in the business, against which, while disclaiming any tenderness for Mrs. Bracegirdle, he protested with much asperity. Hill approached in time to catch the substance of Mountfort's remark, and having hastily said that he could vindicate himself, gave him a blow on the ear, and at the same moment a challenge to fight They both went from the pavement into the middle of the road, and after making two or three passes at each other, Mountfort was mortally wounded He threw down his sword, which broke by the fall, and staggered to his own house, where Mrs. Page, who had gone to concert with Mrs. Mountfort for her husband's safety, hearing a cry of "murder" in the street, threw open the door, and received him pale, bleeding, and exhausted, in her arms. Hill fled and escaped, but Lord Mohun, having surrendered himself, was arraigned before parliament as an accomplice, on the 31st of January, 1693, and, after a laborious, patient, protracted, and impartial trial, acquitted of the crime, in which he certainly bore no conspicuous part. Mountfort languished till noon the next day, and solemnly declared, at the very point of death, that Hill stabbed him with one hand while he struck him with the other, Lord Mohun holding him in conversation when the murder was committed. From the fact, however, of Mountfort's sword being taken up unsheathed and broken, there is no doubt, without insisting upon the testimony to that effect, that he used it; and that he could have used it after receiving the desperate wound of which he died, does not appear, by his flight and exhaustion, to have been possible. Some of his fellow-players, it seems, had sifted the evidence of a material witness, the day after his death, and at this evidence they openly expressed their dissatisfaction. Mountfort, it was indisputably shown, too, *went out of the way to his own house*, in going down Howard-street at all, as he ought to have crossed it, his door being the second from the south-west corner. These circumstances will perhaps support a conjecture that some part of the odium heaped upon Lord Mohun and Hill has proceeded from the cowardice and exasperation of a timid and vindictive fraternity, coupled with the individual artifices of Mrs. Bracegirdle, to redeem a character which the real circumstances of Mountfort's death, dying as her champion, severely affected. Cibber's assurance of her purity, may merely prove the extent of his dulness or dissimulation, for on calmly reviewing this case in all its aspects, chequered as it is by Hill's impetuosity, Mrs. Bracegirdle's lewdness, and Mountfort's presumption, I cannot help inferring that he fell a victim, not unfairly, to one of those casual encounters which mark the general violence of the times. The record of his murder is therefore erroneous, and we may hope to see it amended in every future collection of theatrical lives.[1]

[1] Bellchambers seems to have had a craze on the subject of Mrs. Bracegirdle's character, which he vilifies on every possible opportunity. His opinion here appears to me very questionable

Samuel Sandford.

Samuel Sandford made his first appearance upon the stage, under D'Avenant's authority, in the year 1663,[1] at the time when that company was strengthened by the accession of Smith and Matthew Medbourn. The first part for which he has been mentioned by Downes, is *Sampson*, in "Romeo and Juliet;" he soon after sustained a minor part in the "Adventures of Five Hours," fol. 1663; and when D'Avenant produced his comedy of the "Man's the Master," he and Harris sung an eccentric epilogue in the character of two street ballad-singers. Sandford was the original *Foresight*, in "Love for Love," and though Mr. Cibber has exclusively insisted upon his tragic excellence, he must have been a comedian of strong and diversified humour. When Betterton and his associates seceded to the new theatre in Lincoln's-inn-fields, he refused to join them as a sharer, but was engaged at a salary of three pounds per week. As Sandford is not enumerated by Downes among the actors transferred to Swiney, in the latter end of 1706, when Betterton and Underhill, indeed, are mentioned as "the only remains" of the duke's company, it is clear he must have died during the previous six years, having been referred to by Cibber, as exercising his profession in 1700. His ancestors were long and respectably settled at Sandford, a village in Shropshire; and he seems to have prided himself, absurdly, upon the superiority of his birth.

James Nokes.

James Nokes formed part of the company collected at the "Cockpit," in 1659, and is first mentioned by Downes for *Norfolk*, in "King Henry the Eighth," some time after D'Avenant's opening in Lincoln's-inn-fields. Upon this assumption Mr. Davies has expressed a very reasonable

[1] Sandford played Worm in "The Cutter of Coleman Street" as early as 1661. (L.)

doubt, and conjectured, with much plausibility, that it was sustained by Robert Nokes.

In Cowley's "Cutter of Coleman-street" [1661], the part of *Puny* was allotted to Nokes, whose reputation at that period appears to have been but feebly established, as the more important comic characters were intrusted to Lovel and Underhill. We find the name of Nokes affixed to *Lovis*, in Etherege's "Comical Revenge," 1664, but his performance of that part, whatever merit it might have evinced, acquired no distinction. [This is wrong; Nokes played Sir Nicholas Cully: the part of Lovis was acted by Norris.] The plague then beginning to rage, theatrical exhibitions were suspended, in May, 1665, and the company ceased to act, on account of the great fire, till [about] Christmas, 1666, when their occupation was resumed in Lincoln's-inn-fields, and Lord Orrery produced his play of "Mr. Antony." In this piece there was an odd sort of duel between Nokes and Angel, in which one was armed with a blunderbuss, and the other with a bow and arrow. Though this frivolous incident procured Nokes some accession of public notice, it was Dryden's " Sir Martin Mar-all," [1667,] which developed his powers to their fullest extent, and raised him to the highest pitch of popularity.

According to Downes, the Duke of Newcastle gave a literal translation of Molière's " Etourdi " to Dryden, who adapted the part of *Sir Martin Mar-all* " purposely for the mouth of Mr. Nokes;" and the old prompter has corroborated Mr. Cibber's assertion of his success. Nokes added largely to his reputation, in [1668], by performing *Sir Oliver*, in " She would if she could ;" and strengthened Shadwell's " Sullen Lovers," by accepting the part of *Poet Ninny*.

Nokes acted *Barnaby Brittle* at the original appearance —about 1670—of Betterton's " Amorous Widow," and [in 1671] performed *Old Jorden*, in Ravenscroft's "Citizen turned Gentleman," a part which the king and court were said to have been more delighted with than any other, except *Sir Martin Mar-all*. His *Nurse*, in "Caius Marius," 1680, excited such uncommon merriment, that he carried the name of Nurse Nokes to his grave. In 1688, he supported the hero of Shadwell's "'Squire of Alsatia," a play which was acted in every part with remarkable excellence, and enjoyed the greatest popularity. We find no farther mention of him, subsequent to this period, though included by Cibber among those who were performing under the united patents, in 1690, when he first came into the company According to Brown, who has peculiarly marked out his "gaiety and openness" upon the stage, he kept a "nicknackatory, or toy-shop," opposite the spot which has since received the denomination of Exeter Change. The date of his death is uncertain, but there is some reason to presume that it happened about the year 1692.[1]

WILLIAM PINKETHMAN

The first mention of Pinkethman, by Downes, is for the part of *Ralph*, in "Sir Salomon," when commanded at court, in the beginning of [1704], but he had been alluded to, two years before, in Gildon's "Comparison between the Two Stages," as the "flower of Bartholomew-fair, and the idol of the rabble A fellow that overdoes every thing, and spoils many a part with his own stuff." [He was on the stage as early as 1692] He is again mentioned in the "Roscius Anglicanus" for *Dr. Caius*, in the "Merry Wives of Windsor," and continued to act in the Drury-lane company till his death, about the year 1725

Pinkethman was a serviceable actor, notwithstanding his irregularities, and performed many characters of great importance He was the original *Don Lewis*, in "Love makes a Man," 1701, a proof that his talents were soon and greatly

[1] Cibber says that Nokes, Mountfort, and Leigh, "died about the same year," *viz* 1692

appreciated. His eccentric turn led him, in too many instances, from the sphere of respectability, and we find him in the constant habit of frequenting fairs, for the low purpose of theatrical exhibition. His stage talents were marred, it is true, by an extravagant habit of saying more than had been "set down" for him, and though this abominable blemish is fully admitted, still its toleration proves that Pinkethman must have been an actor of uncommon value. His son was a comedian of merit, who played *Waitwell*, in the "Way of the World," at the opening of Covent-garden theatre, in December, 1732, and died in May, 1740.

Anthony Leigh.

The "famous Mr. Ant ony Leigh," as Downes denominates him, came into the duke's company, about the year [1672], upon the deaths of several eminent actors, whose places he and others were admitted to supply. He played *Bellair, sen*, in Etherege's "Man of Mode," at its production in 1676. In 1681, Leigh supported *Father Dominic*, in Dryden's "Spanish Friar," a piece, which, according to the "Roscius Anglicanus," was "admirably acted, and produced vast profit to the company." Leigh's success was so great in this character, that a full-length portrait was taken of him in his clerical habit, by Sir Godfrey Kneller, for the Earl of Dorset, from which a good mezzotinto engraving is now in the hands of theatrical collectors. In 1685, we find him allotted to *Sir Nicholas Calico*, in "Sir Courtly Nice," in 1688 he supported *Sir William Belfond*, in Shadwell's "Squire of Alsatia," and these parts, with a few others, appear to have constituted his peculiar excellence

The satirical allusions of such a random genius as Brown, are rarely to be relied upon, or we might suspect Leigh, from the following extract, to have been distinguished by pious hypocrisy :—

"At last, my friend Nokes, pointing to a little edifice, which exactly resembles Dr. Burgess's conventicle in Russel-court, says he, 'your old acquaintance Tony Leigh, who turned presbyterian parson upon his coming into these quarters, holds forth most notably here every Sunday'"—"Letters from the Dead to the Living" [1744, ii. 77].

Cave Underhill.

Cave Underhill was a member of the company collected by Rhodes, and which, soon afterwards, submitted to the authority of Sir William D'Avenant. He is first mentioned by Downes, for his performance of *Sir Morglay Thwack*, in the "Wits," after which he sustained the *Grave-digger*, in "Hamlet," and soon testified such ability, that the manager publicly termed him "the truest comedian" at that time upon his stage.[1] Underhill, about this time, strengthened the cast of "Romeo and Juliet," by playing *Gregory*, and though the custom of devoting the best talent which the theatres afford, to parts of minor importance, has ceased, it is a practice to which the managers, were public amusement consulted, might safely recur In Shakspeare's "Twelfth Night," which, says Downes, "had mighty success by its well performance," Underhill soon after supported the *Clown*, a character in which the latter attributes delineated by Cibber, could alone have been employed Underhill's reputation appears to have been speedily established, as we find him intrusted by Cowley, in [1661], with the hero of his "Cutter of Coleman-street ," and he is mentioned by Downes for especial excellence in performing *Jodelet*, in D'Avenant's "Man's the Master." His first new part after the accession of James, was *Hothead*, in "Sir Courtly Nice;" on the 30th of April, 1695, he distinguished himself by his chaste and spirited performance of *Sir Sampson Legend*, in

[1] "Roscius Anglicanus."

Congreve's "Love for Love," and in 1700, closed a long, arduous, and popular career of original parts, by playing *Sir Wilful Witwou'd,* in the "Way of the World." [He continued on the stage till 1710.]

A brief account of this valuable comedian has been furnished by Mr. Davies, which, for the satisfaction of our readers, we shall proceed to transcribe.

"Underhill was a jolly and droll companion, who, if we may believe such historians as Tom Brown, divided his gay hours between Bacchus and Venus, with no little ardour. Tom, I think, makes Underhill one of the gill-drinkers of his time, men who resorted to taverns, in the middle of the day, under pretence of drinking Bristol milk, (for so good sherry was then called) to whet their appetites, where they indulged themselves too often in ebriety. Underhill acted till he was past eighty. He was so excellent in the part of Trinculo, in the Tempest, that he was called Prince Trinculo.[1] He had an admirable vein of pleasantry, and told his lively stories, says Brown, with a bewitching smile. The same author says, he was so afflicted with the gout, that he prayed one minute and cursed the other. His shambling gait, in his old age, was no hindrance to his acting particular parts He retired from the theatre in 1703."—"Dram. Misc.," iii 138.

On the 31st of May, 1709, Underhill applied for a benefit, and procured it, upon which occasion he played his favourite part of the *Grave-digger,* and received the following cordial recommendation from Sir Richard Steele —

"My chief business here [Will's Coffee House] this evening, was to speak to my friends in behalf of honest Cave Underhill, who has been a comic for three generations; my father admired him extremely when he was a boy. There is certainly nature excellently represented in his manner of action; in which he ever avoided that general fault in

[1] I find, on looking over the "Roscius Anglicanus," that *Trinculo* is termed *Duke Trinculo,* in a short reference to the "Tempest."

players, of doing too much. It must be confessed, he has not the merit of some ingenious persons now on the stage, of adding to his authors; for the actors were so dull in the last age, that many of them have gone out of the world, without having ever spoken one word of their own in the theatre. Poor Cave is so mortified, that he quibbles and tells you, he pretends only to act a part fit for a man who has one foot in the grave; *viz.* a *Grave-digger.* All admirers of true comedy, it is hoped, will have the gratitude to be present on the last day of his acting, who, if he does not happen to please them, will have it then to say, that it is the first time "—" Tatler," No 22.

GEORGE POWELL.

The father of George Powell was an actor in the king's company at the time of its junction, in 1682, with the duke's. Powell's access to the theatre was, therefore, easy; and we are intitled to suspect, though the time is not to be ascertained, that he began to act at a very early period.

Even, according to Cibber's allowance, when Powell was appointed to the principal parts abandoned by Betterton and his revolters, they were parts for which, whether serious or comic, he had both elocution and humour It is remarked by Davies,[1] that Cibber "seems to have hated Powell," and if so, we have a ready clue to the neglect and asperity with which he has treated him

Powell succeeded Betterton, it is supposed, in the part of *Hotspur,* when that excellent comedian exchanged its choleric attributes, in his declining years, for the gaiety and humour of *Falstaff. Edgar,* in " King Lear," was also one of his most successful characters, but of this, owing to his irregularities, he was dispossessed by Wilks To such a height, indeed, was the intemperance of this actor carried,

---

[1] "Dramatic Miscellanies," vol ii p 323.

that Sir John Vanbrugh, in his preface to the "Relapse," 4to, 1697, speaking of Powell's *Worthy*, has exposed it in following manner:

> One word more about the bawdy, and I have done. I own the first night this thing was acted, some indecencies had like to have happened; but it was not my fault. The fine gentleman of the play, drinking his mistress's health in Nantes brandy, from six in the morning to the time he waddled on upon the stage in the evening, had toasted himself up to such a pitch of vigour, I confess I once gave up *Amanda* for gone, and am since, with all due respect to Mrs Rogers, very sorry she escaped: for I am confident a certain lady, (let no one take it to herself that is handsome) who highly blames the play, for the barrenness of the conclusion, would then have allowed it a very natural close.

To the folly of intoxication he added the horrors of debt, and was so hunted by the Sheriffs' officers, that he usually walked the streets with a sword (sheathed) in his hand, and if he saw any of them at a distance, he would roar out, "Get on the other side of the way, you dog!" The bailiff, who knew his old customer, would obligingly answer, "We do not want you *now*, Master Powell." Harassed by his distresses, and unnerved by drink, it is hardly to be wondered at if his reputation decreased, and his ability slackened, but that his efforts were still marked by a possession of the very highest qualities that criticism can attest, is proved by the following extract from the "Spectator:"

> Having spoken of Mr. Powell as sometimes raising himself applause from the ill taste of an audience, I must do him the justice to own, that he is excellently formed for a tragedian, and, when he pleases, deserves the admiration of the best judges —No. 40.

Addison and Steele continued their regard for this unhappy man as long as they could render him any service, and that he acted *Portius*, in "Cato," on its appearance in 1713, must have been with the author's approbation. The last trace we have of Powell is confined to a playbill, for his benefit, in the year 1717, since when no vestige has been found of his career. He lies buried, it has been said, in the vault of St. Clement-Danes; but though the period of his death may be fixed not far from the date of this document, it cannot be minutely ascertained. [Genest says Powell died 14th December, 1714.]

In the intervals of excess Powell found time for repeated literary labour, having written four plays, and superintended the publication of three more. His fault was too great a passion for social pleasure, but though the irregularities this passion produced, disabled him from exerting the talents he was allowed to possess, still his excellence on the stage is not to be disputed. He was esteemed at one period of his life a rival to Betterton, and had the prudence of his conduct been equal to the vigour of his genius, he would have held, as well as reached, that lofty station for which nature had designed him.

If the testimony of Aston can be relied on, Powell was born in the year 1658, being incidentally mentioned by that facetious writer, as Betterton's junior by three and twenty years.

JOHN VERBRUGGEN.

John Verbruggen, it appears from the assertion of Mr. Davies, was a dissipated young fellow, who determined, in opposition to the advice of his friends, to be an actor, and accordingly loitered about Drury-lane theatre, at the very time when Cibber was also endeavouring to get admittance, in expectation of employment. On the death of Mountfort, whose widow he married, Verbruggen was intrusted, I have no doubt, with the part of *Alexander*, his fondness for which was such, that he suffered the players and the public, for many years, to call him by no other name. [He seems to have been called Alexander from his first appearing on the stage, till 1694] It is mentioned in more than one pamphlet, that Cibber and Verbruggen were at variance, and hence the animosity and unfairness with which the latter has been treated.[1]

The first part to which Verbruggen can be traced, is *Aurelius*, in "King Arthur," 4to, 1691 [he played *Termagant* ("Squire of Alsatia") in 1688] : in the year 1696, Mr Southern assigned him the character of *Oroonoko*, by the special advice of William Cavendish, the first Duke of Devonshire ; and as the author informs us in his preface, " it was Verbruggen's endeavour, in the performance of that part, to merit the duke's recommendation." A further proof of Mr. Cibber's partiality, is the constant respect paid to Verbruggen by such judges of ability as Rowe and Congreve, for whose pieces he was uniformly selected. His *Mirabel*, in the "Way of the World," and *Bajazet*, in " Tamerlane," were parts of the highest importance, and it will be difficult to show that an ordinary actor could have been intrusted, by writers of equal power and fastidity, with duties of which he was not thoroughly deserving When

---

[1] " That Verbruggen and Cibber did not accord, is plainly insinuated by the author of the Laureat It was known that the former would resent an injury, and that the latter's valour was entirely passive. The temper of Verbruggen may be known, from a story which I have often been told by the old comedians as a certain fact, and which found its way into some temporary publication

"Verbruggen, in a dispute with one of King Charles's illegitimate sons, was so far transported by sudden anger, as to strike him, and call him a son of a whore The affront was given, it seems, behind the scenes of Drury-lane Complaint was made of this daring insult on a nobleman, and Verbruggen was told, he must either not act in London, or submit publicly to ask the nobleman's pardon During the time of his being interdicted acting, he had engaged himself to Betterton's theatre He consented to ask pardon, on liberty granted to express his submission in his own terms He came on the stage dressed for the part of *Oroonoko*, and, after the usual preface, owned that he had called the Duke of St A. a son of a whore. 'It is true,' said Verbruggen, ' and I am sorry for it ' On saying this, he invited the company present to see him act the part of *Oroonoko*, at the theatre in Lincoln's-inn-fields "—" Dramatic Miscellanies," vol. iii. p. 447.

Verbruggen died it is impossible to ascertain. He played *Sullen,* in the "Beaux' Stratagem," at its production in 1707, and as Elrington made his appearance in *Bajazet,* in 1711, there is some reason to conclude that Verbruggen's death occurred during that interval. [He died before April, 1708.]

Though Gildon, a scribbler whose venality was only exceeded by his dulness, has mentioned Verbruggen in the most derogatory terms,[1] there is ample evidence in the bare record of his business, to justify the most unqualified merit we may incline to ascribe. Chetwood alludes to him, in pointing out Elrington's imitation of his excellencies, as "a very great actor in tragedy, and polite parts in comedy,"[2] and the author of the "Laureat" enumerates a variety of important characters, in which he commanded universal applause.

JOSEPH WILLIAMS.

Joseph Williams,[3] who was bred a seal-cutter, came into the duke's company, about the year 1673, when but a boy, and according to the practice of that period, being apprenticed to an eminent actor, "served Mr. Harris." I find him first mentioned by Downes, for *Pylades,* in the serious opera of "Circe," his next character of importance being *Polydore,* in the "Orphan," 1680; and, same year, *Theodosius,* in Lee's tragedy of that name. The Union in 1682, without diminishing his merit, appears to have lessened his value, by the introduction of Kynaston and others, who had more established pretensions to parts of importance.

---

[1] "A fellow with a crackt voice: he clangs his words as if he spoke out of a broken drum."—"Comparison, &c.," 1702

[2] "History of the Stage," p. 136.

[3] There was also a David Williams; perhaps the person who played the *2d Grave-digger,* in "Hamlet." (B.) [Genest gives this part to Joseph Williams.]

The secession of Williams from Betterton's company, just before the opening in 1695, has been noticed and explained by Mr. Cibber, in a subsequent passage. Greatly, as I have no doubt, he has depreciated the merit of this actor, no materials remain of a more recent date than those already quoted, by which we may conjecture his talents, or enforce his estimation. Williams is not to be confounded with an actor of the same appellation, who was at Drurylane theatre in the year 1730, and relieved Cibber of *Scipio*, in Thomson's "Sophonisba," a curious account of which is given in the "Dramatic Miscellanies"

Elizabeth Barry.

Elizabeth Barry, it is said, was the daughter of Edward Barry, Esq., a barrister, who was afterwards called Colonel Barry, from his having raised a regiment for the service of Charles the First, in the course of the civil wars. The misfortunes arising from this engagement, involved him in such distress, that his children were obliged to provide for their own maintenance Lady D'Avenant, a relation of the noted laureat, from her friendship to Colonel Barry, gave this daughter a genteel education, and made her a constant associate in the circle of polite intercourse These opportunities gave an ease and grace to Mrs. Barry's behaviour, which were of essential benefit, when her patroness procured her an introduction to the stage. This happened in the year 1673, when Mrs Barry's efforts were so extremely unpropitious, that the directors of the duke's company pronounced her incapable of making any progress in the histrionic art. Three times, according to Curll's "History of the Stage," she was dismissed, and by the interest of her benefactor, re-instated. When Otway, however, produced his "Alcibiades," in 1675, her merit was such, as not only to excite the public attention, but to command the author's praise, which has been glowingly bestowed upon her in the preface to that production. We find her, next season, filling the lively character of *Mrs. Lovit*, in Etherege's "Man of Mode;" and in 1680, her performance of *Monimia*, in the "Orphan," seems to have raised that reputation to its greatest height, which had been gradually increasing The part of *Belvidera*, two years afterwards, and the heroine of Southern's "Fatal Marriage," in 1694, elicited unrivalled talent, and procured her universal distinction

When Mrs. Barry first resorted to the theatre, her pretensions to notice were a good air and manner, and a very powerful and pleasing voice. Her ear, however, was so extremely defective, that several eminent judges, on seeing her attempt a character of some importance, gave their opinion that she never could be an actress. Upon the authority of Curll's historian, Mr. Davies[1] has compiled what appears to me an apocryphal tale of her sudden rise to the pinnacle of excellence, though there is no reason to dispute her criminal intimacy with the Earl of Rochester. I am not inclined, while doubting the precise anecdote of his assistance, to deny that much advantage might have been derived from his general instructions.

Mrs. Barry was not only remarkable for the brilliancy of her talent, but the earnestness of her zeal, and the ardour of her assiduity Betterton, that kind, candid, and judicious observer, bore this testimony to her eminent abilities, and unyielding good-nature, that she often exerted herself so greatly in a pitiful character, that her acting has given success to plays which would disgust the most patient reader.[2] When she accepted a part, it was her uniform practice to consult the author's intention. Her last new character was the heroine of Smith's "Phædra and Hippolytus," and though Mrs. Oldfield and the poet fell out concerning a few lines in the part of *Ismena*, Mrs. Barry

---

[1] "Dramatic Miscellanies," vol III p 209
[2] "Life of Betterton," p 16

and he were in perfect harmony. [*Valide*, in Goring's "Irene," 1708, was her last new part.]

Mrs. Barry must have closed her career with this performance, being mentioned by Steele, in the "Tatler," when assisting at Betterton's benefit, on Thursday, April 7th, 1709, as "not at present concerned in the house." She died on the 7th of November, 1713, aged fifty-five years, and was buried in Acton church-yard. Mr. Davies ascribes her death to the bite of a favourite lap-dog, who, unknown to her, had been seized with madness, and there seems to be no grounds for disturbing his supposition.

MRS. BETTERTON.

When Sir William D'Avenant undertook the management of the duke's company, he lodged and boarded four principal actresses in his house, among whom was Mrs. Saunderson, the subject of this article

Mrs Saunderson's first appearance in D'Avenant's company, was made as *Ianthe*, in the "Siege of Rhodes," on the opening of his new theatre in Lincoln's-inn-fields, in April, 1662 [should be June, 1661]. She played *Ophelia* soon afterwards, and that part being followed by Shakspeare's *Juliet*, evinces the consideration in which her services were held [About] 1663, she married Mr. Betterton, and not in 1670, as it is erroneously mentioned in the "Biographia Dramatica," and other worthless compilations.[1]

The principal characters sustained by Mrs. Betterton, were *Queen Catharine*, in "Henry the Eighth;" the *Duchess of Malfy;* the *Amorous Widow;* those enumerated in the text, and many others, not less remarkable for their impor-

---

[1] Downes expressly mentions her as Mrs Betterton for *Camilla* [should be *Portia*], in the "Adventures of Five Hours," 1663, and she also acted by that name, a few months after, in the "Slighted Maid" This error originated with the "Biographia Britannica," but Mr Jones, the late slovenly editor of the book alluded to, had ample means to correct it. (B.)

tance than their variety. On the death of her husband, in April, 1710, she was so strongly affected by that event, as to lose her senses, which were recovered, however, a short time previous to her own decease. Mr. Cibber may be right in stating that she only enjoyed the bounty of her royal mistress for about half a year; but, in that case, the pension could not have been granted directly he died, as we find that Mrs. Betterton was alive on the 4th of June, 1711, more than thirteen months after, and had the play of "Sir Fopling Flutter," performed at Drury-lane for her benefit. Mrs Betterton, though prevented from performing, by age and infirmity, enjoyed a sinecure situation in Drury-lane theatre, till she withdrew from it, in 1709, and was paid at the rate of [one pound] a-week. The "Biographia Britannica" says she survived her husband eighteen months, but the precise date of her decease has never been discovered. [Mrs. Betterton made a will on 10th March, 1712. In all probability Bellchambers is right in supposing that the annuity was not granted till some time after her husband's death.]

BENJAMIN JOHNSON.

This excellent actor, who was familiarly known by the appellation of his great namesake, Ben Jonson, came into the Theatre Royal, from an itinerant company, as Mr. Cibber relates, about the year 1695. He was bred a sign painter, but took more pleasure in hearing the actors, than in handling his pencil or spreading his colours, and, as he used to say in his merry mood, left the saint's occupation at last to take that of the sinner.

Johnson's merit was evinced as *Sir William Wisewould*, in Cibber's comedy of "Love's Last Shift," 4to, 1696; but I find him first mentioned by Downes, for *Justice Wary*, in Caryl's "Sir Salomon" [about 1704 or 1705]; the old prompter, in a species of postscript to his valuable tract, then terms him " a true copy of Mr. Underhill," and instances his *Morose, Corbaccio,* and *Hothead,* as very admirable efforts. Johnson passed over to the management of old Swiney, in 1706, with other members of Betterton's company, and established a very high reputation by his chaste and studied manner of acting. When Rich, in 1714, opened his new theatre in Lincoln's-inn-fields, Booth, Wilks, and Cibber, the managers of Drury-lane, solicitous to retain in their service comedians of merit, paid a particular respect to Johnson, by investing him with such parts of Dogget, who had taken leave of them, as were adapted to his powers. Here he continued with fame and profit, till August, 1742, when he expired in the seventy-seventh year of his age. Mr Davies, who appears to have been familiar with his excellencies, has given a description of Johnson, which, for its evident taste and candour, I shall do myself the pleasure to transcribe.

"That chaste copier of nature, Ben Johnson, the comedian, for above forty years, gave a true picture of an arch clown in the *Grave-digger* His jokes and repartees had a strong effect from his seeming insensibility of their force His large, speaking, blue eyes he fixed steadily on the person to whom he spoke, and was never known to have wandered from the stage to any part of the theatre."—" Dram. Misc.," iii 140.

WILLIAM BULLOCK.

This excellent actor came to London, as we see, about 1695, deriving his engagement from the distress in which Drury-lane theatre was involved by the desertion of Betterton, and other principal performers. He quitted this establishment in 1714, owing, as Mr. Cibber insinuates, to the ungovernable temper of Wilks; and passed over to John Rich, at the opening of Lincoln's-inn-fields. He is first mentioned by Downes, for the *Host,* in Shakspeare's "Merry Wives of Windsor" [about 1704 or 1705], and appears to be pointed at in Dennis's "Epistle Dedicatory" to the "Comical

Gallant," where the irascible writer thus addresses the Hon. George Granville :—

"Falstaff's part, which you know to be the principal one of the play, and that which on all the rest depends, was by no means acted to the satisfaction of the audience, upon which several fell from disliking the action, to disapproving the play." [As noted before, p. 252, Bullock was probably not the actor aimed at.]

This piece was printed in 1702, as acted "at the Theatre Royal in Drury-lane;" with a list of the *dramatis personæ*, but the names of the actors not annexed. Bullock, however, sustained the part of *Sir Tunbelly Clumsy*, in Vanbrugh's "Relapse," which had been previously performed under the same auspices, and from its nature, most probably by the same actor.

William Bullock was a comedian of great glee and much vivacity, and in his person large, with a lively countenance, full of humourous information. Steele, in the "Tatler," with his usual kind sensibility, very often adverts to Bullock's faculty of exciting amusement, but sometimes censures his habit of interpolation.[1] In Gildon's "Comparison between the Two Stages," 1702 [p 199], he is termed the "best comedian since Nokes and Leigh, and a fellow that has a very humble opinion of himself." Bullock's abilities have been ratified by the sanction of Macklin, who denominated him a true theatrical genius, and Mr Davies saw him act several parts with great applause, and particularly the *Spanish Friar*, when beyond the age of eighty. He died on the 18th of June, 1733 [Genest, iii. 593, points out that Bullock was acting in 1739.]

JOHN MILLS.

Our first notice of this actor is found in the "Roscius

[1] "You'll have Pinkethman and Bullock helping out Beaumont and Fletcher."—Tatler," No. 89.

Anglicanus," where Downes, who seems anxious to dispatch his subject, says summarily that "he excels in tragedy," but without making the remotest allusion to any characters in which his talent had been displayed.

John Mills the elder was, in person, inclined to the athletic size; his features were large, though not expressive, his voice was full, but not flexible; and his deportment was manly, without being graceful or majestic. He was considered one of the most useful actors that ever served in a theatre, but though invested by the patronage of Wilks with many parts of the highest order, he had no pretensions to quit the secondary line in which he ought to have been placed. Steele[1] taxes him very broadly with a want of "sentiment," and insinuates that by making gesture too much his study, he neglected the better attributes of his art.

On the death of Betterton, or soon after, Wilks, who took upon himself to regulate the theatrical cast, gave *Macbeth*, with great partiality, to Mills, while Booth and Powell were condemned to represent the inferior parts of *Banquo* and *Lenox*. Mills, though he spoke the celebrated soliloquy on time,—

> To-morrow, and to-morrow, etc,

with propriety, feeling, and effect, wanted genius to realise the turbulent scenes in which this character abounds. So much, indeed, was his deficiency perceived, that the indignation of a country gentleman broke out one night, during the performance of this play, in a very odd manner. The 'squire, after having been heartily tired with Mills, on the appearance of his old companion, Powell, in the fourth act, exclaimed, loud enough to be heard by the audience, "For God's sake, George, give us a speech, and let me go home."[2]

I recollect an incident of the same sort occurring at Bristol, where a very indifferent actor, declaimed so long

---

[1] "Tatler," No 201.
[2] "Dramatic Miscellanies," vol II. p 133

and to such little purpose, that an honest farmer, who sat in the pit, started up with evident signs of disgust, and waving his hand, to motion the speaker off, cried out, "Tak' un away, tak' un away, and let's have another."

One of the best parts sustained by Mills, was that of *Pierre*, which he acted so much to the taste of the public, that the applause it produced him exceeded all that was bestowed upon his best efforts in every thing else. He also acted *Ventidius* with the true spirit of a rough and generous old soldier, and in *Bajazet*, by the aid of his strong, deep, melodious voice, he displayed more than ordinary power.

It is supposed that Mills died in [December], 1736, respected by the public as a decent actor, and beloved by his friends as a worthy man

THEOPHILUS KEEN

Theophilus Keen received his first instructions in acting from Mr. Ashbury, of the Dublin theatre, in which he made his appearance about the year 1695 He most probably came into the Drury-lane company with Johnson and others, when Rich had beaten up for recruits. On the opening of the new house in Lincoln's Inn Fields, he went over to it, and, according to Chetwood, had a share not only of the management, but in the profit and loss, which latter speculation proved so disastrous to him, that he died in the year 1719, of a broken heart. He was buried in the church of St. Clement-Danes, and so much does he seem to have been respected, that more than two hundred persons in deep mourning, attended his funeral.

The influence he possessed in the theatre sometimes led him to assume such parts as *Edgar*, *Oroonoko*, and *Essex*, while his excellence lay in *Clytus*, and characters of a similar cast. His figure and voice, though neither elegant nor soft, were good, and his action was so complete, that it obtained for him the epithet of majestic, and when he spoke those lines of the *King*, in "Hamlet," where he descants upon the dignity that "doth hedge" a monarch, his look and whole deportment were so commanding, that the audience accompanied them always with the loudest applause.

MRS. MARY PORTER.

This valuable and respected actress, who was not only an honour to the stage, but an ornament to human nature, obtained the notice of Betterton by performing, when a child, the *Genius of Britain*, in a Lord Mayor's pageant, during the reign of Charles or James the Second It was the custom for fruit-women in the theatre formerly to stand fronting the pit, with their backs to the stage, and their oranges, &c. covered with vine leaves, under one of which Betterton threatened to put his little pupil, who was extremely diminutive, if she did not speak and act as he would have her.

Mrs. Porter was the genuine successor of Mrs Barry, and had an elevated consequence in her manner, which has seldom been equalled. One of her greatest parts was Shakspeare's *Queen Catherine*, in which her sensibility and intelligence, her graceful elocution and dignified behaviour, commanded applause and attention in passages of little importance. When the scene was not agitated by passion, to the general spectator she failed in communicating equal pleasure; her recitation of fact or sentiment being so modulated as to resemble musical cadence rather than speaking. Where passion, however, predominated, she exerted her powers to a supreme degree, and exhibited that enthusiastic ardour which filled her audience with animation, astonishment, and delight.

The dislocation of her thigh-bone, in the summer of 1731, was attended with a circumstance that deserves to be recorded. She lived at Heywood-hill, near Hendon, and, after the play, went home every night in a one-horse chaise, prepared to defend herself against robbery, with a brace of pistols. She was stopped on one of those occasions by a highwayman, who demanded her money, and having the courage to level one of her pistols at him, the assailant, who was probably unfurnished with a similar weapon, assured her that he was no common thief, and had been driven to his present course by the wants of a starving family. He told her, at the same time, where he lived, and urged his distresses with such earnestness, that she spared him all the money in her purse, which was about ten guineas. The man left her, on which she gave a lash to the horse, who suddenly started out of the track, overturned her vehicle, and caused the accident already related Let it be remembered to this good woman's credit, that notwithstanding the pain and loss to which he had, innocently, subjected her, she made strict inquiry into the highwayman's character, and finding that he had told the truth, she raised about sixty pounds among her acquaintance, and sent it, without delay, to the relief of his wretched family. There is a romantic generosity in this deed that captivates me more than its absolute justice.

About the year 1738, Mrs Porter returned to the stage, and acted many of her principal characters, with much vigour and great applause, though labouring under advanced age and unconquerable infirmity. She had the misfortune to outlive an annuity upon which she depended, and died in narrow circumstances, about the year 1762. [She published Lord Cornbury's comedy of "The Mistakes," in 1758, by which she realized a large sum of money.]

Though her voice was harsh and unpleasing, she surmounted its defects by her exquisite judgment. In person she was tall and well shaped, her complexion was fair; and her features, though not handsome, were made susceptible of all that strong feeling could desire to convey.

Her deportment was easy, and her action unaffected; and the testimony upon which the merits of Mrs. Porter are placed, entitles us to rank her in the very first class of theatrical performers.

MRS. ANNE OLDFIELD.

Anne Oldfield was born in the year 1683, and would have possessed a tolerable fortune, had not her father, a captain in the army, expended it at a very early period. In consequence of this deprivation, she went to reside with her aunt, who kept the Mitre tavern, in St James's-market, where Farquhar, the dramatist, one day heard her reading a few passages from Beaumont and Fletcher's "Scornful Lady," in which she manifested such spirit, ease, and humour, that being struck by her evident advantages for the stage, he framed an excuse to enter the room, a little parlour behind the bar, in which Miss Nancy was sitting.

Vanbrugh, who frequented the house, and was known to Mrs. Oldfield's mother, received a communication from that lady of the very great warmth with which his friend Farquhar had extolled her daughter's abilities. Vanbrugh, who seems to have been a zealous and sincere friend to all by whom his assistance was courted, immediately addressed himself to our heroine, and having ascertained that her fancy tended to parts of a sprightly nature, he recommended her to Rich, the manager of Drury-lane, by whom she was immediately engaged, at a salary of fifteen shillings *per* week. Her qualifications soon rendered her conspicuous among the young actresses of that time, and a man of rank being pleased to express himself in her favour, Mr Rich increased her weekly terms to the sum of twenty shillings.

The rise of Mrs. Oldfield was gradual but secure, and soon after the death of Mrs. Verbruggen she succeeded to the line of comic parts so happily held by that popular actress. Her *Lady Betty Modish*, in 1704, before which she was little known, and barely suffered, discovered accomplishments the public were not apprised of, and rendered her one of the greatest favourites upon whom their sanction had ever been bestowed. She was tall, genteel, and well shaped; her pleasing and expressive features were enlivened by large speaking eyes, which, in some particular comic situations, were kept half shut, especially when she intended to realise some brilliant idea; in sprightliness of air, and elegance of manner, she excelled all actresses; and was greatly superior in the strength, compass, and harmony of her voice.

Though highly appreciated as a tragic performer, Mrs. Oldfield, in the full round of glory, used to slight her best personations of that sort, and would often say, "I hate to have a page dragging my train about. Why don't they give Porter those parts? She can put on a better tragedy face than I can." The constant applause by which she was followed in characters of this description, so far reconciled her to Melpomene, that the last new one in which she appeared was Thomson's *Sophonisba*. Upon her action and deportment the author has expressed himself with great ardour in the following lines .

> Mrs. Oldfield, in the character of *Sophonisba*, has excelled what, even in the fondness of an author, I could either wish or imagine. The grace, dignity, and happy variety, of her action have been universally applauded, and are truly admirable.

Thomson's praise, indeed, is not more liberal than just, for we learn, that in reply to some degrading expression of *Massinissa*, relating to Carthage, she uttered the following line,—

> Not one base word of Carthage, for thy soul !—

with such grandeur of port, a look so tremendous, and in a voice so powerful, that it is said she even astonished Wilks, her *Massinissa;* it is certain the audience were struck, and expressed their feelings by the most uncommon applause.[1] Testimony like this is sufficient to protect her claim to tragic excellence, eclipsed as it certainly is by the superiority of her comic reputation.

Lady Townly has been universally adduced as her *ne plus ultra* in acting. She slided so gracefully into the foibles, and displayed so humourously the excesses, of a fine woman too sensible of her charms, too confident in her strength, and led away by her pleasures, that no succeeding *Lady Townly* arrived at her many distinguished excellencies in the character. By being a welcome and constant visitor to families of distinction, Mrs. Oldfield acquired a graceful carriage in representing women of high rank, and expressed their sentiments in a manner so easy, natural, and flowing, that they appeared to be of her own genuine utterance. Notwithstanding her amorous connexions[2] were publicly known, she was invited to the houses of women of fashion, as conspicuous for unblemished character as elevated rank. Even the royal family did not disdain to see Mrs Oldfield at their levees. George the Second and Queen Caroline, when Prince and Princess of Wales, often condescended to converse with her. One day the Princess told Mrs Oldfield, she had heard that General Churchill and she were married: "So it is said, may it please your royal highness," replied Mrs. Oldfield, "but we have not owned it yet."

In private, Mrs Oldfield was generous, humane, witty, and well-bred. Though she disliked the man, and disapproved of his conduct, yet the misfortunes of Savage recommended him to her pity, and she often relieved him

---

[1] "Dramatic Miscellanies," vol. iii. p. 465.

[2] It is supposed that she was engaged in a tender intercourse with Farquhar, and was the "Penelope" of his amatory correspondence. She lived successively with Arthur Mainwaring, one of the most accomplished characters of his age, and General Churchill, by each of whom she had a son.

by a handsome donation. Her influence with Walpole contributed to procure his pardon when convicted, on false evidence, of murder, and adjudged to death, a fate which his most unnatural mother did her utmost to enforce. It is not true that she either allowed this poet an annuity, or admitted his conversation,[1] but still the benefits she did confer upon him were quite numerous enough to warrant his celebration of her memory. The goodness of her heart, and the splendour of her talents, were topics upon which Savage might have ventured to insist, without endangering his piety or wounding his pride. Dr Johnson has sanctioned the silence of this author,[2] on the grounds of Mrs. Oldfield's condition; but that dogmatic man would have shown a truer taste for benevolence, had he recommended the most ardent devotion to individuals of any stamp, who were actuated by so glorious a principle.

Pope, who seems to have persecuted the name of player with a malignancy unworthy of his genius, has stigmatised the conversation of Mrs Oldfield by the word "*Oldfield-ismos*," which he printed in Greek characters; nor can there be a doubt that he meant her by the dying coquette, in one of his epistles. That Mrs. Oldfield was touched by the vanity of weak minds, and drew an absurd importance from the popularity of her low station, may be fairly inferred, and might have been fairly derided;[3] but Pope, with his usual want of candour, has appealed to less

[1] This fact is firmly denied in Cibber's "Lives of the Poets," and with a pointed reference to Johnson's admission of it.—Vol. v. p. 33.

[2] Savage, however, was *not* silent, though he abstained from putting his name to the poem, he indisputably wrote upon Mrs. Oldfield's death. It is preserved in Chetwood's "History"

[3] What can be more ridiculous than the following anecdote?
Mrs Oldfield happened to be in some danger in a Gravesend boat, and when the rest of the passengers lamented their imagined approaching fate, she, with a conscious dignity, told them their deaths would be only a private loss;—"But I am a public concern."—"Dramatic Miscellanies," vol i. p. 227.

tangible failings, and tried, as in most cases, much more to ridicule the person than correct the fault. I do not dispute the brilliancy of his sarcasm, but I would rather hail the rigour of his justice.[1]

Mrs. Oldfield died on the 23d of October, 1730, most sincerely lamented by those to whom her general value was not unknown.

[1] The bitterness of Pope's muse subsided upon no occasion, where the name of Mrs. Oldfield might be aptly introduced. Thus in the "Sober Advice from Horace," one of his inedited poems

> Engaging Oldfield! who, with grace and ease,
> Could join the arts to ruin and to please.

INDEX.

ABBÉ, Monsieur L', a French dancer, i. xxvii, i. 316.

Acting, excellence of, about 1631, i. xlviii.; Cibber's views on versatility in, i 209.

Actors, their names not given in old plays, i. xxv., join Charles I's army, i. xxix, the prejudice against, i. 74-84, taken into society, i. 83; their delight in applause, i 85; entitled Gentlemen of the Great Chamber, i. 88; must be born, not made, i. 89; their private characters influence audiences, i 243-251; their arrangement with Swiney in 1706, ii 9; refused Christian burial by the Romish Church, ii. 29; badly paid, ii. 64, dearth of young, ii. 221

——— the old, played secretly during the Commonwealth, i. xxx.; arrested for playing, i. xxx.; bribed officers of guard to let them play, i. xxx

Actress (Miss Santlow), insulted, i. 76.

Actresses, first English, i. 87, *note* 1, i. 90, i. 119; who were Charles II.'s mistresses, i. 91; difficulty of getting good, ii 222.

Addison, Joseph, i. 245, ii 36, *note* 1, ii. 151, ii. 163, *note* 1, ii. 251; Pope's attack on, i 38, his opinion of Wilks's Hamlet, i. 100, his view regarding humour in tragedy, i 123; his play of "Cato," ii. 120; its great success, ii 127-133; presents the profits of "Cato" to the managers, ii. 129; its success at Oxford, ii 137, his "Cato" quoted, ii. 238, *note* 2.

Admission to theatres, cheap, before 1642, i xxvii.

Adventurers—subscribers to the building of Dorset Garden Theatre, i. 97, *note* 1; their interest in the Drury Lane Patent, ii. 32, *note* 1; Rich uses them against Brett, ii. 57; names of the principal, ii. 57, *note* 1.

Agreement preliminary to the Union of 1682, ii. 324, ii. 328

"Albion Queens, The," ii. 14, *note* 1.

"Alexander the Great," by Lee, i. 105.

Allen, William, an eminent actor, i. xxvi.; a major in Charles I.'s army, i. xxix.

Alleyn, Edward, caused the Fortune Theatre to be built for his company, i. xxviii.; endowed Dulwich College, i. xxviii; Ben Jonson's eulogium of, i. xxviii.

"Amphytrion," by Dryden, i. 113.

Angel, a comedian, ii 347.

Anne, Queen (while Princess of Denmark), deserts her father, James II., i 67, i. 70; pensions Mrs Betterton, i 162, at the play, i. 185; forbids audience on the stage, i. 234, *note* 2; her death, ii 161.

Applause, i. 221; the pleasure of, i. 85.

Archer, William, his investigations regarding the truth of Diderot's "Paradoxe sur le Comédien," i. 103, *note* 1; his "About the Theatre," i. 278, *note* 1.

Aristophanes, referred to, i. 39

Arlington, Earl of, his death, i 31, *note* 1.

Arthur, son of Henry VII., pageants at his marriage, i. xliii.

Ashbury, Joseph, the Dublin Patentee, i. 236, ii. 364; engages Mrs. Charlotte Butler, i. 165, memoir of, i. 165, *note* 1.

Aston, Anthony, quoted, i. 109, *note* 1, i. 110, *note* 1, i. 116, *note* 1, i. 167, *note* 1, i. 167, *note* 2, ii 354, on his own acting of Fondlewife, ii. 312, his "Brief Supplement" to Cibber's Lives of his Contemporaries, reprint of, ii. 297; his description of Mrs. Barry, ii. 302; Betterton, ii. 299; Mrs. Bracegirdle, ii. 303; Dogget, ii 308; Haines, ii. 314, Mrs Mountfort, ii. 313; Sandford, ii. 306; Underhill, ii 307; Verbruggen, ii. 311.

Audience on the stage, i. 234, ii 246

Audiences rule the stage for good or evil, i 112, authors discouraged by their severity, i 176

Authors abusing managers and actors, ii 249, managers' troubles with, ii 249; Cibber censured for his treatment of, ii. 251, *note* 1.

Bacon, Lord, quoted, i. xlv.

Baddeley, Robert, the last actor who wore the uniform of their Majesties' servants, i 88, *note* 3.

INDEX.

Balon, Mons., a French dancer, i. 316.

Banks, John, the excellence of his plots, ii. 15; his "Unhappy Favourite," ii. 244.

Baron, Michael (French actor), i. 175.

Barry, Mrs. Elizabeth, i. 98, i. 110, *note* 1, i. 185, i. 188, i. 192, *note* 1, i. 251, *note* 1, ii. 300, ii. 302, ii. 306, ii. 320, ii. 337, ii. 365; Cibber's account of, i. 158-161; her great genius, i. 158; Dryden's compliment to, i. 158; her unpromising commencement as an actress, i. 159; her power of exciting pity, i. 160; her dignity and fire, i. 160; the first performer who had a benefit, i. 161; her death, i. 161; her retirement, ii. 69; Anthony Aston's description of, ii. 302; Bellchambers's memoir of, ii. 357.

Beaumont and Fletcher's "Wild-Goose Chase," published for Lowin and Taylor's benefit, i. xxxi.

Beeston, Christopher, ii. 326.

"Beggar's Opera," i. 243, i. 318.

Behn, Mrs. Aphra, i. 195.

Bellchambers, Edmund, his edition of Cibber's "Apology" quoted, i. 5, *note* 1, i. 14, *note* 1, i. 35, *note* 2, i. 41, *note* 2, i. 58, *note* 1, i. 71, *note* 1, i. 106, *note* 1, i. 123, *note* 2, i. 133, *note* 1, i. 141, *note* 1, i. 146, *note* 1, i. 152, *note* 1, i. 161, *note* 2, i. 163, *note* 1, i. 170, *note* 1, i. 179, *note* 2, i. 183, *note* 1, i. 197, *note* 3, i. 202, *note* 1, i. 251, *note* 1, i. 278, *note* 1, ii. 17, *note* 1, ii. 51, *note* 1, ii. 88, *note* 1, ii. 185, *note* 1, ii. 252, *note* 1, ii. 254, *note* 1; his memoir of Mrs. Barry, ii. 357; Betterton, ii. 333; Mrs. Betterton, ii. 359; W. Bullock, ii. 361; Estcourt, ii. 331; Goodman, ii. 329; Hart, ii. 322; B. Johnson, ii. 360; Keen, ii. 364; Kynaston, ii. 339; Anthony Leigh, ii. 349; John Mills, ii. 362; Mohun, ii. 326; Mountfort, ii. 341; James Nokes, ii. 346; Mrs. Oldfield, ii. 367; Pinkethman, ii. 348; Mrs. Porter, ii. 365; Powell, ii. 352; Sandford, ii. 346: Smith, ii. 319; Underhill, ii. 350; Verbruggen, ii. 354; Joseph Williams, ii. 356.

Benefits, their origin, i. 161; Mrs. Elizabeth Barry the first performer to whom granted, i. 161, ii. 67; part confiscated by Rich, ii. 66; Rich ordered to refund the part confiscated, ii. 68; amounts realized by principal actors, ii. 78, *note* 1.

Betterton, Mrs. Mary, i. 98, i. 327, ii. 336; said to be the first English actress, i. 90, *note* 1; Cibber's account of, i. 161-162, without a rival in Shakespeare's plays, i. 162; her unblemished character, i. 162; pensioned by Queen Anne, i. 162, her death, i. 162; Bellchambers's memoir of, ii. 359

—— Thomas, i. 98, i 162, i. 175, i. 181, *note* 2, i. 187, *note* 1, i. 188, ii 64, *note* 2, ii. 128, ii. 211, *note* 1, ii. 215, ii. 237, ii 244, *note* 1, ii. 306, ii. 308, ii 311, ii 320, ii. 324, ii. 346, ii 352, ii. 358, ii. 359, ii. 363, ii. 365, improves scenery, i xxii; taken into good society, i. 83, famous for Hamlet, i. 91; Cibber's eulogium of, i. 99-118; his supreme excellence, i. 100; description of his Hamlet, i. 100, Booth's veneration for, i 101, *note* 1, his Hotspur, i. 103, his Brutus, i 103; the grace and harmony of his elocution, i 106; his success in "Alexander the Great," i. 106, i. 108, his just estimate of applause, i 109; his perfect elocution, i. 111, description of his voice and person, i. 116, Kneller's portrait of, i 117; his last appearance, i. 117, his death, i. 118; the "Tatler's" eulogium of, i. 118, *note* 1; Gildon's Life of, i. 118, *note* 2, ii. 324, ii. 337, *note* 1, ii. 358; Mrs. Bracegirdle returns to play for his benefit, i. 174; ill-treated by the Patentees, i. 188, makes a party against them, i. 189; obtains a licence in 1695, i. 192, *note* 1, i 194; mimicked by Powell, i 205, i. 207, *note* 1, his versatility, i. 211; his difficulty in managing at Lincoln's Inn Fields, i. 228; as a prologue-speaker, i 271, inability to keep order in his Company, i. 315, said to be specially favoured by the Lord Chamberlain, ii. 18; declines management in 1709, ii. 69; advertisement regarding his salary (1709), ii. 78, *note* 1; his superiority to Wilks and Booth, ii 245, Anthony Aston's description of, ii. 299; and the puppet-show keeper, ii 301, Bellchambers's memoir of, ii. 333.

Betterton's Company (1695 to 1704), their decline, i. 314, disorders in, i. 315.

Biblical narratives dramatized in the "Ludus Coventriæ," i. xxxvii. *et seq*

Bibliography of Colley Cibber, ii. 289-296

Bickerstaffe, Isaac (author), ii. 288.

INDEX.

Bickerstaffe, John (actor), ii. 77, *note* 1, ii. 94, *note* 1; threatens Cibber for reducing his salary, i. 71, *note* 1.

Bignell, Mrs., ii. 77, *note* 1, ii. 129, *note* 2.

"Biographia Britannica," ii. 360.

"Biographia Dramatica," i. 184, *note* 1, i. 278, *note* 1, i. 330, *note* 1, ii. 14, *note* 1, ii. 332, ii. 336, ii. 337, *note* 1, ii. 359, *note* 1.

Bird, Theophilus, an eminent actor, i. xxvi.

Blackfriar's Company, "men of grave and sober behaviour," i. xxvii.

—— Theatre, i. xxv., i xxvi., i. xxviii., i xlix.; its excellent company, i. xxiv., i. xxvi.

Blanc, Abbé Le, his account of a theatre riot, i. 278, *note* 1.

"Blast upon Bays, A," ii. 266.

"Bloody Brother, The," actors arrested while playing, i. xxx.

Booth, Barton, i. 157, ii. 36, *note* 1, ii. 77, *note* 1, ii. 94, *note* 1, ii. 95, *note* 1, ii. 110, ii. 128, ii 129, *note* 2, ii. 167, ii. 230, ii. 232, ii 320, ii. 361, ii. 363; Memoirs of, published immediately after his death, i. 5; story told by him of Cibber, i. 63, *note* 1; his veneration for Betterton, i. 101, *note* 1; his indolence alluded to by Cibber, i. 103; his reverence for tragedy, i. 121; his Morat, i. 122; his Life, by Theo. Cibber, quoted, i. 122, *note* 1, i. 123, *note* 2, ii. 130, *note* 2, ii. 140, *note* 1; his Henry VIII., i. 123, *note* 2; is warned by Powell's excesses to avoid drinking, i. 260; as a prologue-speaker, i. 271; elects to continue at Drury Lane in 1709, ii. 70; his marriage, ii 96, *note* 1; the reason of the delay in making him a manager, ii. 114, his success as Cato, ii. 130-133; his claim to be made a manager on account of his success, ii. 130; supported by Lord Bolingbroke, ii. 130, *note* 2, his name added to the Licence, ii. 140; the terms of his admission as sharer, ii. 144; his suffering from Wilks's temper, ii. 155, his connection with Steele during the dispute about Steele's patent, ii. 193, *note* 1; Wilks's jealousy of, ii. 223; a scene with Wilks, ii. 234-237; and Wilks, their opinion of each other, ii. 240, his deficiency in humour, ii. 240; formed his style on Betterton, ii. 241; Cibber's comparison of Wilks and Booth, ii. 239-245; his Othello and Cato,

ii. 243; memoir of, ii. 254, *note* 1; Patent granted to him, Wilks, and Cibber, after Steele's death, ii. 257, sells half of his share of the Patent to Highmore, ii. 258.

Booth, Mrs. Barton (see also Santlow, Hester), insulted by Capt. Montague, i. 76-78; sells the remainder of Booth's share to Giffard, ii. 259.

Boswell, James, his "Life of Dr. Johnson," quoted, i. 36, *note* 2, i. 46, *note* 1, i 215, *note* 1, ii. 41, *note* 2, ii. 163, *note* 1.

Bourgogne, Hotel de, a theatre originally used for religious plays, i. xxxv.

Boutell, Mrs, mentioned, i. 161, *note* 1, i. 167, *note* 2.

Bowen, James (singer), ii. 312.

Bowman (actor), memoir of, ii. 211, *note* 1; sings before Charles II., ii. 211.

—— Mrs, ii 211, *note* 1.

Bowyer, Michael, an eminent actor, i. xxvi.

Boy-actresses, i. 90; still played after the appearance of women, i. 119.

Bracegirdle, Mrs. Anne, i. 98, i. 182, i. 188, i. 192, *note* 1, ii. 300, ii. 302, ii. 312, ii. 337; admitted into good society, i. 83; Cibber's account of, i. 170-174; her good character, i. 170-172; her character attacked by Bellchambers, i. 170, *note* 1; Tom Brown's scandal about her, i. 170, *note* 1; attacked in "Poems on Affairs of State," i. 170, *note* 1; her best parts, i. 173; her retirement, i. 174; memoir of her, i. 174, *note* 2; her rivalry with Mrs. Oldfield, i. 174, *note* 2; declines to play some of Mrs. Barry's parts, i. 188-9; her retirement, ii. 69; Anthony Aston's description of, ii. 303, her attempted abduction by Capt. Hill, ii. 342

Bradshaw, Mrs, ii. 77, *note* 1, ii. 94, *note* 1, ii. 303.

Brett, Colonel Henry, a share in the Drury Lane Patent presented to him by Skipwith, ii. 32; his acquaintance with Cibber, ii. 33, Cibber's account of, ii. 34-42; admires Cibber's perriwig, ii. 35, and the Countess of Macclesfield, ii. 39-41; his dealings with Rich, ii 42-49, ii 56-60, makes Wilks, Estcourt, and Cibber his deputies in management, ii. 56, *note* 1; gives up his share to Skipwith, ii. 59

—— Mrs. (see also Miss Mason, and Countess of Macclesfield), Cibber's high opinion of her taste, ii. 41, note 2; his "Careless Husband" submitted to her, ii. 41, *note* 2; her judicious treatment of her husband, ii. 41, *note* 2.

Bridgwater (actor), ii. 260.

Brown, Tom, ii. 348, ii. 350; his scandal on Mrs. Bracegirdle, i. 170, *note* 1.

Buck, Sir George, his "Third University of England," quoted, i. xlviii.

Buckingham, Duke of, ii. 210.

"Buffoon, The," an epigram on Cibber's admission into society, i. 29, *note* 1.

Bullen, A. H., his "Lyrics from Elizabethan Song-books," i. 21, *note* 1.

Bullock, Christopher, ii 169, *note* 2.

—— Mrs. Christopher, i. 136, *note* 2.

—— William, i. 194, i. 313, i 332, ii. 169, *note* 2, ii. 252, *note* 1; Bellchambers's memoir of, ii. 361.

Burbage, Richard, i xxvi.

Burgess, Colonel, killed Horden, an actor, i. 303; his punishment, i. 302, *note* 2.

Burlington, Earl of, ii. 209

Burnet, Bishop, his observations on Nell Gwynne, ii. 212, on Mrs. Roberts, ii. 212.

Burney, Dr., his "History of Music," ii 55, *note* 1, ii. 89, *note* 1; his MSS. in the British Museum, i. 174, *note* 2, ii. 198, *note* 1, ii. 224, *note* 1.

Burt (actor), superior to his successors, i. xxiv.; apprenticed to Shank, i. xxv.; and to Beeston, i. xxv.; a "boy-actress," i. xxv.; a cornet in Charles I.'s army, i. xxix.; arrested for acting, i. xxx.

Butler, Mrs. Charlotte, i. 98, i. 237, ii. 262; Cibber's account of, i 163-165; patronized by Charles II, i. 163; a good singer and dancer, i. 163; a pleasant and clever actress, i. 164; compared with Mrs. Oldfield, i. 164; goes to the Dublin theatre, i. 164; note regarding her, i. 164, *note* 1.

Byrd, William, his "Psalmes, Sonets, etc," i. 21, *note* 1.

Byron, Lord, a practical joke erroneously attributed to him while at Cambridge, i. 59, *note* 1.

Cambridge. See Trinity College, Cambridge.

"Careless Husband," cast of, i 308, *note* 1

Carey, Henry, deprived of the freedom of the theatre for bantering Cibber, ii. 226, *note* 2.

Carlile, James, memoir of, i. 84, *note* 1; is killed at Aughrim, i. 84, *note* 1, i. 85.

Cartwright (actor), belonged to the Salisbury Court Theatre, i. xxiv.

Castil-Blaze, Mons, his "La Danse et les Ballets" quoted, i. 316, *note* 1.

Catherine of Arragon, pageants at her marriage with Prince Arthur, i. xliii.

"Cato," by Addison, cast of, ii. 120, *note* 1; its success, ii 127-133, at Oxford, ii. 137; its influence, ii. 26; Cibber's Syphax in, i. 122

Chalmers, George, his "Apology for the Shakspeare-Believers," i 276, *note* 1, i 277, *note* 1

"Champion" (by Henry Fielding), quoted, i. 1, *note* 1, i. 38, *note* 1, i 50, *note* 2, i 63, *note* 1, i. 69, *note* 1, i. 93, *note* 2, i 288, *note* 1, ii. 54, *note* 2.

Charke, Charlotte, ii. 285.

—— (musician), husband of Cibber's daughter, ii. 285.

Charles II. mentioned, i. 120, i. 133, his escape from Presbyterian tyranny, i. 22; Cibber sees him at Whitehall, i 30; writes a funeral oration on his death while still at school, i. 31, Patents granted by him to Davenant and Killigrew, i. 87, wittily reproved by Killigrew, i. 87, *note* 2, called Anthony Leigh "his actor," i. 154,

his Court theatricals, ii. 209; and Bowman the actor, ii. 211; his opinion of Sandford's acting, ii 306.

Chesterfield, Lord, his powers of raillery, i. 13, i 14, refers ironically to Cibber in "Common Sense," i. 71, *note* 1, opposes the Licensing Act of 1737, i. 289

Chetwood, William Rufus, Cibber acts for his benefit, ii. 265; his "History of the Stage," i. 165, *note* 1, i. 207, *note* 1, i. 244, *note* 1, ii. 140, *note* 1, ii. 169, *note* 3, ii. 319-320, ii 331, ii. 356, ii. 364.

"Children of her Majesty's Chapel," i. xxxvi.

"Children of Paul's," i xxxvi.

Churchill, General, ii. 369, *note* 2.

—— Lady (Duchess of Marlborough), i 67, Cibber attends her at table, i. 68; his admiration of her, i. 68, her beauty and good fortune, i 69.

Cibber, Caius Gabriel, father of Colley Cibber, i. 7, *note* 2; his statues and other works, i. 8; his marriage, i. 8, *note* 1; his death, i. 8, *note* 1; presents a statue to Winchester College, i. 56; employed at Chatsworth, i. 58; statues carved by him for Trinity College Library, Cambridge, i 59.

Cibber, Colley, Account of his Life:—

His Apology written at Bath, i. 1, *note* 1; his reasons for writing his own Life, i. 5, i. 6; his birth, i. 7; his baptism recorded, i. 7, *note* 2, sent to school at Grantham, i. 9; his character at school, i. 9; writes an ode at school on Charles II.'s death, i. 31; and on James II.'s coronation, i. 33; his prospects in life, i. 55, his first taste for the stage, i. 58; stifles his love for the stage and desires to go to the University, i. 58, serves against James II in 1688, i. 61, attends Lady Churchill at table, i. 68, his admiration of her, i. 68; disappointed in his expectation of receiving a commission in the army, i. 71; petitions the Duke of Devonshire for preferment, i. 73; determines to be an actor, i. 73; hangs about Downes the prompter, i. 74, *note* 1; his account of his own first appearances, i. 180; his first salary, i. 181; description of his personal appearance, i. 182; his first success, i. 183; his marriage, i. 184, plays Kynaston's part in "The Double Dealer," i. 185, remains with Patentees in 1695, i. 193; writes his first Prologue, i. 195; not allowed to speak it, i. 196; forced to play Fondlewife, i. 206, plays it in imitation of Dogget, i. 208, his slow advancement as an actor, i. 209, i 215; writes his first play, "Love's Last Shift," i 212; as Sir Novelty Fashion, i 213; encouraged and helped by Vanbrugh, i 215; begins to advance as an actor, i. 218, better in comedy than tragedy, i. 221; tragic parts played by him, i. 222; his Iago abused, i. 222, *note* 1; description of his Justice Shallow, i. 224, *note* 2, leaves Drury Lane for Lincoln's Inn Fields, i 232, *note* 1, returns to Drury Lane, i. 232, *note* 1; his "Love in a Riddle" condemned, i. 244-250; accused of having Gay's "Polly" vetoed, i 247, his Damon and Philhda, i. 249, *note* 1; consulted by Rich on matters of management, i. 253; his disputes with Wilks, i. 258; his "Woman's Wit" a failure, i. 264; distinguished by

Cibber, Colley, Account of his Life—*continued*.

Dryden, i 269; attacked by Jeremy Collier, i 274; his adaptation of "Richard III.," i. 139; his "Richard III." mutilated by the Master of the Revels, i 275, attacked by George Chalmers, i. 276, *note* 1, i 277, *note* 1; declines to pay fees to Killigrew, Master of Revels, i. 277; his surprise at Mrs Oldfield's excellence, i 307, writes "The Careless Husband" chiefly for Mrs Oldfield, i 308, finishes "The Provoked Husband," begun by Vanbrugh, i. 311, *note* 1, invited to join Swiney at the Haymarket, i 333; leaves Rich and goes to Swiney, i 337; his "Lady's Last Stake," ii. 2; his "Double Gallant," ii. 3, his "Marriage à la Mode," ii 5, declines to act on the same stage as rope-dancers, ii. 7; advises Col. Brett regarding the Patent, ii 33, ii. 42; his first introduction to him, ii. 33; his account of Brett, 34-42; as Young Reveller in "Greenwich Park," ii 41; made Deputy-manager by Brett, ii. 56, *note* 1; advertisement regarding his salary, 1709, ii. 78, *note* 1, made joint manager with Swiney and others in 1709, ii. 69; and his fellow-managers, Wilks and Dogget, ii. 110, ii. 117, ii. 121, ii. 127; mediates between Wilks and Dogget, ii. 122; his troubles with Wilks, ii. 124; his views and conduct on Booth's claiming to become a manager, ii. 131-133, ii. 140-143, his meetings with Dogget after their law-suit, ii 150, his "Nonjuror," i. 177, *note* 1, ii. 185-190; accused of stealing his "Nonjuror," ii 186, *note* 1; makes the Jacobites his enemies, ii. 185-187; reported dead by "Mist's Weekly Journal," ii. 188; his "Provoked Husband" hissed by his Jacobite enemies, ii 189; his appointment as Poet Laureate in 1730, i. 32, *note* 1; the reason of his being made Laureate, ii. 190, his "Ximena," ii 163, *note* 1; his suspension by the Duke of Newcastle, ii. 193, *note* 1; his connection with Steele during the dispute about Steele's Patent, ii. 193, *note* 1; his account of a suit brought by Steele against his partners, ii. 196-208; his pleading in person in the suit brought by Steele, ii. 199-207; his success in pleading, ii. 198, *note* 1, ii. 207; assisted Steele in his "Conscious Lovers," ii. 206; his playing of Wolsey before George I., ii. 216; admitted into good society, i. 29; elected a member of White's, i. 29, *note* 1; an epigram on his admission into good society, i. 29, *note* 1; Patent granted to Cibber, Wilks, and Booth after Steele's death, ii. 257; sells his share of the Patent to Highmore, ii. 258; his sale of his share in the Patent, i. 297; his shameful treatment of Highmore, ii. 259; his retirement, ii. 255; gives a reason for retiring from the stage, i. 178, i. 179, *note* 1; his appearances after his retirement, ii. 261, ii. 263, ii. 264, ii. 268; his remarks on his successful reappearances, i. 179; his last appearances, i. 6, *note* 1; his adaptation of "King John," i. 6, *note* 1; his "Papal Tyranny in the Reign of King John" withdrawn from rehearsal, ii. 263; his "Papal Tyranny" produced, ii. 268; its success, ii. 270; his quarrel with Pope, ii. 270-283; and Horace Walpole, ii. 284; his death and burial, ii. 284; list of his plays, ii. 286-7; bibliography of, ii. 289-296; Anthony Aston's "Supplement" to, ii. 297.

Cibber, Colley, Attacks on him :—

Commonly accused of cowardice, i. 71, *note* 1; threatened by John Bickerstaffe, for reducing his salary, i. 71, *note* 1; accused of "venom" towards Booth, i. 123, *note* 2; abused by Dennis, i. 66, *note* 1, ii. 168, *note* 1; his offer of a reward for discovery of Dennis, i. 41, *note* 1, ii. 168, *note* 1; charged with envy of Estcourt, i. 115, *note* 2; Fielding's attacks upon, quoted (see under Fielding, Hy.); his galling retaliation on Fielding, i. 286; said to have been thrashed by Gay, i. 71, *note* 1; "The Laureat's" attacks upon (see "Laureat"); satirized on his appointment as Laureate, i. 46; epigrams on

Cibber, Colley, Attacks on him—*continued.*

his appointment quoted, i. 46, *note* 1, writes verses in his own dispraise, i. 47; his Odes attacked by Fielding, i. 36, *note* 2; and by Johnson, i 36, *note* 2; charges against him of levity and impiety, i. 58, *note* 1; accused of negligence in acting, i. 241, *note* 1, attacked by the daily papers, i. 41; his disregard of them, i. 41, i. 44, *note* 1; on newspaper attacks, ii. 167; on principle never answered newspaper attacks, ii. 168; his famous quarrel with Pope, ii. 270; "The Nonjuror" a cause of Pope's enmity to Cibber, ii. 189, *note* 1, attacked by Pope for countenancing pantomimes, ii. 182, *note* 1; his reply, ii 182, *note* 1; his first allusion to Pope's enmity, i. 21; his opinion of Pope's attacks, i. 35; his Odes, i. 36, *note* 2, supposed to be referred to in Preface to Shadwell's "Fair Quaker of Deal," ii. 95, *note* 1; attacked for mutilating Shakespeare, ii. 263; accused of stealing "Love's Last Shift," i. 214, and "The Careless Husband," i. 215, *note* 1; satirized by Swift, i. 52, *note* 2; his defence of his follies, i. 2, i. 19.

Cibber, Colley, Criticisms of Contemporaries:—

On the production of Addison's "Cato," ii. 120, ii. 127-133; his description of Mrs Barry, i. 158-161; on the excellence of Betterton and his contemporaries, i. 175; his eulogium of Betterton, i. 99-118; his description of Mrs Betterton, i 161-162; his account of Booth and Wilks as actors, ii 239-245, his description of Mrs. Bracegirdle, i. 170-4; his description of Mrs. Butler, i. 163-165; his high opinion of Mrs. Brett's taste, ii. 41, *note* 2; submits every scene of his "Careless Husband" to Mrs. Brett, ii 41, *note* 2; on his own acting, i 220-226; his "Epilogue upon Himself," ii. 265, on Dogget's acting, ii. 158; his low opinion of Garrick, ii. 268, his description of Kynaston, i 120-127; his description of Leigh, i. 145-154; his description of Mrs. Leigh, i. 162-3, his description of Mountfort, i. 127-130; his description of Mrs. Mountfort, i. 165-169; his praise of Nicolini, ii. 51; his description of Nokes, i. 141-145; his hyperbolical praise of Mrs. Oldfield's Lady Townly, i. 51, i. 312, *note* 3; on Rich's misconduct, ii. 46; his description of Sandford, i. 130; his description of Cave Underhill, i. 154-156; his unfairness to Verbruggen, i. 157, *note* 2; his account of Wilks and Booth as actors, ii. 239-245; on Wilks's Hamlet, i. 100; praises Wilks's diligence, ii. 160, ii. 239; on Wilks's love of acting, ii. 225; on Wilks's temper, ii. 155, ii. 171; a scene with Wilks, 234-237.

Cibber, Colley, Reflections and Opinions:—

On acting, i. 209, i. 221; on acting villains, i. 131-135, i. 222; on the prejudice against actors, i. 74-84; his advice to dramatists, ii. 14; on applause, i. 221, ii. 214; on the severity of audiences, i. 175; on politeness in audiences, ii. 247; on troubles with authors, ii. 249; on the effect of comedy-acting, i. 140; on Court influence, ii. 103; on criticism, i. 52; on his critics, ii. 220; on humour in tragedy, i. 121; on the Italian Opera, ii. 50-55; on the difficulty of managing Italian singers, ii. 88; on laughter, i. 23; on the liberty of the stage, i. 289; on the validity of the Licence, i. 284; on the power of the Lord Chamberlain, ii. 10-23; his principles as manager, i. 190; on management, ii. 60; on judicious management, ii. 74; on the duties and responsibilities of management, ii. 199-207; on the success of his management, ii. 245; on morality in plays, i. 265, i. 272; on the power of music, i. 112; on Oxford theatricals, ii. 133-139; on pantomimes, i. 93, ii. 180; on prologue-speaking, i. 270; on the difficulties of promotion in the theatre, ii. 223; on the Queen's Theatre in the Haymarket, i. 322; on raillery, i. 11; on the Revolution of 1688, i. 60-63; on satire, i. 37; on the reformation of the

Cibber, Colley, Reflections and Opinions—*continued.* stage, i. 81; on making the stage useful, ii. 24-31; on the benefit of only one theatre, i. 92, ii. 139, ii. 178-185; on the shape of the theatre, ii. 84; on his own vanity, ii. 182

—— Miscellaneous ——

Profit arising from his works, i. 3, *note* 2; frequently the object of envy, i 33; his obtrusive loyalty, i 33, *note* 1, i 66, banters his critics by allowing his "Apology" to be impudent and ill-written, i. 43, his easy temper under criticism and abuse, i 50, confesses the faults of his writing, i. 50; his "quavering tragedy tones," i. 110, *note* 1, his playing of Richard III an imitation of Sandford, i 139; his "Careless Husband" quoted, i. 148, *note* 1; his wigs, ii. 36, *note* 1, his treatment of authors, ii. 37, *note* 1; reproved by Col Brett for his treatment of authors, ii 37, *note* 1, his dedication of the "Wife's Resentment" to the Duke of Kent, ii. 46; censured for his treatment of authors, ii. 251, *note* 1; his satisfaction in looking back on his career, ii. 115; his acknowledgment of Steele's services to the theatre, ii. 162; his dedication of "Ximena" to Steele, ii. 163, *note* 1; his omission of many material circumstances in the history of the stage, ii. 193, *note* 1, Wilks his constant supporter and admirer, ii 226, *note* 1, his "Odes," ii. 283, hissed as Phorbas, ii. 309, Aston on Cibber's acting, ii. 312

Cibber, Mrs Colley, her marriage, i 184; her character, i. 184, *note* 1; her father's objection to her marriage, i. 184, *note* 1

—— Lewis (brother of Colley), admitted to Winchester College, i. 56, Cibber's affection for, i. 57; his great abilities, i. 57; his death, i 57.

—— Susanna Maria (wife of Theophilus), ii. 267, *note* 1, ii. 270, ii. 285; her speaking described, i. 110, *note* 1.

—— Theophilus, ii 187, *note* 1, ii 262; mentioned ironically by Lord Chesterfield, i. 71, *note* 1; in "Art and Nature," i. 152, *note* 1; acts as his father's deputy in management, ii. 258; heads a mutiny against Highmore, ii. 259; account of him, ii. 285; his "Life of Booth" quoted, i. 122, *note* 1, i. 123, *note* 2, ii. 130, *note* 2, ii. 140, *note* 1.

"Circe," an opera, i. 94.

Civil War, the, closing of theatres during, i. 89.

Clark, actor, memoir of, i. 96, *note* 3.

Cleveland, Duchess of, and Goodman, ii. 330.

Clive, Mrs. Catherine, ii. 260, ii. 268, *note* 1, ii. 269; her acting in "Love in a Riddle," i. 244, *note* 1.

Clun, a "boy-actress," i. xxiv.

Cock-fighting prohibited in 1654, i. lii.

Cockpit, The (or Phœnix), i. xxv.; its company, i. xxvi., i. xxviii., i. xlix.; Rhodes's Company at, i. xxviii.; secret performances at, during the Commonwealth, i. xxx.

Coke, Rt. Hon. Thomas, Vice-Chamberlain, his interference in Dogget's dispute with his partners, ii. 146.

Coleman, Mrs., the first English actress, i. 90, *note* 1.

Colley, the family of, i. 8, i. 9.

—— Jane, mother of Colley Cibber, i. 8, *note* 1.

Collier, Jeremy, i. 170, *note* 1, i. 268, *note* 2, i. 273, i. 274, ii. 233, *note* 2; his "Short View of the Profaneness, &c., of the English Stage," i. xxi., i. xxxiii., i. 272, i. 289; his arguments confuted, i. xxxiii.

Collier, William, M.P., i. 97, *note* 2, ii. 172, ii. 175; procures a licence for Drury Lane, ii. 91; evicts Rich, ii. 92; appoints Aaron Hill his manager, ii. 94, *note* 1; his unjust treatment of Swiney, ii. 101, ii. 107; takes the control of the opera from Swiney, ii. 102; farms the opera to Aaron Hill, ii. 105; forces Swiney to resume the opera, ii. 107; made partner with Cibber, Wilks, and Dogget at Drury Lane, ii. 107; his shabby treatment of his partners, ii. 108, ii. 141; his downfall, ii. 109; replaced by Steele in the Licence, ii. 164.

Comedy-acting, the effect of, i. 140.

"Common Sense," a paper by Lord Chesterfield, quoted, i. 71, *note* 1.

"Comparison between the two Stages," by Gildon, i. 189, *note* 1, i. 194, *note* 1, i. 194, *note* 5, i. 214, *note* 1, i. 216, *note* 1, i. 218, *note* 2, i. 231, *note* 2, i. 232, *note* 2, i. 233, *note* 1, i. 254, *note* 1, i. 303, *note* 1, i. 306, *note* 1, i. 316, *note* 2, ii. 328, *note* 2, ii. 348, ii. 356, *note* 1, ii. 362.

Complexion, black, of evil characters on the stage, i. 133.

Congreve, William, i. 185, 1. 274, 1. 284, ii. 36, *note* 1, ii. 110, ii. 159, ii 251, 11. 302; Memoir of, mentioned, 1 5, *note* 1, his "Love for Love," i. 155, 1 197; scandal about him and Mrs. Bracegirdle, 1 170, *note* 1; a sharer with Betterton in his Licence in 1695, i. 192, *note* 1, 1. 197; his "Mourning Bride," i 199, his "Way of the World," 1 200; his opinion of "Love's Last Shift," 1 220, and Vanbrugh manage the Queen's Theatre, 1 320, 1. 325; gives up his share in the Queen's Theatre, 1 326, and Mrs. Bracegirdle, 11 304.

Cooper, Lord Chancellor, 11. 149, 11. 174.

Coquelin, Constant, his controversy with Henry Irving regarding Diderot's "Paradoxe sur le Comédien," i. 103, *note* 1.

Corelli, Arcangelo, ii 247

Cory (actor), 11. 169, *note* 2.

Court, theatrical performances at, see Royal Theatricals; interference of the, in the management of the stage, i. 89

Covent Garden, Drury Lane theatre sometimes described as the theatre in, i. 88, *note* 1.

Covent Garden Theatre, i 92, *note* 1.

Coventry, the old Leet Book of, i. xl

Craggs, Mr. Secretary, ii 96, *note* 1, ii. 165, 11. 333; chastises Captain Montague for insulting Miss Santlow, i 77

Craufurd, David, his account of the disorders in Betterton's company, i. 315, *note* 2.

Crawley, keeper of a puppet-show, 11. 301.

Creation, the, dramatized in the "Ludus Coventriæ," 1 xxxviii.

Cromwell, Lady Mary, i. 267, *note* 1.

Cross, Mrs., i. 334, *note* 1.

—— Richard, prompter of Drury Lane, 1 181, *note* 2.

Crowne, John, his masque of "Calisto," 11. 209

Cumberland, Richard, his description of Mrs. Cibber's speaking, 1 110, *note* 1.

Cunningham, Lieut.-Col. F., doubts if Ben Jonson was an unsuccessful actor, i. 85, *note* 1.

Curll, Edmund, his "History of the Stage," i. 96, *note* 4, 1. 174, *note* 2, 11. 357, his "Life of Mrs. Oldfield," i. 305, *note* 2; his memoirs of Wilks, i. 5, *note* 1.

Curtain Theatre, the, mentioned by Stow as recently erected, i. xlviii.
Cuzzoni, Francesca, her rivalry with Faustina, ii. 89.
"Cynthia's Revels," played by the Children of her Majesty's Chapel, i. xxxvi.

"Daily Courant," quoted, ii. 175, *note* 1.
Daly, Augustin, his Company of Comedians, ii. 289.
Dancers and singers introduced by Davenant, i. 94.
Davenant, Alexander, ii. 32, *note* 1; his share in the Patent, i. 181, *note* 1.
—— Dr. Charles, ii. 324.
—— Sir William, i. 181, *note* 1, i. 197, *note* 3, ii. 179, *note* 1, ii. 334; first introduces scenery, i. xxxii.; copy of his patent, i. liii.; Memoir of, i. 87, *note* 1; Poet Laureate, i. 87, *note* 1; receives a patent from Charles I., i. 87, *note* 1; from Charles II., i. 87; his company worse than Killigrew's, i. 93; he introduces spectacle and opera to attract audiences, i. 94; unites with Killigrew's, i. 96; his "Macbeth," ii. 229, *note* 1.
Davies, Thomas, his "Dramatic Miscellanies," i. 3, *note* 2, i. 41, *note* 1, i. 58, *note* 1, i. 71, *note* 1, i. 74, *note* 1, i. 90, *note* 1, i. 101, *note* 1, i. 153, *note* 1, i. 166, *note* 1, i. 179, *note* 1, i. 181, *note* 2, i. 192, *note* 1, i. 214, *note* 2, i. 222, *note* 1, i. 224, *note* 2, i. 241, *note* 1, i. 273, *note* 1, i. 274, *note* 1, i. 302, *note* 2, i. 330, *note* 1, ii. 36, *note* 1, ii. 211, *note* 1, ii. 216, *note* 1, ii. 226, *note* 1, ii. 230, *note* 1, ii. 233, *note* 3, ii. 240, *note* 1, ii. 263, *note* 1, ii. 268, *note* 1, ii. 325, *note* 1, ii. 335, *note* 1, ii. 351, ii. 352, ii. 354, ii. 355, *note* 1, ii. 358, ii. 361, ii. 363, ii. 369; his "Life of Garrick," i. lv., *note* 1, i. 283, *note* 2, ii. 259.
Davis, Mary (Moll), i. 91, *note* 1.
Denmark, Prince of, his support of William of Orange, i. 67, i. 70.
Dennis, John, i. 41, *note* 2, ii. 361; abuses Cibber for his loyalty, i. 66, *note* 1; accuses Cibber of stealing his "Love's Last Shift," i. 215; his attacks on Steele and Cibber, ii. 168, *note* 1, ii. 176, *note* 1; attacks Wilks, ii. 226, *note* 2; abuses one of the actors of his "Comic Gallant," ii. 252, *note* 1.
"Deserving Favourite, The," i. xxv.

Devonshire, Duke of, ii. 305 ; his quarrel with James II., i 72, Cibber presents a petition to, i. 73

Diderot, Denis, his "Paradoxe sur le Comédien, i. 103, note 1.

Dillworth, W. H , his "Life of Pope," ii. 278, note 1.

Dixon, a member of Rhodes's company, 1. 163, note 1

Dobson, Austin, his "Fielding" quoted, i. 286, note 1, i. 287, note 3, 1 288, note 1.

Dodington, Bubb, mentioned by Bellchambers, 1. 14, note 1

Dodsley, Robert, purchased the copyright of Cibber's "Apology," 1 3, note 2

Dogget, Thomas, 1 157, ii 110, ii. 227, ii 314, ii. 361, his excellence in Fondlewife, i. 206 ; Cibber plays Fondlewife in imitation of, i. 208 ; his intractability in Betterton's Company, 1 229, deserts Betterton at Lincoln's Inn Fields, and comes to Drury Lane, i 229, arrested for deserting Drury Lane, ii. 21, defies the Lord Chamberlain, ii. 21 ; wins his case, ii. 22 , made joint manager with Swiney and others in 1709, ii 69 ; his characteristics as a manager, ii 111, ii 117 ; his behaviour on Booth's claiming to become a manager, ii. 131, ii 141 ; retires because of Booth's being made a manager, ii 143 ; his refusal to come to any terms after Booth's admission, ii. 145 ; goes to law for his rights, ii. 149 , the result, ii. 150 ; Wilks's temper, the real reason of his retirement, ii. 150-155 , shows a desire to return to the stage, ii 157 ; his final appearances, ii. 158 ; Cibber's account of his excellence, ii. 158 , Anthony Aston's description of, ii. 308.

Doran, Dr. John, his "Annals of the Stage," i 88, note 3, 1 130, note 1, 1. 161, note 3, ii 62, note 1, ii 284

Dorset, Earl of, ii. 305 ; has Leigh's portrait painted in "The Spanish Friar," 1. 146 ; when Lord Chamberlain, supports Betterton in 1694-1695, i 192 ; compliments Cibber on his first play, i. 214.

Dorset Garden, Duke's Theatre, i. xxxii.

—— Theatre, built for Davenant's Company, 1. 88, note 2 , the subscribers to, called Adventurers, i. 97, note 1.

"Double Dealer, The," 1. 185, note 1

"Double Gallant," cast of, ii. 3, note 2.

Downes, John, his "Roscius Anglicanus," i. 83, *note* 1, i. 84, *note* 1, i. 96, *note* 3, i. 114, *note* 1, i. 127, *note* 2, i. 130, *note* 1, i. 141, *note* 1, i. 146, *note* 1, i. 163, *note* 1, i. 181, *note* 2, i. 187, *note* 2, i. 192, *note* 1, i. 197, *note* 1, i. 197, *note* 2, i. 316, *note* 2, i. 320, *note* 2, i. 333, *note* 1, ii. 158, *note* 3, ii. 320, ii. 323, ii. 328, ii. 330, ii. 332, ii. 334, ii. 340, ii. 341, ii. 342, ii. 346, ii. 347, ii. 348, ii. 349, ii. 350, ii. 356, ii. 359, ii. 360, ii. 361, ii. 362; attended constantly by Cibber and Verbruggen in hope of employment on the stage, i. 74, *note* 1; the "Tatler" publishes a supposed letter from, ii. 75.

"Dramatic Censor," 1811, ii. 57, *note* 1, ii. 79, *note* 2.

Dramatists, Cibber's advice to, ii. 14.

Drury Lane Theatre, i. 92, *note* 1; opened by King's Company, i. xxxii.; built for Killigrew's Company, i. 88; sometimes called "the theatre in Covent Garden," i. 88, *note* 1; desertion from in 1733, i. 283; Company (1695), their improvement, i. 314; its Patent, ii. 31; its original construction, ii. 81; why altered, ii. 81; under W. Collier's management, 1709, ii. 91; report on its stability, ii. 176-7.

Dryden, John, ii. 163, *note* 1, ii. 210, ii. 251; his prologue on opening Drury Lane, 1674, i. 94, *note* 2, i. 322, *note* 1; a bad elocutionist, i. 113; his Morat ("Aurenge-Zebe"), i. 124; his high praise of Mrs. Elizabeth Barry, i. 158; his prologue to "The Prophetess," i. 187, *note* 1; his "King Arthur," i. 187, *note* 2; a sharer in the King's Company, i. 197; his address to the author of "Heroic Love" quoted, i. 231, *note* 1, ii. 238, *note* 3; his indecent plays, i. 267; his epilogue to "The Pilgrim," i. 268; his "Secular Masque," i. 268, *note* 1; his prologue to "The Prophetess" vetoed, ii. 13; his prologues at Oxford, ii. 134, ii. 136, *note* 1, ii. 137, *note* 1; expensive revival of his "All for Love," ii. 175.

Dublin, Wilks's success in, i. 235.

"Duchess of Malfy," i. xxv.

Dugdale, Sir William, his "Antiquities of Warwickshire" quoted, i. xxxvi.; mentions the "Ludus Coventriæ," i. xxxviii.

Duke's Servants, The, i. 87, *note* 1, i. 88.

Duke's Theatre, ii. 336; first theatre to introduce scenery, i. xxxii.

Dulwich College, built and endowed by Edward Alleyn, i. xxviii.

"Dunciad, The," i 36, *note* 1, ii 181, *note* 1, ii. 182, *note* 1, ii. 270; on Italian opera, i. 324, *note* 1.

Dyer, Mrs, actress, i. 136, *note* 2.

Edicts to suppress plays, 1647-1648, ii. 322

Edward, son of Henry VI., pageant played before, i. xl.

—— son of Edward IV, pageant played before, i xlii

Edwin, John, his "Eccentricities" quoted, ii 78, *note* 1.

E——e, Mr. [probably Erskine], his powers of raillery, i. 13, i. 14, *note* 1, i 16

Egerton, William, his memoirs of Mrs. Oldfield, i 5, *note* 1

"Egotist, The," i lv., *note* 1, i. 36, *note* 2, i 41, *note* 2, i. 43, *note* 1, i. 45, *note* 1, i. 46, *note* 1, i. 53, *note* 1, ii 265

Elephants on the stage, ii 7, *note* 1.

Elizabeth, Queen, and the Spanish Armada, allusion to, i. 64; her rule of government, i 65.

Elocution, importance of, i. 110

Elrington, Thomas, his visit to Drury Lane in 1714, ii. 121, *note* 1; Cibber said to have refused to let him play a certain character, ii. 193, *note* 1.

Ely, Bishop of, and Joe Haines, ii. 315.

Erskine, Mr., probably the person mentioned by Cibber, i. 13, i. 14, *note* 1, i. 16.

Estcourt, Richard, i. 166, i. 237, i. 332, i. 334, *note* 1; a marvellous mimic, i 114, yet not a good actor, i. 115; said to be unfairly treated by Cibber, i. 115, *note* 2, could not mimic Nokes, i. 142, his "gag" on the Union of the Companies in 1708, i 301, his first coming to London, i 304; made Deputy-manager by Brett, ii. 56, *note* 1, advertisement regarding his salary, 1709, ii. 78, *note* 1; his Falstaff, ii. 300; Bellchambers's memoir of, ii 331.

Eusden, Laurence, poet laureate, his death, i. 32, *note* 1.

Evans, John, his visit to Drury Lane in 1714, ii. 121, *note* 1; his Falstaff, ii. 300.

"Faction Display'd," ii. 233, *note* 2.

"Fair Maid of the West, The," i. xxv.

Fairplay, Francis, a name assumed by Cibber on one occasion, i. 48.
"Fairy Queen," preface to, quoted, i. 110, *note* 1.
Farinelli (singer), ii. 88.
Farquhar, George, ii. 251, ii. 367, ii. 369.
Fashionable nights, ii. 246.
Faustina (Faustina Bordoni Hasse), her rivalry with Cuzzoni, ii. 89.
Fees for performances at Court, ii. 218.
Fenwick, Sir John, ii. 62.
Fideli, Signor, i. xxvii.
Field, Nathaniel, originally a "Chapel boy," i. xxxvii.
Fielding, Henry, i. 202, *note* 1, i. 287, *note* 4, i. 288, *note* 1, ii. 269; attacks Cibber in "The Champion," i. 1, *note* 1, i. 38, *note* 1, i. 50, *note* 2, i. 63, *note* 1, i. 69, *note* 1, i. 93, *note* 2, i. 288, *note* 1, ii. 54, *note* 2; in "Joseph Andrews," i. 10, *note* 1, i. 50, *note* 2, i. 61, *note* 1; in "Pasquin," i. 36, *note* 2; attacks Cibber for mutilating Shakespeare, ii. 263; manager of a company at the Haymarket, i. 92, *note* 1; Cibber's retaliation on, i. 286; Austin Dobson's memoir of, quoted, i. 286, *note* 1, i. 287, *note* 3, i. 288, *note* 1; said to have caused the Licensing Act of 1737, i. 286.

Fitzgerald, Percy, his "New History of the English Stage," i. 90, *note* 1, i. 320, *note* 1, ii. 11, *note* 1, ii. 32, *note* 1, ii. 49, *note* 1, ii. 56, *note* 1, ii. 79, *note* 2, ii. 94, *note* 1, ii. 148, *note* 1.
Fitzharding, Lady, i. 68.
Fitzstephen, William, his "Description of the City of London," i. xxxvii.
Fleetwood, Charles, ii. 264; purchases from Highmore and Mrs. Wilks their shares of the Patent, i. 285, ii. 261; the deserters return to him, ii. 261.
Fletcher, John, his plays, i. xxv.
Footmen, admitted gratis to Drury Lane, i. 233; this privilege abolished, i. 234, *note* 1.
Fortune Theatre, i. xxvi., i. xxix.
Fox, Bishop, had charge of pageants in which sacred persons were introduced, i. xlv.
French actors at Lincoln's Inn Fields, ii. 180, *note* 1.
—— audience, conduct of, ii. 247.
"Funeral, The," i. 263.

Gaedertz, Herr, his "Zur Kenntniss der altenglischen Bühne," ii. 84, *note* 1.

INDEX.

"Gammer Gurton's Needle," one of the earliest regular comedies, i. xlvii.

Garrick, David, i. 110, *note* 1, i. 278, *note* 1, ii. 259, ii. 270; his influence in reforming the stage, ii 263; Cibber plays against, ii. 268; Cibber's low opinion of, ii. 268, Davies's Life of, i lv, *note* 1, i. 283, *note* 2, ii. 259.

Gaussin, Jeanne Catherine, ii. 248.

Gay, John, said to have thrashed Cibber, i. 71, *note* 1; his "Beggar's Opera," i. 243, his "Polly" forbidden to be played, i. 246, i. 278, *note* 1.

Genest, Rev. John, his "Account of the English Stage," i. 83, *note* 1, i 88, *note* 3, i 91, *note* 2, i. 91, *note* 4, i. 97, *note* 1, i 110, *note* 1, i. 149, *note* 2, i 156, *note* 2, i 174, *note* 2, i. 203, *note* 1, i. 220, *note* 1, i 230, *note* 1, i 267, *note* 2, i. 268, *note* 1, i. 269, *note* 1, i. 296, *note* 1, i. 326, *note* 3, ii. 5, *note* 1, ii. 7, *note* 1, ii. 56, *note* 1, ii 79, *note* 2, ii 96, *note* 1, ii 98, *note* 1, ii. 123, *note* 1, ii. 165, *note* 1, ii 169, *note* 3, ii. 171, *note* 1, ii 186, *note* 1, ii. 186, *note* 2, ii. 187, *note* 1, ii. 198, *note* 1, ii. 210, *note* 1, ii 251, *note* 1, ii 267, ii. 269, ii. 324; his opinion of Cibber's Richard III., i. 139, *note* 2.

"Gentleman's Magazine," ii. 284.

Gentlemen of the Great Chamber, actors entitled, i. 88.

George I. has theatrical performances at Hampton Court, ii. 208; his amusement at a scene of "Henry VIII.," ii. 216; his present to the actors for playing at Court, ii 218.

—— II., i. 32, ii. 219

Giffard, Henry, i. 92, *note* 1, i. 283, *note* 1, his theatre in Goodman's Fields, i. 282, *note* 2, purchases half of Booth's share of the Patent, ii. 259.

Gifford, William, doubts if Ben Jonson was an unsuccessful actor, i 85, *note* 1

Gildon, Charles, his Life of Betterton, i 118, *note* 2, ii. 324, ii. 337, *note* 1, ii. 358.

Globe Theatre, i. xxvi, i. xxix.

Goffe, Alexander, a "boy-actress," i xxx; employed to give notice of secret performances during the Commonwealth, i xxx.

"Golden Rump, The," a scurrilous play, i. 278, *note* 1.

Goodman, Cardell, mentioned, i. 83, *note* 1, i. 96; prophesies Cibber's success as an actor, i. 183, a highway robber, ii. 61, ii. 63; his connection with the Fenwick and Charnock Plot, ii.

62, he and Captain Griffin have one shirt between them, ii. 63; Bellchambers's memoir of, ii. 329.

Goodman's Fields, unlicensed theatre in, i. 281; attempt to suppress it, i. 282; Odell's theatre, i. 282, *note* 1; Giffard's theatre, i. 282, *note* 2.

—— Theatre, i. 92, *note* 1, closed by Licensing Act (1737), i. 92, *note* 1.

Grafton, Duke of, ii. 260, blamed for making Cibber Laureate, i 46, *note* 1.

Grantham, Cibber sent to school at, i. 9.

Griffin, Captain (actor), i. 334, *note* 1; admitted into good society, i 83, memoir of, i. 83, *note* 1, and Goodman have one shirt between them, ii. 63.

Griffith, Thomas, his visit to Drury Lane in 1714, ii. 121, *note* 1.

"Grub Street Journal," ii. 258, *note* 1

Guiscard, his attack on Lord Oxford referred to, i 291.

Gwyn, Nell, i. 91, *note* 1, i. 182, *note* 1, ii 323; and Charles II., ii. 211; Bishop Burnet's opinion of, ii. 212.

Haines, Joseph, ii. 252, *note* 1, his *bon mot* on Jeremy Collier, i. 273; account of his career, i. 273, *note* 1; Aston's description of, ii. 314; his pranks, ii. 315, ii. 325; Life of, ii. 325, *note* 1.

Halifax, Lord, i. 217, ii. 311; a patron of the theatre, ii. 4, his testimonial to Mrs. Bracegirdle, ii. 305.

Hamlet, incomparably acted by Taylor, i. xxvi; Betterton as, i. 100; Wilks's mistakes in, i. 100.

Hammerton, Stephen, a famous "boy-actress," i. xxvi.; played Amyntor, i. xxvi.

Hampton Court, theatrical performances at, ii. 208, ii. 214, ii. 219

"Hannibal and Scipio," i xxv.

Harlequin, Cibber's low opinion of the character, i. 150-152, played without a mask by Pinkethman, i. 151.

"Harlequin Sorcerer," a noted pantomime, ii 181, *note* 1.

Harper, John, arrested as a rogue and vagabond, i 283; trial, ii. 260, the result of his trial, i. 284; his Falstaff, ii 300.

Harris, ii. 334, ii 346.

Harrison, General, murders W. Robinson the actor, i. xxix

Hart, Charles, i. 125, *note* 2, ii. 134, ii. 137, *note* 1, superior to his successors, i. xxiv, apprenticed to Robinson, i. xxiv., a "boy-actress," i.

xxiv.; a lieutenant in Charles I.'s army, i xxix ; arrested for acting, i. xxx.; grows old and wishes to retire, i. xxxii.; his acting of the Plain Dealer, i. 83, *note* 1, famous for Othello, i 91; his retirement, i 96; Bellchambers's memoir of, ii. 322.

Haymarket, Little Theatre in the, i. 92, *note* 1, opened by the mutineers from Highmore in 1733, ii. 259; closed by Licensing Act (1737), i. 92, *note* 1.

—— the Queen's Theatre in the (now Her Majesty's), i. 319; its history, i. 319, *note* 1; opened for Betterton's Company, i. 320, defects in its construction, i. 320, i 326, inconvenience of its situation, i. 322.

Hemming, John, i xxvi.

"Henry VIII.," ii 215.

Heron, Mrs, ii. 262.

Hewett, Sir Thomas, his report on the stability of Drury Lane, ii. 177.

Highmore, John, at variance with his actors, i. 283; his purchase of the Patent, i. 283, *note* 1; the price he paid for the Patent, i. 297, *note* 1; purchases half of Booth's share of the Patent, ii. 258; purchases Cibber's share, ii. 258 · his actors mutiny, ii. 259; he summons Harper as a rogue and vagabond, ii. 260, sells his share in the Patent, ii. 261.

Hill, Aaron, on "tone" in speaking, i. 110, *note* 1; appointed by W. Collier to manage Drury Lane, ii. 94, *note* 1, defied and beaten by his actors, ii. 94, *note* 1; farms the opera from Collier, ii. 105, on Booth's lack of humour, ii. 240, *note* 2.

—— Captain Richard, his murder of Mountfort, i. 130, *note* 1, ii 342

"Historia Histrionica," reprint of, i. xix.; preface to, i xxi.

"Historical Register for 1736," ii 263.

Hitchcock, Robert, his "Historical View of the Irish Stage," i 165, *note* 1.

"Holland's Leaguer," i xxv

Holt, Lord Chief Justice, ii 22.

Horden, Hildebrand, a promising actor, killed in a brawl, i. 302.

Horton, Mrs., ii. 260.

Howard, J. B., plays Iago in English to Salvini's Othello, i. 325, *note* 1.

—— Sir Robert, i 192, *note* 1.

Hughes, Margaret, said to be the first English actress, i. 90, *note* 1.

Hutton, Laurence, his "Literary Landmarks of London" quoted, i. 7, *note* 3, ii. 284, *note* 1.

Irving, Henry, his controversy with Constant Coquelin regarding Diderot's "Paradoxe sur le Comédien," i. 103, *note* 1 ; restores Shakespeare's "Richard III." to the stage, ii. 287.
Italian Opera, introduced into England, i. 324 ; "The Dunciad" on, i 324, *note* 1.

Jackson, John, his "History of the Scottish Stage" referred to, ii 181, *note* 1
Jacobites attacked in Cibber's "Nonjuror," ii. 185, repay Cibber for his attack by hissing his plays, ii. 187, hiss his "Nonjuror," ii 189.
James II, ii. 134, Cibber, at school, writes an Ode on his coronation, i 33; Cibber serves against, at the Revolution, i. 60; his flight to France, i. 70, his quarrel with the Duke of Devonshire, i. 72.
Jekyll, Sir Joseph, ii. 198
Jevon, Thomas, i. 151, *note* 1.
Johnson, Benjamin (actor), i. 99, *note* 1, i. 194, i 313, i. 332, ii 129, *note* 2, ii. 252, *note* 1, ii. 262, ii. 308 ; Bellchambers's memoir of, ii. 360.
Johnson, Dr. Samuel, i. 215, *note* 1, ii. 163, *note* 1; his opinion of Cibber's Odes, i. 36, *note* 2 ; his epigram on Cibber's Laureateship quoted, i. 46, *note* 1; his "Life of Pope," ii. 275, ii. 276, ii. 280, *note* 1, ii. 281, *note* 1; his "Lives of the Poets," ii 27, *note* 1, ii. 128, *note* 1, ii. 370, his famous Prologue (1747) quoted, i. 113, *note* 1.
Jones, Inigo, ii. 209.
Jonson, Ben, i. 245, out of fashion in 1699, i xviii.; no actors in 1699 who could rightly play his characters, i xxiv.; his plays, i xxv, his epigram on Alleyn, i. xxviii.; on Sal Pavy, i xxxvi.; said by Cibber to have been an unsuccessful actor, i 85 ; this denied by Gifford and Cunningham, his editors, i. 85, *note* 1 ; his Masques, ii 209.
Jordan, Thomas, his "Prologue to introduce the first woman that came to act on the stage," 1660, i 90, *note* 1, i. 119, *note* 1.
"Joseph Andrews" quoted, i 10, *note* 1, i. 50, *note* 2, i. 61, *note* 1.
"Julius Cæsar," special revival of, in 1707, ii 5.

Keen, Theophilus, i. 332, ii. 77, *note* 1, ii. 94, *note* 1, ii. 129, *note* 2, ii. 169, *note* 2; Bellchambers's memoir of, ii. 364.

Kemble, John P., mentioned, i. lv, *note* 1.

Kent, Duke of, ii. 46.

—— Mrs, ii. 169, *note* 2.

Killigrew, Charles, ii. 32, *note* 1, his share in the Patent, i. 181, *note* 1.

—— Thomas, i. 181, *note* 1, i 197, *note* 3; granted a Patent similar to Davenant's, i. liii, i. 87; memoir of, i 87, *note* 2, his witty reproof of Charles II., i. 87, *note* 2; his Company better than Davenant's, i. 93; unites with Davenant's, i 96.

"King and no King," special revival of, in 1707, ii 5

"King Arthur," i 187.

"King John" mutilated by Colley Cibber, ii 268.

"King John and Matilda," i. xxv.

King's Servants, The, i. 87, *note* 2, i 88; before 1642, i. xxvi.; after the Restoration, i. xxxi.

Kirkman, Francis, his "Wits," ii. 84, *note* 1.

Knap, ii. 169, *note* 2

Kneller, Sir Godfrey, his portrait of Betterton, i 117; his portrait of Anthony Leigh, i. 146, ii. 349; imitated by Estcourt, ii. 333.

Knight, Mrs. Frances, ii. 77, *note* 1, ii. 94, *note* 1, ii. 169, *note* 2.

—— Joseph, his edition of the "Roscius Anglicanus" referred to, i. 87, *note* 1, i. 90, *note* 1.

Knip, Mrs., i. 182, *note* 1

Kynaston, Edward, i. 98, i. 119, ii. 324, ii. 334, i. 185, i 327, petted by ladies of quality, i. 120, the beauty of his person, i. 121, his voice and appearance, i 121, his bold acting in inflated passages, i 124, his majesty and dignity, i. 125-6, lingered too long on the stage, i. 126, Bellchambers's memoir of, ii. 339.

Lacy, John, superior to his successors, i xxiv.

Lady of title, prevented by relatives from becoming an actress, i 75

"Lady's Last Stake," cast of, ii. 3, *note* 1.

Langbaine, Gerard, his "Account of the English Poets," ii 13, *note* 1.

Laughter, reflections on, i. 23.

"Laureat, The" (a furious attack on Cibber), i. 3, *note* 2, i. 14, *note* 1, i. 35, *note* 2, i. 48, *note* 1, i 78, *note*

1, i. 101, *note* 2, 1. 122, *note* 1, i. 123, *note* 1, i. 140, *note* 1, i. 157, *note* 2, i. 174, *note* 2, i. 182, *note* 2, i 191, *note* 2, i 222, *note* 1, 1. 224, *note* 1, i. 238, *note* 1, i 239, *note* 1, 1. 242, *note* 1, 1 256, *note* 1, i. 258, *note* 2, i. 264, *note* 1, i 273, *note* 2, 1. 300, *note* 1, i. 312, *note* 2, ii. 30, *note* 1, ii 37, *note* 1, ii. 121, *note* 1, ii. 148, *note* 1, ii. 160, *note* 1, ii. 163, *note* 1, ii. 251, *note* 1, ii. 256, *note* 1, ii. 335, *note* 1, ii 356.

Lebrun, Charles, painter, alluded to, i. 106.

Lee, Charles Henry, Master of the Revels, ii 260.

—— Mrs. Mary, i. 163, *note* 1.

—— Nathaniel, ii. 327; his "Alexander the Great," i. 105; a perfect reader of his own works, i. 113, Mohun's compliment to him, i. 114, failed as an actor, i. 114.

Leigh, Anthony, 1. 98, i 142, 1. 304, 1. 327, Cibber's account of, i. 145-154; his exuberant humour, 1 145; in "The Spanish Friar," 1. 145; painted in the character of the Spanish Friar, 1. 146; his best characters, i. 146, i. 149; and Nokes, their combined excellence, 1. 147, his superiority to Pinkethman, 1. 149; the favourite actor of Charles II., i. 154; compared with Nokes, 1. 154; his death, i 154, i. 188, his "gag" regarding Obadiah Walker's change of religion, ii. 134; Bellchambers's memoir of, ii. 349.

Leigh, Mrs. Elizabeth, 1. 98; Cibber's account of, i. 162-163; her peculiar comedy powers, 1. 162; note regarding her, i. 163, *note* 1.

—— Francis, ii. 77, *note* 1, ii. 94, *note* 1, ii. 169, *note* 2, ii 170, *note* 1.

Leveridge, Richard, ii. 169, *note* 3.

Licence granted by King William in 1695, 1. 98

Licensing Act of 1737, 1. 278, *note* 1, i. 286, i 287, *note* 4, ii. 262.

"Lick at the Laureat," said to be the title of a pamphlet, i 35, *note* 2.

Lincoln's Inn Fields, Duke's old Theatre in, 1 xxxii, i. 88, *note* 2.

—— Betterton's theatre in, i. 194; its opening, 1 196; its success at first, i. 227; its speedy disintegration, 1 228.

—— Rich's theatre in, ii. 79, ii. 100; its exact situation, ii. 101, *note* 1; Rich's Patent revived at, ii 165; its opening, ii. 166, *note* 1, ii. 171, *note* 1; actors desert Drury Lane to join, ii 169.

INDEX.

"London Cuckolds," i. 267.
"London News-Letter," i. 302, *note 2*
Lord Chamberlain, Cibber on the power of the, ii. 10-23, ii. 74; his name not mentioned in the Patents, ii. 10; Sir Spencer Ponsonby-Fane on the power of, ii. 11, *note 1*, his power of licensing plays, ii. 11; plays vetoed by him, ii. 12-14; actors arrested by his orders, ii. 17-22; his edicts against desertions, ii. 17, *note 1*, ii. 18, *note 1*; said to favour Betterton at the expense of rival managers, ii. 18, various edicts regarding Powell, ii. 19, *note 1*, ii. 20, *note 1*, ii. 94, *note 1*; warrant to arrest Dogget, ii 21, *note 1*; his edict separating plays and operas in 1707, ii. 49, *note 1*, interferes on behalf of actors in their dispute with the Patentees in 1709, ii. 68; silences Patentees for contumacy, ii 72, his order for silence, 1709, quoted, ii. 73, *note 1*.
Lord Chamberlain's Records, i. 229, *note 1*, i. 315, *note 2*, ii. 17, *note 1*, ii. 18, *note 1*, ii 19, *note 1*, ii. 20, *note 1*, ii. 21, *note 1*, ii. 49, *note 1*, ii. 50, *note 1*, ii. 69, *note 1*, ii. 73, *note 1*, ii 79, *note 2*, ii 94, *note 1*, ii. 102, *note 1*,

ii. 108, *note 2*, ii. 171, *note 1*, ii. 193, *note 1*, ii. 218, *note 1*, ii. 219, *note 1*, ii. 257, *note 1*.
Lorraine, Duke of, ii. 219
Louis XIV., mentioned, i. 6.
—— Prince, of Baden, ii. 228.
"Love in a Riddle," cast of, i. 244, *note 1*.
Lovel (actor), ii. 347.
Lovelace, Lord, ii. 304.
"Love's Last Shift," cast of, i. 213, *note 1*.
Lowin, John, ii. 335; arrested for acting, i. xxx., superior to Hart, i. xxiv.; his chief characters, i xxvi , too old to go into Charles I 's army, i. xxix.; becomes an innkeeper, and dies very poor, i. xxxi
"Lucius Junius Brutus," by Lee, vetoed, ii. 13.
"Ludus Coventriæ," i xxxviii; these plays acted at other towns besides Coventry, i. xxxviii., a description of them, i xxxviii *et seq*
"Lunatick, The," ii. 252, *note 1*
Luttrell's Diary quoted, i. 302, *note 2*.

Macaulay, Lord, his "History of England" referred to, ii. 134, *note 3*.
"Macbeth" *in the nature of an opera*, i. 94, *note 1*; ii. 228, ii. 229, *note 1*.

Macclesfield, Countess of, ii. 39 See also Mrs. Brett.

Macklin, Charles, ii 270, ii. 362; his first coming to London, ii. 261; a great reformer, ii. 262.

Macready, William C, mentioned, i. 135, *note* 1.

MacSwiney, Owen. See Swiney, Owen.

"Maid's Tragedy" vetoed in Charles II.'s time, ii. 12; played with altered catastrophe, ii. 12.

Mainwaring, Arthur, ii. 369, *note* 2.

Malone, Edmond, i 185, *note* 1, i. 197, *note* 3, ii. 32, *note* 1, ii. 138, *note* 1.

Management, Cibber on the duties and responsibilities of, ii. 199-207.

Margaret, Queen of Henry VI, pageant played before her, i. xl.

Marlborough, Duchess of. See Churchill, Lady

—— Duke of, ii. 96, *note* 1, ii. 130, ii 164, ii 228.

"Marriage à la Mode," by Cibber, cast of, ii. 5, *note* 1.

Marshall, Anne, i. 161, *note* 1, said to be the first English actress, i. 90, *note* 1.

—— Julian, his "Annals of Tennis" quoted, i. 315, *note* 1.

Mary, the Virgin, and Joseph, characters in the "Ludus Coventriæ," i xxxix.

—— Queen, her death, i. 193.

"Mary, Queen of Scotland," by Banks, vetoed, ii. 14.

Masculus, a comedian, who was a Christian martyr, i. xxii.

Masks, Ladies wearing, at the theatre, i. 266; ultimately the mark of a prostitute, i. 267, *note* 1.

Mason, Miss. See Countess of Macclesfield, and Mrs. Brett.

Masques, enormous expense of, ii. 209.

Master of the Revels. See Revels.

Mathews, Charles (the elder), his powers of imitation referred to, i 115, *note* 1

Mathias, St, the choosing of, as an apostle, dramatized in the "Ludus Coventriæ," i. xxxviii.

Matthews, Brander, ii. 289, *note* 1.

Maynard, Serjeant, a Whig lawyer, satirized, i. 149, *note* 2.

Medbourn, Matthew, ii. 346.

Melcombe, Lord, mentioned, i. 14, *note* 1.

"Mery Play between the Pardoner and the Frere, the Curate and Neybour Pratte, A," described, i. xlv.

Miller, James, his "Art and Nature" failed, i. 152, *note* 1.
—— Josias (actor), ii. 262.
Mills, John, i. 332, ii. 70, *note* 2, ii. 129, *note* 2, ii. 259, *note* 1, ii. 262; his friendship with Wilks, i. 259, ii. 223; his honesty and diligence, i. 260; his large salary, i. 260; advertisement regarding his salary, 1709, ii. 78, *note* 1; Bellchambers's memoir of, ii. 362; and the country squire, ii. 363.
Milward, William, i. 224, *note* 2.
Mist, Nathaniel. See "Mist's Weekly Journal."
"Mist's Weekly Journal," ii. 163, *note* 1, ii. 167, ii. 187.
Mohun, Lord, ii. 314; implicated in Mountfort's death, i. 130, *note* 1, ii. 342.
—— Michael, superior to his successors, i. xxiv.; apprentice to Beeston, i. xxv.; acted Bellamente, i. xxv.; a captain in Charles I.'s army, i. xxix.; his death, i. 96; his admiration of Nat. Lee's elocution, i. 114; Bellchambers's memoir of, ii. 326.
Montague, Captain, insults Miss Santlow, i. 76; chastised by Mr. Craggs, i. 77.
Moore, Mrs., ii. 77, *note* 1, ii. 94, *note* 1.

Morley, Professor Henry, his edition of the "Spectator," ii. 54, *note* 1.
Mountfort, William, i. 98, i. 108, i. 170, *note* 1, i. 237, ii. 314; taken into good society, i. 83; Cibber's account of, i. 127-130; his voice and appearance, i. 127; his Alexander the Great, i. 127; his excellent acting of fine gentlemen, i. 127; his delivery of witty passages, i. 128; his Rover, i. 128; his versatility, i. 128, i. 210; his Sparkish ("Country Wife") and his Sir Courtly Nice, i. 129; copied by Cibber in Sir Courtly Nice, i. 129; his tragic death, i. 130, i. 188; memoir of him, i. 130, *note* 1; Tom Brown on his connection with Mrs. Bracegirdle, i. 170, *note* 1; his comedy of "Greenwich Park," ii. 41; copied by Wilks, ii. 241; Bellchambers's memoir of, ii. 341; full account of his death by the hands of Capt. Hill, ii. 342-345.
—— Mrs., i. 98, i. 237, ii. 343, ii. 367; Cibber's account of, i. 165-169; her variety of humour, i. 165; her artistic feeling, i. 166; her acting of the Western Lass, i. 166; in male parts, i. 167; plays Bayes with success, i. 167;

the excellence of her Melantha, i. 167; memoir of, i. 169, *note* 1, leaves Betterton's company in 1695, i. 200; her death, ii. 306; Anthony Aston's description of, ii. 313.
Mountfort, Susanna, i. 334, *note* 1.
Music in the theatre, i. xxxii.

Newcastle, Duke of, ii. 219; (Lord Chamberlain), his persecution of Steele, ii. 193, *note* 1.
Newington Butts, i xlix.
Newman, Thomas, actor, one of their Majesties' servants, i 88, *note* 3.
Nichols, John, his "Theatre, Anti-Theatre, &c.," ii 66, *note* 2, ii. 168, *note* 1, ii. 174, *note* 2, ii. 176, *note* 1, ii. 177, *note* 1, ii. 193, *note* 1.
Nicolini (Nicolo Grimaldi), singer, ii. 48, ii. 51; Cibber's high praise of, ii. 51; praised by the "Tatler," ii. 52.
Noblemen's companies of players, i xlvii.
Nokes, James, i. 98; Cibber's description of, i. 141-145; his natural simplicity, i. 141, could not be imitated, i. 142; his best characters, i. 142; his ludicrous distress, i. 143; his voice and person, i. 145; and Leigh, their combined excellence, ii.

i. 147; compared with Leigh, i. 154; his death, i. 188; Bellchambers's memoir of, ii. 346; why called "Nurse Nokes," ii. 348.
Nokes, Robert, i. 141, *note* 1, i 143, *note* 2, ii. 346.
"Nonjuror, The," a line in the epilogue quoted, i. 49; cast of, ii. 185, *note* 2.
Norris, Henry, ii. 77, *note* 1, ii. 94, *note* 1.
—— Mrs., said to be the first English actress, i 90, *note* 1.
Northey, Sir Edward, his "opinion" on the Patent, ii. 32, *note* 1

Oates, Titus, i. 133.
Odell, Thomas, his theatre in Goodman's Fields, i. 282, *note* 1.
"Old and New London," referred to, ii. 104, *note* 1.
Oldfield, Mrs. Anne, i. 157, i 251, *note* 1, i. 332, ii 69, ii 129, *note* 2, ii. 358, memoirs of, published immediately after her death, i. 5; her acting of Lady Townly praised in highflown terms by Cibber, i. 51, i. 312, *note* 3; admitted into good society, i 83; her unpromising commencement as an actress, i. 159, i. 305; compared with Mrs. Butler, i. 164; her rivalry with Mrs.

Bracegirdle, i. 174, *note* 2; Cibber's account of, i. 305-312; her good sense, i. 310; her unexpected excellence, i. 306; Cibber writes "The Careless Husband" chiefly for her, i. 308; her perfect acting in it, i. 309; and Wilks playing in same pieces, i. 314; proposed to be made a manager, ii. 69, gets increased salary instead, ii. 71; advertisement regarding her salary, 1709, ii. 78, *note* 1; riot directed against, ii. 166; settles a dispute between Wilks, Cibber, and Booth, ii. 236; her death, ii. 254; copied Mrs Mountfort in comedy, ii. 313; Bellchambers's memoir of, ii. 367; and Richard Savage, ii. 369.

Opera, i. 111; control of, given to Swiney, ii. 48.

—— Italian, account of its first separate establishment, ii. 50-55, decline of Italian, ii. 87-91.

Otway, Thomas, his failure as an actor, i. 114, *note* 1; his "Orphan," i. 116, *note* 2.

Oxford, visited by the actors in 1713, ii. 133, ii. 135, Dryden's Prologues at, ii. 134, ii. 136, *note* 1, its critical discernment, ii. 136.

—— Lord, Guiscard's attack on, referred to, i. 291.

Pack, George, ii. 77, *note* 1, ii. 94, *note* 1, account of, ii. 169, *note* 3.

Pageants formed part in receptions of princes, &c., i. xl. *et seq.*

Painting the face on the stage, i. 182, *note* 1.

Pantomimes, the origin of, ii. 180, Cibber's opinion of, ii. 180; "The Dunciad" on, ii. 181, *note* 1.

"Papal Tyranny in the Reign of King John," cast of, ii. 269, *note* 1.

Parish-clerks, play acted by, in 1391, i. xxxv.

Parliamentary reports on the theatres, i. 278, *note* 1.

"Parson's Wedding, The," played entirely by women, i. xxxii.

"Pasquin" quoted, i. 36, *note* 2

Patent, copy of, granted to Sir William Davenant in 1663, i. liii.; Steele's, ii. 174

Patentees, the, their foolish parsimony, i. 164; their ill-treatment of Betterton and other actors, i. 187; the actors combine against them, i. 189; their deserted condition, i. 194. (For transactions of the Patentees, see also Rich, C.)

Pavy, Sal, a famous child-actor, i. xxxvi; Ben Jonson's epigram on, i. xxxvi.

Pelham, Hon. Henry, Cibber's "Apology" dedicated to, i. lv., *note* 1.
Pembroke, Earl of, ii. 105, *note* 1.
Pepys, Samuel, his "Diary," i. 119, *note* 1, i. 161, *note* 2, i. 182, *note* 1, i. 267, *note* 1, i. 303, *note* 1.
Percival (actor), i. 183, *note* 1.
Perkins, an eminent actor, i. xxvi.; his death, i. xxxi
Perrin, Mons. (of the Théâtre Français), ii. 221, *note* 1, ii. 246, *note* 1.
Perriwigs, enormous, worn by actors, ii. 36, *note* 1.
Phœnix, the, or Cockpit, i xxvi.
"Picture, The," i. xxv.
Pinkethman, William, i 313, i. 334, *note* 1, ii. 129, *note* 2, ii. 252, *note* 1; his inferiority to Anthony Leigh, i. 149; his liberties with the audience, i. 152; hissed for them, i. 153, *note* 1; his lack of judgment, i. 150; plays Harlequin without the mask, i. 151; his success as Lory in "The Relapse," i. 230, Bellchambers's memoir of, ii. 348.
—— the younger, ii. 349.
Plays, value of old, for information on manners, i. xxi.; old, no actors' names given, i xxv; originally used for religious purposes, i. xxxiv., i. xxxv.; their early introduction, i. xxxvii., began to alter in form about the time of Henry VIII., i. xlv.; origin of, in Greece and England, i. xlviii.; the alteration in their subjects noticed by Stow in 1598, i xlviii.; temporarily suspended, i. xlix.; arranged to be divided between Davenant's and Killigrew's companies, i. 91; expenses of, i. 197, *note* 3.
Players defended regarding character, i. xxii.; not to be described as rogues and vagabonds, i. xlix.; entirely suppressed by ordinances of the Long Parliament, i. li.
Playhouses, large number of, in 1629, i. xlix.
"Poems on Affairs of State," quoted, i. 170, *note* 1.
"Poetaster, The," played by the Children of her Majesty's Chapel, i. xxxvi
Poet Laureate, Cibber appointed, 1730, i. 32, *note* 1.
Pollard, Thomas, a comedian, i. xxvi.; superior to Hart, i. xxiv.; too old to go into Charles I.'s army, i. xxix, arrested for acting, i. xxx., his retirement and death, i xxxi.
Pollixfen, Judge, ii. 315.
Ponsonby-Fane, Sir Spencer, his memorandum on the

power of the Lord Chamberlain, ii. 11, *note* 1.
Pope, Alexander, ii. 151; Cibber's "Letter" to, quoted, i. 3, *note* 1, Cibber's first allusion to Pope's enmity, i. 21; an epigram comparing Pope and Cibber in society, i. 29, *note* 1; Cibber's opinion of Pope's attacks, i. 35; some of Pope's attacks quoted, i. 36, *note* 1; his attack on Atticus (Addison), i. 38; Cibber's "Letter" to, quoted, i. 44, *note* 1, i. 45, *note* 2; epigram attributed to him, on Cibber's Laureateship, i. 46, *note* 1; his "Moral Essays," quoted, i. 307, *note* 3; attacks Cibber for countenancing pantomimes, ii. 182, *note* 1, "The Nonjuror" a cause of his enmity to Cibber, ii. 189, *note* 1; his "Epistle to Dr Arbuthnot," ii. 189, *note* 1, his quarrel with Cibber, ii. 270-283; Cibber's "Letter" to him, ii. 271, his famous adventure, ii. 278, Cibber's second "Letter" to, ii. 281, his portrait of Betterton, ii. 339, his attacks on Mrs. Oldfield, ii. 370. (See also "Dunciad")
Porter, Mrs. Mary, ii. 129, *note* 2, ii. 303, ii. 368; Dogget plays for her benefit after his retirement, ii. 158; accident to, ii. 254, ii. 365; Bellchambers's memoir of, ii. 365.
Portuguese, the, and religious plays, i. xxxv.
"Post-Boy Rob'd of his Mail," i. 328, *note* 1, i. 329, *note* 1.
Powell, George, i. 157, i. 193, i. 203, *note* 1, i 228, i. 259, i 334, *note* 1, ii. 77, *note* 1, ii. 94, *note* 1, ii. 129, *note* 2, ii. 238, ii. 301, ii. 311, ii. 363, offered some of Betterton's parts, i. 188, his indiscretion as a manager, i 204; mimics Betterton, i. 205, i 207, *note* 1; the contest between him and Wilks for supremacy at Drury Lane, i. 237-243, i. 251-256; his carelessness, i. 240, i 243; deserts Drury Lane, i. 239; returns to Drury Lane, i 239; arrested for deserting his manager, ii. 18; arrested for striking young Davenant, ii. 19; discharged for assaulting Aaron Hill in 1710, ii. 94, *note* 1; Bellchambers's memoir of, ii. 352.
Price, Joseph, account of him by Bellchambers, i. 146, *note* 1.
Prince's Servants, The, before 1642, i. xxvi.
Pritchard, Mrs., ii. 268, *note* 1.

Profits made by the old actors, i. xxxii.; of the theatre, how divided in 1682, i. 97.
Prologue-speaking, the art of, i. 271
"Prophetess, The," i. 187.
"Provoked Husband," cast of, i. 311, *note* 1.
"Provoked Wife," altered, ii. 233.
"Psyche," an opera, i. 94.
Puppet-show in Salisbury Change, i. 95
Purcell, Henry, i. 187, *note* 1, ii. 312.

Quantz, Mons., ii. 89, *note* 1.
Queen's Servants, The, before 1642, i. xxvi.
—— Theatre in the Haymarket, success of Swiney's company in, ii. 1, set aside for operas only, ii 48, its interior altered, ii. 79; opened by the seceders from Drury Lane in 1709, ii. 87.
Quin, James, i. 224, *note* 2, ii. 259, *note* 1, the chief actor at Garrick's appearance, ii. 262.

Raftor, Catherine. See Clive.
—— James, i. 330, *note* 1.
Raillery, reflections on, i. 11.
Raymond, his "opinion" on the Patent, ii. 32, *note* 1.
Red Bull Theatre, i. xxvi., i. xxix.; used by King's Company after the Restoration, i. xxxi.; drawing of the stage of the, ii. 84, *note* 1.
Reformation of the stage, Cibber on, i. 81.
Rehan, Ada, a great comedian, ii. 289.
Religion and the stage, i. xxi., i. xxxiii.
"Renegado, The," i. xxv.
Revels, Master of the, his unreasonableness to Cibber, i. 275; his fees refused to be paid, i. 277.
Rhodes, the prompter, ii. 333, ii 339, his company, at the Cockpit, i xxviii, his company of actors engaged by Davenant, i. 87, *note* 1.
Rich, Christopher, Patentee of Drury Lane, i. 181, *note* 1, ii 336, ii. 361, ii. 367, description of, i. 233, *note* 1, admits servants to theatre gratis, i 233, his treatment of his actors, i 252, consults Cibber on matters of management, i 253, his principles of management, i. 262, ii. 6-8, his tactics to avoid settling with his partners, i. 328, his objections to an union of the two companies, i. 329, permits Swiney to rent the Queen's Theatre, i 331, his foolish neglect of his actors, i 334; declines to execute his agree-

ment with Swiney, i. 336;
wishes to bring an elephant
on the stage, ii. 6; introduces rope-dancers at Drury
Lane, ii. 7; silenced for
receiving Powell, ii 19, *note*
1; his share in the Patent,
ii. 32, *note* 1, ii. 98; his
dealings with Col. Brett, ii.
42-49, ii. 56-60, Cibber on
his misconduct, ii. 46, his
foolish mismanagement, ii.
60, ii 65, confiscates part
of his actors' benefits, ii.
66; ordered to refund this,
ii. 68, silenced by the Lord
Chamberlain (1709), ii. 72;
his proceedings after being
silenced, ii. 77, ii. 79, *note* 2,
an advertisement issued by
him regarding actors' salaries
in 1709, ii. 78, *note* 1;
evicted by Collier from
Drury Lane (1709), ii 92,
his Patent revived in 1714,
ii. 79, ii 165; his extraordinary behaviour to the
Lord Chamberlain, ii 98;
Genest's character of him,
ii. 98, *note* 1; rebuilds Lincoln's Inn Fields Theatre,
ii. 100, his death, ii. 166,
note 1

Rich, John, ii 79, ii 98, *note* 2,
opens Lincoln's Inn Fields
Theatre, ii 166, *note* 1, an
excellent Harlequin, ii 181,
note 1, manages the Lincoln's Inn Fields company,
ii 262; opens Covent Garden, ii. 262.

"Richard III.," Cibber's adaptation of, i. 139, his playing
in, i. 139, i. 275; cast of,
ii 288, *note* 1.

Richardson, Jonathan, ii. 276.

Roberts, Mrs, one of Charles
II.'s mistresses, ii. 212.

Robins, a comedian, i. xxvi.

Robinson, William, ii. 322,
Hart apprenticed to, i. xxiv.,
a comedian, i xxvi; murdered by Harrison, i. xxix.

Rochester, Lord, ii. 138, *note*
1, ii. 303

Rogers, Mrs., 1 332, ii. 129,
note 2, ii. 169, *note* 2, ii. 353;
her affectation of prudery,
i. 135; becomes Wilks's
mistress, 1 136, her eldest
daughter, 1 136, riot caused
by, ii. 166.

Rogues and vagabonds, players
not to be described as, i.
xlix, i. l.

"Roman Actor, The," i. xxv.

Roman Catholic religion, attacked by Cibber, i. 80.

Rope-dancers on the stage,
ii. 7.

"Roscius Anglicanus." See
Downes, John.

Rose Tavern, the, i. 303,
note 1.

Rowe, Nicholas, in love with
Mrs Bracegirdle, i. 172;
complains of French dancers, i. 317.

Royal Theatricals during George I's reign, ii. 208; during previous reigns, ii. 209; effect of audience on actors, ii. 214, fees for, ii. 218.

Rymer, Thomas, ii. 324.

Sacheverel, Doctor, his trial hurtful to the theatres, ii. 91.

St. Giles's-in-the-Fields, Colley Cibber christened at, i. 7, *note 2*.

"St. James's Evening Post," ii. 198, *note 1*.

St. Paul's Singing School, i. xlix.

Salisbury Court, the private theatre in, i. xxiv., i. xxvi, i. xxviii.

Salvini, Tommaso, the great Italian tragedian, plays in Italian, while his company plays in English, i. 325, *note 1*.

Sandford, Samuel, i. 98, i. 327, ii 244, *note 1*; the "Spagnolet" of the theatre, i. 130; Cibber's account of him, i. 130-1; his personal appearance, i. 131; an actor of villains, i. 131, i. 137; his Creon ("Œdipus"), i. 131; the "Tatler" on his acting, i. 132, *note 1*; anecdote of his playing an honest character, i. 132; "a theatrical martyr to poetical justice," i. 137; his voice and manner of speaking, i. 138; would have been a perfect Richard III., i. 138; Cibber plays Richard III. in imitation of, i. 139, Anthony Aston's description of, ii. 306; Bellchambers's memoir of, ii 346.

Santlow, Hester, her first appearance as an actress, ii. 95; her manner and appearance, ii. 95; her character, ii 96, *note 1*; her marriage with Booth, ii. 96, *note 1* (See also Booth, Mrs. Barton.)

Satire, reflections on, i. 37; Cibber's opinion regarding a printed and an acted, i. 289

Saunderson, Mrs. See Betterton, Mrs.

Savage, Richard, ii. 39, *note 1*, and Mrs Oldfield, ii 369.

Scenes, first introduced by Sir William Davenant, i. xxxii., i. 87, *note 1*

"Secular Masque, The," i. 268, *note 1*.

Sedley, Sir Charles, Kynaston's resemblance to, ii. 341.

Senesino (singer), ii. 53.

Sewell, Dr. George, his "Sir Walter Raleigh," ii. 186, *note 1*.

Shadwell, Charles, his "Fair Quaker of Deal," ii 95.

—— Thomas, his comedy of "The Squire of Alsatia," i. 148.

Shaftesbury, first Earl of, i. 134, *note* 1.

Shakespeare, William . (see also names of his plays), a better author than actor, i. xxv, i. 89; his plays, i. xxv.; his plays depend less on women than on men, i. 90; expenses of plays in his time, i. 197.

"Sham Lawyer, The," ii. 252, *note* 1.

Shank, John, a comedian, i. xxvi; played Sir Roger ("Scornful Lady"), i xxvi.

Shatterel, ii. 326; superior to his successors, i. xxiv.; apprentice to Beeston, i. xxv.; a quartermaster in Charles I's army, i. xxix.

Shelton, Lady, ii 303

Shore, John, brother-in-law of Colley Cibber, i. 184, *note* 1.

—— Miss. See Cibber, Mrs. Colley, i. 184, *note* 1.

"Shore's Folly," i 184, *note* 1.

"Silent Woman," i. xxiv.

Singers and dancers introduced by Davenant, i 94; difficulty in managing, ii 88.

Skipwith, Sir George, ii 60.

—— Sir Thomas (one of the Patentees of Drury Lane), ii. 109, does Vanbrugh a service, i. 217; receives "The Relapse" in return, i 217; a sharer in the Drury Lane Patent, ii 31; assigns his share to Colonel Brett,

ii. 32, his friendship for Brett, ii. 39; claims his share from Brett, ii. 59.

Smith, William, i. 327, ii 324, ii 346; insulted by one of the audience, i. 79; defended by the King, i. 79; driven from the stage because of the King's support of him, i. 79; taken into good society, i. 83, Bellchambers's memoir of, ii. 319.

Sophocles, his tragedies, ii. 29.

Southampton House, Bloomsbury, i. 7, *note* 3.

Southerne, Thomas, ii. 311; prophesies the success of Cibber's first play, i. 212; his "Oroonoko," i. 216, *note* 1.

Spaniards, the, and religious plays, i xxxv.

"Spectator," ii. 353.

Spiller, James, ii. 169, *note* 2.

Stage, and religion, i. xxi, i. xxxiii; the, Cibber on the reformation of, i. 81; audience on, forbidden, i. 234, Cibber on the influence of, ii. 24-31; shape of the, described, ii. 84; doors, ii. 84, *note* 1.

Statute regarding rogues and vagabonds, i. l., against profanity on the stage, i l.; against persons meeting out of their own parishes on

Sundays for sports, etc., i. l. ; entirely suppressing players, i li

Steele, Sir Richard, i. 97, *note* 2, i. 276, ii. 36, *note* 1, ii. 109, ii. 128, ii. 151, ii 217, ii. 251, ii. 257 ; substituted for Collier in the Licence, ii. 162 ; the benefits he had conferred on Cibber and his partners, ii. 162 ; Dennis's attacks on, ii. 168, *note* 1 ; receives a Patent, ii. 173 ; assigns equal shares in the Patent to his partners, ii. 174 ; account of his transactions in connection with the theatre which are ignored by Cibber, ii. 193, *note* 1 ; persecuted by the Duke of Newcastle, then Lord Chamberlain, ii. 193, *note* 1 ; his Licence revoked, ii. 193, *note* 1 ; restored to his position, ii. 193, *note* 1 ; the expiry of his Patent, ii. 193, *note* 1 ; assigns his share of the Patent, ii. 196 ; brings an action against his partners, ii. 196 ; account of the pleadings, ii. 196-208 ; his recommendation of Underhill's benefit, ii. 351.

Stow, John, his "Survey of London" quoted, i. xxxv., i. xlviii.

Strolling players, i. xl., i. xlvii., i. l.

Subligny, Madlle., a French dancer, i. 316.

"Summer Miscellany, The," ii. 272, *note* 1.

Sumner, an eminent actor, i. xxvi. ; his death, i. xxxi.

Sunderland, Lady (the Little Whig), i. 320.

Swan Theatre, drawing of the stage of the, ii. 84, *note* 1.

Swanston, Eliard, acted Othello, i. xxvi ; the only actor that took the Presbyterian side in the Civil War, i. xxix.

Swift, Jonathan, an attack on Cibber by him in his "Rhapsody on Poetry" quoted, i. 52, *note* 2.

Swiney, Owen, i. 97, *note* 2, ii. 43, ii. 223, ii. 267 ; his "Quacks," i. 247, *note* 1, account of his character, i. 329 ; memoir of, i. 330, *note* 1 ; rents the Queen's Theatre from Vanbrugh, i. 330, i. 333, *note* 1, his agreement with Rich about renting the Queen's Theatre, i. 331 ; Rich declines to execute it, i. 336, his success at the Queen's Theatre in 1706-7, ii. 1 ; his arrangement with his actors in 1706, ii 9 ; control of the opera given to, ii. 48, his gain by the opera in 1708, ii. 55 ; has joint control of plays and operas (1709), ii. 69, forced to hand over the opera to Collier, ii. 102; forced to resume the opera, ii. 107; goes abroad on account of debt, ii 108; his return to England, ii. 108, Cibber plays for his benefit, ii. 262.

"Tatler," the, i. 38, i. 132, *note* 1, ii 75, ii. 93, ii. 229, *note* 1, ii. 244, *note* 1, ii. 244, *note* 2, ii. 328, ii. 362, ii 363, its eulogium of Betterton, i. 118, *note* 1; recommends Cave Underhill's benefit, i 155, praises Nicolini, ii 52; its influence on audiences, ii. 162.

Taylor, John, his "Records of my Life" quoted, i. lxv, *note* 1.

——— Joseph, ii 334; superior to Hart, i. xxiv., his chief characters, i. xxvi.; too old to go into Charles I.'s army, i. xxix.; arrested for acting, i xxx, his death, i xxxi.

"Tempest, The," as an opera, i. 94, revival of, ii 227.

Theatre, the, mentioned by Stow as recently erected, i. xlviii.

Théâtre Français, ii. 221, *note* 1, ii 246, *note* 1.

Theatres, number of, before 1642, i. xxvi.; more reputable before 1642, i. xxvii.; less reputable after the Restoration, i. xxvii.; evil, artistically, of multiplying, i. 92.

Theobald, Lewis, deposed from the Throne of Dulness, ii 280.

Thomson, James, his "Sophonisba," ii. 368.

Tofts, Mrs. Katherine, i 334, *note* 1, ii. 51; Cibber's account of, ii. 54.

"Tone" in speaking, i. 110, *note* 1.

Trinity College, Cambridge, Caius Cibber's statues on the Library, i. 59; particulars regarding these, i. 59, *note* 1

Underhill, Cave, i 98, i. 142, i. 327, ii 307, ii. 346, ii. 347, ii. 361; his chief parts, i 154-155, Cibber's account of, i 154-156; his particular excellence in stupid characters, i. 154; the peculiarity of his facial expression, i 155, his retirement and last appearances, i. 155, *note* 2; his death, i. 156, Anthony Aston's description of, ii. 307; Bellchambers's memoir of, ii. 350.

Underwood, John, originally a "chapel boy," i. xxxvii.

Union of Companies in 1682, i. xxxii., i. 96; in 1708, i. 301; causes that led up to, ii. 45, ii. 48.

Valentini (Valentini Urbani), singer, i. 325, ii. 51, ii. 55.
Vanbrugh, Sir John, i. 269, i. 274, i. 284, ii. 107, ii. 110, ii. 190, ii. 337, ii. 353, ii. 367; his opinion of Cibber's acting of Richard III., i. 139; his "Relapse," i. 216, i. 218; his high opinion of Cibber's acting, i. 216; his "Provoked Wife," i. 216-217; in gratitude to Sir Thomas Skipwith presents him with "The Relapse," i. 217, his "Æsop," i. 216, i. 218, his great ability, i. 219; alters his "Provoked Wife," ii 233; his share in the "Provoked Husband," i 311, *note* 1, builds the Queen's Theatre, i. 319; and Congreve manage the Queen's Theatre, i. 320, i. 325, his "Confederacy," i. 325; "The Cuckold in Conceit" (attributed to him), i. 326, his "Squire Trelooby," i. 326; his "Mistake," i. 327, sole proprietor of the Queen's Theatre, i. 326; lets it to Swiney, i. 330, i. 333, *note* 1.
Vaughan, Commissioner, ii. 278, *note* 1.

"Venice Preserved," ii. 224, *note* 1.
Verbruggen, John, i 108, *note* 2; mentioned, i. 157, i. 193; hangs about Downes, the prompter, i. 74, *note* 1; note regarding, i. 157, *note* 2; Anthony Aston's description of, ii. 311; Bellchambers's memoir of, ii. 354.
—— Mrs. See Mrs. Mountfort.
Vere Street, Clare Market, theatre in, i. xxxii.
Versatility, Cibber's views on, i. 209
Victor, Benjamin, ii. 259; a story told by him of Cibber's cowardice, i 71, *note* 1; his "History of the Theatres," i 110, *note* 1, i. 297, *note* 1, ii. 259, *note* 2, ii. 260, *note* 1, ii 261, *note* 1, ii 264, ii 270, his "Letters" quoted, i. 58, *note* 1; his "Life of Booth," i. 5, *note* 1, ii. 240, *note* 2
Villains, Cibber's views on, i. 131; Macready's views on, referred to, i 135, *note* 1, E. S. Willard mentioned as famous for representing, i. 135, *note* 1, on the acting of, i 222.
Vizard-masks (women of the town), i. xxvii. See also Masks.
Voltaire, his "Zaire," ii. 248.

Walker, Obadiah, his change of religion, ii. 134.
Waller, Edmund, altered the last act of the "Maid's Tragedy," ii. 12.
Walpole, Horace, and Cibber, ii. 284.
Warburton, Bishop, mentioned, i 106, *note* 1, ii 281.
Ward, Professor A W., his "English Dramatic Literature," i. 187, *note* 1
Warwick, Earl of, his frolic with Pope and Cibber, ii. 278.
Weaver, John, his "Loves of Mars and Venus," ii 180, *note* 2.
Webster, Benjamin, i. 88, *note* 3.
"Wedding, The," i xxv.
"Weekly Packet" quoted, ii 171, *note* 1.
Welsted, Leonard, satirically mentioned by Swift, i. 52, *note* 2.
Westminster Bridge, difficulties in getting permission to build, ii. 104.
Whig, the Little (Lady Sunderland), i 320
White's Club, Cibber a member, i. 29, *note* 1.
Whitefriars, i. xlix
"Whitehall Evening Post," Cibber sends verses to, regarding himself, i. 47
Whitelocke's "Memorials," ii 209, *note* 2.

Wigs. See Perriwigs.
Wildair, Sir Harry, i. 318.
"Wild-Goose Chase, The," i. xxv.
Wilks, Robert, i. 108, *note* 2, i. 157, i. 270, i. 332, ii. 36, *note* 1, ii. 167, ii. 176, ii. 300, ii. 352, ii. 361, ii. 363, ii. 368, memoirs published immediately after his death, i. 5 ; mistakes in his Hamlet, i. 100, *note* 1 ; lives with Mrs. Rogers, i. 136, distressed by Pinkethman's "gagging," i 153, *note* 1, his impetuous temper, i. 190, i. 191, *note* 1, i. 191, *note* 2, ii 127, ii. 150-155, ii. 171, his return to Drury Lane from Dublin, i 235 ; his commencing as actor, i. 235, the contest between him and Powell for supremacy at Drury Lane, i. 237-243, i. 251-256; his wonderful memory, i 240, i. 242 ; his diligence and care, i. 240, ii. 160 ; his good character, i 243, made chief actor at Drury Lane, under Rich, i. 256 ; his energy in managing, i. 257, his disputes with Cibber, i. 258 ; his friendship with Mills, i 259, as a prologue-speaker, i. 271 ; the occasion of his coming to London, i 304 ; and Mrs. Oldfield playing in same pieces,

i. 314; made Deputy-manager by Brett, ii. 56, *note* 1; made joint-manager with Swiney and others in 1709, ii. 69; advertisement regarding his salary, 1709, ii. 78, *note* 1; his characteristics as a manager, ii. 111, ii 117; his patronage of his friends, ii. 121; his behaviour on Booth's claiming to become a manager, ii 131, ii. 141; his favour for Mills, ii. 223, his connection with Steele during the dispute about Steele's Patent, ii. 193, *note* 1; his love of acting, ii. 225; a genuine admirer of Cibber, ii. 226, *note* 1; attacked by Dennis, ii. 226, *note* 2; his excellence as Macduff, ii. 228; gives the part to Williams, ii. 229; but withdraws it, ii 230; complains of acting so much, ii. 232; a scene between him and his partners, ii. 234-237, benefits arising from his enthusiasm for acting, ii. 237; and Booth, their opinion of each other, ii. 240, formed his style on Mountfort's, ii. 241, Cibber's comparison of Booth and Wilks, ii. 239-245; his Othello, ii. 244; death of, ii. 254; memoir of, ii. 254, *note* 4; Patent granted to him, Cibber, and Booth, after Steele's death, ii. 257.

Wilks, Mrs., inherits Wilks's share in the Patent, ii. 258; delegates her authority to John Ellys, ii. 258; her share sold to Fleetwood, ii. 261

Willard, E. S., mentioned, i. 135, *note* 1.

William of Orange, Cibber a supporter of, at the Revolution, i. 60; made king, i. 70; gives a Licence to Betterton, i 192, *note* 1.

Williams, Charles, Wilks gives him the part of Macduff, ii. 229, but withdraws it, ii. 230, hissed in mistake for Cibber, i. 179, *note* 1.

—— Joseph, mentioned, i. 157, i 200; Bellchambers's memoir of, ii. 356.

Wiltshire (actor), leaves the stage for the army, i. 84, killed in Flanders, i. 85.

Winchester College, Cibber stands for election to, and is unsuccessful, i. 56, his brother, Lewis Cibber, is afterwards successful, i. 56, his father presents a statue to, i. 56; communication from the Head Master of, i. 56, *note* 2.

Wintershal (actor), belonged to the Salisbury Court Theatre, i. xxiv.

Woffington, Margaret, her artistic feeling, i. 166, *note* 1; an anecdote wrongly connected with her, ii. 266.

"Woman's Wit," cast of, i. 264, *note* 1.

Women, their first introduction on the stage, i. xxxii., i. 89, *note* 1, i. 90

Wren, Sir Christopher, the designer of Drury Lane Theatre, ii. 82.

Wright, James, his "History of Rutlandshire," i. 8; quoted, i. 9, *note* 1; his "Historia Histrionica," i. xix.

Wykeham, William of, Cibber connected with by descent, i. 56.

"Ximena," cast of, ii. 163, *note* 1.

York, Duke of (James II), at Whitehall, i 30

Young, Dr. Edward, his "Epistle to Mr. Pope" quoted, i. 54, *note* 1.

Young actors, dearth of, ii 221.

END OF VOL. II.

CHISWICK PRESS:—C. WHITTINGHAM AND CO., TOOKS COURT,
CHANCERY LANE.

Lightning Source UK Ltd.
Milton Keynes UK
UKOW01f0607131017
310923UK00005B/315/P